D0605395

PR
1203
.09
Date Due
COLLEGE OF MARIN LIBRARY
COLLEGE AVENUE
KENTFIELD, CA 94904
PRINTED IN U.S.A.
23-521-002

MIDDLE ENGLISH POETRY

THE LIBRARY OF LITERATURE

A SELECTION OF POETRY
WRITTEN IN ENGLISH
FROM THE XIIITH
TO THE EARLY XVITH
CENTURIES

MIDDLE ENGLISH POETRY

AN ANTHOLOGY

EDITED WITH AN INTRODUCTION
AND COMMENTARY
BY

LEWIS J. OWEN
Occidental College
AND
NANCY H. OWEN
Westridge School

THE BOBBS-MERRILL COMPANY, INC.
INDIANAPOLIS · NEW YORK

Library of Congress Catalog Card Number 76–138662
Printed in the United States of America
First Printing

For Gwyneth & Geoffrey

PREFACE

WE ARE indebted to the Trustees of the British Museum; the Trustees of the National Library of Scotland; the Dean and Chapter of Lincoln Cathedral; the Librarian of Lambeth Palace Library; the University Library, Cambridge; the Librarian, Trinity College, Cambridge; the Pepys Library, Magdalene College, Cambridge; the Bodleian Library, Oxford; the Master and Fellows of Balliol College, Oxford, for their several permissions to use manuscripts and books in their possession as bases for the texts in this edition. We are also most grateful to the authorities and staff of the Huntington Library for the use of their resources and congenial surroundings; to the President and Board of Trustees of Occidental College for a generous grant-in-aid; and to Ian Watt for his guidance as our work progressed, and for his patience when it did not.

CONTENTS

GENERAL INTRODUCTION

Principles of Selection

THE POEMS in this collection have been chosen because they suggest something of the range of Middle English poetry, and because they are significant works of art. As much as possible we have used complete poems; when we have had to use parts of very long poems, we have chosen sections which possessed some unity of their own. We have excluded Chaucer from our selections because most students will already possess a collection of his poetry; and in order to include other poetry not so accessible, we have reluctantly also excluded the Gawain poet, whose two major works are now so readily available in good, inexpensive editions.

The large categories under which the poems are grouped do not establish absolute divisions but simply identify important elements which the poems have in common. There is indeed much overlapping: verse chronicle and romance merge in *The Alliterative Morte Arthure;* the lyric *As I went on Yol Day* makes use of burlesque; Gower's dream vision includes a romance; the debate between the Thrush and the Nightingale depends heavily upon allegory. Similarly, although there is no separate group of didactic or homiletic poems, almost all of the poems include a didactic purpose. Although this element is most conspicuous in such a poem as Henryson's *Bludy Serk* with its appended "Moralitas," it is present to some degree in even the most secular poems. And in Gower's *Confessio* this didacticism assumes an almost homiletic form with Genius's explanations and exempla of the Deadly Sins.

Glossaries

A glossary has been placed at the foot of each page to be immediately available. Since these are intended to be complete for each poem no general glossary is included at the back. The glossaries for any one poem therefore never assume knowledge of the glossaries of other poems in the book. A word that reappears often throughout a poem may not be glossed every time, but it will have been glossed in several early appearances. Whenever a difficulty extends beyond individual words, the full line or passage is translated as literally as possible. The whole selection from Layamon's *Brut* is translated because its difficulty seemed to require more than a gloss of individual words and phrases. All Biblical references which appear in the glossaries are to the Douay version.

Texts

All texts have been checked against the original manuscript (or a photographic copy) of the basic text, and this source is given as the first part of the commentaries at the back of the book. Departures from the basic text occur only when absolutely necessary, and are always noted either in the textual note or in the glossaries.

In preparing the texts we have tried, while preserving the sounds and rhythms of the original, to make the meaning and pronunciation clear to readers who are not specialists in Middle English. To this end, we have *usually* adopted these practices:

1. Revised capitalization and punctuation to accord with modern practice;
2. Replaced obsolete letters: *thorn* (þ) = th; *eth* (ð) = th; *yogh* (ȝ) = y, gh, or s;
3. Reduced variant spellings to that closest to modern English, so long as the modern form does not encourage mispronunciation or misunderstanding, specifically:
   a. These pairs of interchangeable letters have been regularized to accord with modern usage: w/u, v/u, y/i, i/j, initial c/k;
   b. The unstressed vowel in inflectional endings of nouns and verbs has generally been reduced to *e* (its usual modern equivalent) except where some other vowel appears so consistently as to become a characteristic of the language, as for example the *i* in Scottish texts, which has been retained;
   c. The verbal prefix i- or y- is recorded as it appears in the manuscript;

d. The stem vowel *i* or *y* which is retained in some Middle English verbs (Old English weak verbs, class II) is recorded as it appears in the manuscript;

e. The following miscellaneous spellings have been regularized to accord with modern usage:

s, ss, sch, ch > sh	quh > wh	to > too
of > off; off > of	by-, bi- > be-	qw > qu

and some double consonants have been reduced;

f. Spelling of these pronouns has been regularized: I, me, my, min(e); thou, thee, thy, thin(e); but ic, ich have been retained;

g. Spelling of proper names has not been altered;

h. Final -e has never been altered.

We have, however, departed from these practices whenever a particular poem or line seemed to require us to do so — to preserve, for example, the appearance of rhyme or alliteration, or the distinctive character of a dialect or of a very early text. (The text of Layamon raised special problems, and since it was to be accompanied by a complete translation, we have been more conservative in our modifications of the manuscript readings.) Our purpose has been to provide texts which will be as readable as possible while preserving those qualities of language upon which critical analysis depends: meaning, sound, rhythm. It goes without saying that this text is not intended for the linguistic specialist but for the student, undergraduate or graduate, who requires a text suitable for responsible literary analysis.

Introductions and Commentaries

The Introductions and Commentaries supplement each other. The Introductions preceding each section supply general information about the various categories; the Commentaries at the back of the book provide textual information, a brief description of the form, and a short critical analysis of each poem. No single analysis considers all the elements of a poem, but taken together, the analyses touch upon most of the important elements in Middle English poetry. A biographical note is given for each known poet; for those poets who appear more than once, this note accompanies the following poems: Charles d'Orleans — *The New Lady*; Robert Henryson — *The Testament of Cresseid*; William Dunbar — *Hale! sterne superne.*

Prosody

Middle English poetry, which was generally meant to be heard, not to be read silently, drew on two different prosodic traditions: the accentual, unrhymed, alliterative poetry of the Anglo-Saxons; and the syllabic, rhymed, stanzaic poetry of the French — a poetry that became extremely influential after the Norman conquest of England in 1066. It should be recognized, however, that the decline of native English poetry after the Norman occupation was due partly to a decline in the English poetic impulse itself, a decline which was apparent in England long before 1066. If French influence dominated poetry in England for the next century and a half, this was a consequence not only of military victory and occupation, but of a lack of vitality within the native tradition itself.

The basic metrical unit of Old English poetry was a short verse line containing at least one, but usually two, stressed syllables, or "lifts," with a varying number of unstressed syllables, or "dips." Most frequently these short lines occurred in pairs to make a single line whose two parts were separated by a pronounced pause, or "caesura," but were connected to each other by one or more alliterative sounds that carried over from the first part of the line into the second. The key in this system was the third stress, which normally alliterated with the first stress, often with the second, rarely also with the fourth.

French poetry was syllabic: that is, a verse or line contained a fixed number of syllables, not just a fixed number of *stressed* syllables, as in Old English poetry; and the stresses occurred in regular pattern which remained more or less constant through a fixed number of lines. These stressed syllables were determined by the accent they received in pronunciation, rather than by their length or their grammatical importance, both of which had influenced Old English stress. Finally, these lines were bound together by terminal rhyme that linked them into couplets or into stanzas of varying length and rhyme pattern.

Once poetry in English began to reappear significantly, in the thirteenth century — the same century that saw the English language begin to supersede French in other areas of life, largely because of the loss of Normandy to France and a growing identification of the Normans with their new island kingdom — it might derive almost exclusively from one or the other tradition: as Layamon's *Brut* seems almost wholly in the Old English tradition, while the equally early *Owl and the Nightingale* seems almost totally French. More often, however, the poetry combined the resources of both traditions, as, for example, *The Auntirs of Arthure at the Terne Wathelyn* uses a version of the Old English alliterative line but also uses terminal rhyme and gathers its lines into fairly regular stanzas.

In the mid- and late fourteenth century, pure alliterative verse enjoyed what has been called a "revival," but it should be recognized that this native verse form had never completely died out, but had continued in an unbroken — if not always prolific or distinguished — tradition, especially in those areas of England remote from Norman influence — the north and the west. Some of this late alliterative poetry, like the poems of the Gawain poet, is collected into stanzas; in others, like *The Alliterative Morte Arthure* and *Piers Plowman,* the alliterative lines still stand independently, as they had done in Old English poetry. But in either case the alliterative line itself has been modified from its prototype in *Beowulf.* It is generally longer and more flexible. In *Beowulf,* the stresses or "lifts" normally had to fall on syllables that were long and grammatically important; in such a poem as *Gawain and the Green Knight,* since the rhythmic movement is accentual, stress need no longer be associated with syllabic length or grammatical function. Moreover, the number of stresses and the number of alliterations within a single line are often increased to five or six. The greater cohesiveness provided by this rich alliteration in turn makes possible a greater number of unstressed syllables. The result, then, is a line that is longer, that carries a greater number of stresses, and whose alliteration may fall on almost any syllable. Sometimes, indeed, the same alliterating sound carries through several lines (*e.g., Morte Arthure,* ll. 3842–47), thus tying groups of these unrhymed lines into loose units despite the absence of terminal rhyme or stanza divisions.

Pronunciation

Because of the diversity of the English dialects over several hundred years, and because of the limitations of space, it is impossible to present a complete description of the vowel and consonant sounds in Middle English. The following description, however, offers an approximate guide to the pronunciation of Middle English.

VOWELS

sound	spelling	as pronounced in Modern English	Middle English
a	a	hot (Am.)	*saḳ, that, balle*
aː	a, aa	calm	*name, dame, caas*
ɛ	e	bed	*bed, dette; senne* (sin)
e	e, ee	claim	*sleepen, clene, prechen, pite; brede* (bride)
ə	e, i	*a*bout	*sleepen, wallis*
ɪ	i	thing	*thing, his, sinne, riche*
i	i, y, ii	seen	*time, cry, wiis, bride*
ɒ	o	hot (Br.)	*folḳ, ḳnotten, robben*
ɔ	o, oo	all	*ston, stoon, cote*
o	o, oo	hope	*boḳ, booḳ, moven*
ʊ	o, u	put	*yong, yung, turnen*
u	u, ou, ow	moon	*hus, hous, down, flour*
ʏ	u	Germ. Münster	*sunne* (sin)
y	u	Germ. Schüler	*brude* (bride)

In Scottish texts vowel length is often indicated by adding *i* after the vowel, as Sc. *gaist* (ghost), *seid* (seed), *rois* (rose), *luiḳ* (look).

DIPHTHONGS

sound	spelling	Middle English
æɪ	ai, ay, ei, ey	*main, may, seil, wey*
aʊ	au, aw	*naught, clawe*
ɒʊ	ou, ow	*doughter, blowen*
ɛu	eu, ew	*sleuthe, fewe*
ɪu	iw, ew, eu; u	*sniwen, snewen, reu; vertu*
ɔɪ	oi, oy	*chois, joy*

CONSONANTS

sound	spelling	as pronounced in Modern English	Middle English
b	b	but	*but*
d	d	drink	*drinḳen*
f	f	five	*five*

dʒ	j, g, gg	judge, lodge	*jugen, logge*
g	g, gg	go	*gon, frogges*
h	h	hat	*hat*
tʃ	ch	chin	*chin*
k	k, c	king, cold	*king, cold*
l	l	long	*long, half*
m	m	man	*man*
n	n	name	*name*
p	p	peace	*pes*
r	r (sometimes trilled)	run	*runnen*
s	s, c	song, city	*song, citee*
ʃ	sh	shall	*shall*
t	t	tooth	*tooth*
v	v; f	visage	*visage;* final [v] in Scottish often spelled *f, ff, haif* (have)
w	w	wind	*wind*
j	y	young	*yong*
z	s, rarely z	rise	*risen*
θ	th	bath	*bath*
ð	th	bathe	*bathen*
ç	gh, h, ch	Germ. ich	*night, niht, nicht*
x	gh, h, ch	Germ. doch	*thought, thoht, thocht*

A few consonants are not pronounced:

v, written u between vowels in Scottish: *deuill*
l, after a or o sometimes unpronounced in Scottish: *chalmir*
g, of gn in French words; gn pronounced as [n]: *resigne*
h, silent in French words: *honour, throne*

Certain combinations of consonant sounds are pronounced as follows:

ks	x	wax	*wax*
ŋg	ng	finger	*singen*
ŋk	nk	drink	*drinken*
kw	qu	quake	*quak*
kn	kn		*knight*
hw	wh, quh (Scottish)	what	*what, quhat* (with greater aspiration)
gn	gn		*gnawen*

ABBREVIATIONS OF TITLES AND SERIES

BMS	*The Bannatyne Manuscript,* ed. W. Tod Ritchie, 4 vols., Edinburgh: W. Blackwood and Sons, 1928–34, *STS.*
EEC	*The Early English Carols,* ed. Richard L. Greene, Oxford: Oxford University Press, 1935.
EEL	*Early English Lyrics,* ed. E. K. Chambers and F. Sidgwick, London: Sidgwick and Jackson, 1907.
EETS	Early English Text Society.
EME	*Early Middle English Verse and Prose,* ed. J. A. W. Bennett and G. V. Smithers, Oxford: Oxford University Press, 1966.
HL	*The Harley Lyrics,* ed. G. L. Brook, Manchester: Manchester University Press, 1948.
Index	*The Index of Middle English Verse,* ed. Carleton Brown and Rossell Hope Robbins, New York: Columbia University Press, 1943.
MEL	*Medieval English Lyrics,* ed. R. T. Davies, Evanston: Northwestern University Press, 1964.
MEP	Speirs, John. *Medieval English Poetry,* London: Faber and Faber, Ltd., 1957.
ML	Kane, George. *Middle English Literature,* London: Methuen and Co., Ltd., 1951.
MWD	*The Poems of William Dunbar,* ed. W. Mackay Mackenzie, Edinburgh: The Porpoise Press, 1932.
OML	*One Hundred Middle English Lyrics,* ed. Robert D. Stevick, Indianapolis: The Bobbs-Merrill Co., Inc., 1964.
PFRH	*The Poems and Fables of Robert Henryson,* ed. David Laing, Edinburgh: W. Patterson, 1865.
PRH	*The Poems of Robert Henryson,* ed. G. Gregory Smith, 3 vols., Edinburgh: W. Blackwood and Sons, 1906–14, *STS.*

PWD *The Poems of William Dunbar,* ed. David Laing, 2 vols., Edinburgh: Laing and Forbes, 1834.

RHP *Robert Henryson: Poems,* ed. Charles Elliott, Oxford: Oxford University Press, 1963.

SCM *Songs, Carols, and Other Miscellaneous Poems,* ed. Roman Dyboski, Oxford: Oxford University Press, 1908, *EETS.*

SL Moore, Arthur K. *The Secular Lyric in Middle English,* Lexington, Ky.: University of Kentucky Press, 1951.

SO *Sir Orfeo,* ed. A. J. Bliss, 2nd ed., Oxford: Oxford University Press, 1966.

SPWD *The Poems of William Dunbar,* ed. John Small, 3 vols., Edinburgh: W. Blackwood and Sons, 1893, *STS.*

STS Scottish Text Society.

TA Matthews, William. *The Tragedy of Arthur,* Berkeley: University of California Press, 1960.

WDP *William Dunbar: Poems,* ed. James Kinsley, Oxford: Oxford University Press, 1958.

WN Manning, Stephen. *Wisdom and Number,* Lincoln, Neb.: University of Nebraska Press, 1962.

WPFH *The Poems and Fables of Robert Henryson,* ed. H. Harvey Wood, 2nd ed., Edinburgh: Oliver and Boyd, 1958.

XIII *English Lyrics of the XIIIth Century,* ed. Carleton Brown, Oxford: Oxford University Press, 1932.

XIV *Religious Lyrics of the XIVth Century,* ed. Carleton Brown, 2nd ed., Oxford: Oxford University Press, 1952.

XIV-XV *Secular Lyrics of the XIVth and XVth Centuries,* ed. Rossell Hope Robbins, 2nd ed., Oxford: Oxford University Press, 1955.

XV *Religious Lyrics of the XVth Century,* ed. Carleton Brown, Oxford: Oxford University Press, 1939.

Texts of the Poems

LYRIC POETRY

THE Middle English lyric, both sacred and secular, appeared at least as early as the twelfth century. Three brief hymns have been attributed to St. Godric (d. 1170), and the twelfth-century chronicler Thomas of Ely includes four lines of a song composed by King Canute as he listened from his boat to the sweet singing of the monks on the banks of the River Ouse. The popularity of secular love poetry at the end of the twelfth century is indicated by an amusing anecdote, told by Giraldus Cambrensis in his *Gemma Ecclesiastica,* of a parish priest in Worcestershire who was so hypnotized by the refrain of a love song which had been echoing outside his window all night that on the following day he inadvertently dismissed his congregation with the injunction, "Sweetheart have mercy," instead of the more conventional, "God be with you." Apart from these brief references and examples from the twelfth century, the bulk of extant English lyrics date from the early thirteenth century through the fifteenth.

More sacred than secular lyrics have survived, but this does not prove that they were either more numerous or more popular. The monks and other religious persons who were at first largely responsible for compiling manuscripts would naturally have chosen to record religious works, and even the man of the world, though he might not share the Church's distaste for secular lyrics, would probably have agreed with the monastic distinction between poetry to be enjoyed and poetry to be piously and laboriously preserved in fine manuscripts. After Chaucer's day an increasing number of secular lyrics were written down, but of the surviving Middle English lyrics the religious still outnumber the secular by about three or four to one. The early lyrics usually circulated orally before and after they were recorded, so that poems which appear in several different manuscripts will appear in variant forms. Although one manuscript might be copied from another it was more likely for each manuscript version to derive from its own oral source. Lyrics dating from the earlier half of the thirteenth century generally appeared in texts where they stand alone. After 1250 they tended more and more to be gathered together in extensive groups within single manuscript collections, of which Trinity College, Cambridge, MS 323; Harley MS 2253; and Bodleian, Digby MS 86, are three of the most noteworthy.

The earliest lyrics are often, though not always, quite short. Moreover, the presence of musical notation that frequently accompanies the texts of poems in manuscripts dating from the thirteenth century indicates that these lyrics were often intended to be sung. Secular lyrics were also often accompanied by a dance. Both dance and music became increasingly less frequent during the fourteenth century, the century of the "literary" lyric; it is not until the appearance of the carol in the fifteenth century that a considerable number of lyrics are again provided with a musical accompaniment.

The influences on the English lyric are uncertain. A number of the early sacred lyrics are translations from the Latin, and Latin hymns may also have suggested rhythms and stanzaic forms. Generally, however, the influence of Latin hymns on the sacred English lyric does not appear to have been great, and Latin rhetoric is not a significant influence until the appearance of aureate verse in the fifteenth century. More important were the direct influences of the Bible itself, the liturgy of the service, and the rich tradition of patristic writings. Similarly, although the secular lyrics of the thirteenth century reveal strong French influence, the bulk of later English secular lyrics were not substantially influenced by the French. As Rossell H. Robbins has pointed out, most of the "tricks and devices" of these poems are ones which could have been developed independently by any poet who was even superficially aware of French and Continental fashions (*XIV–XV*, pp. *lii–iii*). And Arthur Moore, in discussing the *pastourelle* as it appears in the Harley collection, is chiefly impressed with how much the English poets modified the French formula (*SL*, p. 55). Such adornments as alliteration derive most of all from the native traditions of English poetry, while the elaborate devices in the later aureate verse derive not from the French, but from Latin rhetoric.

The range of the medieval English lyric is almost inexhaustible. The distinction between sacred and secular indicates only the largest subdivision, and even this neglects an equally important vertical division between courtly and popular. There is political verse and practical verse. There are popular drinking songs and popular love songs, epitaphs and presentation verses. And there is a vast range of courtly love lyrics. Within religious poetry, there are moral poems and devotional poems, with the latter appearing in such various forms as prayers, meditations, and mystical visions.

The Middle English poet, who before the fifteenth century was usually anonymous, wrote in a lyric voice that might be intensely personal but rarely individual, in the sense that a lyric by John Donne or by Dylan Thomas is individual. Whether a poem is sacred or secular, the description of an event or the account of a psychological state of mind, it becomes an invitation for the reader to participate in a response which is assumed to be universal. We do not feel that we are being introduced to a uniquely personal perception of experience, but rather being reminded of a commonly shared experience whose nature and value are already established and familiar. The assumption that certain topics are in themselves emotionally self-sufficient and that responses to them are automatic could lead an indifferent poet to take his responsibilities too lightly, to feel that his verse was only a useful reminder. (See *ML* p. 125.) But for the good poet this danger turns to advantage. Since his subjects are familiar and the attitudes towards them traditional, he can work with great economy—he does not need to inform or explain, but simply to manipulate familiar materials so as to revivify, reintensify the response to them. In this he is also assisted by a view of the world which sees all experience as both interrelated and expressive of larger meanings that lie behind the literal appearance of things. Thus every event no matter how remote in time or place can become startlingly present; every object, no matter how trivial or commonplace, can shimmer into new life, can evoke stunning, resonant associations, if only it is managed properly.

Definition of terms

In reading the lyrics it will be useful to have a few terms defined.

A *pastourelle* is a narrative poem in which the poet wanders into the country, usually in springtime, meets a lady with whom he converses and often makes love – with or without success; *e.g., Now skrinketh rose and lilye flour.*

A *reverdie* is a lyric celebrating the return of spring. The celebration may stand alone, as an independent poem, but it may also serve as the opening sections of another form — the *pastourelle,* for example; *e.g., Sumer is i-cumen in.*

A *carol* is a poem intended to be sung, often with an accompanying dance. It therefore comprises a number of uniform stanzas and a burden, which is sung at the beginning and then again after every stanza. A frequent variation on this basic formula uses a couplet burden that rhymes with the last line of a quatrain stanza rhyming *aaab.* A medieval carol is thus defined by its metrical form, not by its subject. Although many carols were written about Christmas and Easter events, they were also written on other subjects; *e.g. Lullay, lullay, litel child.*

A *burden* is distinguished from a *refrain* by the fact that it is sung at the beginning of the poem, as well as after each stanza; *e.g. As I went on Yol Day* uses both.

Aureate verse is consciously and elaborately ornamented with rhetorical devices of all sorts, but especially alliteration and assonance and, often, new words coined expressly to provide more of these devices. The style depends heavily upon Latin rhetoric as in Dunbar's *Hale! sterne superne.*

LYRICS

1 *(Early 13th c.)*

Now goth sonne under wod:
Me reweth, Marie, thy faire rode.
Now goth sonne under tre:
Me reweth, Marie, thy sone and thee.

2 *(Later 13th c.)*

Foweles in the frith,
The fishes in the flod,
And I mon waxe wod:
Mulch sorw I walke with
5 For beste of bon and blod.

3 *(13th c.)*

Wen the turuf is thy tuur,
And thy put is thy bour,
Thy wel and thy wite throte
Shulen wormes too note.
5 Wat helpit thee thenne
Al the worilde wenne?

(1) [1] Now goes the sun behind the wood (the Son under the Cross).
[2] I feel pity, Mary, for your fair face.
[3] Now goes the sun behind the tree (the Son under the Cross).
[4] I feel pity, Mary, for your son and you.

(2) [1] *Foweles,* birds; *frith,* woods [3] And I must go mad.
[4] Much sorrow I live with; *Mulch,* MS *multh.*
[5] Because of the best of bone and blood (the best man alive, *i.e.,* Christ)

(3) [1] *Wen,* When [2] *put,* pit, grave [3] *wel,* skin; *wite,* white
[4] Worms shall also note. [5] *Wat,* What
[6] *worilde wenne,* world's joy, wealth, MS *wnne*

4 *(Ca. 1230–40)*

Sumer is i-cumen in,
Lhude sing, cuccu!
Groweth sed and bloweth med
And springth the wude nu –
5 Sing, cuccu!

Awe bleteth after lomb,
Lhouth after calve cu,
Bulluc sterteth, bucke verteth –
Murie sing, cuccu!
10 Cuccu, cuccu,
Wel singes thu, cuccu!
Ne swik thou naver nu!

Sing, cuccu, nu! Sing, cuccu!
Sing, cuccu! Sing, cuccu, nu!

5 *(Late 13th, early 14th c.)*

Betwene Mersh and Averil
When spray beginneth to springe,
The lutel fowl hath hire wil
On hire lud to singe.
5 Ich libbe in love longinge
For semlokest of alle thinge,
He may me blisse bringe;
Ich am in hire baundoun.
An hendy hap ichabbe y-hent –

(4) 1–5 Spring has come, Sing loudly, cuckoo! Seed grows and meadow blooms and the woods spring to life now. Sing, cuckoo! 4 *wude,* MS *wde*
6-12 Ewe bleats after lamb, cow lows after calf, bullock leaps, buck farts – Merrily sing, cuckoo! Cuckoo, cuckoo, well sing thou, cuckoo! Now never stop.
(5) 1 *Mersh and Averil,* March and April
2 *spray,* twigs; *to springe,* to grow 3 *wil,* wish 4 *On,* In; *lud,* language
5 *Ich libbe,* I live 6 *semlokest,* fairest; *thinge,* creatures 7 *He,* She
8 *baundoun,* power
9–12 A fair fortune I have received – I know from Heaven it is sent to me! From all women my love is removed and has settled on Alisoun.

THE LIBRARY OF LITERATURE

UNDER THE GENERAL EDITORSHIP OF

John Henry Raleigh and Ian Watt

Library of Congress Catalog Card Number 76-138662
Printed in the United States of America
First Printing
4-29-77

10 Ichot from Hevene it is me sent!
From alle wimmen my love is lent,
And light on Alisoun.

On hew hire her is fair inogh,
Hire browe browne, hire eye blake;
15 With lossum chere he on me logh,
With middle small and wel y-make.
Bote he me wolle to hire take
Forte buen hire owen make,
Longe to liven ichulle forsake
20 And feye fallen adown.
An hendy hap ichabbe y-hent—
Ichot from Hevene it is me sent!
From alle wimmen my love is lent,
And light on Alisoun.

25 Nightes when I wende and wake—
Forthy min wonges waxeth won—
Levedy, al for thine sake
Longinge is y-lent me on!
In world nis non so witer mon
30 That al hire bounte telle con:
Hire swire is whittore then the swon,
And feirest may in towne.
An hendy hap ichabbe y-hent—
Ichot from Hevene it is me sent!
35 From alle wimmen my love is lent,
And light on Alisoun.

Icham for wowing al forwake,
Wery so water in wore,

[13] In hue her hair is very fair. [14] *browe,* eyebrows
[15] *lossum chere,* lovely look; *he,* she; *logh,* laughed
[16] *middle,* waist; *y-make,* formed [17] *he,* she [18] *make,* mate
[19–20] I shall forsake (long life) living for a long time and doomed (shall) fall down.
[25] *wende,* turn [26] Therefore my cheeks turn pale. [27] *Levedy,* Lady
[28] Desire is come on me. [29] In the world there is no man so wise
[30] *bounte,* excellence [31] *swire,* neck [32] *may,* maid
[37] *forwake,* worn out with lying awake [38] Weary as water in a troubled pool

Lest eny reve me my make
40 Ichabbe y-yirned yore.
Betere is tholien while sore
Then mournen evermore.
Geinest under gore,
Herkne to my roun!
45 An hendy hap ichabbe y-hent —
Ichot from Hevene it is me sent,
From alle wimmen my love is lent,
And light on Alisoun.

6 *(Ca. 1314–1340)*

Now skrinketh rose and lilye flour,
That whilen ber that swete savour
In somer that swete tide;
Ne is no quene so stark ne stour,
5 Ne no levedy so bright in bour,
That ded ne shall byglide.
Whoso wol fleysh lust forgon
And Hevene blis abide,
On Jesu be is thoght anon,
10 That therled was is side.

From Petresbourgh in o morewening,
As I me wende o my pleying,
On my folye I thoghte;
Menen I gon my mourning

39 *reve*, rob 40 *y-yirned yore*, yearned for a long time
41–42 It is better to suffer sorely for a while than grieve forever.
43 Fairest under clothes 44 Listen to my song!
(6) 1 *skrinketh*, withers (MS *skrnketh*)
2 *whilen*, formerly 3 *tide*, time 4 *Ne is no*, There is no; *stour*, haughty
5 *levedy*, lady; *bour*, chamber 6 That death shall not overtake
7 Whoever will forgo fleshly pleasure 8 And await Heaven's bliss
9 *is*, his; *anon*, at once 10 *therled*, pierced; *is*, his
11 *o morewening*, one morning 12 As I went about my amusement
13 *folye*, lustful (?) folly 14 I go to lament my grief.

15 To hire that ber the Hevene King,
Of mercy hire besoghte:
"Ledy, preye thy sone for ous,
That us duere boghte,
And shild us from the lothe hous
20 That to the fend is wroghte."

Mine herte of dedes wes fordred,
Of sinne that I have my fleish fed
Ant folewed al my time,
That I not whider I shall be led
25 When I ligge on dethes bed —
In joye ore into pine.
On o Ledy min hope is,
Moder ant virgine;
We shulen into Hevene blis
30 Thurgh hire medicine.

Betere is hire medicin
Then eny mede or eny win;
Hire erbes smulleth swete.
From Catenas into Divelin
35 Nis ther no leche so fin
Oure serewes to bete.
Mon that feleth eny sor,
And his folye wol lete,
Withoute gold other eny tresor
40 He may be sound ant sete.

Of penaunce is his plastre al,
Ant ever serven hire I shal,
Now and al my live.

18 *düere,* dear 19 *lothe,* loathsome 20 *to,* for
21 My heart was frightened for the deeds (I had done).
24 *not,* do not know 25 *ligge,* lie 26 *In,* Into; *pine,* pain, suffering
29 *We shulen,* We shall go (MS *whe*) 32 *mede,* meed
34 From Caithness to Dublin 36 Our sorrows to amend 37 *sor,* grief
38 *wol lete,* will leave 39 *other,* or 40 *sete,* content, serene
41 *his, i.e., Mon,* l. 37 43 *live,* life

Now is fre that er wes thral,
45 Al thourgh that Levedy gent and smal —
Heried be hir joyes five!
Wherso eny sek is,
Thider hie blive:
Thurgh hire beoth y-broght to blis
50 Bo maiden ant wive.

For he that dude is body on tre
Of oure sinnes have piete,
That weldes Heovene boures.
Wimmon, with thy jolifte,
55 Thou thench on Godes shoures:
Thagh thou be whit and brith on ble,
Falewen shule thy floures.
Jesu, have mercy of us,
That al this world honoures. Amen

7 *(1372)*

Love me brouthte
And love me wrouthte,
Man, to be thy fere.

Love me fedde
5 And love me ledde
And love me lettet here.

44 *er,* formerly 45 *gent and smal,* noble and slim
46 *Heried,* Praised; *joyes five:* the five joys of the Virgin are variously the Annunciation, the Nativity, the Epiphany, Easter, her Death, her Assumption.
47 *sek,* sick 48 Thither let him hurry quickly.
49–50 Through her are brought to bliss both maiden and wife.
51 Because of him who put his body on the cross 52 *piete,* pity
53 *weldes,* rules 54 *Wimmon,* Women; *jolifte,* gaiety
55 You think about God's pains.
56 *whit,* fair; *brith on ble,* radiant in complexion 57 Your bloom shall fade.
(7) 1 *brouthte,* brought 2 *wrouthte,* fashioned 3 *fere,* companion
6 *lettet,* abandoned, left, allowed

Love me slow
And love me drow
And love me leide on bere.

10 Love is my pes,
For love I ches
Man to bygen dere.

Ne dred thee nouth,
I have thee south
15 Bothen day and nith.

To haven thee,
Well is me,
I have thee wonnen in fith.

8 *(15th c.)*

I have a newe garden
And newe is begunne:
Swich another garden
Know I not under sunne.

5 In the middis of my garden
Is a peryr set,
And it wele non per bern
But a per Jenet.

The fairest maide of this town
10 Preyed me
For to griffen her a grif
Of mine pery tre.

7 *slow,* slew 8 *drow,* drew 9 *leide on bere,* laid on a bier 10 *pes,* peace
11 *ches,* chose 12 *bygen dere,* buy at great cost 13 Fear nothing
14 *south,* sought 15 *nith,* night 18 *fith,* fight
(8) 3 *Swich,* Such 5 *middis,* midst 6 *peryr,* pear tree
8 Except an early pear 11 To graft her a graft

Whan I hadde hem griffed
Alle at her wille,
15 The win and the ale
She dede in fille.

And I griffed her
Right up in her home,
And by that day twenty wowkes
20 It was qwik in her womb.

That day twelfve month,
That maide I met;
She seid it was a per Robert,
But non per Jonet!

9 *(15th c.)*

Kyrie, so Kyrie,
Jankyn singit merye,
With Aleyson.

As I went on Yol Day in our procession,
Knew I joly Jankyn by his mery ton.
Kyrieleyson.

Jankyn began the offis on the Yol Day,
5 And yit me thinkit it dos me good, so merye gan he say,
"Kyrieleyson."

Jankyn red the Pistil ful fair and ful wel,

13 *hem,* them 14 *wille,* wish 16 She filled me with
18 *home* (Robbins emends), MS *honde,* membrane? 24 *Jonet,* MS *Ion*
(9) *Kyrie:* a part of the Mass. The order of the Mass is Introit, Kyrie, Gloria, Epistle, Gradual, Prayer, Gospel, Credo, Offertory, Sanctus, Canon of the Mass, Consecration, Communion, Agnus Dei, Benediction.
3 *Kyrieleyson,* Lord have mercy 7 *Pistil,* Epistle

And yit me thinkit it dos me good, as evere have I sel.
Kyrieleyson.

10 Jankyn at the Sanctus crakit a merye note,
And yit me thinkit it dos me good, I payed for his cote.
Kyrieleyson.

Jankyn crakit notes an hunderid on a knot,
And yit he hackit hem smaller than wortes to the pot.
15 Kyrieleyson.

Jankyn at the Angnus berit the pax brede;
He twinkeled, but said nout, and on min fot he trede.
Kyrieleyson.

Benedicamos Domino, Crist fro shame me shilde;
20 *Deo gracias,* therto — alas, I go with childe.
Kyrieleyson.

10 *(Early 15th c.)*

I sing of a maiden
That is makeles:
King of alle kinges
To her sone she ches.

5 He cam also stille
Ther his moder was,

[8] *sel,* good fortune [10, 13] *crakit,* trills [13] *on a knot,* at a time
[14] *wortes,* herbs
[16] *pax brede,* silver or gilt disk used in giving the kiss of peace to the congregation
[17] *twinkeled,* winked [19] *Benedicamos Domino,* Let us praise the Lord
[21] *Deo gracias,* Thanks be to God. These two Latin phrases occur together at the end of a Mass when a procession follows the Mass.
(10) [2] *makeles,* matchless, mateless
[4] *ches,* chose [5] *also,* as [6] *Ther,* Where

As dew in Aprille
That fallit on the gras.

He cam also stille
10 To his moderes bour,
As dew in Aprille
That fallit on the flour.

He cam also stille
Ther his moder lay,
15 As dew in Aprille
That fallit on the spray.

Moder and maiden,
Was never non but she:
Wel may swich a Lady
20 Godes moder be.

11 *(Ca. 1500)*

Lully, lulley, lully, lulley,
The fawcon hath born my mak away

He bare him up, he bare him down,
He bare him into an orchard brown.

In that orchard ther was an hall,
That was hanged with purpill and pall.

5 And in that hall ther was a bede:
It was hanged with gold so rede.

And in that bed ther lythe a knight,
His woundes bleding day and night.

[10] *bour,* chamber (womb) [16] *spray,* branch [19] *swich,* such
(11) *fawcon,* falcon; *mak,* mate
[4] *pall,* white linen cloth to cover chalice

By that bedes side ther kneleth a may,
10 And she wepeth both night and day.

And by that bedes side ther stondeth a ston,
Corpus Christi wreten theron.

12 (*1372*)

Lullay, lullay, litel child,
Why wepest thou so sore?

Lullay, lullay, litel child:
Thou that were so sterne and wild
Now art become meke and mild,
To saven that was forlore.

5 But for my senne I wot it is
That Godes sone suffret this:
Mercy, Lord, I have do mis;
Iwis I wile no more.

Ayenis my fadres wille I ches
10 An appel with a rewful res;
Werfore min heritage I les,
And now thou wepest therfore.

An appel I tok off a tre —
God it hadde forboden me;
15 Wherfore I shulde dampned be,
Yef thy weping ne wore.

Lullay for wo, thou litel thing,
Thou litel barun, thou litel king;

[9] *may,* maiden [12] *Corpus Christi,* the body of Christ
(12) [5] *senne,* sin; *wot,* know [7] *do mis,* done wrong [8] *Iwis,* Certainly
[9] *Ayenis,* Against; *ches,* chose [10] *res,* rashness [11] *les,* lost
[16] *Yef,* If; *ne wore,* were not

Mankinde is cause of thy murning,
20 That thou hast loved so yore.

For man that thou hast ay loved so
Yet shaltou suffren peines mo,
In heved, in feet, in hondes to,
And yet wepen wel more.

25 That peine us make of senne fre,
That peine us bringe Jesu to thee,
That peine us helpe ay to fle
The wickede fendes lore. Amen.

13 *(Ca. 1500)*

William Dunbar

(*Ca.* 1460–*ca.* 1513)

Hale! sterne superne. Hale! in eterne,
In Godis sicht to shine.
Lucerne in derne forto discerne
Be glory and grace devine.
5 Hodiern, modern, sempitern,
Angelicall Regine,
Our tern inferne forto dispern
Helpe, rialest rosine!
Ave! Maria, gracia plena.
10 Haile! freshe floure feminine,
Yerne us, guberne, virgin matern,
Of reuth baith rute and rine.

20 *so yore,* for so long 21 *ay,* always 22 *mo,* more 23 *heved,* head
(13) 1 *sterne superne,* star on high; *eterne,* eternity
3 Lamp which looks into darkness 4 *Be,* By, Through 5 Today, now, forever
6 *Regine,* Queen 7 *tern inferne,* trouble below; *dispern,* disperse
8 *rosine,* rose 9 Hail! Mary, full of grace. 11 *Yerne,* Desire; *guberne,* govern
12 Of pity both root and rind

Haile! ying bening, freshe flurishing,
    Haile! Alphais habitakle;
15 Thy ding ofspring maid us to sing
    Befor his tabernakle.
All thing maling we downe thring
    Be sicht of his signakle,
Whilk King us bring unto his ring
20   Fro dethis dirk umbrakle.
Ave! Maria, gracia plena.
    Haile! moder and maide, but makle,
Bricht sing glading our languishing
    Be micht of thy mirakle.

25 Haile! bricht be sicht in Hevin on hicht,
    Haile! day sterne orientale,
Our licht most richt in clud of nicht
    Our dirkness forto scale.
Hale! wicht in ficht, puttar to flicht
30   Of fendis in battale;
Haile! plicht but sicht, hale! mekle of micht,
    Haile! glorius virgin, hale!
Ave! Maria, gracia plena.
    Haile! gentill nichttingale,
35 Way stricht, cler dicht to wilsome wicht
    That irke bene in travale.

Hale! Quene serene, hale! most amene,
    Haile! hevinlye hie empris;

13 *ying bening,* young gentle one (MS *yhyng*); *flurishing,* flowering
14 *Alphais habitakle,* Alpha's (Christ's) habitation 15 *ding,* worthy
17 *maling,* malign; *thring,* throw 18 *signakle,* sign of the cross
19 *Whilk,* Which; *ring,* kingdom 20 *umbrakle,* shade
22 *but makle,* without spot 23 *sing,* sign 26 *orientale,* eastern
28 *scale,* drive away 29 *wicht,* creature
31 *plicht but sicht,* support without sight, unseen; *mekle,* great
35 The strait way, clearly made ready for a straying creature
36 That weary are in labor 37 *amene,* gentle 38 *hie,* high

Haile! shene unseyne with carnale eyne,
40 Haile! Ros of Paradis.
Haile! clene, bedene, ay till conteyne,
Haile! fair freshe flour-de-lyce;
Haile! grene daseyne, Hale! fro the splene
Of Jesu genitrice.
45 *Ave! Maria, gracia plena.*
Thou bair the Prince of Pris,
Our teyne to meyne and ga betweyne,
As humile oratrice.

Hale! more decore than of before,
50 And swetar be sic sevine;
Our glore forlore forto restor
Sen thou art Quene of Hevin—
Memore of sore, stern in aurore,
Lovit with angellis stevine—
55 Implore, adore, thou indeflore,
To mak ous oddis evine.
Ave! Maria, gracia plena.
With lovingis loude ellevin,
Whill store and hore my youth devor,
60 Thy name I shall ay nevine.

Emprice of pris, Imperatrice,
Bricht, polist, precious stane,
Victrice of vice, hie genitrice
Of Jesu, Lord soveraine;
65 Our wis pavis fro enemis
Agane the feindis traine.

39 *shene,* beautiful; *eyne,* eyes 41 Hail! purity, now, always to remain
43 *grene daseyne,* flowering (?) daisy; *splene,* spleen (the seat of the affections)
47 *teyne to meyne,* misery to lessen 48 As humble spokesman
49 *decore,* becoming 50 *be sic sevine,* through such seven 52 *Sen,* Because
53 Remembrance of pain, star of morning 54 Praised by angel's shout (song?)
55 *indeflore,* undeflowered 58 With praises loudly extolled
59 *store and hore,* trouble and age 60 *nevine,* call (upon)
65 *wis pavis,* wise shield 66 *Agane,* Against; *traine,* treachery

Oratrice, mediatrice, salvatrice,
To God gret suffragane.
Ave! Maria, gracia plena.
70 Haile! sterne meridiane,
Spice, flour-de-lice of Paradis,
That baire the glorius graine.

Imperiall wall, place palestrall,
Of peirles pulcritud,
75 Triumphale hall, hie trone regall
Of Godis celsitud;
Hospitall riall, the Lord of all
Thy closet did include,
Bricht ball cristall, ros virginall,
80 Fulfillit of angell fude.
Ave! Maria, gracia plena.
Thy birth has, with his blude,
Fra fall mortall, originall,
Us raunsound on the Rude.

14 *(Ca. 1500)*

William Dunbar

Rorate celi desuper!
Hevins, distill your balmy shouris,
For now is rissin the bricht day ster
Fro the ros Mary, flour of flouris.
5 The cleir sone, whome no clud devouris,
Surmunting Phebus in the est,

68 *suffragane,* one who stands in place of another, co-adjutor
70 *meridiane,* noon 72 *graine,* seed (Christ) 73 *palestrall,* palatial
75 *trone,* throne 76 *celsitud,* greatness 77 *Hospitall,* Inn
78 Thy womb did contain 80 *Fulfillit,* Filled; *angell fude, i.e.,* Christ
82 *birth,* child

(14) 1 Drop down dew, ye heavens, from above (Isaiah, 45:8).
3 *ster,* star 5 *clud,* cloud 6 *Surmunting,* Surpassing

Is cumin of his hevinly touris
Et nobis Puer natus est.

Archangellis, Angellis, and Dampnationis,
10 Tronis, Potestatis, and Marteiris seir,
And all ye hevinly operationis,
Ster, planeit, firmament, and speir,
Fire, erd, air, and watter cleir,
To him gife loving, most and lest,
15 That come in to so meik maneir
Et nobis Puer natus est.

Synnaris, be glaid and pennance do,
And thank your Makar hairtfully,
For he that ye micht nocht cum to
20 To you is cumin full humly
Your saulis with his blud to by,
And lous you of the feindis arrest,
And only of his awin mercy
Pro nobis Puer natus est.

25 All clergy, do to him incline,
And bow unto that barne bening,
And do your observance devine
To him that is of kingis King;
Ensence his altar, reid, and sing
30 In haly kirk, with mind degest,
Him honouring attour all thing
Qui nobis Puer natus est.

[8] And unto us a Child is born (Isaiah, 9:6).

[9–10] Archangels, Angels, Dominations, Thrones, and Powers are five of the nine orders of medieval angelology. The other four are the Seraphim, Cherubim, Principalities, and Virtues.

[10] *seir,* various [11] *operationis,* works [12] *speir,* sphere [13] *erd,* earth

[14] *loving,* praise; *most and lest,* highest and lowest

[18] *hairtfully,* from the heart [20] *humly,* humbly [21] *by,* buy

[22] *lous,* set free; *arrest,* thralldom [23] *awin,* own [24] *Pro,* For

[26] *barne bening,* gentle bairn [30] *degest,* fixed

[31] *attour,* above [32] *Qui,* Who

Celestiall fowlis in the air,
Sing with your nottis upoun hicht;
35 In firthis and in forrestis fair
Be mirthfull now, at all your micht,
For passit is your dully nicht:
Aurora hes the cluddis perst,
The Son is rissin with glaidsum licht
40 *Et nobis Puer natus est.*

Now spring up, flouris, fra the rute,
Revert you upwart naturaly
In honour of the blissit frute
That rais up fro the rose Mary;
45 Lay out your levis lustely,
Fro deid tak life now at the lest
In wirship of that Prince wirthy
Qui nobis Puer natus est.

Sing, Hevin imperiall, most of hicht,
50 Regions of air, mak armony;
All fishe in flud and fowll of flicht,
Be mirthfull and mak melody:
All *Gloria in excelsis* cry —
Hevin, erd, se, man, bird, and best:
55 He that is crownit abone the sky
Pro nobis Puer natus est.

15 *(Ca. 1500)*

William Dunbar

Done is a battell on the dragon blak!
Our campioun Christ confoundit hes his force;

33 *air,* MS *are* 34 *nottis,* music 35 *firthis,* arms of the sea 37 *dully,* sorrowful
38 *perst,* pierced 39 *glaidsum,* bringing gladness 41 *rute,* root
42 *Revert,* Turn 44 *rais,* rose 45 *Lay out,* Put forth; *lustely,* joyfully
46 *deid,* death 53 *Gloria in excelsis,* Glory (to God) in the highest
55 *abone,* above
(15) 1 *dragon,* Satan 2 *hes,* has

The yettis of Hell ar brokin with a crak,
The signe triumphall rasit is of the croce,
5 The divillis trimmillis with hiddous voce,
The saulis ar borrowit and to the blis can go;
Christ with his blud our ransonis dois indoce:
Surrexit Dominus de sepulchro.

Dungin is the deidly dragon Lucifer,
10 The crewall serpent with the mortall stang;
The auld kene tegir with his teith on char
Whilk in a wait hes lyne for us so lang,
Thinking to grip us in his clowis strang,
The mercifull Lord wald nocht that it wer so —
15 He maid him forto felye of that fang:
Surrexit Dominus de sepulchro.

He for our saik that sufferit to be slane
And lik a lamb in sacrifice wes dicht,
Is lik a lione rissin up agane,
20 And as giane raxit him on hicht;
Sprungin is Aurora, radius and bricht,
On loft is gone the glorius Appollo,
The blisfull day departit fro the nicht:
Surrexit Dominus de sepulchro.

25 The grit victour agane is rissin on hicht,
That for our querrell to the deth wes woundit;
The sone that wox all paill now shinis bricht,
And, dirknes clerit, our faith is now refoundit;
The knell of mercy fra the Hevin is soundit,

[3] *yettis,* gates [4] *rasit,* raised; *croce,* cross [5] *trimmillis,* tremble; *voce,* voice
[6] *borrowit,* redeemed [7] *dois indoce,* does endorse
[8] The Lord is risen from the tomb: first versicle for matins on Easter Sunday.
[9] *Dungin,* Overcome [10] *stang,* sting [11] *auld,* old; *on char,* open
[12] *in a wait,* watching; *lyne,* lain [13] *clowis,* claws [15] *felye,* fail; *fang,* booty
[18] *dicht,* prepared [20] *giane raxit,* giant stretches
[21] *Aurora,* Morning Star (Christ) [22] *Appollo,* Sun (Christ)
[26] *querrell,* cause [28] *refoundit,* reestablished
[29] *knell of mercy,* ringing of bells on Easter Sunday

30 The Cristin ar deliverit of thair wo,
The Jowis and thair errour ar confoundit:
Surrexit Dominus de sepulchro.

The fo is chasit, the battell is done ceis;
The presone brokin, the jevellouris fleit and flemit;
35 The weir is gon, confermit is the peis;
The fetteris lowsit, and the dungeoun temit;
The ransoun maid, the presoneris redemit;
The feild is win, ourcumin is the fo,
Dispulit of the tresur that he yemit:
40 *Surrexit Dominus de sepulchro.*

16 *(Ca. 1440)*

Charles d'Orleans
(1394–1465)

A pak, a pak, Madame, my lode alight,
Forwhy, allas, I bere too hevy, lo!
And without you I may no ferthir go.
So helpe me sett my croked burthen right,
5 Or ellis ye are to blame, by God almight,
For me mysilf wolde helpe you, bare ye so.
A pak, a pak, Madame, my lode alight,
Forwhy, alas, I bere too hevy, lo!
There is no mo to calle now here in sight,
10 So helpe or ellis attonis become my foo.
Now, mercy! swete, but will ye, lo, or noo,
Have pite now upon me, poore wight?

33 *done ceis,* caused to cease 34 *jevellouris,* jailers; *fleit and flemit,* fled and banished
35 *weir,* war; *peis,* peace 36 *lowsit,* loosed; *temit,* emptied
39 *Dispulit,* Despoiled; *yemit,* kept
(16) 1 *pak,* package, bundle; *alight,* lighten
2 *Forwhy,* Because; *too hevy,* too much; *lo,* lo 9 *mo,* more; *calle,* call on
10 *attonis,* at once 11 *or noo,* or not 12 *wight,* creature

A pak, a pak, Madame, my lode alight,
Forwhy, alas, I bere too hevy, lo!

17 *(Ca. 1440)*

Charles d'Orleans

The mede is flowe, the grace is goon,
The hert is chaunged from his place:
    Where I had wende hem be, ne nas;
    Thus Mirthe and I are comen foon.
5   But, fy! allas, that a wise oon
    Shulde "hay!" or they se what to chas.
The mede is flowe, the grace is goon,
The hert is chaunged from his place.
    Yet trust I, lo, to finde aloon
10   An hert, if that I have the grace;
    And if I onis may that purchace
    Then "hay on hardely, everichoon!"
The meede is flowe, the grace is goon,
The hert is chaunged from his place.

(17) 1 *mede,* reward (with pun on meadow); *grace,* grace (with pun on grass)
2 *hert,* heart (with pun on hart); *his,* its
3 Where I had thought them to be, they were not. 4 *comen foon,* become foes
6 Should shout "hey!" before they see what to chase
11 *purchace,* obtain 12 *hay,* shout "hey!"

VERSE CHRONICLE

A VERSE CHRONICLE is a detailed and continuous verse history, generally written by one author over a short period of time. There are eight extant in Middle English, all of them written between the thirteenth and the fifteenth centuries. Of these, Layamon's *Brut* is the most famous, as well as the earliest and perhaps the best. The only other with much literary merit is John Barbour's *Bruce,* written in 1375.

All the Middle English verse chronicles are expressions of national pride, whether British, English, or Scottish; and either by direct statement or by implication they proposed to teach their national history to those who could not read it themselves. Many, like Layamon's *Brut,* begin with the traditional fable of the founding of Britain by Aeneas' legendary great-grandson, Brut, and continue to the author's own time.

18 *(Early 13th c.)*

From LAYAMON'S BRUT

The Round Table

Layamon
(fl. early 13th c.)

And seide that he wolde ayæin to thisse londe
And iseon Wenhaiver, the wuneliche quene.
Bemen he lette blawen and bonnien his ferden,
And to shipen wenden wunder blithe theines.
5 Wind heom stod on willen, weder alse heo wolden;
Blithe heo weoren alle forthi; up heo comen at Grimesbi.
That iherden sone tha hæhste of thissen londe;
And to thære quene com tidende of Arthure than kinge,
That he wes isund icumen, and his folc on selen.
10 Tha weoren inne Bruttene blissin inowe:

[Arthur has just completed a series of short, successful campaigns that have brought under his control Ireland, Iceland, the Orkneys, Gothland (either southern Sweden or the island of Gotland off the east coast of Sweden), and Winetland (the territory south of the Baltic between the Oder and Vistula rivers, inhabited by the Wends). He is now anxious to return to Britain ("thisse londe") and to Guinevere (Wenhaiver), whom he had married only the winter before. The following literal translation is based on that of Sir Frederic Madden.]

And [Arthur] said that he would [go] again to this land
and see Wenhaiver, the lovely queen.
He had trumpets blown and his army assembled,
and to ship went the wondrously blithe thanes.
5 The wind stood at their will, weather as they wished;
blithe they all were therefore; up they came at Grimesby.
Soon the highest of this land heard that;
and to the queen came tidings of Arthur the king,
that he was safely come, and his people in prosperity.
10 Then were in Britain joys enough:

(18) 6 *Grimesbi,* Grimsby, a town on the Humber estuary in NE Lincs.

Her wes fithelinge and song; her wes harpinge imong —
Pipen and bemen murie ther sungen;
Scopes ther sungen of Arthure than kingen
And of than muchele wurthshipe the he iwunnen hafeden.
15 Folc com to hirede of feole cunne theode;
Widen and siden folc wes on selen.
Al that Arthur isæh, al hit him to bæh,
Riche men and povere, swa the hayel valleth;
Nef ther nan swa wræcche Brut that he nes awælyed.
20 Her mon mai arede of Arthure than king,
Hu he twelf yere seothen wuneden here
Inne grithe and inne frithe, in alle væyernesse.
Na man him ne faht with, no he ne makede nan unfrith.
Ne mihtẹ navere nan man bithenchen of blissen
25 That weoren in ai theode mare than i thisse;
Ne mihte navere mon cunne nan swa muchel wunne
Swa wes mid Arthure and mid his folke here.
Ich mai sugge hu hit iwarth, wunder thæh hit thunche.
Hit wes in an Yeol-dæie that Arthur in Lundene lai;

here was fiddling and song; here was harping among [them] —
pipes and trumpets sang there merrily;
scops sang there of Arthur the king
and of the great honor that he had won.
15 People came all together from many kinds of lands;
far and wide the people were in prosperity.
All that Arthur saw, all bowed to him,
rich men and poor, as the hail falls;
there was no Briton so wretched who was not enriched.
20 Here man may tell of Arthur the king,
how afterwards he lived here for twelve years
in peace and in concord, in all fairness.
No man fought with him, nor did he cause any strife.
No man might ever imagine joys
25 that were in any country greater than in this;
nor might man ever know so much joy
as was with Arthur and with his people here.
I may say how it happened, wondrous though it seems.
It was on a Yule-day that Arthur lay in London;

[13] *Scopes,* scops — *i.e.,* poets or minstrels

30 Tha weoren him to icumen of alle his kinerichen —
Of Brutlonde, of Scotlonde, of Irlonde, of Islonde,
And of al than londe the Arthur hæfede an honde —
Alle tha hæxte theines mid horsen and mid sweines.
Ther weoren seoven kingene sunes mid seoven hundred
knihten icumen,
35 Withuten than hired the herede Arthure.
Ælc hafede an heorte leches hehe,
And lette that he weore betere than his ivere.
That folc wes of feole londe; ther wes muchel onde,
For the an hine talde hæh, tha other muche herre.
40 Tha bleou mon tha bemen and tha bordes bradden;
Water me brohte an vloren mid guldene læflen,
Seothen clathes soften, al of white seolke.
Tha sat Arthur adun, and bi him Wenhaver tha quene.
Seothen sete tha eorles, and ther after tha beornes;
45 Seothen tha knihtes, al swa mon heom dihte.
Tha hehe iborne thene mete beoren
Æfne forth rihten tha to than knihten,
Tha touward than thæinen, tha touward than sweinen,

30 then were come to him from all his kingdoms —
from Britain, from Scotland, from Ireland, from Iceland,
and from all the lands that Arthur had in hand —
all the highest thanes with horses and with swains.
There were seven kings' sons with seven hundred knights come,
35 not counting the people who served Arthur.
Each had in his heart proud thoughts,
and allowed that he was better than his fellow.
That folk was from many a land; there was much envy,
because the one counted himself high, the other much higher.
40 Then men blew the trumpets and spread the tables;
men brought water onto the floor with golden bowls,
afterwards soft clothes, all of white silk.
Then Arthur sat down, and by him Wenhaver the queen.
Then the eorls sat down, and after that the nobles;
45 then the knights, as men arranged them.
The high born carried the meat
directly to the knights,
then to the thanes, then to the swains,

Tha touward than bermonnen, forth at than borden.
50 Tha duwethe wærth iwrathed; duntes ther weoren rive.
Ærest tha laves heo weorpen, tha while tha heo ilæsten,
And tha bollen seolverne mid wine ivulled,
And seothen tha vustes vusden to sweoren.
Tha leop ther forth a yung mon the ut of Winetlonde com —
55 He wes iyefen Arthur to halden to yisle,
He wes Rumarettes sune, thas kinges of Winette.
Thus seide the kniht there to Arthure kinge:
"Laverd Arthur, buh rathe into thine bure,
And thy quene mid the, and thine mæies cuthe;
60 And we this comp shullen todelen with thas uncuthe kempen."
Æfne than worde he leop to than borde,
Ther leien tha knives biforen than leodkinge;
Threo knifes he igrap, and mid than anæ he smat
I there swere the kniht the ærest bigon that ilke fiht,
65 That his hefved i thene flor hælde to grunde.
Sone he sloh ænne other, thes ilke theines brother.
Ær tha sweordes comen seoven he afelde.

then to the porters, forth to the table.
50 The nobles became angry; blows were rife there.
First they threw the loaves, while they lasted,
and then silver bowls filled with wine,
and next the fists struck at throats.
Then there leapt forth a young man who came from Wendland —
55 he was given to Arthur to hold as a hostage,
he was Rumareth's son, the King of Wendland.
Thus said the knight there to King Arthur:
"Lord Arthur, go quickly into your room,
and your queen with you, and your known relatives;
60 and we shall decide this fight against these foreign warriors."
Even [with] these words he leapt to the table,
where the knives lay before the king;
he seized three knives, and with one he smote
in the throat the knight who first began that same fight,
65 so that his head fell to the ground on the floor.
Quickly he slew another, this same thane's brother.
Before the swords came he felled seven.

53 *seothen,* MS *seodden*

Ther wes fæht swithe græt; ælc mon other smat;
Ther wes muchel blod gute; balu wes an hirede.
70 Tha com the king buwen ut of his buren,
Mid him an hundred beornen mid helmen and mid burnen;
Ælc bar an his riht hond whit stelene brond.
Tha cleopede Arthur, athelest kingen:
"Sitteth, sitteth swithe, elc mon bi his live!
75 And wa swa that nulle don, he shal fordemed beon!
Nimeth me thene ilke mon tha this feht ærest bigon,
And doth withe an his sweore and draweth hine to ane more
And doth hine in an ley ven; ther he shal liggen.
And nimeth al his nexte cun tha ye mawen ivinden,
80 And swengeth of tha hafden mid breoden eouwer sweorden!
Tha wifmen tha ye mawen ifinden of his nexten cunden,
Kerveth of hire neose, and heore wlite ga to lose!
And swa ich wulle al fordon that cun that he of com!
And yif ich avere mare seothen ihere
85 That æi of mine hirede, of hehe na of lowe,
Of thissen ilke slehte æft sake are,

There was a very great fight; each man smote the other;
there was much bloodshed; death was among the people.
70 Then the king came out of his room,
with him a hundred nobles with helms and burnies;
each bare in his right hand a white steel sword.
Then Arthur called out, noblest of kings:
"Sit [down], sit quickly, each man by his life!
75 And whoso will not do that, he shall be destroyed!
Seize for me that same man who first began his fight,
and put a withy rope on his neck and draw him to a moor
and put him in a low fen; there he shall lie.
And seize all his nearest kin that you may find,
80 and strike off the heads with your broad swords.
The women that you may find of his nearest kin,
carve off their noses, and their beauty go to destruction.
And so I will completely destroy that race from which he came!
And if I evermore afterwards hear
85 that any of my people, of high or of low [degree],
[because] of this same slaughter again raise strife,

72 *brond,* MS *brod*

Ne shulde him neother gon fore, gold ne na gærsume,
Hæh hors no hære shrud, that he ne shulde beon ded,
Other mid horsen todrawen. That is elches swiken lawen!
90 Bringeth thene halidom and ich wulle swerien theron;
Swa ye shullen, knihtes the weoren at thissen fihte,
Eorles and beornes, that ye hit breken nulleth."
Ærst sweor Arthur, athelest kingen;
Seothen sworen eorles; seothen sweoren beornes;
95 Seothen sweoren theines; seothen sweoren sweines,
That heo navere mare the sake nulde arere.
Me nom alle tha dede and to leirstowe heom ladden.
Seothen me bleou bemen mid swithe murie dremen.
Weoren him leof, weoren him læd, elc ther feng water and clæd,
100 And seothen adun æten sæhte to borden,
Al for Arthure æi ye, athelest kingen.
Birles ther thurngen, gleomen ther sungen,
Harpen gunnen dremen, duwethe wes on selen.
Thus fulle seoveniht wes than hirede idiht.
105 Seothen, hit seith in there tale, the king ferde to Cornwale.

[there] shall go for him [*i.e.*, ransom him] neither gold nor any treasure,
great horse nor war garment, that he shall not be dead,
or drawn to pieces with horses. That is the law for each traitor!
90 Bring the holy relics and I will swear thereon;
so shall you, knights who were at this fight,
eorls and nobles, that you will not break it."
First swore Arthur, noblest of kings;
then swore the eorls; than swore the nobles;
95 then swore the thanes; then swore the swains,
that they nevermore would raise strife.
Men took all the dead and carried them to the graveyard.
Afterward men blew trumpets with a very merry sound.
Were he willing, were he loath, each there took water and cloth,
100 and then sat down at table to eat,
all for dread of Arthur, noblest of kings.
Cupbearers thronged there, gleemen sang there,
harps began to sound, the people were in joy.
Thus for a full sevennight were the people furnished.
105 Afterwards, it says in the tale, the king went to Cornwall.

89 *Other*, MS *orðer*

Ther him com to anan that wæs a crafti weorcmon,
And thene king imette, and feiere hine grætte:
"Hail seo thu, Arthur, athelest kinge!
Ich æm thin awe mon; moni lond ich habbe thurh gan;
110 Ich con of treowrekes, wunder feole craftes.
Ich iherde suggen biyeonde sæ neowe tidende,
That thine knihtes at thine borde gunnen fihte
A midewinteres dæi; moni ther feollen
For heore muchele mode morthgomen wrohten,
115 And for heore hehe cunne ælc wolde beon withinne.
Ah ich the wulle wurche a bord swithe hende
That ther mawen sitten to sixtene hundred and ma,
Al turn abuten, that nan ne beon withuten —
Withuten and withinne, mon toyæines monne.
120 Whenne thu wult riden, with the thu miht leden.
And setten hit whar thu wulle, after thine iwulle.
And ne dert thu navere adrede, to there worlde longen,
That ævere æine modi kniht at thine borde makie fiht,
For ther shal the hehe beon æfne than lowe."

There came to him one that was a crafty workman,
and met the king, and greeted him fair:
"Hail be you, Arthur, noblest king!
I am your own man; many lands I have gone through:
110 I know of treeworks [carpentry], wondrous many crafts.
I heard told beyond the sea new tidings,
that your knights at your table began to fight
on a midwinter's day; many fell there
because their great pride created murder-games,
115 and because of their high lineage each wished to be within.
But I will make for you a table so handsome
that there may sit at [it] sixteen hundred and more,
all turn about, so that none be without —
without and within, man facing man. [Since the table is round,
no man will be placed below another; hence degree at
table can no longer exist to cause strife.]
120 When you wish to ride, you might carry it with you,
and set it where you wish, after your will.
And you need never fear, to the world's ends,
that any proud knight at your table will ever cause [a] fight,
for there shall the high be even with the low."

125 Timber me lete biwinnen, and that beord biginnen;
To feouwer wikene virste that wrec wes ivorthed.
To ane hehe dæie that hired wes isomned,
And Arthur himseolf beh sone to than borde,
And hehte alle his knihtes to than borde forth rihtes.
130 Tho alle weoren iseten, knihtes to heore mete.
That spæc ælc with other alse hit weore his brother:
Alle heo seten abuten; nef ther man withuten.
Ævereælches cunnes kniht there wes swithe wel idiht;
Alle heo weoren bi ane, the hehe and tha lawe;
135 Ne mihten ther nan yelpen for othere kunnes shenchen,
Other his iveren the at than beorde weoren.
This wes that ilke bord that Bruttes of yelpeth,
And suggeth feole cunne lesinge bi Arthure than kinge.
Swa deth aver alc mon the other luvien ne con:
140 Yif he is him to leof, thenne wule he liyen,
And suggen on him wurthshipe mare thennehe beon wurthe;
Ne beo he no swa luther mon that his freond him wel ne on.
Æft yif on volke feondshipe arereth,
An æver æi time bitweone twon monnen,

125 Men had timber brought and the table begun;
in four weeks' time the work was finished.
On a high day [feast day] the people were assembled,
and Arthur himself came quickly to the table,
and ordered all his knights to the table immediately.
130 When all were seated, the knights at their meat,
then each spoke with other as [if] it were his brother:
they all sat around [the table]; there was no man without.
Every kind of knight was very well provided there;
all were [treated] the same, the high and the low;
135 no one there might boast of any other kind of drink,
other than [that of] his comrades who were at that table.
This was that same table that Britons boast about,
and tell all kinds of lies about Arthur the king.
So always does each man who cannot love other:
140 if he is too dear to him, then he will lie,
and say of him more honor than he is worth;
nor is there a man so evil that his friend will not act well to him.
On the other hand, if among people strife arises,
in ever any time between two men,

145 Me con bi than læthe lasinge suggen
Theh he weore bezste mon the ævere æt at borde;
The mon the him weore lath, him cuthe last finden.
Ne al soh ne al les that leodscopes singeth,
Ah this is that sothe bi Arthure than kinge:
150 Nes næver ar swulc king swa duhti thurh alle thing.
For that sothe stod a than writen, hu hit is iwurthen
Ord from than ænden of Arthure than kinge,
No mare no lasse buten alse his lawen weoren.
Ah Bruttes hine luveden swithe and ofte him on liyeth
155 And suggeth feole thinges bi Arthure than kinge
That nævere nes iwurthen a thissere weorlderichen.
Inoh he mai suggen, the soth wule vremmen,
Seolcuthe thinges bi Arthure kinge.
Tha wes Arthur swithe heh, his hired swithe hende,
160 That nas na kniht wel itald no of his tuhlen swithe bald
Inne Wales no in Ænglelond, inne Scot no in Irlond,
In Normandie no inne France, inne Flanders no inne Denemarc,
No in navere none londe the a theos halfe Mungiu stondeth,

145 men can tell lies of the hated one
though he were the best man who ever ate at table;
the man who was hateful to him, him he can find last.
Neither all truth nor all lies that minstrels sing,
but this is the truth about Arthur the king:
150 there was never before such a king so powerful in all things.
For that truth stood in those writings, how it has happened
from beginning to the end of Arthur the king,
no more nor less but as his laws were.
But Britons loved him greatly and often lie about him
155 and say many things about Arthur the king
that never happened in this world's realm.
He may say enough, who wishes to speak truth,
wonderful things about Arthur the king.
Then was Arthur most high, his people most fair,
160 that there was no knight well accounted nor of his manners so assured
in Wales nor in England, in Scotland nor in Ireland,
in Normandy nor in France, in Flanders nor in Denmark,
nor in ever any land that on this side of Mountjoy stands,

[163] *Mungiu,* Mountjoy: Great St. Bernard Pass, Haute-Savoie

Thet weoren ihalde god kniht no his deden itald oht,
165 Bute of he cuthe of Arthure and of athelen his hirede,
His wepnen and his weden and his hors leden,
Suggen and singen: of Arthure than yinge
And of his hired knihten, and of hehe heore mihten
And of heore riche dome, and hu wel hit heom bicomen.
170 Thenne weore he wilcume a thissere weorlderichen,
Come ther he come; and theh he weore i Rome,
Al that iherde of Arthure telle,
Heom thuhte muchel seollic of selen than kinge.
And swa hit wes ivuren iboded, ær he iboren weoren:
175 Swa him sæide Merlin, the witeye wes mære,
That a king shulde cume of Uthere Pendragune;
That gleomen shulden wurchen burd of thas kinges breosten,
And ther to sitten scopes swithe sele
And eten heore vullen ær heo thenne fusden,
180 And winshenches ut teon of theos kinges tungen,
And drinken and dreomen daies and nihtes.
This gomen heom shulde ilasten to there weorlde longe.

who was held a good knight nor his deeds accounted anything,
165 unless he could of Arthur and of his noble people,
his weapons and his clothes and his horsemen,
speak and sing: of Arthur the young
and of his knights, and of their great might,
and of their wealth, and how well it became them.
170 Then were he welcome to this world's realm,
no matter where he came from; and though he were in Rome,
all that heard Arthur spoken of,
to them it seemed a great wonder of the good king.
And so it was earlier forboded, before he was born:
175 so said Merlin, who was a great prophet,
that a king should come of Uther Pendragon;
that gleemen should make a table from this king's breast,
and thereat [should] sit very good scops
and eat their fill before they departed thence,
180 and wine draughts draw out from this king's tongue,
and drink and revel day and night.
This play should last them to the world's end.

176 *Uthere Pendragune,* Uther Pendragon. Arthur was the child of Uther and Ygaerne, wife of the Earl of Cornwall. 177 *Kinges,* MS *Kiges*

And yet him seide Marlin mare that wes to comene:
That al that he lokede on to foten him shulde buwen.
185 Tha yet him sæide Mærlin a sellic the wes mare,
That shulde beon unimete care of thas kinges forth fare.
And of thas kinges ende nulle hit na Brut ileve,
Buten hit beon the leste dæth at than muchele dome,
Thenne ure drihte demeth alle volke.
190 Ælles ne cunne we demen of Arthures dethen,
For he seolf sæide to sele his Brutten,
Suth inne Cornwale, ther Walwain wes forfaren
And himseolf wes forwunded wunder ane swithe,
That he varen wolde into Avalune,
195 Into than æitlond, to Argante there hende;
For heo shulde mid haleweie helen his wunden,
And thenne he weore al hal, he wolde com heom.
This ilefde Bruttes, thet he wule cumen thus,
And lokieth a whenne he cume to his londe
200 Swa he heom bihahte ar he heonne wende.

And yet Merlin said more that was to come:
that all that he [Arthur] looked on should bow down to his feet.
185 Then again Merlin said a wonder that was greater,
that there should be heavy sorrow at this king's departure.
And of this king's end no Briton will believe it,
unless it is the last death at the great doom,
when our Lord judges all people.
190 Otherwise we cannot judge of Arthur's death,
for he himself said to his good Britons [that he would go]
south to Cornwall, where Walwain was slain
and himself was wounded very severely,
that he would go to Avalon,
195 to that island, to Argante the beautiful;
for she should with balsam heal his wounds,
and when he was all whole, he would come to them.
This the Britons believed, that he will thus come,
and [they] look to [the time] when he [will] come to his land
200 as he promised them before he went from it.

192 *Walwain,* Gawain, who, according to Layamon, later died at Romney in Kent

195 *Argante,* Morgan Le Fay, Arthur's half-sister

ROMANCE

THE TERM *romance* originally referred to the vernacular language of France, as distinct from the Latin from which it derived and which continued throughout the Middle Ages to be the international language of learning, religion, politics, and the law. *Romance* therefore referred to anything written in French, but increasingly it became associated with stories of knightly adventure, regardless of the language in which they were actually written, because such stories were associated especially with France.

The chivalric romance almost certainly developed out of an earlier epic tradition that in England had produced such heroic tales as *Beowulf,* and in France was still producing *chansons de geste* like *Roland.* Like the epic before it, the romance usually centers on the adventures of a warrior hero; but because of the influences of a feudal aristocracy whose entertainments were increasingly luxurious and increasingly influenced by women, the romances have a very different tone. While the epic hero was motivated by male allegiances — to his lord or to his comrades — and was almost exclusively occupied with warfare of one sort or another, the chivalric knight is motivated also, and even more importantly, by love for his lady and devotion to his God, and his occupations may include the soft dalliances of love as well as the rigors of battle. (The transition appears in *Roland,* in which appear significant religious influences, but not yet the influence of women.) While the epic hero undertook adventures which were forced upon him, the chivalric knight is increasingly required to seek out adventures simply for their own sake, wandering in search of encounters that will prove him worthy as his lady's — or God's — knight. Even when his adventures seem to force themselves upon him, as the Green Knight forces his challenge on Arthur's court, the antagonist often proves to be only an artificial threat constructed to prove a point, rather than a threat that emerges naturally from the substance of actual human experience (natural or supernatural), as Grendel and the dragon emerge in *Beowulf,* or the Saracens in *Roland.*

The subjects of medieval romance have traditionally been classified under various national themes, or "matters," especially those three *matières* enumerated by Jean Bodel at the end of the twelfth century: the Matter of France (Charlemagne and his Frankish knights), the Matter of Britain (Arthur and his knights of the Round Table), and the Matter of Rome the Great (the Trojan War, the Siege of Thebes, Alexander the Great, *etc.*). Later a fourth classification was added, the Matter of England (Guy of Warwick, Athelstan, Gamelyn, *etc.*). Actually, these categories do not begin to exhaust the subjects of medieval romance, which could in fact come from any source — folk lore, oriental tales, religious legend. What defines a romance is not so much the source of the story as the manner in which the story is treated.

Like most medieval literature the romance often included a didactic element, but its first purpose was to entertain a courtly audience made up of both men and women. To this end, its characters, properties, and setting, regardless of their historical or geographical origin, were thoroughly medievalized. The characters become medieval kings and knights and ladies whose actions are directed by the social and ethical ideals of medieval chivalry. The adventures are motivated by the love of a lady or, less frequently, the love of God, by loyalty to one's king or simple devotion to knightly ideals, by the love of adventure itself, or by a combination of all these. The fabric of adventure is enriched by elaborate descriptions — the sumptuous details of a banquet, the elaborate decorations of armor or dress, the rich appointments of a chamber within the castle or of a jousting yard outside. The setting is a sort of wonderland, in which vividly natural details stand side by side with the most extravagant enchantments and marvels, not the least of which is the disappearance of those economic and linguistic difficulties which beset real travellers, no matter how grand. Similarly, the familiar relationships of time and space are violated whenever it seems convenient. Usually, but not always, the romance has a happy ending.

All these characteristics invite the exaggerations which have often led modern readers to suppose that medieval romance is by nature unable to deal significantly with human experience. However, the chivalric ideals and even the marvels can make these stories more real instead of "romantically" remote. It has, indeed, been suggested that romances may have been so popular because, "unlike so much of the Latin literature known to medieval readers, they were up to date in their ideas and their properties."[1] Although these romances were intended to entertain by providing an escape, the best ones did so not by removing themselves from real life, but by heightening real life. Armor was richer, gowns more gorgeous, feasts more sumptuous, marvels more abundant than in real life. But all of these elements, including the marvelous, were first of all the ingredients of actual experience; and their heightening was, by the best writers, managed so as to emphasize and then intensify the familiarity, not the remoteness of things. By this heightening and arranging of materials drawn from familiar experience, the writer of medieval romance can thus be working toward that ordering and intensifying of human experience which we recognize to be one of the chief businesses of art.

The romances of chivalry appeared in France in the twelfth century and flourished into the thirteenth. Romances came to England through the Normans, but because of the long predominance of French as the language of the English court, few romances were written in English until about the middle of the thirteenth century, much later than the great period of the French romances which inspired them. The English romances were frequently translated from or at least based on a French original, but usually the English versions reveal relatively less interest in the minute psychology of love, relatively more in the knightly adventures which such love inspired. There are roughly fifty surviving romances in Middle English, more or fewer depending upon one's definition of a genre that can easily merge with verse chronicle or the didactic tale. The earlier English romances were in verse of various metrical and stanzaic forms, but the octosyllabic couplet and tail-rhyme stanzas were perhaps most common. (*A tail-rhyme stanza* consists of rhymed groups of lines which are followed by lines of different length — usually shorter, hence "tails" — which rhyme with each other: *e.g.,* aab ccb ddb eeb, with the "b" line often carrying four stresses, the others, three stresses. See *The Tournament of Tottenham* for use of this stanza form in burlesque.) After the middle of the fourteenth century romances might be written in either verse or prose; after the middle of the fifteenth they were almost always written in prose. Verse romances generally extended from 1000 to 5000

[1] Dorothy Everett, *Essays on Middle English Literature* (London: Oxford University Press, 1951), p. 6. See generally pp. 4–13.

lines, though they might be shorter or longer. Prose romances were usually very long, sometimes running into several volumes.

A special, briefer type of medieval romance is the Breton Lay. The origins of this form are associated with Marie de France, an early twelfth-century poetess about whom we know very little except that she was apparently French but lived and wrote in England. Marie wrote a number of short romances whose source, she claimed, was *lais* sung by Breton minstrels, though the word *lai* itself indicates that the tradition extended behind the Bretons to the Celts of Ireland and Wales, who sang short tales to the accompaniment of a musical instrument like the harp or viol. After Marie, the form became popular in France, but it was not until the fourteenth century that the vogue became established in England, well after its popularity in France had declined. The distinguishing characteristics of a Breton lay, as it was understood by English poets of the fourteenth century, are set forth in the beginning of *Sir Orfeo* and in Chaucer's "Franklin's Tale." They are short enough for recitation at one sitting; the adventures are often set in Brittany; the emphasis is more on love than on battle; and they rely heavily on Celtic færy lore and enchantment. Most of the so-called English Breton lays do incorporate at least some of these characteristics, but the differences among these romances suggest that the form was only vaguely defined in the minds of the English poets, and that the designation of a romance as a Breton lay was mainly intended to take advantage of the popularity enjoyed by this form.

19 (*Ca. 1350–1400*)

From THE ALLITERATIVE MORTE ARTHURE

The Fall of Arthur

Than this roy royall reherses theis wordes:
"Now may we revell and riste, fore Rome es oure awen!
Make oure ostage at ese, thise avenaunt childiren,
And luk ye honden them all that in min oste lenges.
3210 The Emperour of Almayne and alle theis este marches,
We shall be overlinge of all that on the erthe lenges.
We wille by the Crosse Dayes encroche theis londes,
And at the Cristenmesse Daye be crowned theraftere;
Ryngne in my ryalltes and holde my Rounde Table
3215 Withe the rentes of Rome, as me beste likes;
Sine graithe over the grette see with gud men of armes
To revenge the renke that on the rode diede."
Thane this comliche kinge, as cronicles telles,
Bounnes brathely to bede with a blithe herte.
3220 Off he slinges with sleghte and slakes girdill,
And fore sleuthe of slomoure on aslepe falles.
Bot be ane aftire midnighte all his mode changede:
He mett in the morne-while full mervailous dremes,
And when his dredefull drem whas drefen to the ende,
3225 The kinge dares for doute, die as he sholde,

(19) 3206 *roy,* Arthur 3207 *riste,* rest; *awen,* own
3208 *ostage,* hostages; *avenaunt childiren,* handsome nobles
3209 *honden,* hold; *oste,* host; *lenges,* remains
3210 *Almayne,* Germany; *marches,* regions 3211 *overlinge,* ruler
3212 *Crosse Dayes,* Rogation Days, the three days before Ascension Day, which is forty days after Easter; *encroche,* seize
3214 *Ryngne,* Reign
3215 *rentes,* revenues; *as me beste likes,* as it best pleases me
3216 *Sine,* Then; *graithe,* prepare to go 3217 *renke,* man
3218 *comliche,* fair 3219 *Bounnes brathely,* Hurries quickly
3220 *sleghte,* dexterity; *slakes,* loosens 3221 *sleuthe,* sloth; *slomoure,* slumber
3222 *be ane,* at one 3223 *mett,* dreamed; *morne-while,* morning-time
3224 *whas drefen,* was driven 3225 The king cowers for fear, as though he should die.

Sendes aftire philosophers and his affraie telles.
"Sen I was formede, in faith, so ferde whas I never!
Forthy, raunsakes redily and rede me my swefenes,
And I shall redily and righte rehersen the sothe.
3230 Me thoughte I was in a wode, willed min one,
That I ne wiste no waye whedire that I sholde,
Fore wolves and whilde swine and wikkede bestes
Walkede in that wasterne, wathes to seche.
Thare liouns full lothely likkede theire tuskes
3235 All fore lapinge of blude of my lele knightes.
Thurghe that foreste I flede, thare floures whare heghe,
For to fele me for ferde of tha foule thinges;
Merkede to a medowe with montaingnes enclosede,
The merieste of medillerthe that men mighte beholde.
3240 The close was in compas casten all aboute,
With claver and clereworte clede even over.
The vale was enverounde with vines of silver
All with grapes of golde — gretter ware never,
Enhorilde with arborye and alkins trees,
3245 Erberes full honeste and hirdes thereundire.
All froites foddemed was that floreshede in erthe,
Faire frithed in fraunke, appon tha free bowes.
Whas thare no dounkinge of dewe that oghte dere sholde;

3226 *affraie,* fear 3227 *Sen,* Since; *ferde,* afraid
3228 Therefore, investigate readily and interpret my dreams.
3229 *righte,* rightly; *sothe,* truth
3230 It seemed to me I was in a wood, lost alone by myself.
3231 *ne wiste,* did not know
3233 *wasterne,* wasteland; *wathes to seche,* seeking prey 3235 *lele,* loyal
3236 *thare,* where; *whare heghe,* were high
3237 To lay low (conceal myself) for fear of those hideous things
3238 *Merkede,* Went 3239 *medillerthe,* middle-earth, the world
3240 *close,* enclosure; *compas,* circumscribed area; *casten,* laid out in order
3241 With clover and small clover covered evenly over
3242 *enverounde,* surrounded, MS *euenrownde*
3244 *Enhorilde,* Edged; *arborye,* shrubs; *alkins,* all kinds of
3245 *Erberes,* Arbors; *honeste,* genuine; *hirdes,* shepherds
3246 *froites,* fruits; *foddemed,* produced
3247 *frithed in fraunke,* protected in an enclosure
3248 *that oghte dere sholde,* that could harm anything

With the droughte of the daye all drye ware the flores.
3250 "Than discendes in the dale down fra the cloudes
A Duches dereworthily dighte in diaperde wedes,
In a surcott of silke full selcouthely hewede,
All with loyotour overlaide lowe to the hemmes
And with ladily lappes the lenghe of a yerde,
3255 And all redily reverssede with rebanes of golde;
With bruches and besauntes and other brighte stones
Hir bake and hir breste was brochede all over,
With kelle and with corenall clenliche arrayede,
And that so comly of colour on knowen was never.
3260 Aboute sho whirllede a whele with hir whitte hondes,
Overwhelme all quaintely the whele as sho sholde.
The rowell whas rede golde with ryall stones,
Railede with reched and rubies inewe;
The spekes was splentede all with speltes of silver
3265 The space of a spere lenghe springande full faire.
Thereone was a chaiere of chalke-whitte silver
And chekerde with charebokle, chaunginge of hewes.
Appon the compas ther clewede kinges one rawe
With corowns of clere golde that crakede in sondire.
3270 Sex was off that setill full sodainliche fallen,
Ilke a segge by himselfe, and saide theis wordes:
'That ever I rengnede on thir rog me rewes it ever.
Was never roye so riche that regnede in erthe:

3251 *dereworthily dighte,* richly arrayed; *diaperde,* patterned
3252 *selcouthely hewede,* unusually colored 3253 *loyotour,* embroidery
3254 *ladily lappes,* ladylike folds 3255 *reverssede,* trimmed
3256–7 MS *Bruches . . ./ With hir . . .*
3256 *bruches and besauntes,* ornamental fastenings and bezants
3257 *brochede,* brocaded 3258 *kelle,* cap; *corenall,* coronet
3259 *on,* one (like it) 3261 *Overwhelme,* Turns over; *quaintely,* skillfully
3262 *rowell,* rim of the wheel
3263 *Railede,* Arrayed; *reched,* riches(?); *inewe,* in abundance
3264 The spokes were splinted with thin strips of silver.
3265 *springande,* springing (-and, -ande = -ing) 3267 *charebokle,* carbuncle
3268 *compas,* outer rim; *clewede,* clung; *one rawe,* in a row, in order
3270 *Sex,* Six; *setill,* seat 3271 *Ilke a segge,* Each man
3272 That ever I reigned on this wheel, I regret it forever.

Whene I rode in my route, roughte I noghte ells
3275 Bot revaye and revell and raunson the pople;
And thus I drife forthe my dayes, whills I dreghe mighte,
And therefore derfliche I am dampnede forever.'
The laste was a litill man that laide was benethe:
His leskes laye all lene and latheliche to shewe,
3280 The lokkes liarde and longe the lenghe of a yerde;
His lire and his ligham lamede full sore.
The tone eye of the bierin was brightere than silver;
The tother was yalowere then the yolke of a naye.
" 'I was lorde,' quod the lede, 'of londes inewe,
3285 And all ledes me louttede that lengede in erthe;
And nowe es lefte me no lappe my ligham to hele,
Bot lightly now am I loste, leve iche mane the sothe.'
"The secunde sir, forsothe, that sewede them aftire
Was sekerare, to my sighte, and saddare in armes;
3290 Ofte he sighede unsounde and said theis wordes:
'On yone see hafe I sitten als soveraine and lorde,
And ladys me lovede to lappe in theire armes;
And nowe my lordshippes are loste and laide for ever.'
The thirde thorowely was throo and thikke in the shuldirs,
3295 A thra man to threte off, there thretty ware gaderede;
His diadem was droppede down, dubbede with stones,
Endente all with diamaundes and dighte for the nones:

3274 *route,* company; *roughte I noghte ells,* I cared for nothing else
3275 *revaye,* hunting or hawking; *raunson,* to oppress with taxes; *pople,* people
3276 *dreghe,* endure 3277 *derfliche,* terribly
3279 *leskes,* loins; *latheliche,* ugly 3280 *liarde,* gray
3281 *lire,* muscles; *ligham,* body
3282 *tone eye,* one eye, MS *two eyne*; *bierin,* man
3283 *a naye,* an egg 3284 *lede,* man 3285 *louttede,* bowed to
3286 *lappe,* clothing; *hele,* cover 3287 *lightly,* easily; *leve iche,* believe each
3288 *sewede,* followed 3289 *sekerare,* more assured; *saddare,* more vigorous
3290 *unsounde,* heavily 3291 *see,* seat; *als,* as 3292 *lappe,* clasp
3293 *laide,* set down 3294 *throo,* fierce
3295 *thra,* fierce; *threte,* threaten; *there thretty,* where thirty
3296 *dubbede,* adorned
3297 *Endente,* Notched; *dighte,* adorned; *for the nones,* metrical tag

'I was dredde in my dayes,' he said, 'in diverse rewmes,
And now dampnede to the dede, and dole es the more.'
3300 "The fourte was a faire mane and forsesy in armes,
The faireste of fegure that fourmede was ever:
'I was frekke in my faithe,' he said, 'whills I one foulde regnede,
Famous in ferre londes and floure of all kinges.
Now es my face defadede, and foule es me hapnede,
3305 For I am fallen fro ferre and frendles belevede."
"The fifte was a faire man than fele of thies other,
A forsesy man and a ferse, with fomand lippes;
He fongede faste on the feleighes and failed his armes,
Bot yit he failede and fell a fifty fote large.
3310 Bot yit he sprange and sprente and spradden his armes,
And one the spere-lenghe spekes, he spekes thire wordes:
'I was in Surrye a sir, and sett be min one
As soveraine and seingnour of sere kinges londes.
Now off my solace I am full sodanly fallen,
3315 And for sake of my sin yone sete es me rewede.'
"The sexte had a Sautere semliche bounden
With a surepel of silke sewede full faire,
A harpe, and a hande-slinge with harde flinte stones;
What harmes he has hente he halowes full sone:
3320 " 'I was demede in my dayes,' he said, 'of dedes of armes
One of the doughtieste that dwellede in erthe,
Bot I was merrede one molde in my moste strenghethes
With this maiden so milde that mofes us all.'

3298 *dredde,* feared; *rewmes,* realms 3299 *dede,* death; *dole,* grief
3300 *forsesy,* violent 3302 *frekke,* eager; *foulde,* earth
3304 *foule es me hapnede,* evil has come to me
3305 *belevede,* abandoned 3306 *fele,* many
3308 *fongede,* held; *feleighes,* rims of the wheel; *failed,* a mistake for another f-alliterating word (?)
3309 *Bot yit,* But yet; *large,* full 3310 *sprente,* leapt 3311 *spekes,* spokes
3312 *Surrye,* Syria; *be min one,* by myself alone 3313 *sere,* sundry
3314 *off,* from 3315 *rewede,* taken from
3316 *Sautere,* Psalter; *semliche,* handsomely 3317 *surepel,* cover
3319 *hente,* received; *halowes,* shouts
3322 *merrede one molde,* destroyed on earth 3323 *With,* By; *mofes,* moves

"Two kinges ware climbande and claverande one heghe;
3325 The creste of the compas they covette full yerne.
'This chaire of charbokle,' they said, 'we chalange hereaftire,
As two of the cheffeste chosen in erthe.'
The childire ware chalke-whitte, chekes and other,
Bot the chaiere abounne chevede they never.
3330 The forthirmaste was freely with a frount large,
The faireste of fyssnamy that fourmede was ever;
And he was buskede in a blee of a blewe noble
With flour-de-lice of golde floreshede al over.
The tother was cledde in a cote all of clene silver,
3335 With a comliche crosse corven of golde,
Foure crosselettes crafty by the crosse ristes.
And therby knewe I the king, that cristnede him semede.
"Than I went to that wlonke and winly hire gretes,
And sho said, 'Welcom iwis! wele arte thou founden.
3340 Thee aughte to wirshipe my will, and thou wele couthe,
Of all the valiant men that ever was in erthe,
Fore all thy wirshipe in werre by me has thou wonnen.
I hafe bene frendely, freke, and fremmede till other.
That has thou founden, in faithe, and fele of thy biernes.
3345 Fore I felled down Sir Frolle with frowarde knightes,
Forethy the fruites of Fraunce are freely thine awen.
Thou shall the chaiere escheve — I chese thee myselfen,
Before all the cheftaines chosen in this erthe.'
Sho lifte me up lightly with hir lene hondes
3350 And sette me softely in the see, the septre me rechede.

3324 *claverande,* clinging 3325 *creste,* top; *compas,* rim; *yerne,* eagerly
3328 *childire,* nobles 3329 *abounne,* above; *chevede,* reached
3330 *freely,* pleasant; *frount,* forehead 3331 *fyssnamy,* physiognomy
3332 *buskede,* dressed; *blee,* color; *noble,* splendid
3336 *crafty,* skillfully crafted; *ristes,* rest 3337 *him semede,* he seemed
3338 *wlonke,* glorious one; *winly,* pleasantly; *hire,* her
3339 *sho,* she; *iwis,* indeed; *founden,* endowed
3340 *and thou wele couthe,* if you well understand (how things are)
3342 *wirshipe,* honor 3343 *freke,* man; *fremmede,* alien, hostile; *till,* to
3344 *faithe,* truth; *fele,* many 3345 *Fore,* Because; *Sir Frolle,* King of France
3347 *escheve,* achieve
3350 *see,* seat; *rechede,* gave

Craftely with a cambe sho cembede min hevede,
That the crispande croke to my crownne raughte;
Dressed onne me a diademe that dighte was full faire,
And sine profres me a pome pighte full of faire stones,
3355 Enamelde with azoure, the erth thereon depaintede,
Serkilde with the salte see appone sere halfes,
In signe that I sothely was soveraine in erthe.
"Than broght sho me a brande with full brighte hiltes
And bade me braundishe the blade: 'The brande es min awen.
3360 Many swain with the swinge has the swette levede;
For whills thou swanke with the swerde it swikkede thee never.'
Than raikes sho with roo, and riste when hir likede,
To the rindes of the wode, richere was never.
Was no pomarye so pighte of princes in erthe,
3365 Ne nonne apparaill so proude, bot Paradis one.
Sho bad the bewes sholde bewe down and bring to my hondes
Of the beste that they bare one braunches so heghe.
Than they heldede to hir heste all holly at ones,
The hegheste of iche a hirste, I hette you forsothe.
3370 Sho bade me firthe noghte the fruite bot fonde whills me likede:
'Fonde of the fineste, thou freliche bierne,
And reche to the ripeste and riotte thyselven.
Riste, thou ryalle roye, for Rome es thin awen!
And I shall redily roll the roo at the gaineste,
3375 And reche thee the riche wine in rinsede coupes.'

3351 *Craftely,* Artfully; *cembede,* combed; *hevede,* head
3352 *crispande croke,* curling locks; *crownne,* crown of head; *raughte,* reached
3354 *sine,* then; *pome,* globe; *pighte,* stuck
3356 *Serkilde,* Circled, MS *selkylde*; *sere halfes,* all sides
3358 *brande,* sword 3360 *swain,* men; *swette,* blood, MS *swtte*; *levede,* lost
3361 *swanke,* worked; *swikkede,* failed
3362 *raikes,* walked; *roo,* wheel; *hir likede,* she wants 3363 *rindes,* borders
3364 *pomarye,* orchard; *pighte,* adorned 3365 *apparaill,* dress; *one,* alone
3368 *heste,* command 3369 *a hirste,* grove of trees; *hette,* assure
3370 *firthe,* spare; *fonde,* try 3372 *reche,* reach
3374 *roo,* wheel; *gaineste,* quickest

Than sho wente to the welle by the wode eves,
That all wellede of wine and wondirliche rinnes,
Caughte up a coppefull and coverde it faire:
Sho bad me dereliche drawe and drinke to hirselfen.
3380 And thus sho lede me aboute the lenghe of an oure,
With all likinge and luffe that any lede sholde,
Bot at the middaye full evin, all hir mode chaungede,
And mad miche manace with mervaillous wordes.
When I criede appon hire, sho cest down hir browes:
3385 'King, thou carpes for noghte, be Criste that me made,
For thou shall lose this laike, and thy life aftire.
Thou has liffede in delitte and lordshippes inewe!'
"Aboute sho whirles the whele, and whirles me undire,
Till all my quarters that whille whare quaste al to peces;
3390 And with that chaiere my chine was chopped in sondire,
And I hafe cheverede for chele sen me this chance happenede.
Than wakkenede I, iwis, all wery fordremede —
And now wate thou my woo, worde as thee likes."
"Freke," says the philosophre, "thy fortune es passede.
3395 For thou shall find hir thy foo, fraiste when thee likes.
Thou arte at the hegheste, I hette thee forsothe;
Chalange nowe when thou will, thou cheves no more.
Thou has shedde miche blode and shalkes distroyede
Sakeles, in cirquitrie, in sere kinges landes.
3400 Shrife thee of thy shame and shape for thin ende.
Thou has a shewinge, Sir Kinge; take kepe yif thee like,
For thou shall fersely fall within five winters.
Founde abbayes in Fraunce — the froites are thein awen —

3376 *eves,* ends 3377 *wondirliche rinnes,* marvelously runs
3379 *dereliche,* deeply 3380 *oure,* hour
3381 *luffe,* love; *lede sholde,* man should have 3382 *full evin,* exactly
3385 *carpes,* complains 3386 *laike,* pleasure
3389 *quarters,* four parts of the body; *whille,* moment; *quaste,* crushed
3391 *cheverede,* shivered; *chele,* cold 3392 *fordremede,* weary from dreaming
3393 *wate,* know; *worde,* speak 3395 *fraiste when thee likes,* try as you may
3396 *hette,* promise 3397 *cheves,* achieves 3398 *shalkes,* men
3399 Innocent, in (your) pride, in many kings' lands 3400 *ende,* death
3401 *shewinge,* sight; *take kepe yif thee like,* pay attention if you wish
3402 *fersely,* violently 3403 *froites,* fruits; *awen,* own

Fore Froill and for Ferawnt, and for thir ferse knighttes,
3405 That thou fremedly in Fraunce has faye belevede.
Take kepe yitte of other kinges and caste in thine herte,
That were conquerours kidde and crownnede in erthe.
The eldeste was Alexandere, that all the erthe louttede;
The tother Ector of Troye, the chevalrous gume.
3410 The thirde Julyus Cesare, that geant was holden,
In iche jorne gentill ajuggede with lordes.
The ferthe was Sir Judas, a justere full nobill,
The maysterfull Makabee, the mighttieste of strenghes.
The fifte was Josue, that joly mane of armes,
3415 That in Jerusalem oste full miche joye limppede.
The sexte was David the dere, demed with kinges
One of the doughtieste that dubbede was ever,
For he slewe with a slinge, be sleighte of his handes,
Golyas the grette gome, grimmeste in erthe;
3420 Sine endittede in his dayes all the dere psalmes
That in the Sautire ere sette with selcouthe wordes.
"The two climbande kinges, I knawe it forsothe,
Shalle Karolus be callede, the king son of Fraunce:
He shall be crouell and kene, and conquerour holden,
3425 Covere be conqueste contres inewe;
He shall encroche the crowne that Crist bare himselfen;
And that lifeliche launce that lepe to his herte
When he was crucifiede one crose, and all the kene nailes,
Knightly he shall conquere to Cristen men hondes.
3430 "The tother shall be Godfraye, that Gode shall revenge
One the Gud Fridaye, with galiarde knightes;
He shall of Lorrayne be lorde, be leefe of his fadire,

3404 *Ferawnt,* ally of the Romans
3405 *fremedly,* unkindly; *faye belevede,* left fated (to die)
3406 *yitte,* still; *caste,* look 3407 *kidde,* famous 3408 *louttede,* bowed to
3409 *Ector,* Hector; *gume,* man 3411 *jorne,* military expedition; *gentill,* noble
3412 *justere,* fighter 3414 *Josue,* Joshua.
3415 *oste,* host; *limppede,* encountered 3420 *Sine,* Afterwards
3421 *selcouthe,* wonderful 3423 *Karolus,* Charlemagne
3425 Gain by conquest many countries 3426 *encroche,* seize
3427 *lifeliche,* life-giving, living 3429 *to,* for, into
3430 *Godfraye,* Godfrey of Bouillon 3431 *galiarde,* valiant 3432 *leefe,* leave

And sine in Jerusalem miche joye happen,
For he shall cover the crosse be craftes of armes
3435 And sinne be corownde kinge with crysome enointtede.
Shall no duke in his dayes siche destanye happen,
Ne siche mischefe dreghe when treuthe shall be triede.
Forethy Fortune thee fetches to fulfill the noumbire,
Alls nine of the nobileste namede in erthe:
3440 This shall in romance be redde with ryall knighttes,
Rekkenede and renounde with riotous kinges,
And demed one Domesdaye, for dedes of armes,
For the doughtieste that ever was dwelland in erthe —
So many clerkes and kinges shall carpe of youre dedes
3445 And kepe youre conquestes in cronicle forever.
Bot the wolfes in the wode and the whilde bestes
Are some wikkede men that werrayes thy rewmes;
Es entirde in thin absence to werraye thy pople,
And alienes and ostes of uncouthe landes.
3450 Thou getes tidandes, I trowe, within ten dayes
That some torfere es tidde sen thou fro home turnede.
I rede thou rekken and reherse unresonable dedes
Ore thee repenttes full rathe all thy rewthe werkes.
Mane, amende thy mode or thou mishappen,
3455 And mekely aske mercy for mede of thy saule."
Than rises the riche king and raughte on his wedes:
A reedde acton of rosse, the richeste of floures,
A pesane and a paunson and a pris girdill;

3433 *sine,* afterward 3434 *cover,* recover 3435 *crysome,* consecrated oil
3437 *dreghe,* endure; *treuthe,* faith, loyalty 3538 *Forethy,* Thus
3439 The Nine Worthies were the three pagans, three Jews, and three Christians just enumerated.
3441 *Rekkenede,* Counted; *riotous,* fond of fighting 3444 *carpe,* speak
3447 *werrayes,* harass 3449 *ostes,* hosts; *uncouthe,* uncivilized
3451 *torfere es tidde,* trouble has happened; *sen,* since 3452 *rekken,* count up
3453 *Ore,* Ere; *rathe,* quickly; *rewthe werkes,* works for which you should feel remorse
3454 *mode,* way; *or,* ere; *mishappen,* meet with misfortune 3455 *mede,* reward
3456 *raughte,* put 3457 *reedde acton of rosse,* red jacket of rose
3458 *pesane,* upper chest and neck armor; *paunson,* lower armor(?); *pris,* valuable

And one he henttes a hode of sharlette full riche,
3460 A paves pillion hatt that pighte was full faire
With perry of the Orient and precious stones,
His gloves gayliche gilte and graven by the hemmes
With graines of rubies full gracious to shewe,
His bede grehounde, and his bronde, ande no bierne ells,
3465 And bounnes over a brode mede with breth at his herte;
Furth he stalkes a stye by tha still eves,
Stotais at a hey strette, studyande him one.
Att the surs of the sone he sees there commande,
Raikande to Romewarde the rediestе wayes,
3470 A renke in a rounde cloke with righte rowme clothes,
With hatte, and with heyghe shone homely and rounde.
With flatte ferthinges the freke was floreshede all over;
Manye shredes and shragges at his skirttes hinnges,
With scrippe ande with slavin and scalopes inewe,
3475 Both pike and palme, alls pilgram him sholde.
The gome graithely him grette and bade gode morwen.
The king, lordelye himselfe, of langage of Rome,
Of Latin corroumppede all, full lowely him menes:
"Whedire wilnes thoue, wye, walkande thin one?
3480 Whills this werlde es o werre, a waughte I it holde.

3459 *henttes,* puts; *sharlette,* scarlet
3460 *paves pillion hatt,* wide hat; *pighte,* adorned 3461 *perry,* jewels
3462 *graven,* ornamented 3463 *graines,* beads
3464 *bede grehounde,* bed greyhound; *bronde,* sword
3465 *bounnes,* hurries; *breth,* rage
3466 Forth he walks along a path by the quiet edge of the wood.
3467 *Stotais,* Hesitates; *studyande him one,* reflecting by himself
3468 *surs,* rising; *commande,* coming
3469 *Raikande,* Walking; *rediestе,* shortest 3470 *renke,* man; *rowme,* ample
3471 *shone,* shoes 3473 *shragges,* rags; *hinnges,* hang
3474 *scrippe,* pilgrim's wallet; *slavin,* mantle; *scalopes,* cockleshells worn by pilgrims who had been to the shrine of St. James of Compostella
3475 Both staff and palm branch, as a pilgrim should have
3476 *graithely,* properly
3478 *Latin corroumppede,* Latin corrupted, *i.e.,* vulgar Latin; *menes,* says
3479 *wilnes,* wish; *wye,* man; *thin one,* by yourself alone
3480 *waughte,* danger

Here es ane enmye with oste undire yone vines;
And they see thee, forsothe, sorowe thee betiddes.
Bot yif thou hafe condethe of the kinge selfen,
Knaves will kill thee and keppe at thou haves;
3485 And if thou halde the hey waye, they hente thee also,
Bot if thou hastily hafe helpe of his hende knighttes."
Than carpes Sir Cradoke to the kinge selfen:
"I shall forgiffe him my dede, so me Gode helpe,
Onye grome undire Gode that one this grounde walkes.
3490 Latte the keneste come that to the king langes;
I shall encountire him as knighte, so Criste hafe my saule.
For thou may noughte reche me ne areste, thyselfen,
Thoffe thou be richely arayede in full riche wedes;
I will noghte wonde for no werre to wende whare me likes,
3495 Ne for no wy of this werlde that wroghte es on erthe.
Bot I will passe in pilgremage this pas unto Rome,
To purchese me pardone of tha Pape selfen,
And of paines of Purgatorye be plenerly assoillede.
Thane shall I seke sekirly my soveraine lorde,
3500 Sir Arthure of Inglande, that avenaunt bierne,
For he es in this empire, as hathell men me telles,
Ostayande in this Oriente with awfull knightes."
"Fro qwin come thou, kene man," quod the kinge than,
"That knawes Kinge Arthure and his knighttes also?
3505 Was thou ever in his courte qwills he in kith lengede?
Thou carpes so kindly it comforthes min herte.
Well wele has thou wente and wisely thou seches,
For thou arte Bretoune bierne, as by thy brode speche."

3482 *And,* If 3483 *Bot yif,* Unless; *condethe,* safe-conduct; *selfen,* himself
3484 *keppe at thou haves,* seize what you have 3485 *hente,* take
3486 *hende,* courteous 3487 *Sir Cradoke,* Cradoc, keeper of Caerleon
3488 *dede,* death 3489 *grome,* man 3490 *keneste,* bravest; *langes,* belongs
3492 *reche,* touch; *ne areste, thyselfen,* nor stop me yourself
3494 *wonde,* hesitate; *werre,* war 3495 *wy,* warrior 3496 *pas,* way
3498 *plenerly,* fully 3499 *sekirly,* certainly 3500 *avenaunt bierne* noble man
3501 *hathell,* noble 3502 *Ostayande,* Waging war; *Oriente,* East
3503 *qwin,* whence; *quod,* said
3505 *qwills,* while; *kith,* native country; *lengede,* remained
3507 *wele,* honorably; *wente,* traveled

"Me aughte to knowe the kinge; he es my kidde lorde,
3510 And I calde in his courte a knighte of his chambire.
Sir Craddoke was I callede in his courte riche,
Kepare of Karlyon under the kinge selfen.
Nowe am I cachede outt of kith with care at my herte,
And that castell es caughte with uncouthe ledes."
3515 Than the comliche kinge caughte him in armes,
Ceste off his ketill hatte and kissede him full sone,
Saide, "Welcom, Sir Craddoke, so Criste mott me helpe!
Dere cosin of kinde, thoue coldes min herte:
How fares it in Bretaine with all my bolde berens?
3520 Are they brettenede or brinte or broughte oute of live?
Ken thou me kindely whatte caase es befallen.
I kepe no credens to crafe; I knawe thee for trewe."
"Sir, thy wardane es wikkede and wilde of his dedes,
For he wandreth has wroghte sen thou awaye passede.
3525 He has castells encrochede and corownde himselven,
Caughte in all the rentes of the Rounde Tabill.
He devisede the rewme and delte as him likes,
Dubbede of the Danmarkes dukes and erlles,
Disseverede them sondirwise, and cites distroyede.
3530 To Sarazenes and Sessoynes, appon sere halves,
He has semblede a sorte of selcouthe berines,
Soveraines of Surgenale, and soudeours many
Of Peightes and painims, and provede knighttes
Of Irelande and Orgaile, outlawede berenes.
3535 All thaa laddes are knighttes that lange to the mountes,

3509 *kidde,* renowned 3513 *cachede,* driven
3514 *caughte with,* possessed by; *uncouthe ledes,* strange men
3518 *kinde,* kindred; *coldes,* chills 3520 *brettenede or brinte,* killed or burned
3521 *Ken,* Tell; *kindely,* thoroughly; *caase,* chance
3522 *I kepe no credens to crafe,* I do not crave assurance.
3523 *wardane, i.e.,* Mordred. 3524 *wandreth,* distress 3527 *devisede,* divided
3530 *Sarazenes,* Saracens; *Sessoynes,* Saxons; *sere halves,* sundry sides
3531 *semblede,* assembled; *sorte,* company; *selcouthe,* strange
3532 *Surgenale,* Syria or Surluse (Scilly Isles, South Wales?); *soudeours,* soldiers
3533 *Peightes,* Picts; *painims,* pagans 3534 *Orgaile,* Argyll
3535 *thaa laddes,* those men; *lange,* belong

And ledinge and lordeshipe has all, alls themselfe likes —
And there es Sir Childrike, a cheftaine holden.
That ilke chevalrous man, he chargges thy pople.
They robbe thy religeous and ravishe thy nonnes,
3540 And redy riddes with his routte to raunsone the poure;
Fro Humbyre to Hawyke he haldes his awen,
And all the countre of Kentt, be covenaunte entaillede:
The comliche castells that to the corown langede,
The holttes and the hare-wode and the harde bankkes,
3545 All that Henguste and Hors hent in theire tim.
Att Southampton on the see es seven score shippes,
Fraughte full of ferse folke out of ferre landes
For to fighte with thy frappe when thou them assailes.
Bot yitt a worde, witterly; thou watte noghte the werst:
3550 He has weddede Waynore and hir his wieffe holdes,
And wonnes in the wilde boundes of the weste marches,
And has wroghte hire with childe, as wittnesse telles.
Of all the wyes of this worlde, woo motte him worthe
Alls wardaine unworthye women to yeme:
3555 Thus has Sir Modrede merrede us all!
Forthy I merkede over thees mountes to mene thee the sothe."
Than the burliche kinge, for brethe at his herte
And for this botelesse bale, all his ble chaungede.

3536 *ledinge,* commanding 3537 *Childrike,* Childric, King of the Saxons
3538 *ilke,* same; *chargges,* burdens 3539 MS *ravichse*
3540 *riddes,* rides; *routte,* company; *raunsone,* exact payment from
3541 *Hawyke,* Hawick (Scotland)
3542 *be covenaunte entaillede,* by agreement bequeathed
3543 *langede,* belonged
3544 *holttes,* woods; *hare-wode,* hoar-wood; *bankkes,* hillside
3545 *Henguste and Hors,* Hengest and Horsa; *hent,* seized
3547 *Fraughte,* Laden 3548 *frappe,* crowd 3549 *witterly,* truly; *watte,* know
3550 *He, i.e.,* Mordred; *Waynore,* Guinevere 3551 *wonnes,* lives
3553 *wyes,* men; *woo motte him worthe,* may woe come to him
3554 *yeme,* look after
3555 *Modrede,* Mordred, son of Lott (elsewhere he is Arthur's incestuously begotten son); *merrede,* injured.
3556 *merkede,* came; *mene,* tell 3557 *burliche,* noble; *brethe,* fury
3558 *botelesse bale,* irremediable evil; *ble,* color

"By the rode," says the roye, "I shall it revenge.
3560 Him shall repente full rathe all his rewthe werkes!"
All wepande for woo he went to his tentes;
Unwinly this wyesse kinge he wakkenesse his berens,
Cleped in a clarione kinges and othire,
Calles them to concell and of this cas telles:
3565 "I am with treson betrayede, for all my trewe dedes,
And all my travaile es tint, me tides no bettire.
Him shall torfere betide, this tresone has wroghte,
And I may traistely him take, as I am trew lorde.
This es Modrede, the mane that I moste traistede
3570 Has my castells encrochede and corownde himselven
With renttes and reches of the Rounde Table,
Has made all his retenewes of renaiede wreches
And devised my rewme to diverse lordes,
To soudeours and to Sarazenes outte of sere londes.
3575 He has weddede Waynore and hir to wiefe holdes,
And a childe es eshapede, the chaunce es no bettire.
They hafe semblede on the see seven score shippes
Full of ferrom folke to feghte with min one.
Forthy to Bretaine the Brode buske us behoves,
3580 For to bretten the berene that has this bale raisede.
Thare shall no freke men fare bott all one freshe horses,
That are fraistede in fighte and floure of my knighttes.
Sir Howell and Sir Hardolfe here shall beleve,
To be lordes of the ledes that here to me lenges:

3562 *Unwinly,* Unjoyfully 3563 *Cleped in a clarione,* Called on a trumpet
3566 And all my labor is lost, nothing better happens to me.
3567 To him shall trouble come, who has wrought this treason.
3568 *And,* If; *traistely,* confidently 3571 *reches,* riches
3572 *renaiede,* renegade 3576 *eshapede,* issued; *chaunce,* luck
3578 *ferrom,* distant
3579 Therefore to Britain the Broad (Great Britain) it behooves us to hurry.
3580 *bretten,* butcher 3581 *freke,* eager; *bott,* except
3582 *fraistede,* experienced
3583 *Howell,* a kinsman of Arthur; *Hardolfe,* Hardolf, a knight of Arthur; *beleve,* remain
3584 *lenges,* belongs

3585 Lokes into Lumbardye that thare no lede chaunge,
And tendirly to Tuskayne take tente alls I bide;
Resaive the rentes of Rome when thay are rekkenede;
Take sesen the same daye that laste was assignede,
Or ells all the ostage withoutten the walles
3590 Be hinggede hye appon highte all holly at ones."
Nowe bounes the bolde kinge with beste knightes,
Gers trome and trusse, and trines forth aftire;
Turnes thorowe Tuskayne, taries bot littill,
Lighte noghte in Lumbarddye bot when the lighte failede,
3595 Merkes over the mountaines full mervailous wayes,
Ayres thurghe Almaygne evene at the gaineste,
Ferkes evene into Flawndreshe with his ferse knighttes.
Within fiftene dayes his flete es assemblede,
And thane he shoupe him to shippe and shounnes no lengere,
3600 Sheres with a sharpe winde over the shire waters;
By the roche with ropes he rides on ankkere.
Thare the false men fletede and one flode lengede,
With chefe chaines of chare chokkede togedirs,
Charggede even chekefull of chevalrous knightes;
3605 And in the hinter one heghte, helmes and crestes,
Hatches with haithen men hilled ware thare undire,
Proudliche purtrayede with paintede clothes,
Iche a pece by pece prikkede till other,
Dubbede with dagswainnes, doublede they seme.

3585 *Lumbardye,* Lombardy 3586 *Tuskayne,* Tuscany; *tente,* charge
3588 *sesen,* possession 3590 *hinggede,* hanged 3591 *bounes,* hurries
3592 Equips troops and baggage, and afterwards marches away
3594 *Lighte noghte,* Alights not; *bot when,* until
3596 *Ayres,* Marches; *evene at the gaineste,* directly by the shortest route
3597 *Ferkes,* Moves quickly; *Flawndreshe,* Flanders
3599 *shoupe him,* prepared himself; *shounnes,* holds back
3600 *Sheres,* Cleaves; *shire,* clear
3602 *fletede,* floated; *one flode lengede,* waited for the tide
3603 Locked together with heavy loading chains(?)
3604 *chekefull,* chock-full 3605 *hinter one heghte,* rear aloft
3606 *hilled,* concealed 3607 *purtrayede,* adorned 3608 *prikkede till,* stitched to
3609 *Dubbede with dagswainnes,* Adorned with rough shaggy fabric; *doublede,* doubled in size (or number)

3610 And thus the derfe Danamarkes had dighte all theire shippes
That no dinte of no darte dere them ne shoulde.
Than the roye and the renkes of the Rounde Table
All ryally in rede arrayes his shippes.
That daye, ducheries he delte and doubbede knighttes,
3615 Dresses dromoundes and dragges, and drawen upe stones.
The toppe-castells he stuffede with toyeles, as him likede,
Bendes bowes of vis brothly thareaftire.
Toloures tentily takell they rightten,
Brasen hedes full brode buskede one flones,
3620 Graithes for garnisons — gomes arrayes,
Grime gaddes of stele, ghyves of iren,
Stightteles steren one sterene with stiffe men of armes.
Mony lufliche launce appon lofte stonndes,
Ledes one leburde; lordes and other
3625 Pighte paivese one porte, paintede sheldes
One hindire hurdace, one highte, helmede knightes.
Thus they sheften fore shotes one thas shire strandes,
Ilke shalke in his shroude — full sheen ware theire wedes.
The bolde kinge es in a barge and aboutte rowes,
3630 All bare heuvede for besye with beveren lokkes,
And a beren with his bronde and ane helme beten,
Mengede with a mauncelet of mailes of silver,

3611 *dere them ne shoulde,* should harm them 3614 *ducheries,* duchies
3615 *dromoundes,* long ships; *dragges,* rafts, barges
3616 *toppe-castells,* a protected platform at the top of the mast; *toyeles,* tools (of war)
3617 Bends cross-bows quickly thereafter
3618 They skillfully prepare tillers (made out) of cross-bows.
3619 *buskede one flones,* fastened on arrows
3620 Prepares for garrisons — arrays men
3621 *gaddes,* spikes, goads; *ghyves,* gyves, fetters
3622 MS *Stirttelys*; Supplies stern after stern with stout men of arms
3624 *Ledes,* Men; *leburde,* leeboard
3625 *Pighte paivese one porte,* Fastened shields on port-side
3626 *hindire hurdace,* rear palisade
3627 *sheften,* make arrangements; *one,* on; *shire strandes,* bright shores
3628 Each man in his dress — very bright were their garments
3630 All bareheaded because of his activity, with reddish-brown locks
3631 *beren,* warrior 3632 *Mengede with,* Joined to; *mauncelet,* mantelet

Compaste with a coronall and covererde full riche;
Caires to iche a cogge to comfurthe his knighttes.
3635 To Clegys and Cleremownde he cries one loude:
"O Gawayne! O Galyran! thies gud mens bodies."
To Loth and to Lyonell full lovefly he meles,
And to Sir Lawncelot de Lake, lordliche wordes:
"Lat us covere the kithe — the coste es oure ownn —
3640 And gere them brotheliche blenke, all yone blodhondes!
Britten them within-bourde, and brinne them thareaftire!
Hewe down hertly yone heithen tikes!
Thay are harlotes halfe, I hette you min honnde!"
Than he coveres his cogge and caches one ankere,
3645 Caughte his comliche helme with the clere mailes,
Buskes baners one brode, beten of goules
With corowns of clere golde clenliche arrayede;
Bot thare was chosen in the chefe a chalke-whitte maiden,
And a childe in hir arme, that chefe es of Hevine.
3650 Withoutten changing in chace, thies ware the cheefe armes
Of Arthure the avenaunt whills he in erthe lengede.
Thane the marinerse melles, and maisters of shippes,
Merily iche a mate menes till other.

3633 *Compaste,* Encircled; *coronall,* crowned helmet
3634 *Caires,* Goes; *cogge,* ship
3635 *Clegys and Cleremownde,* Clegis and Clarrus of Clere Mounte, knights of Arthur
3636 *Gawayne,* Gawain, Lott's son and Arthur's nephew, one of Arthur's foremost knights; *Galyran,* Galeron of Galway, knight of the Round Table
3637 *Loth,* Lott, King of Lothian and Orkney, married Arthur's half sister; *Lyonell,* Lionel, kinsman of Launcelot; *lovefly he meles,* affectionately he speaks
3638 *Lawncelot de Lake,* in French romance, one of the foremost knights of the Round Table, Guinevere's lover, and eventual hermit and priest
3639 *covere,* recover; *kithe,* land; *coste,* coast
3640 *gere,* make; *brotheliche blenke,* flinch violently
3641 *Britten,* Butcher; *brinne,* burn 3642 *tikes,* dogs
3643 *harlotes halfe,* on the scoundrel's side; *hette,* give
3644 *coveres his cogge,* returns to his own ship; *caches one,* weighs
3646 Unfurls banners inlaid with red
3648 *chefe,* main (banner) 3650 *in chace,* during battle
3651 Of Arthur the noble, as long as he lived (in contrast to Mordred, who disguised himself) 3652 *melles,* converse 3653 *menes,* talks

Of theire termes they talke, how thay ware tidd,
3655 Towen trussell one trete, trussen upe sailes,
Bet bonettes one brede, bettrede hatches,
Braundeste brown stele, braggede in trompes;
Standes stiffe one the stamen, steres one aftire;
Streken over the streme thare strivinge beginnes,
3660 Fro the wagande winde oute of the weste risses,
Brethly bessomes with birre in berens sailles,
With hir bringges one burde burliche cogges,
Whills the bilinge and the beme brestes in sondire;
So stouttly the forsterne one the stam hittes,
3665 That stokkes of the stere-burde strikkes in peces.
Be than cogge appon cogge, crayers and other,
Castes crepers one crosse als to the crafte langes;
Thane was hede-rapes hewen that helde upe the mastes.
Thare was conteke full kene and crachinge of shippes,
3670 Grett cogges of campe crasseches in sondire,
Mony caban clevede, cabills destroyede.
Knightes and kene men killede the braines.
Kidd castells were corven with all theire kene wapen,
Castells full comliche, that coloured ware faire.
3675 Upkynes eghelinge thay ochen thareaftire,
With the swinge of the swerde sweys the mastes;

[3654] *termes,* technical language; *how thay ware tidd,* how they were faring
[3655] Tug at furled sails continuously, furl up (other) sails
[3656] *Bet bonettes one brede,* Spread extra canvas abroad; *bettrede,* battened down
[3657] *braggede in trompes,* sounded trumpets
[3658] One stands boldly in the prow, one steers aft.
[3659] *thare,* where [3660] *wagande,* shaking; *risses,* rises
[3661–65] Quickly sweeps in gusts into the warriors' sails, so that it brings stout ships together until the prow and beam break asunder; so violently does the prow hit the stern, that the starboard beams are shattered in pieces.
[3666] *Be than,* Then; *crayers,* small trading vessels
[3667] Cast grappling hooks across skillfully
[3668] *hede-rapes hewen,* head-ropes cut [3670] *campe,* war
[3671] *caban,* cabins; *cabills,* cables [3672] *braines,* furious ones (?)
[3673] *Kidd castells,* Splendid towers (on the ships)
[3675] Upwards (upkynes = upkydes?) they hack thereafter with the edge of the sword.

Ovirefalles in the firste frekes and othire,
Frekke in the forshipe fey es belevefede.
Than brothely they bekire with boustouse tacle,
3680 Brushese boldlye on burde briniede knightes —
Out of botes one burd was buskede with stones —
Bett down of the beste, bristes the hetches.
Som gomes thourghe-girde with gaddes of iren
Gomes gayliche clede — englaimous wapen.
3685 Archers of Inglande full egerly shottes,
Hittes thourghe the harde stele full hertly dinnttes.
Sonne hotchen in holle the hethene knightes,
Hurte thourghe the harde stele, hele they never.
Than they fall to the fighte, foines with speres,
3690 All the frekkeste one frounte, that to the fighte langes;
And ilkon freshely fraistes theire strenghes,
Were to fighte in the flete with theire fell wapen.
Thus they dalte that daye, thire dubbede knightes,
Till all the Danes ware dede and in the depe throwen.
3695 Than Bretons brothely with brondes they hewen,
Lepes in upone lofte lordeliche berenes;
When ledes of out-lonndes leppen in waters,
All oure lordes one loude laughen at ones.
Be thane speres whare spronngen, spaldded shippes,
3700 Spanioles spedily sprentede overburdes;
All the kene men of campe, knightes and other,
Killed are colde dede and casten overburdes.
Theire swiers sweiftly has the swete levede,

3677 *in the,* at; *frekes,* men
3678 Bold ones in the prow are abandoned (to die).
3679 *brothely,* fiercely; *bekire,* fight; *boustouse,* massive
3680 *Brushese,* Rush 3681 One of the ships was stocked with stones (?).
3682 *Bett,* Beat 3683 *thourghe-girde with gaddes,* strike through with goads
3684 *clede,* clad; *englaimous,* bloodying (the)
3687 *hotchen,* move up and fall back; *holle,* hold
3690 *frekkeste,* fiercest; *langes,* is proper 3691 *fraistes,* tests
3692 *Were,* Where; *flete,* water, fleet 3695 *brothely,* fiercely
3699 By then spears were splintered, ships split in pieces.
3700 *Spanioles,* Spaniards; *sprentede,* sprang 3701 *campe,* the force
3703 *swiers,* squires; *swete levede,* lifeblood left

Hethene hevande on hatche, in ther hawe rises,
3705 Sinkande in the salte see seven hundrethe at ones.
Thane Sir Gawayne the Gude, he has the gree wonnen,
And all the cogges grete he gafe to his knightes;
Sir Geryn and Sir Grifswolde and othir gret lordes
Garte Galuth, a gud gome, girde off thaire hedes.
3710 Thus of the false flete appon the flode happenede,
And thus theis ferene folke fey are belevede.
Yitt es the traitoure one londe with triede knighttes,
And all trompede they trippe one trappede stedes,
Shewes them undir shilde one the shire bankkes;
3715 He ne shounttes for no shame, bot shewes full heghe.
Sir Arthure and Gawayne aviede them bothen
To sexty thosandes of men that in theire sighte hovede.
Be this the folke was fellede, thane was the flode passede;
Thane was it slike a sloude in slakkes full hugge,
3720 That let the king forto lande, and the lawe watire;
Forthy he lengede one laye for lesinng of horseses,
To loke of his lege men and of his lele knightes,
Yif any ware lamede or loste, life yife they sholde.
Than Sir Gawayn the Gude of galaye he takes
3725 And glides up at a gole with gud men of armes;
When he groundede, for grefe he girdes in the watere
That to the girdill he gos in all his gilte wedes,
Shottes upe appon the sonde in sighte of the lordes,
Sengly with his soppe; my sorowe es the more.

3704 *on,* up; *hawe,* enclosure 3706 *gree,* victory
3708 *Geryn, Grifswolde,* Mordred's knights, slain by Gawain
3709 *Garte,* Caused; *Galuth,* Gawain's sword; *girde,* to strike
3711 *fey are belevede,* are left dead 3713 *trompede,* deceived
3714 *shire,* bright 3715 *shounttes,* goes away
3716 *aviede them,* made their way 3717 *hovede,* appeared
3718 *Be this,* By the time that; *flode passede,* tide out
3719 *slike,* slick; *a sloude,* meaning unknown; *slakkes,* mud flats
3720 *let,* hindered
3721 Therefore he waited on the water for fear of losing the horses.
3722 *of,* over 3723 *life yife they sholde,* if they might live
3725 *gole,* channel 3726 *groundede,* ran aground; *grefe,* anger; *girdes,* springs
3728 *Shottes,* Rushes 3729 *soppe,* troop

3730 With baners of his bages, beste of his armes,
He braides upon the banke in his brighte wedes.
He biddes his baneoure, "Buske thou belife
To yone brode bataile that one yone banke hoves,
And I ensure you sothe I shall you sewe aftire.
3735 Loke ye blenke for no bronde ne for no brighte wapen,
Bot beres down of the beste and bring them odawe.
Bees noghte abaiste of theire boste, abide on the erthe;
Ye have my baneres borne in batailles full hugge.
We shall fell yone false, the fende hafe theire saules!
3740 Fightes faste with the frape — the felde shall be oures.
May I that traitoure overtake, torfere him tiddes
That this treson has timbirde to my trewe lorde.
Of siche an engendure full littill joye happens,
And that shall in this journee be juggede full even."
3745 Now they seke over the sonde this soppe at the gaineste,
Sembles one the soudeours and settes theire dintes.
Thourghe the sheldes so shene shalkes they touche,
With shaftes sheverede shorte of thas shene launces;
Derfe dinttes they dalte with daggande speres.
3750 One the danke of the dewe many dede ligges,
Dukes, and duszeperes, and dubbede knighttes;
The doughttieste of Danemarke undone are forever.
Thus thas renkes in rewthe rittes theire brenies
And reches of the richeste unreken dinttes,
3755 Thare they thronge in the thikke, and thristes to the erthe
Of the thraeste men thre hundrethe at ones.

3731 *braides,* rushes
3732 *baneoure,* banner-man; *Buske thou belife,* Go quickly
3733 *hoves,* appears 3734 *sewe,* follow 3735 *blenke,* flinch
3736 *bring them odawe,* put them to death 3737 *abaiste,* frightened
3740 *frape,* rabble 3741 *May,* If; *torfere,* trouble
3742 *timbirde,* caused 3743 *engendure,* creation 3744 *journee,* day's battle
3745 *soppe,* (Mordred's) host; *at the gaineste,* the quickest way
3746 *Sembles one,* Falls on 3747 *shalkes,* men 3748 *sheverede,* splintered
3749 *Derfe,* Strong; *dalte,* dealt; *daggande,* piercing 3750 *ligges,* lie
3751 *duszeperes,* illustrious knights 3753 *rittes,* split; *brenies,* byrnies
3754 And strike (or receive) from the strongest uncounted blows
3756 *thraeste,* fiercest

Bot Sir Gawayne for grefe mighte noghte againestande,
Umbegrippes a spere, and to a gome rinnes
That bare of goules full gaye with gouces of silvere.
3760 He girdes him in at the gorge with his grim launce,
That the grounden glaife graithes in sondire;
With that boistous braide he bounes him to die –
The King of Gutlande it was, a gude man of armes.
Thaire avawwarde than all voides thareaftire,
3765 Alls venqueste verraiely with valiant berenns,
Metes with medilwarde, that Modrede ledes.
Oure men merkes them to, as them mishappenede,
For hade Sir Gawayne hade grace to halde the grene hill,
He had wirshipe iwis wonnen forever.
3770 Bot than Sir Gawayne, iwisse, he waites him wele
To wreke him on this werlaughe that this werre movede,
And merkes to Sir Modrede amonge all his berens,
With the Mowntagus and other gret lordes.
Than Sir Gawayne was grevede, and with a gret will
3775 Fewters a faire spere and freshely ascries:
"Fals fosterde foode, the fende have thy bones!
Fy one thee, felone, and thy false werkes!
Thou shall be dede and undon for thy derfe dedes
Or I shall dy this daye, yif destanye worthe!"
3780 Thane his enmye with oste of outlawede berenns
All enangills aboute oure excellente knighttes,
That the traitoure be tresone had triede himselven.
Dukes of Danemarke he dighttes full sone,
And leders of Lettowe, with legions inewe,

3757 *againestande,* resist 3758 *Umbegrippes,* Grasps
3759 Who bore (a heraldic device) of red, very gay, with tear drops of silver
3760 *girdes,* strikes 3761 *grounden glaife,* sharpened spear; *graithes,* falls
3762 *boistous braide,* stout blow; *bounes,* hurries 3764 *avawwarde,* vanguard
3766 *medilwarde,* middleguard 3767 *merkes,* go 3770 *waites,* watches
3771 *wreke,* avenge; *werlaughe,* oath-breaker
3773 *Mowntagus,* the Montagu family, who support Mordred
3775 *Fewters,* puts in rest; *ascries,* calls out 3776 *foode,* creature
3778 *derfe,* terrible 3779 *worthe,* come to pass
3781 *enangills aboute,* surrounds 3782 *triede,* tested
3783 *dighttes,* prepares 3784 *Lettowe,* Lithuania

3785 Umbelappede oure men with launces full kene,
Soudeours and Sarazenes oute of sere landes:
Sexty thosande men semlily arrayede
Sekerly assembles thare one sevenscore knightes
Sodainly in dischaite by tha salte strandes.
3790 Thane Sir Gawayne grette with his gray eghen
For grefe of his gud men that he gide shulde.
He wiste that thay wondede ware and wery forfoughtten,
And what for wondire and woo all his witte failede.
And thane sighande he saide with silande teres:
3795 "We are with Sarazenes besett appon sere halfes!
I sighe noghte for myselfe, sa helpe oure Lorde!
Bot for to us supprisede my sorowe es the more.
Bes doughtty todaye; yone dukes shall be youres!
For dere Drightten this daye, dredes no wapen.
3800 We shall ende this daye alls excellent knighttes,
Aiere to endelesse joye with angells unwemmede.
Thofe we hafe unwittily wastede oureselfen,
We shall wirke all wele in the wirshipe of Criste.
We shall for yone Sarazenes, I sekire you my trowhe,
3805 Souppe with oure Saveoure solemply in Heven
In presence of that precious Prince of all other,
With prophetes and patriarkes and apostles full nobill,
Before his freliche face that fourmede us all.
Yondire to yone yaldsons he that yeldes him ever,
3810 Qwhills he es quikke and in querte unquellede with handes,
Be he never mo savede ne socourede with Criste,
Bot Satanase his saule mowe sinke into Helle!"

3785 *Umbelappede,* Surrounded 3789 *dischaite,* deceit
3790 *grette,* wept; *eghen,* eyes 3792 *forfoughtten,* worn out with fighting
3794 *silande,* falling 3795 *sere halfes,* all sides 3797 *for to us,* because we are
3798 *Bes,* Be 3799 *Drightten,* God 3800 *alls,* as
3801 *Aiere,* Go; *unwemmede,* unspotted
3802 *Thofe,* Though; *unwittily,* unwittingly, or unwisely
3804 *sekire you my trowhe,* give you my word 3808 *freliche,* beautiful
3809 *yaldsons,* old sons (term of contempt); *he that yeldes him ever,* whoever yields
3810 *Qwhills,* While; *quikke,* alive; *querte,* health
3811 *mo,* more 3812 *mowe,* may

Than grimly Sir Gawayne grippes his wapen,
Againe that gret bataille he graithes him sone;
3815 Radly of his riche swerde he reghttes the cheines,
In he shokkes his shelde, shountes he no lengare.
Bot alls unwise, wodewise, he wente at the gaineste,
Wondes of thas wedirwins with wrakfull dinttes:
All welles full of blode thare he awaye passes,
3820 And thofe him ware full woo he wondes bot littill,
Bot wrekes at his wirshipe the wrethe of his lorde.
He stekes stedes in stoure and sterenefull knighttes,
That steren men in theire sterapes stone-dede thay ligge;
He rives the ranke stele, he rittes the mailes.
3825 Thare mighte no renke him areste, his reson was passede;
He fell in a fransye for fersenesse of herte.
He feghttes and felles down that him before standes;
Fell never fay man siche fortune in erthe.
Into the hale bataile hedlinngs he rinnes
3830 And hurtes of the hardieste that one the erthe lenges;
Letande alls a lion, he launches them thorowe,
Lordes and ledars, that one the launde hoves.
Yit Sir Wawayne for wo wondes bot littill,
Bot woundes of thas wedirwins with wonderfull dintes
3835 Alls he that wold wilfully wasten himselfen;
And for wondsom and will all his wit failede,
That wode alls a wilde beste he wente at the gaineste,
All walewede one blode thare he awaye passede:
Iche a wy may be warre, be wreke of another.

3814 *graithes,* advances 3815 *Radly,* Quickly; *reghttes,* adjusts
3816 *shokkes,* thrusts; *shountes,* holds back
3817 But like a fool, a madman, he went most directly.
3818 *Wondes of,* Wounds some of; *wedirwins,* enemies; *wrakfull,* vengeful
3819 *thare,* where; *awaye,* by 3820 *wondes,* hesitates
3821 *wrekes,* avenges; *at his wirshipe,* to his honor; *wrethe,* wrath
3822 *stekes,* pierces; *stoure,* fight; *sterenefull,* bold
3824 *rives,* splits; *ranke,* stout; *rittes,* rips
3825 *renke,* man 3828 *fay,* doomed 3829 *hale,* whole; *hedlinngs,* headlong
3830 *of,* some of 3831 *Letande,* Behaving 3832 *hoves,* remains
3833 *Wawayne,* Gawain 3836 *wondsom,* sorrow 3837 *wode,* mad
3839 *wy,* man; *be wreke,* by the calamity

3840 Than he moves to Sir Modrede amange all his knighttes
And mett him in the mide-shelde and malles him thorowe.
Bot the shalke for the sharpe he shounttes a littill;
He share him one the shorte ribbes a shaftmonde large.
The shafte shoderede and shotte in the shire beren,
3845 That the shadande blode over his shanke rinnes
And shewede on his shinbawde that was shire burneste.
And so they shifte and shove, he shotte to the erthe:
With the lusshe of the launce, he lighte one his shuldirs
Ane akere-lenghe one a launde, full lothely wondede.
3850 Than Gawayne girde to the gome and one the groffe falles;
Alls his grefe was graithede, his grace was no bettire.
He shokkes outte a shorte knife shethede with silvere
And sholde have slotted him in, bot no slitte happenede;
His hand slepped and slode o slante one the mailes,
3855 And the tother slely slinges him undire.
With a trenchande knife the traitoure him hittes,
Thorowe the helme and the hede, one heyghe one the braine.
And thus Sir Gawaine es gon, the gude man of armes,
Withoutten rescheue of renke, and rewghe es the more.
3860 Thus Sir Gawayne es gon, that giede many othire,
Fro Gowere to Gernesay, all the gret lordes
Of Glamour, of Galys-londe, this galiarde knightes,
For glent of gloppenning glade be they never.
King Froderike of Fres faithely thareaftire

3841 *malles,* strikes
3842 *shalke,* man; *sharpe,* sharp blow; *shounttes,* withdraws
3843 *share,* cut; *shaftmonde,* handbreadth 3844 *shire,* noble
3845 *shadande,* flowing 3846 *shinbawde,* leg-armor; *shire,* brightly
3848 *lusshe,* blow 3849 *Ane akere-lenghe,* Full-length
3850 *girde to the gome,* struck at the man; *groffe,* rough terrain
3851 *grefe,* anger; *graithede,* aroused; *grace,* luck
3852 *shokkes outte,* snatches out
3853 *slotted him in,* stabbed him in (the throat); *slitte,* cut
3855 *slely,* cleverly 3856 *trenchande,* keen
3859 *rescheue of,* rescue by; *renke,* man; *rewghe,* pity 3860 *giede,* guided
3861 *Gowere,* peninsula of Gower, South Wales; *Gernesay,* Isle of Guernsey
3862 *Glamour,* Glamorganshire, Wales; *Galys-,* Welsh-; *galiarde,* brave
3863 *glent of gloppenning,* glimpse of sorrow, MS *gloppyngnyng*
3864 *Froderike of Fres,* Frederick of Friesland; *faithely,* truly

3865 Fraines at the false mane of oure ferse knighte.
"Knew thou ever this knighte in thy kithe riche?
Of whate kinde he was comen, beknowe now the sothe.
What gome was he, this with the gaye armes,
With this griffoune of golde, that es one grouffe fallen?
3870 He has grettly greffed us, sa me Gode helpe,
Girde down oure gude men and grevede us sore.
He was the sterenneste in stoure that ever stele werrede,
Fore he has stonaiede oure stale and stroyede forever."
Than Sir Mordrede with mouthe meles full faire:
3875 "He was makles one molde, mane, be my trowhe.
This was Sir Gawayne the Gude, the gladdeste of othire,
And the graciouseste gome that undire God liffede;
Mane hardieste of hande, happieste in armes,
And the hendeste in hawle undire Heven-riche,
3880 The lordelieste of leding whills he liffe mighte,
Fore he was lione allossede in londes inewe.
Had thou knawen him, Sir King, in kithe thare he lengede,
His coninge, his knighthode, his kindly werkes,
His doing, his doughtinesse, his dedes of armes,
3885 Thou wolde hafe dole for his dede the dayes of thy life."
Yit that traitour alls tite teres lete he fall,
Turnes him furthe tite and talkes no more,
Went wepand awaye and weries the stoundes
That ever his werdes ware wroghte siche wandrethe to wirke.
3890 Whene he thoghte on this thinge, it thirllede his herte;
For sake of his sibb blode sigheande he rides.

3865 *Fraines at,* Asks; *of,* about 3866 *kithe,* country 3867 *beknowe,* tell
3869 *grouffe,* ground 3871 *Girde,* Struck 3872 *stoure,* battle; *werrede,* wore.
3873 *stonaiede oure stale,* stunned our men; *stroyede,* destroyed (them)
3874 *meles,* speaks
3875 *makles one molde,* matchless on earth; *trowhe,* truth.
3876 *gladdeste,* most cheerful 3878 *happieste,* most fortunate
3879 *hendeste,* most courteous; *hawle,* hall; *Heven-riche,* Heaven's kingdom
3881 *allossede,* praised 3882 *kithe,* land; *thare,* where; *lengede,* lived
3883 *coninge,* knowledge 3885 *dede,* death 3886 *alls tite,* quickly
3887 *tite,* immediately 3888 *weries the stoundes,* curses the hour
3889 *werdes,* fates; *wandrethe,* misery; *wirke,* create 3890 *thirllede,* pierced
3891 *sibb,* related

When that renaiede renke remembirde himselven
Of reverence and riotes of the Rounde Table,
He remed and repent him of all his rewthe werkes,
3895 Rode awaye with his route, ristes he no lengere,
For rade of oure riche kinge rive that he sholde.
Than caires he to Cornewaile, carefull in herte
Because of his kinsemane that one the coste ligges;
He taries tremlande ay, tidandes to herken.
3900 Than the traitoure treunted the Tyseday tharaftire,
Trinnes in with a traine treson to wirke,
And by the Tambire that tide his tentes he reres.
And thane in a mette-while a messangere he sendes,
And wraite unto Waynor how the werlde chaungede,
3905 And what comliche coste the king was arivede,
One floode foughten with his fleete and felled them o life,
Bade hir ferken oo ferre and flee with hir childire
Whills he mighte wile him awaye and win to hir speche,
Aiere into Irelande, into thas oute-mountes,
3910 And wonn thare in wildernesse within tha wastlandes.
  Than sho yermes and yee at Yorke in hir chambire,
Grones full grisely with gretand teres,
Passes oute of the palesse with all hir price maidenes —
Towarde Chestyre in a charre thay chese hir the wayes,
3915 Dighte hir even forto die with dule at hir herte.
Sho caires to Karelyone and caughte hir a vaile,

3892 *renaiede renke,* renegade man 3893 *riotes,* revels
3894 *remed,* lamented; *rewthe,* pitiable
3896 For fear that he should be torn apart by our powerful king
3897 *caires,* goes; *carefull,* sorrowful 3898 *ligges,* lies
3899 *tremlande ay,* always trembling; *tidandes to herken,* tidings to hear
3900 *treunted,* departed (?) 3901 *Trinnes,* Marches; *traine,* group of followers
3902 *Tambire,* River Tamar, between Cornwall and Devon; *tide,* time
3903 *in a mette-while,* in the meantime 3906 *o,* of
3907 *ferken oo ferre,* hurry far away
3908 *Whills,* Until; *wile him,* draw himself; *to hir,* her to
3909 *Aiere,* Go; *oute-mountes,* distant mountains 3910 *wonn,* live
3911 *yermes and yee,* wails and cries 3912 *gretand,* flowing 3913 *price,* noble
3914 *charre,* cart 3915 *Dighte hir,* Prepared herself; *dule,* dole
3916 *caires,* goes; *Karelyone,* Caerleon-upon-Usk, often Arthur's chief seat

Askes thare the habite in the honoure of Criste,
And all for falsede and fraude and fere of hir loverde.
 Bot whene oure wiese kinge wiste that Gawayne was landede,
3920 He al towrithes for woo, and wringande his handes
Gers launche his botes appon a lawe watire,
Londes als a lion with lordliche knightes,
Slippes in the sloppes o-slante to the girdill,
Swalters upe swiftly with his swerde drawen,
3925 Bounnes his bataile and baners displayes,
Buskes over the brode sandes with breth at his herte,
Ferkes frekkly one felde thare the feye ligges.
Of the traitours men one trappede stedes,
Ten thosandes ware tinte, the trewghe to acount,
3930 And certane on oure side seven score knightes
In soite with theire soveraine unsounde are belevede.
 The king comly overceste knightes and othire,
Erlles of Awfrike and Estriche berenes,
Of Orgaile and Orekenay, the Ireshe kinges,
3935 The nobileste of Norwaye, noumbirs full hugge,
Dukes of Danamarke, and dubbed knightes;
And the Guchede kinge in the gay armes
Lys gronande on the grounde, and girde thorowe even.
The riche kinge ransakes with rewthe at his herte
3940 And up ripes the renkes of all the Rounde Tabill,

3918 *loverde,* lord 3920 *towrithes,* writhes terribly 3921 *Gers,* Prepares to
3923 *sloppes,* mud holes 3924 *Swalters,* Wades
3925 *Bounnes,* Prepares; *bataile,* troops 3926 *Buskes,* Hurries; *breth,* wrath
3927 *frekkly,* eagerly; *feye,* dead; *ligges,* lie 3929 *tinte,* lost
3931 In attendance with their lord (Gawain) mortally wounded are left
3932 *comly overceste,* gently turned over 3933 *Estriche,* Austrian (?)
3937 *Guchede kinge:* Since *Guchede* is capitalized in the MS, and since the scribe is careful in his use of capitalization, the phrase probably refers to the King of Guthland whom Gawain had speared in the throat (l. 3760). Elaborate armor and the proximity of Danish knights, which appear in both references, support the reading.
3938 *girde thorowe even,* struck right through
3939 *ransakes,* searches
3940 *up ripes,* searches out

Ses them all in a soppe in soute by them one,
With the Sarazenes unsounde enserclede aboute;
And Sir Gawayne the Gude in his gaye armes,
Umbegrippede the girse and one grouffe fallen,
3945 His baners braiden down, beten of goulles,
His brand and his brade shelde al blody beronen.
Was never oure semliche kinge so sorowfull in herte
Ne that sanke him so sade, bot that sighte one.
Than gliftes the gud kinge and glopens in herte,
3950 Grones full griseley with gretande teres,
Kneles down to the cors and caught it in armes,
Castes upe his umbrere and kisses him sone,
Lokes one his eyeliddes that loukkede ware faire,
His lippes like to the lede and his lire falowede.
3955 Than the corownde king cries full loude:
"Dere cosin o kinde, in care am I levede,
For nowe my wirshipe es wente and my were endede.
Here es the hope of my hele, my happinge of armes;
My herte and my hardines hale one him lengede,
3960 My concell, my comforthe that kepede min herte.
Of all knightes the kinge, that under Criste lifede,
Thou was worthy to be kinge thofe I the corown bare.
My wele and my wirshipe of all this werlde riche
Was wonnen thourghe Sir Gawayne, and thourghe his witt one.
3965 "Allas," saide Sir Arthure, "Nowe ekes my sorowe;
I am uttirly undon in min awen landes.
A! douttouse, derfe dede, thou dwelles too longe!

3941 Sees them all in a group in company by themselves 3942 MS *enserchede*
3944 Grasped the grass and face downward fallen
3945 *braiden,* flung; *goulles,* gules (heraldic red) 3946 *beronen,* smeared
3948 *Ne that sanke,* Nor (anything) that made; *one,* alone
3949 *gliftes,* looks; *glopens,* sorrows 3950 *gretande,* flowing
3952 *umbrere,* visor 3953 *loukkede,* closed
3954 *lire falowede,* flesh grown pale 3956 *o kinde,* natural; *levede,* left
3957 *wirshipe,* honor 3958 *hele,* prosperity; *happinge,* fortune
3959 *hale,* wholly; *lengede,* remained 3960 *kepede,* nourished
3964 *witt,* intelligence; *one,* alone 3965 *ekes,* increases
3967 Oh, terrible, cruel death, you linger too long.

Why drawes thou so one dreghe? thou drownnes min herte!"
Than sweltes the swete kinge and in swoun falles,
3970 Swafres up swiftely and swetly him kisses
Till his burliche berde was blody beroun,
Alls he had bestes birtenede and broghte out of life.
Ne had Sir Ewayne comen and othire grete lordes,
His bolde herte had brousten for bale at that stounde.
3975 "Bline!" says thies bolde men, "Thou blondirs thyselfen;
This es botles bale, for bettir bees it never.
It es no wirshipe, iwisse, to wring thin hondes;
To wepe als a woman it es no witt holden.
Be knightly of contenaunce, als a king sholde,
3980 And leve siche clamoure, for Cristes lufe of Heven!"
"For blode," said the bolde king, "blin shall I never,
Or my braine tobriste or my breste other.
Was never sorowe so softe that sanke to my herte;
Itt es full sibb to myselfe, my sorowe es the more.
3985 Was never so sorowfull a sighte sein with min eyghen;
He es sakles supprisede for sin of min one."
Down kneles the kinge and cries full loude;
With carefull contenaunce he carpes thes wordes:
"O rightwis riche Gode, this rewthe thou beholde!
3990 This ryall rede blode rin appon erthe,
It ware worthy to be shrede and shrinede in golde,
For it es sakles of sin, sa helpe me oure Lorde."
Down kneles the king with care at his herte,
Caughte it upe kindly with his clene handes,
3995 Caste it in a ketill-hatte and coverde it faire,
And caires furthe with the cors in kihte thare he lenges.

3968 *drawes thou so one dreghe,* do you linger so tediously
3969 *sweltes,* faints, MS *swetes*
3970 *Swafres,* Staggers 3971 *burliche,* noble; *beroun,* besmeared
3972 *Alls,* As though; *birtenede,* slaughtered
3973 *Ne had,* Had not; *Ewayne,* Ywain, son of Urien or Henry
3974 *stounde,* place 3975 *Bline,* Stop; *blondirs,* confound
3976 *botles bale,* useless grief 3981 *For blode,* For (his) blood
3982 *tobriste,* burst in pieces; *other,* else 3983 *so softe that,* that so easily
3984 *sibb,* relative 3985 *eyghen,* eyes 3986 *sakles supprisede,* innocent betrayed
3988 *carpes,* speaks 3991 *shrede,* removed
3996 *caires,* goes; *in kihte,* into the country; *lenges,* belongs

"Here I make min avowe," quod the kinge than,
"To Messie and to Marie, the milde Quenne of Heven:
I shall never revaye, ne racches uncoupill
4000 At roo ne rainedere that rinnes appone erthe,
Never grewhounde late glide, ne gossehawke latt flye,
Ne never fowle see fellede that flieghes with wenge,
Faucon ne formaille appon fiste handill,
Ne yitt with gerefaucon rejoise me in erthe,
4005 Ne regnne in my royaltes, ne halde my Rounde Table
Till thy dede, my dere, be deuly revengede;
Bot ever droupe and dare, whills my life lastes,
Till Drighten and derfe dede hafe don whate them likes."
Than caughte they upe the cors with care at theire hertes,
4010 Caried one a coursere with the kinge selfen.
The waye unto Wynchestre thay wente at the gaineste,
Wery and wandsomdly with wondede knightes.
Thare come the prior of the plas and professede monnkes,
Apas in processione, and with the prince metes;
4015 And he betuke tham the cors of the knighte noble.
"Lokes it be clenly keped," he said, "and in the kirke holden,
Done for derygese as to the ded falles,
Menskede with messes for mede of the saule;
Loke it wante no waxe ne no wirshipe ells,
4020 And at the body be baumede and one erthe holden.
Yiff thou kepe thy covent, encroche any wirshipe
At my coming againe, yif Crist will it thole.
Abide of the beryenge till they be broughte undire

3998 *Messie,* Messiah 3999 *revaye,* hunt and hawk; *racches,* hunting dogs
4000 *roo,* roe (deer)
4003 *Faucon,* Falcon; *formaille,* formel hawk, the female hawk
4004 *gerefaucon,* gerfalcon 4006 *dede,* death
4007 *droupe and dare,* droop and pine
4008 *Drighten,* God; *derfe dede,* cruel death 4012 *wandsomdly,* falteringly
4014 *apas,* at once 4015 *betuke tham,* entrusted to them
4016 *keped,* cared for; *holden,* watched over
4017 *Done for derygese,* Dirges undertaken
4018 *Menskede,* Honored; *mede,* reward 4019 *waxe,* candles
4020 *at,* that; *baumede,* enbalmed; *holden,* guarded
4021 *covent,* promise; *encroche,* (you may) claim (?) 4022 *thole,* allow

That has wroghte us this woo and this werre movede."
4025 Than says Sir Wychere the wy, a wiese mane of armes:
"I rede ye warely wende and wirkes the beste.
Sojorne in this cete and semble thy berenes,
And bidde with thy bolde men in thy burghe riche;
Get out knighttes of contres that castells holdes,
4030 And out of garisons grete gude men of armes,
For we are faithely too fewe to feghte with them all
That we see in his sorte appon the see bankes."
With creuell contenance thane the king carpes theis wordes:
"I praye thee care noghte, Sir Knighte, ne caste thou no dredes.
4035 Hadde I no segge bot myselfe one undir sone,
And I may him see with sighte or one him sette hondes,
I shall even amange his mene malle him to dede
Are I of the stede stire halfe a stede lenghe.
I shall [strike] him in his stoure and stroye him forever,
4040 And thareto make I min avowe devottly to Criste
And to his Modire Marie, the milde Quene of Heven.
I shall never sojourne sounde ne saughte at mine herte
In cete ne in subarbe sette appon erthe,
Ne yitt slomire ne slepe with my slawe eyghne,
4045 Till he be slaine that him slowghe, yif any sleighte happen;
Bot ever pursue the payganes that my pople distroyede
Whills I may pare them and pinne in place thare me likes."
Thare durste no renke him areste of all the Rounde Table,
Ne none paye that prince with plesande wordes,
4050 Ne none of his lige mene luke him in the eyghne,

4025 *Wychere,* one of Arthur's knights; *wy,* man 4027 *cete,* city
4028 *bidde,* wait; *burghe,* city 4029 *Get out, i.e.,* Get knights out of . . .
4030 *garisons,* strongholds 4031 *faithely,* surely 4032 *sorte,* company
4034 *ne caste thou no dredes,* nor have any fear 4035 *segge,* man; *one,* only
4036 *And,* If 4037 *malle,* maul, beat
4038 Before I stir half a steed's length out of the place (or, from my steed)
4039 *strike,* MS *om.*; *stoure,* fight; *stroye,* destroy
4042 *sojourne sounde,* dwell securely; *saughte,* peacefully
4044 *slawe eyghne,* heavy eyes
4045 *yif any sleighte happen,* if any stratagem happens (to work)
4047 *pare,* injure; *pinne,* torment 4048 *areste,* stop
4049 *paye,* pacify

So lordely he lukes for losse of his knighttes.
Thane drawes he to Dorsett and dreches no langere,
Derefull, dredlesse, with drouppande teres,
Caieres into Kornewayle with care at his herte.
4055 The trays of the traitoure he trines full evene
And turnes in be the Treyntes the traitoure to seche,
Findes him in a foreste the Fridaye thereaftire.
The king lighttes one fott and freshely ascries,
And with his freliche folke he has the felde nommen.
4060 Now issheues his enmye undire the wode eives,
With ostes of alines full horrebill to shewe.
Sir Mordrede the Malebranche with his miche pople
Foundes out of the foreste appon fele halfes,
In seven grett batailles semliche arrayede,
4065 Sexty thousande men, the sighte was full hugge.
All fightande folke of the ferre laundes
Faire fettede one frounte be tha freshe strondes;
And all Arthurs oste was amede with knightes
Bot aughtene hundrethe of all, entrede in rolles.
4070 This was a mache unmete, bot mighttes of Criste,
To melle with that multitude in thase man londes.
Than the royall roy of the Rounde Table
Rides on a riche stede, arrayes his berens,
Buskes his avaumwarde als him beste likes.
4075 Sir Ewayne and Sir Errake and othire gret lordes
Demenes the medilwarde menskefully thareaftire,

4052 *dreches,* delays 4053 *Derefull, dredlesse,* Sorrowful, fearless
4054 *Caieres,* Marches 4055 *trays,* track; *trines,* follows
4056 *Treyntes,* River Trent 4058 *freshely ascries,* fiercely cries out
4059 *freliche,* noble; *nommen,* taken 4060 *eives,* edges
4061 *ostes,* hosts; *alines,* foreigners
4063 *Foundes,* Rushes; *appon fele halfes,* on many sides
4064 *batailles,* divisions; *semliche,* handsomely
4067 Fairly drawn up in a battle line by the fresh banks
4068 *amede,* reckoned 4069 *Bot aughtene,* Only eighteen
4070 *unmete,* unequal; *bot,* except for 4071 *melle,* engage
4074 *Buskes his avaumwarde,* Arranges his vanguard
4075 *Errake,* knight of the Round Table
4076 Direct the middleguard honorably thereafter

With Merrake and Meneyduke, mightty of strenghes;
Idirous and Alymere, thire avenaunt children,
Aiers with Arthure, with seven score of knightes.
4080 He reules the rerewarde redily thareaftire,
The rekeneste redy men of the Rounde Table,
And thus he fittes his folke and freshely ascries,
And sien conforthes his men with knightliche wordes:
"I beseke you, Sirs, for sake of oure Lorde,
4085 That ye doo wele todaye and dredes no wapen.
Fighttes fersely nowe and fendes youreselven;
Felles down yone feye folke — the felde shall be ours!
They are Sarazenes, yone sorte, unsounde motte they worthe!
Sett one them sadlye for sake of oure Lorde.
4090 Yif us be destaynede to dy todaye one this erthe,
We shall be hewede unto Heven or we be halfe colde.
Loke ye lett for no lede lordly to wirche.
Layes yone laddes lowe be the laike ende.
Take no tente unto me, ne tale of me rekke;
4095 Bes besy one my baners with youre brighte wapens
That they be strenghely stuffede with steren knightes,
And holden lordly one lofte ledes to shewe;
Yif any renke them arase, reshoue them sone,
Wirkes now my wirshipe, todaye my werre endes.
4100 Ye wotte my wele and my woo; wirkkes as you likes.
Crist comly with crown conforthe you all
For the kindeste creatours that ever kinge ledde.

4077 *Merrake and Meneyduke,* Arthur's knights (though Meneyduke had apparently been slain earlier — l. 1919)
4078 Idrus (son of Ywain) and Alymere, these handsome nobles
4079 *Aiers,* March 4081 *rekeneste redy,* most resourceful, prepared
4082 *fittes,* arrays; *freshely ascries,* fiercely cries out 4083 *sien,* then
4086 *fendes,* defend 4087 *feye,* doomed 4088 *sorte,* group; *worthe,* become
4089 *sadlye,* resolutely 4091 *hewede,* raised; *or,* before
4092 See that you do not fail, on account of any man, to fight nobly.
4093 *laike,* stream
4094 Pay no attention to me, nor believe any rumor about me (my death).
4095 *one,* around 4096 *stuffede,* furnished
4097 And hold (them) nobly on high for all men to see
4098 *arase,* lay low; *reshoue,* rescue 4100 *wotte,* know
4102 *kindeste,* most loyal

I giffe you all my blissing with a blithe will,
And all Bretouns bolde, blithe mote ye worthe."
4105 They pipe upe at prime time, approches them nere;
Pris men and priste proves theire strenghes.
Bremly the brethemen bragges in troumppes,
In cornettes comlily, when knighttes assembles,
And thane jolily enjoines theis gentill knighttes.
4110 A joliere journe ajuggede was never,
When Bretons boldly enbraces theire sheldes,
And Cristen encroissede them and castes in fewtire.
Than Sir Arthure oste his enmye ascries,
And in they shokke theire sheldes, shontes no lengare,
4115 Shotte to the shiltrons and shouttes full heghe.
Thorowe sheldes full shene shalkes they touche.
Redily thas ridde men of the Rounde Table
With ryall rannke stele rittes theire mailes,
Bryneis broudden they briste and burneste helmes,
4120 Hewes haithen men down, halses in sondre,
Fightande with fine stele, the feye blod rinnes;
Of the frekkeste of frounte, unfers ere belevede.
Ethens of Argayle and Irishe kinges
Enverounes oure avaumwarde with venimmos berenns;
4125 Peghttes and Painimes with perilous wapens,
With speres disspetousely disspoilles oure knighttes
And hewede down the hendeste with hertly dinttes:

4104 *worthe,* be 4105 *pipe upe,* sound the attack; *prime time,* early morning
4106 *Pris men and priste,* Valiant and proved men
4107 Fiercely the trumpeters blow on their trumpets.
4109 *jolily enjoines,* gaily engage 4110 *joliere journe,* braver day's battle
4112 *castes in fewtire,* put lances in rest 4113 *ascries,* challenges
4114 *shokke,* thrust; *shontes,* wait
4115 *Shotte to the shiltrons,* Rushed against the close-packed troops
4116 *shalkes,* men; *touche,* pierce 4117 *ridde,* ready
4118 *rannke,* strong; *rittes,* rip open
4119 Burst open woven coats of mail and burnished helmets 4120 *halses,* necks
4121 *feye,* doomed 4122 The boldest in the front (lines) are left tamed.
4123 *Ethens,* Heathens 4124 *Enverounes,* Surrounds 4125 *Peghttes,* Picts
4126 *disspetousely,* mercilessly 4127 *hendeste,* most skillful; *hertly,* spirited

Thorow the holle bataile they holden theire wayes.
Thus fersly they fighte appon sere halfes,
4130 That of the bolde Bretons miche blode spilles.
Thare durste non rescoue them, for reches on erthe,
The steren ware thare so stedde and stuffede wit othire.
He durste noghte stire a steppe, bot stodde for himselven
Till thre stales ware stroyede be strenghe of him one.
4135 "Idrous," quod Arthure, "aire thee behoves!
I see Sir Ewayne oversette with Sarazenes kene—
Redy thee for rescous, arraye thee sone!
Hie thee with hardy men in helpe of thy fadire!
Sett in one the side and socoure yone lordes!
4140 Bot they be socourrede and sounde, unsaughte be I never!"
Idrous him answers ernestly thareaftire:
"He es my fadire in faithe, forsake shall I never;
He has me fosterde and fedde and my faire bretheren.
Bot I forsake this gate, so me Gode helpe,
4145 And sothely all sibreden bot thyselfe one,
I breke never his bidding for beren one life,
Bot ever bouxum as beste blethely to wirke.
He commande me kindly with knightly wordes
That I shulde lelely one thee lenge, and one noo lede ells;
4150 I shall his commandement holde, yif Criste wil me thole.
He es eldare than I and ende shall we bothen:
He shall ferkke before and I shall come aftire.
Yiffe him be destaynede to dy todaye one this erthe,
Criste comly with crown take kepe to his saule!"
4155 Than remes the riche king with rewthe at his herte,
Hewes his handes one heghte and to the Heven lokes:

4128 *holle,* whole 4129 *sere halfes,* all sides 4131 *reches,* riches
4132 The warriors there were so beset and so clogged with others
4134 *stales,* squadrons 4135 *aire thee behoves,* it behooves you to go
4140 *Bot,* Unless; *unsaughte,* dissatisfied 4144 *Bot,* Unless; *gate,* position
4145 *sibreden,* kinship 4147 But always cheerfully obeyed him, as best I could
4148 *commande,* commanded
4149 *lelely one thee lenge,* loyally stay by you; *lede,* man
4150 *thole,* allow 4152 *ferkke,* go 4155 *remes,* weeps

"Whithen hade Drighttin destaynede at his dere will
That he hade demed me todaye to dy for you all!
That had I lever than be lorde all my life tim
4160 Of all that Alexandere aughte whills he in erthe lengede."
Sir Ewayne and Sir Errake, thes excellente berens,
Enters in one the oste and egerly strikes
The ethenes of Orkkenaye and Irishe kinges;
Thay gobone of the gretteste with groundene swerdes,
4165 Hewes one thas hulkes with theire harde wapens,
Layed down thas ledes with lothely dinttes.
Shuldirs and sheldes thay shrede to the haunches,
And medills thourghe mailes thay merken in sondire.
Siche honoure never aughte none erthely king
4170 At theire ending daye, bot Arthure himselven.
So the droughte of the daye driede theire hertes,
That both drinkles they die, dole was the more.
Now melles oure medillwarde and mengen togedire
Sir Mordrede the Malebranche with his miche pople;
4175 He had hide him behinde within thas holte eives,
With halle bataile on hethe, harme es the more.
He hade sene the conteke al clene to the ende,
How oure chevalrye chevede be chaunces of armes;
He wiste oure folke was forfoughtten, that thare was feye levede —
4180 To encountere the kinge he castes him sone,
Bot the churles cheken hade chaungede his armes;
He had sothely forsaken the sauturoure engrelede,
And laughte upe thre lions all of whitte silvire,

4157 Would that God had destined by his precious will 4158 *demed,* appointed
4159 *lever,* rather 4160 *aughte,* possessed; *lengede,* remained
4164 *gobone,* hew into gobbets 4165 *hulkes,* huge people
4167 *shrede to the haunches,* hack clear through
4168 *medills,* waists; *merken,* strike 4169 *aughte,* had
4173 *melles,* engages; *mengen,* mingle 4175 *holte eives,* edges of the wood
4176 *halle bataile,* whole battalion 4178 *chevede,* performed
4179 *wiste,* knew; *forfoughtten,* weary with fighting; *feye levede,* left doomed
4180 *castes him,* contrived 4181 *cheken,* chicken
4182 *sauturoure engrelede,* x-shaped cross with scalloped edges
4183 *laughte,* taken

Passande in purpre, of perrie full riche,
4185 For the king shulde noghte knawe the cautelous wriche.
Because of his cowardis he ceste off his atire,
Bot the comliche king knewe him full swithe,
Carpes to Sir Cadors thes kindly wordes:
"I see the traitoure come yondir trinande full yerne;
4190 Yone ladde with the liones es like to himselfene.
Him shall torfere betide, may I touche ones,
For all his treson and traine, alls I am trew lorde.
Today Clarente and Caliburne shall kithe them togedirs,
Whilke es kenere of cerfe or hardare of eghge.
4195 Fraiste shall we fine stele appone fine wedes.
Itt was my derlinge dainteuous and full dere holden,
Kepede fore encorownmentes of kinges enointtede;
One dayes when I dubbede dukkes and erlles,
It was burliche borne be the brighte hiltes;
4200 I durste never dere it in dedes of armes,
Bot ever kepede clene because of myselven.
For I see Clarent unclede, that crowne es of swerdes,
My wardrop of Walyngfordhe I wate es distroyede.
Wist no wy of wone bot Waynor hirselven;
4205 Sho hade the kepinge hirselfe of that kidde wapen,
Of cofres enclosede that to the crown lengede,
With ringes and relikkes and the regale of Fraunce

4184 *Passande in purpre,* Walking with raised forepaw in purple background; *perrie,* gems
4185 *For,* So; *cautelous wriche,* deceitful wretch
4189 *trinande full yerne,* marching very eagerly
4191 *torfere,* trouble 4192 *traine,* treachery
4193 *Clarente,* Arthur's sword which Guinevere gave to Mordred; *kithe,* demonstrate
4194 *Whilke,* Which; *cerfe,* cutting 4195 *Fraiste,* Test
4196 *Itt,* Clarente; *dainteuous,* dainty; *dere holden,* carefully guarded
4199 *burliche,* nobly 4200 *dere,* venture
4202 *For,* Because; *unclede,* unsheathed
4203 *wardrop of Walyngfordhe,* armor room at Wallingford (Berks.); *wate,* know
4204 No man knew of (its) place but Guinevere herself.
4205 *kidde,* famous 4206 *lengede,* belonged 4207 *regale,* regalia

That was founden on Sir Froll when he was feye levede."
Than Sir Marrike in malincoly metes him sone,
4210 With a melled mace mightily him strikes;
The bordour of his bacenett he bristes in sondire,
That the shire rede blode over his brene rinnes.
The beren blenkes for bale and all his ble chaunges,
Bot yitt he biddes as a bore and brimly he strikes.
4215 He braides oute a brande brighte als ever ony silver
That was Sir Arthure awen, and Utere his fadirs;
In the wardrop of Walyngfordhe was wonte to be kepede.
Tharewith the derfe dogge siche dinttes he rechede
The tother withdrewe one dreghe and durste do non other,
4220 For Sir Marrake was man merrede in elde
And Sir Mordrede was mighty and his moste strenghes;
Come non within the compas, knighte ne non other,
Within the swing of swerde that ne he the swete leved.
That persaifes oure prince and presses too faste,
4225 Strikes into the stoure by strenghe of his handes,
Metes with Sir Mordrede, he meles unfaire:
"Turne, traitoure untrewe, thee tides no bettire!
Be gret Gode, thou shall dy with dint of my handes!
Thee shall rescoue no renke ne reches in erthe!"
4230 The king with Calaburn knightly him strikes;
The cantell of the clere shelde he cerfes in sondire
Into the shuldire of the shalke a shaftmonde large,
That the shire rede blode shewede one the mailes.
He shodirde and shrenkes and shontes bott littill,

4208 *feye levede,* left doomed (to die) 4209 *him,* Mordred
4210 *melled,* hammered 4211 *bacenett,* helmet
4212 *shire,* clear; *brene,* coat of mail
4213 The man flinches at the pain and changes color.
4214 *biddes,* stands firm; *brimly,* fiercely 4215 *He braides,* Mordred draws
4216 *Utere,* Uther 4217 *wonte,* accustomed 4218 *derfe,* cruel; *rechede,* struck
4219 *one dreghe,* to a distance 4220 *merrede,* marred 4221 *and,* and (in)
4223 *swete,* life-blood; *leved,* left 4225 *stoure,* struggle
4226 *meles unfaire,* speaks roughly 4227 *thee tides,* it betides you
4229 Neither man nor earthly riches shall rescue you. 4231 *cantell,* corner
4232 *shalke,* man; *shaftmonde,* handbreadth 4233 *shewede,* showed
4234 *shontes,* shies

4235 Bott shokkes in sharpely in his shene wedes.
The felonne with the fin swerde freshely he strikes:
The felettes of the ferrere side he flashes in sondire;
Thorowe jopoun and jesseraunte of gentill mailes
The freke fichede in the fleshe an halfe fotte large.
4240 That derfe dint was his dede, and dole was the more
That ever that doughtty shulde dy, bot at Drighttens will.
Yitt with Calyburn his swerde full knighttly he strikes,
Castes in his clere shelde and coveres him full faire,
Swappes off the swerde hande, als he by glentes;
4245 Ane inche fro the elbowe he ochede it in sondire,
That he swounnes one the swarthe and one swim falles,
Thorowe bracer of brown stele and the brighte mailes,
That the hilte and the hande appon the hethe ligges.
Thane fresheliche the freke the fente upe rereres,
4250 Broches him in with the bronde to the brighte hiltes;
And he braules one the bronde and bounes to die.
"In faye," says the feye kinge, "sore me forthinkkes
That ever siche a false theefe so faire an ende haves."
When they had feniste this feghte thane was the felde wonnen,
4255 And the false folke in the felde feye are belevede.
Till a foreste they fledde and fell in the greves,
And fers feghtande folke folowes them aftire,
Hountes and hewes down the heithen tikes,
Mourtheres in the mountaignes Sir Modrede knightes.
4260 Thare chapede never no childe, cheftaine ne other,

4235 *shokkes,* thrusts; *shene wedes,* bright clothes (armor)
4237 *felettes,* loins; *ferrere,* farther; *flashes,* slashes
4238 *jopoun,* tunic; *jesseraunte,* splint armor; *gentill,* supple
4239 *freke,* man; *fichede,* pierced 4240 *derfe dint,* terrible blow; *dede,* death
4244 *Swappes off,* Chops off; *glentes,* glides 4245 *ochede,* cut
4246 *swarthe,* grass; *swim,* swoon
4247 *bracer,* wrist guard, MS *brater*; *brown,* burnished 4248 *ligges,* lie
4249 Then eagerly the man lifts up the throat opening.
4250 *Broches,* Thrusts 4251 *braules,* screams; *bounes,* prepares
4252 *faye,* faith; *feye,* doomed; *sore me forthinkkes,* it displeases me sorely
4256 *Till,* To; *greves,* thickets
4258 *tikes,* dogs
4260 *chapede,* escaped; *childe,* noble

Bot choppes them down in the chace, it charges bot littill.
Bot when Sir Arthure anon Sir Ewayne he findes,
And Errake the avenaunt and other grett lordes,
He caughte up Sir Cador with care at his herte,
4265 Sir Clegis, Sir Cleremonde, thes clere men of armes,
Sir Lothe, and Sir Lyonell, Sir Lawncelott, and Lowes,
Marrake and Meneduke, that mighty ware ever;
With langoure in the launde thare he layes them togedire,
Lokede on theire lighames and with a loude steven,
4270 Alls lede that liste noghte life and loste had his mirthes.
Than he stotais for made and all his strenghe failes,
Lokes upe to the lifte, and all his lire chaunges;
Downne he sweys full swithe and in a swoun falles,
Upe he coveres one knees and cries full often:
4275 "King comly with crowne, in care am I levede;
All my lordshipe lawe in lande es laide undire,
That me has gifen guerdons be grace of himselven,
Maintenede my manhede be mighte of theire handes,
Made me manly one molde and maister in erthe!
4280 In a tenefull tim this torfere was rererede,
That for a traitoure has tinte all my trewe lordes.
Here ristes the riche blude of the Rounde Table,
Rebukkede with a rebaude, and rewthe es the more!
I may helples one hethe house be min one,
4285 Alls a wafull wedowe that wanttes hir beren.
I may werye and wepe and wringe min handes,
For my witt and my wirshipe awaye es forever.
Of all lordships I take leve to min ende.

4261 *it charges bot littill,* it makes no difference 4268 *langoure,* sorrow
4269 *lighames,* bodies; *steven,* cry 4270 *Alls lede,* Like a man; *liste,* wished
4271 *stotais for made,* staggers like a madman
4272 *lifte,* heavens; *lire,* countenance 4273 *sweys,* sinks; *swithe,* quickly
4274 *coveres,* recovers 4275 *levede,* left
4276 *lordshipe,* company of lords; *lawe,* low 4279 *molde,* earth
4280 In a sorrowful time this trouble was raised.
4281 *for,* on account of; *tinte,* caused the loss of
4283 *Rebukkede with a rebaude,* Beaten down by a villain
4284 *house be min one,* dwell by myself
4285 *Alls,* As; *wanttes,* lacks; *beren,* man 4286 *werye,* curse

Here es the Bretons blode broughte out of life,
4290 And nowe in this journee all my joy endes."
Thane relies the renkes of all the Rounde Table,
To the ryall roy thay ride tham all;
Than assembles full sone seven score knightes
In sighte to thaire soveraine that was unsounde levede.
4295 Than kneles the crownede kinge and cries one loude:
"I thanke thee, Gode, of thy grace, with a gud will,
That gafe us vertue and witt to vencous this berens,
And us has grauntede the gree of theis gret lordes!
He sent us never no shame ne shenshipe in erthe,
4300 Bot ever yit the overhande of all other kinges.
We hafe no laisere now these lordes to seke,
For yone laithely ladde me lamede so sore.
Graithe us to Glashenbery, us gaines non other;
Thare we may riste us with roo and raunsake oure wondes.
4305 Of this dere day werke the Drightten be lovede,
That us has destaynede and demed to dye in oure awen."
Thane they holde at his heste hally at ones
And graithes to Glasshenberye the gate at the gaineste,
Entres the Ile of Aveloyne, and Arthure he lighttes,
4310 Merkes to a manere there, for mighte he no forthire.
A susgin of Salerne enserches his wondes;

4290 *journee,* day's battle 4291 *relies,* rally
4294 *unsounde levede,* left wounded 4297 *vencous,* vanquish
4298 *gree of,* victory over 4299 *shenshipe,* disgrace
4300 *overhande,* upper hand 4301 *seke,* pursue
4302 *laithely ladde,* hateful fellow
4303 *Graithe us,* Let us go; *Glashenbery,* Glastonbury, Somerset; *us gaines,* profits us
4304 *roo,* peace; *raunsake,* examine
4305 For this bold day's work may God be esteemed.
4306 Who has destined and judged us to die among our own
4307 *heste,* command; *hally,* wholly
4308 *the gate at the gaineste,* by the quickest way
4309 *Ile of Aveloyne,* Avalon, here simply an island near Glastonbury; *lighttes,* alights
4310 *Merkes,* Proceeds; *mighte he,* might he (go)
4311 *susgin,* surgeon; *Salerne,* Salerno, Italy; *enserches,* examines carefully

The king sees be asaye that sounde bese he never,
And sone to his sekire men he said theis wordes:
"Doo calle me a confessour with Criste in his armes;
4315 I will be houselde in haste, whate happe so betiddes;
Constantyn, my cosin, he shall the corown bere
Alls becommes him of kinde, yife Criste will him thole.
Beren, fore my benison thoue berye yone lordes
That in baitaille with brondes are broughte oute of life;
4320 And sithen merke manly to Mordrede children,
That they bee sleighely slaine and slongen in waters:
Latt no wikkede wede waxe ne writhe one this erthe.
I warne fore thy wirshipe, wirke alls I bidde!
I foregiffe all greffe, for Cristes lufe of Heven.
4325 Yife Waynor hafe wele wroghte, wele hir betidde."
He saide *In manus* with maine one molde whare he ligges,
And thus passes his sperit, and spekes he no more.
The baronage of Bretayne thane, beshopes and othire,
Graithes them to Glashenbery with gloppennande hertes,
4330 To bery thare the bolde kinge and bringe to the erthe,
With all wirshipe and welthe, that any wy sholde.
Throly belles thay ringe and *Requiem* singes,
Dosse messes and matins with mournande notes:

4312 *be asaye,* by the examination 4313 *sekire,* true
4314 *Doo calle me,* Have called to me
4315 *be houselde,* receive the communion; *whate happe so betiddes,* whatever may happen
4316 *Constantyn,* Constantine, son of Cador
4317 *of kinde,* rightfully; *thole,* allow
4318 *Beren,* Men; *fore my benison,* for the sake of my blessing
4320 *sithen,* afterwards; *merke manly to,* pursue boldly
4321 *sleighely,* secretly
4322 *wede wax ne writhe,* weed grow nor flourish 4324 *greffe,* injury
4325 If Guinevere has acted well, may she have good fortune.
4326 *In manus,* Into (your) hands (O God, I commend my spirit); *with maine,* strongly; *molde,* earth
4328 *beshopes,* bishops 4329 *gloppennande,* sorrowing
4331 *wy,* man
4332 *Throly,* Vigorously; *Requiem,* Rest (first word in the entrance hymn in a mass for the dead)
4333 *Dosse,* Perform

Religeous reveste in theire riche copes,
4335 Pontificalles and prelates in preciouse wedes,
Dukes and dusszeperes in theire dule-cotes,
Countasses knelande and claspande theire handes,
Ladys languessande and lourande to shewe;
All was buskede in blake, birdes and othire,
4340 That shewede at the sepulture with silande teres.
Whas never so sorowfull a sighte seen in theire tim.
Thus endes King Arthure, as auctors alegges,
That was of Ectores blude, the kinge son of Troye,
And of Sir Pryamous, the prince, praisede in erthe;
4345 Fro theythen broghte the Bretons all his bolde eldirs
Into Bretayne the Brode, as the Bruytte telles.

Hic jacet Arthurus, rex quondam rex que futurus.

4334 *Religeous reveste,* Holy men arrayed
4335 *Pontificalles,* Church dignitaries
4336 *dusszeperes,* nobles; *dule-cotes,* mourning-coats
4338 Ladies languishing and downcast to see
4339 *buskede,* draped; *birdes,* maidens 4340 *silande,* flowing
4345 *theythen,* thence; *eldirs,* ancestors
4346 *Bruytte, Brut:* any of the various stories about Brutus, the legendary founder of Britain who was descended from the royal Trojan line
4347 Here lies Arthur, the once and future king; *quondam,* MS *qondam*

20 *(Ca. 1350–1400)*

HERE BEGINNES THE AUNTIRS OF ARTHURE AT THE TERNE WATHELYN

In King Arthure tim ane auntir betide
By the Terne Wahethelyn, als the buke telles,
Als he to Carelele was commen, that conqueroure kide,
With dukes and with ducheperes that with that dere dwelles,
5 Forto hunnte at the herdes that lange hase bene hide.
And one a daye thay tham dighte to the depe delles
To felle of the femmales in the foreste wele frithede,
Faire in the fernisone-time by frithes and felles.
Thus to the wode are thay wente, the wlonkeste in wedes,
10 Bothe the kinge and the quene
And all the doghety bedene;
Sir Gawane, gayeste one grene,
Dame Gayenoure he ledes.

And thus Sir Gaweane the gay Dame Gayenour he ledes,
15 In a gleterande gide that glemet full gaye,

(20) Here Begins the Adventures of Arthur at the Tarn Wadling (lake in Cumberland associated with Arthurian tradition)

1 *auntir,* adventure; *betide,* happened 2 *als,* as

3 *Carelele,* Carlisle, Cumberland; *kide,* renowned

4 *ducheperes,* nobles: originally Charlemagne's twelve peers (douze peers); *dere,* worthy one

5 *hide,* hidden 6 *tham dighte,* go

7 To kill some of the does in the well enclosed forest

8 *Faire,* Lovely (?), To pursue (?); *fernisone-time,* fermison-time, term of venery, meaning the season between Martinmas and Candlemas, during which female deer only could be killed. See *Sir Gawain and the Green Knight,* l. 1156; *frithes and felles,* woods and hills

9 *wlonkeste,* fairest 11 *doghety,* brave ones; *bedene,* together

12 *Gawane,* Gawain, one of the greatest knights of the Round Table and Arthur's nephew; *one grene,* on the green (or, clothed in green)

13 *Gayenoure,* Guinevere, Arthur's wife

15 *gleterande gide,* bright dress; *glemet,* gleamed

With riche rebanes reverssede, who that righte redes,
Railede with rubes one royalle arraye.
Hir hude was of hawe heue that hir hede hides,
Wroghte with peloure and palle and perrye to paye,
20 Shruedede in a shorte cloke that the raine shrides,
Sett over with safirs, full sothely to saye,
And thus wondirfully was all the wightes wedes;
Hir sadill semede of that ilke,
Semlely sewede with silke.
25 One a muile als the milke
Gayely sho glides.

Thus alle in gleterande golde gayely sho glides
The gates with Sir Gawane by a grene welle;
Nane bot himselfe one a blonke by that birde bides,
30 That borne was in Burgoyne, by buke and by belle.
He ledde that lady so lange by those landes sides;
Sithen undir a lorere sho lighte lawe by a felle.
Sir Arthure with his erles full erenestly rides,
To teche tham to thaire tristes, trewely to telle.
35 To thaire tristes he tham taughte, who that righte trowes;
Ilke a lorde withoutten lett
At his triste was he sett,

16 *reverssede,* trimmed; *who that righte redes,* who understands rightly
17 *Railede,* Adorned 18 *hawe heue,* dark blue hue; *hir,* her
19 Made with fur and fine linen and jewels to please
20 *Shruedede,* Clothed; *shrides,* keeps off
21 *full sothely to saye,* to speak very truthfully 22 *wightes,* creature's
23 *that ilke,* the same 24 *Semlely,* Neatly 25 On a mule (white) as milk
26 *sho glides,* she goes 28 *gates,* way
29 *blonke,* horse; *birde,* lady; *bides,* remains
30 *That:* prob. refers to the horse, not to Guinevere; *Burgoyne,* Burgundy; *by buke and by belle,* by book and bell (a metrical tag, deriving from the phrase "bell, book, and candle" traditionally used in the act of excommunication)
31 *by those landes sides,* beside (through) those countrysides
32 Afterwards under a laurel she alighted at the bottom of a hill.
34 *teche,* guide; *tristes,* hunting stations
35 *righte trowes,* rightly believes
36 *Ilke a,* Each; *lett,* delay

With bowe and with barcelett
Undir those bewes.

40 Undir those bewes thay bade, those berens so bolde,
To bekire at those barraine in bankes so bare;
Thay ceste off thaire copills in cliffes so calde,
Thay recomforthed thaire kenettes to kele tham of care.
Thare mighte hirdmen hendely, forsothte, herdes behalde,
45 Herken huntinge with hornnes in holtes so hare.
Thay fellede downe the femmalls full thikke folde;
With freshe hundes and felle, felonosly thay fare.
Thay questede and quelles
By frithes and felles
50 That the dere dwelles
And darkes and dares.

Alle darkes the dere and to down showes,
And for the doute of the dede droupes the daa;
And by the stremes so strange that swiftly swoghes
55 Thay wery the wilde swine and wirkkes tham waa;
Thay hunte and halowes in holttes and hilles,
And till thaire riste raches relies on thaire raye:
Thay gafe no gamen no grithe that one grounde growes –
Grete hundes full gladly gan gaa.
60 Thus thies gomes thay ga in greves so grene,

38 *barcelett,* hound 39 *bewes,* boughs 40 *bade,* waited; *berens,* men
41 *bekire at,* attack; *barraine,* hinds not bearing young
42 *copills,* coupled collars
43 *recomforthed thaire kenettes,* encouraged their hounds; *kele,* relieve
44 *hirdmen,* retinue; *hendely, forsothte,* readily, in truth
45 *holtes so hare,* woods so gray 46 *full thikke folde,* in great numbers
47 *felle,* fierce; *felonosly,* viciously 48 They hunted and killed
49 Through woodland and moorland 50 *That,* So that; *dwelles,* hesitates
51 And lurks and cowers 52 *down,* hilly ground; *showes,* throng
53 And for fear of death the does lie hid. 54 *strange,* strong; *swoghes,* rush
55 *wery,* worry; *swine,* boars; *waa,* woe 56 *halowes,* halloo
57 And to their resting place (they) rally the hounds in order.
58 They gave no sport nor rest that grows on ground (a metrical tag).
59 *gan gaa,* set out 60 *gomes,* men; *greves,* groves

And boldly blawes rechaise,
And folowes faste one the trase
With many sergeaunte of mace,
Swilk solauce to sene.

65 Thus with solace thay semelede, the proudeste in palle,
And sew to the soveraigne in cleves so clene.
Nane bot Sir Gawane, the gayeste of alle,
Beleves with Dame Gaynour in those greves grene;
Undir a lorrere sho laye, that lady so smalle,
70 Of Boxe and of Barborane biggede full bene.
Faste before undrene this ferly gun falle,
And this mekill mervelle that I of mene;
Now will I of this mervelle men, yif I mote.
The daye wexe als dirke
75 Als it were midnighte mirke;
Therof Sir [Arthur] was irke
And lighte one his fote.

Thus one fote are thay lighte, those frekes unfaine,
And fledde faste to the foreste and to the fawe felles;
80 Thay rane faste to the roches for reddoure of the raine,
For the slete and the snawe that snaippede tham so snelle.
Thare come a lowe one the loughe, in lede es noghte to laine,
In the likness of Lucyfere, laietheste in Helle,

61 *rechaise,* recall 62 *trase,* path 63 *sergeaunte of mace,* attendants
64 *Swilk solauce,* Such pleasure 65 *semelede,* assembled; *palle,* rich cloth
66 *sew,* follow; *cleves,* ravines 68 *Beleves,* Remains
69 *lorrere,* laurel tree. In the Ireland MS the second half of this line reads *vndur a lefe sale* (under a leafy bower), thus providing an object which can reasonably be modified by the phrase in l. 70.
70 Of boxwood and barberry built very trimly
71 Just before noon this wonder befell. 72 *mekill,* great; *of mene,* tell of
73 *men, yif I mote,* tell, if I may 76 *Arthur,* MS *Gawane*
78 *frekes unfaine,* men unwillingly 79 *fawe felles,* colored moorlands
80 *for reddoure,* because of the violence
81 *snaippede tham so snelle,* stung them so sharply
82 There came a flame on the lake, it is not to be denied.
83 *laietheste,* most loathsome

And gliddes to Dame Gaynoure the gates full gaine,
85 Yollande yamirly with many loude yelle.
It yellede, it yamede, with vengeance full wete,
And saide, ofte sighande full sare:
"I ame the body that thee bare!
Allas! now kindils my care;
90 I gloppen and I grete!"

Thane gloppenede and grett Dame Gaynoure the gaye,
And askede Sir Gawayne whatt was his beste rede.
"It es the clippes of the mone, I herde a clerke saye";
And thus he comforthede the quene with his knightehede.
95 "Sir Cadore, Sir Caduke, Sir Costarde, Sir Kaye,
Thir knightes are uncurtaise, by crose and by crede,
That thus me hase lefte in this erthe at my dede daye
With the griselieste gaste that ever herde I grete!"
"At this gaste," quod Sir Gaweayne, "Greve youe no more.
100 I shalle speke with yone spirete
In yone wayes so wete;
If I maye, the bales bete
Of yone body bare."

Bare was hir body and blake to the bone,
105 Alle beclaggede in claye, uncomlily clede.
It weryet, it wayemettede, like a woman
That nouther one hede ne one hare hillinge it hade.
It stottede, it stounnede, it stode als a stane;

[84] *the gates full gaine,* by the shortest path
[85] *Yollande yamirly,* Shrieking lamentably
[86] *vengeance:* apparently an error for some word like cheeks or face, perhaps *wonges*
[90] I sorrow and weep. [92] *rede,* advice [93] *clippes,* eclipse
[95] All knights of the Round Table
[96] *Thir,* These; *by crose and by crede,* by cross and by faith
[97] *dede,* death [98] *gaste,* ghost; *grete,* weep [102] *bales bete,* torments relieve
[105] *beclaggede in,* beclotted with; *clede,* clad
[106] *weryet,* cursed; *wayemettede,* lamented [107] *one,* on; *hillinge,* covering
[108] *stottede,* stuttered; *stounnede,* stood astounded

It marrede, it mournede, it moissede for made.
110 Unto that grisely gaste Sir Gaweayne es gane.
He raikede to it one a rase, for he was never rade;
For rade was he never, nowe who that righte redes.
One the chefe of the cholle
A tade piket one hir polle;
115 Her eghne ware holkede full holle,
Glowand als gledes.

Alle glowede als gledes the gaste whare sho glides,
Umbeclede in a cloude with clethinge unclere,
Cerkelett with serpentes that satt by hir sides:
120 To telle the dedes therone my tonge were too tere.
The beren braundeshe oute his brande and the body bides;
Therefore that chevalrous knighte thoghte it no chere.
The hunndes are to hilles and thaire hedes hides
For that grisely gaste made so grime bere;
125 The grete grewhundes were agayste for that grim bere.
The birdes one the bewes
That one that gaste gewes
Thay clime in the clewes,
That hedous when thay here.

130 Who that mighte that hedous see, hendeste in haulle,
How hir cholle chatirede, hir chaftes and hir chinne!

[109] It was bewildered, it mourned, it stared like a madman.
[111] *raikede,* went; *rase,* rush; *rade,* afraid
[112] *nowe who that righte redes,* whoever now reads rightly
[113–16] On the top of her jowl a toad pecked at her head; her eyes were sunken very hollowly, glowing like coals.
[118] *Umbeclede,* Wrapped up; *clethinge unclere,* dingy covering
[120] *tere,* too difficult [121] *beren,* knight; *bides,* awaits [122] *no chere,* no joy
[123] *are,* are (fled) [124] *bere,* clamor [127] *gewes,* gaze
[128] *clewes,* ravines: The line is probably corrupt. The Ireland MS reads, *Thei skryke in the skowes* (They shriek in the woods).
[129] *hedous,* hideous one
[130] *Who that,* Whoever; *hendeste in haulle,* noblest in the hall (reference to the audience)
[131] *cholle,* upper jaw; *chaftes,* lower jaw

Thane conjurede hir that knighte and one Criste gun he calle:
"Alls thou was crucifiede one croise to save us fra sin!
Thou spirette, saye me the sothe – whedir that thou shall,
135 And why that thou walkes thies wayes thies woddes withinn?"
"I was of fegure and of fleshe the faiereste of alle,
Cristenede and crysommede with kinges in my kin;
I hafe kinges in my kin, knawen kide full kene.
God hase sent me this grace
140 To drie my paines in this place,
And nowe am I commen one a pase
To speke with your quenne.

"Quene was I whilome, wele brighttere of browes
Than Beryke or Brangwayne, the birdes so balde
145 Of any gamnes or gudes that one the grounde growes;
Wele grettere than Gaynour of garsommes and of golde,
Of pales, of poundes, of parkes, of plewes,
Of townnes, of towres, of tresoures untolde,
Of conntres, of castells, of cragges, of clewes.
150 And nowe am I cachede oute of kithe in cares so colde;
In care am I cachede and couchede in claye.
Loo, curtaise knighte,
How that dede hase me dighte!
Nowe giffe me anes a sighte
155 Of Gayenour the gaye."

134 *sothe,* truth; *whedir,* whither
137 *crysommede,* anointed with chrism, a consecrated oil
138 *knawen kide full kene,* well known (to be) very brave 140 *drie,* endure
141 *pase,* journey 142 *quenne,* queen 143 *whilome,* formerly
144 *Beryke or Brangwayne:* Berike is unknown, possibly an error for *beryl,* a precious stone; Brangwaine is the maid of Isoud; *birdes so balde,* maidens so noble
145 *gamnes or gudes,* games or pleasant things
146 *grettere,* greater; *garsommes,* treasure
147 Of enclosed grounds, of ponds, of parks, of ploughed lands
149 *of cragges, of clewes,* of crags, of ravines
150 *cachede oute,* driven out; *kithe,* native land 151 *couchede,* stretched out
153 How death has treated me 154 *anes,* once

Nowe to Gayenour the gaye Sir Gaweayne es gane,
And to that body hase he broghte that birde then so brighte.
"Welecome! Waynour," sho says, "Thou worthye in wane!
Loo, howe that dulefull dede hase thy dame dighte!
160 I was reddere in rode than rose in the raine,
My lire als the lely, lufely to sighte;
And nowe I am a grisely gaste and grimly granes.
With Lucefere in a lake lawe ame I lighte;
Thus am I like to Lucefere — takes witnes by mee:
165 For all youre freshe favoure,
Now moise one this mirroure;
For, bothe kinge and emperoure,
Thus shall ye bee.

"And thus dede will you dighte, takes witnesse by me;
170 And thereone hertly takes hede whils that thou es here.
When thou es richely arrayede and rides in a route,
Hafe than pete and mind one the pore, for thou arte of powere.
Berens and birdes are besye thee aboute;
When thy body es baumede and broghte appone bere,
175 Thane will thay leve thee lightely that nowe will thee loute,
And thane helpes thee no thinge bot halye prayere:
The prayere of the pore chasses thee from Helle.
Of thase that yelles at thy yate
When thou sittes in thy sette
180 With alle mirthes at thy mete,
Some daintes thou dele.

157 *birde,* lady 158 *Waynour,* Guinevere; *wane,* dwelling place
159 *dulefull dede,* doleful death; *dame,* mother; *dighte,* abused
160 *rode,* countenance 161 *lire,* complexion; *lely,* lily 162 *granes,* groans
163 *lawe ame I lighte,* low have I descended 165 *favoure,* beauty
166 *moise one,* meditate on 170 *hertly,* heartily 171 *route,* company
172 *pete and mind,* pity and thought
173 Knights and ladies are busy in attendance on you.
174 *baumede,* embalmed; *bere,* bier 175 *lightely,* quickly; *loute,* bow to
176 *halye,* holy 178 *Of,* To; *yate,* gate
179 *sette,* throne, seat 181 *dele,* distribute

"With dainteths one desse thy dietes are dighte,
And thus in daungere and dole I downe and I dwelle,
Nasty and nedfull and nakede one nighte.
185 There folowes me a ferde of fendes full felle;
Thay harle me unhendely and hewes me one highte:
In brasse and in bromstane I burne als a belle.
Was never wroghte in this werlde a wafullere wighte;
It were tore till any tonge my tourmenttes to telle!
190 Bot now will I of my tourment talke or I gaa.
Thinke hertly on this:
Now fande to mende of thy mis,
For thou erte warnede iwisse;
Be warre now be my waa!"

195 "Now wo es me for thy waa!" said Waynour, "iwisse!
Bot a worde wolde I wete, and thy will ware:
Giff matinns or messes mighte oghte menden thy misse,
Or any mobills on molde, my mirthes ware the mare;
Or bedes of beshopes mighte bringe thee to blisse,
200 Or covenntes in cloisters might kele thee of care;
For, if thou be my modir, grete mervelle it es
That thy burliche body es blakenede so bare."
"I bare thee of my body, whate bote es to lie?
Be that to takeninge thou trowe
205 I brake a solempne avowe
That none wiste bot I and thoue,
And therfore dole I drie."

182 With dainty dishes on the high table your repasts are prepared.
183 *daungere*, bondage; *dole*, sorrow; *downe*, languish 184 *nedfull*, in want
185 *ferde*, crowd; *felle*, terrible
186 *harle*, drag down; *unhendely*, cruelly; *hewes*, heave
188 *wafullere wighte*, woefuller person 189 *tore*, torment; *till*, for
190 *or I gaa*, before I go 192 Now try to mend your misdeeds.
193 *iwisse*, truly 194 Beware now by my woe!
196–98 Only one word would I know, if it were your will: if matins or masses might in any way amend your misfortune, or any goods on earth, my pleasure would be the greater.
199 *bedes*, prayers 200 *covenntes*, groups of monks; *kele*, assuage
202 *burliche*, noble 203 *bote*, help 204 Let that be a token you believe (that)
205 *avowe*, vow, oath 207 *drie*, suffer

"Telle me now sothely what may safe thy sites,
And I shall garre seke saintes for thy sake.
210 Bot of thase balefull bestes that one thy body bites,
Alle blendes my blode, thy blee es soo blake!"
"This es it to luffe paramoures and lustes and lites;
That gerse me lighte and lenge so lawe in this lake.
For alle the welthe of this werlde thus awaye wites;
215 This werlde es wandrethe — that wirkes me wrake,
For wrake it me wirkes now, Waynoure, iwisse!
Were thritty trentalls donne
Betwixen undrone and nonne,
My saule were salvede full sone,
220 And broghte into blisse."

"To blisse bringe thee that barne that dere hase thee boghte,
That was crucifiede one croise and crownnede with thorne,
Cristennede and crysommede with candills and coude,
Fullede in funnstane full frely beforne.
225 Mary, that es mighty and mildeste of mode,
That bare that blisshede in Bedleme was borne,
Giffe me grace forto grete thy saule with some gude,
And mene thee with messes and matinnes one morne!"
"To mene me with messes grete menske nowe it were.
230 For him that riste one the rode,
Giffe nowe faste of thy gude

208 *safe thy sites,* remedy your torments
209 *garre seke,* cause to be importuned 210 *of,* because of
211 *blendes,* curdles; *blee,* color
212–13 Thus is it to enjoy illicit lovers and pleasures and delights; that causes me to descend and linger so low in this lake.
214 *wites,* vanishes 215 This world is sorrow — that works my ruin.
217 *trentalls,* series of thirty masses 218 *undrone,* mid-morning
221–33 appear in the Thornton MS following l. 259. 221 *barne,* child
223 *crysommede,* anointed; *coude,* chrism-cloth
224 Baptised in the fontstone very nobly before 225 *mode,* mood
226 Who bore that blessed one (who) in Bethlehem was born
227 *grete,* greet 228 *mene,* remember; *one morne,* in the morning
229 *menske,* honor 230 *riste,* rested
231 Give now quickly of your goods

To folke that failes the fude,
Whills that thou erte here!"

"Now here hertly one hande I hete thee to halde,
235 With a melionne of messes to make thy meninge.
Bot one worde," saide Dame Waynour, "Nowe wiete that I walde:
What greves Gode moste of any kins thinge?"
"Pride with apparementes, als prophetes have tolde
Before the pople appertly in thaire prechinge.
240 The bowe is full bittire, thareof be thou balde;
It makes berens full balde to breke his biddinge.
Whoso his biddinge brekes, bare he es of blisse;
Bot thay be salved of that sare,
Certes, or thay hethen fare,
245 Thay mon wiete of calde care,
Waynoure, iwis."

"Telle me," saide Waynour, "A worde, yif thou woste:
Whate dedes mighte me beste into blisshe bringe?"
"Mekenesse and mercy," sho saide, "Tho are the moste.
250 Hafe pete one the pore, thane pleses thou oure Kinge;
Sithen after that, do almous dedes of alle other thinge.
Thies aren the gud giftes of the Holy Goste
That enspires alle sperites, withoutten spillinge,
Forto come to that blisse that ever more shall laste.
255 Of thies sperituale thinges spire me na mare;
Whills thou arte quene in thy quarte

232 *failes,* lack 233 *Whills that,* While
234 Now here heartily by my hand I promise you to keep (my word).
235 *meninge,* remembrance 236 *wiete that I walde,* I should like to know
237 *kins,* kind of 238 *apparementes,* adornments 239 *appertly,* openly
240 *bowe,* branch, MS *om.*; *balde,* sure
241 *berens,* knights; *biddinge,* command 243 *Bot,* Unless; *sare,* sore
244–45 Certainly, before they fare hence, they must experience cold sorrow.
246 *iwis,* surely 247 *woste,* know 250 *Hafe pete,* Have pity
251 *Sithen,* Next; *almous,* alms 253 *spillinge,* failure
255 *spire,* ask 256 *quarte,* joy

Halde thies wordes in thin herte,
For thou shall liffe bot a starte;
Hethen shall thou fare."

260 "How shall we fare," saide the freke, "that foundes to fighte,
That ofte [defouleth] the folkes in fele kinges landes,
That riche rewmes overrines againes the righte,
And winnes wirshippes and welthes by wightenes of handes?"
"Youre kinge es too covetous, I tell thee, Sir Knighte;
265 Maye no man stere him of strenghe whills the whele standes.
When he es in his mageste hegheste and maste es of mighte,
He shall lighte full lawe appone the see sandes.
Thus youre chevalrous kinge chefe shalle a chaunce,
False fortune in fighte;
270 That wondirfull whele-wrighte
Mase lordes lawe forto lighte —
Takes witnes by Fraunce.

"Fraunce hafe ye frely with your fighte wonnen:
The Frollo and the Farnaghe es frely belevede,
275 Bretayne and Burgoyne es bothe to you bounden,
And alle the dugepers of Fraunce with the din drevede.
Giane may greten that the werre was begounnen;

258 For you shall live but a moment. 259 *Hethen,* Hence

260 *freke,* man (*i.e.,* Gawain); *foundes,* journey

261 *defouleth,* MS *foundes*; *fele,* many

262 That overrun rich realms unlawfully 263 *wightenes,* valor

265 No man may displace him by force while the wheel (Fortune's) stands still.

266 *mageste hegheste,* very highest 267 *lighte,* fall

268 *chefe,* achieve; *shalle,* shall (experience)

271 Makes lords descend low 273 *frely,* nobly

274 *Frollo,* King of France; *Farnaghe:* possibly one of Frollo's knights, possibly a corruption of Feraunt, an ally of the Romans against Arthur, possibly a corruption of *farnet,* meaning "band" or "company"; *frely belevede,* joyfully left (for dead), though *frely* is possibly an error for *feye,* doomed

275 Brittany and Burgundy are both bound to you.

276 *dugepers,* nobles (see gloss l. 4 above); *with the din drevede,* confounded by the noise of battle

277 *Giane,* Guyenne; *greten,* weep

Es noghte a lorde in that lande appon life levede.
Yete shall the riche Romaynes with you ben overronnen,
280 And alle the Rounde Tabill thaire rentes be revede.
Thay shall yitt be Tybire timbire you tene.
Gete thee, Sir Gawayne:
Turne thou to Tuskayne,
For [lese] thou shall Bretayne
285 With a knighte kene.

"A knighte shall kenly closen the crowne
And at Carelyone be crownede for kinge;
That sege shall be sesede at a sesone,
That mekill bale and barete till Inglande shall bringe.
290 Ther shall in Tuskayne be tallde of that tresonne,
Ane torne home ayaine for that tidinge;
And ther shall the Rounde Tabille losse the renowne,
Beside Ramessaye full righte at a ridinge;

278 *appon life levede,* left alive

279–81 The sense of these lines is confused, but seems to require the following translation: In addition the Romans shall be overrun by you, and all their possessions (*rentes*) be seized by the Round Table. (*Alle* is apparently a mistake for the *atte* and *with* which appear in the other MSS.) Thereafter, they (*i.e.,* Mordred and his followers) shall cause you grief (*timbire you tene*) by the Camel River. (*Tybire* could not reasonably refer to the Tiber in Rome, since Arthur's invasion did not get that far south, and since the Romans did not cause him distress either here or elsewhere. However, *The Alliterative Morte Arthure* speaks of Mordred raising his tents by the Tambire River, while both Wace and Layamon render Geoffrey's *glumen Cambula* as *Tamble* or *Tanbre.*)

282 *Gete thee,* Get away

283 Turn toward Tuscany (the province lying immediately to the north of Viterbo — hence the direction Arthur and Gawain must travel as they hurry back to England to confront Mordred)

285 *With,* By means of 286 *kenly closen,* boldly seize

287 *Carelyone,* Caerleon-upon-Usk, Arthur's chief residence

288–89 That man shall be invested at a (certain) time, that much grief and strife to England shall bring.

293 *Ramessaye:* no such place is mentioned in the chronicles. The author may be referring to Romney, where Arthur first landed and where Gawain was killed.

And at Dorsett shall dy the doghetieste of alle.
295 Gette thee, Sir Gawayne,
The baldeste of Bretayne,
For in a slake thou shall be slaine –
Swilke ferly shall falle.

"Siche ferly shall falle withoutten any fabille
300 Apponne Cornewayle coste with a knighte kene;
Arthure the avenante, that honeste es and abill,
Shall be wonded I wisse, full wathely I wene.
[And all the ryal route of the Round Table
Shall die on a day, the doghting bedene,]
305 Supprisede with a sugette that beres of sabille
A Sautire engrelede of silver full shene;
He beres of sabille, sothely to saye.
In King Arthures haulle
The childe playes him at the balle
310 That shall outtraye you alle
Full derfely a daye.

"Hafe gud daye, Dame Gaynour, and Gawayne the gude!
I hafe no langare time mo tales to telle,
For me buse wende one my waye thoroute this wode
315 Unto my wonninge wane, in waa forto welle.
For him that rewfully rase and rente was one rude,

294 Neither Arthur nor Gawain died in Dorsetshire, though this shire is mentioned in the account of Arthur's pursuit of Mordred (*Allit. M.A.*, l. 4052).
296 *baldeste,* boldest 297 *slake,* hollow 298 Such a marvel shall happen.
300 *with,* by means of 301–2 and 303–4 transposed in MS. 301 *avenante,* bold
302 *wisse,* tell; *wathely,* severely
304 *doghting* (error for *doghty*?) *bedene,* the brave ones together
305–6 Surprised by a subject who bears an indented diagonal cross of bright silver on a sable background (the false heraldic device under which Mordred will disguise himself in the last battle). See *Allit. M.A.*, ll. 4181–85.
309 *childe,* young noble, possibly child 310 *outtraye,* outrage
311 Full terribly one day 314 *For me buse,* For I must
315 Unto my dwelling place in woe to boil
316 For Him that pitifully was raised and torn on the cross

Thinke one the daungere and the dole that I in dwelle,
And fede folke, for my sake, that fautes the fude,
And mene me with messes and matins i-melle.
320 [Messes be medicine to hem that bale bides:]
Us thinke a messe als swete
Als any spice that ever thou ete."
And thus with a grisely grete
The gaste awaye glides,

325 [And gothe with a greting in greves so grene.]
The winde and the wedirs than welken in hides;
Than unclosede the clouddes, the sonne shane shene.
The kinge his bogill hase blowen and on the bent bides;
His faire folke in firthes flokkes in fere.
330 Alle that royalle route to the quene rides
And meles to hir mildely one thaire manere,
[Knightes and squiers on everich sides.]
The wyes on swilke wondirs awondirde thaire were.
The princes proudeste in palle,
335 Dame Gaynour and alle,
Wente to Randolfe-sett Haulle
To thaire sopere.

The kinge was sett to the supere and servede in sale
Undir a seloure of silke full daineteuousely dighte,
340 With alle the wirshipe to welde, and wine forto wale,

317 *daungere,* bondage 318 *fautes,* lack
319 *i-melle,* together. After l. 319, a variation of ll. 229–33 was inserted; then ll. 321 ff. followed. L. 320, here supplied from the Lambeth MS, was somehow lost.
320 *hem,* them; *bale bides,* suffer torment 323 *grete,* cry
326 *wedirs,* stormy weather; *welken in hides,* hide away in the sky
328 *bogill,* bugle; *on the bent bides,* waits in the meadow
329 *firthes,* enclosed woods; *in fere,* together 330 *route,* company
331 *meles,* speaks; *one thaire manere,* in their fashion
333 The men were there amazed at such wonders.
336 *Randolfe-sett Haulle,* possibly Randalholme on the Tyne River
338 *sale,* hall 339 *seloure,* canopy; *dighte,* adorned
340 *wirshipe to welde,* honor to dispense; *wale,* select

Birdes in brede of brint golde brighte.
Ther come two setolers in with a symbale,
A lady, lufsome of late, ledande a knighte.
Sho rides up to the heghe desse, before the royalle,
345 And askede Sir Arthure full hendely one highte;
Sho saide to that soveraine, wlonkeste in wedes:
"Manne moste of mighte,
Here es comen ane armed knighte:
Now do him resoune and righte
350 For thy manhede."

The mane in his mantill sittes at his mete,
In paulle purede with pane, full preciousely dighte,
Trofelete and traverste with trewloves in trete;
The tasee was of topas that therto was tighte.
355 He glifte upe with his eghne that graye ware and grete,
With his burely berde, one that birde brighte.
He was the soveraineste sir sittande in sette
That ever any segge saughe or sene was with sighte.
Thus the king, crowned in kithe, carpes hir till:
360 "Welcome, worthily wighte!
Thou shall hafe resone and righte.
Whithen es this comly knighte,
If it be thy will?"

341 Birds (baked) in bread of bright burnished gold (possibly the last phrase is intended to refer to the serving dishes — *cf.* l. 484)
342 *setolers,* players of the citole (a small lute); *symbale,* cymbal
343 *lufsome of late,* lovely of countenance; *ledande,* leading
344 *Sho,* She; *desse,* dais; *royalle,* royal person
345 *hendely one highte,* courteously on high
346 *wlonkeste in wedes,* fairest in garments
347 *Manne,* Man (Arthur) 350 *For,* For the sake of
352–53 In rich cloth adorned with strips of different colored cloths very preciously adorned, with trefoils and crossed with true-love knots in a row
354 *tasee,* clasp; *tighte,* fastened 355 *glifte,* looked; *eghne,* eyes
356 *burely,* noble; *birde,* maiden 357 *sir,* man 358 *segge,* man; *sene,* seen
359 *kithe,* land; *carpes hir till,* speaks to her
360 *worthily wighte,* worthy person
362 *Whithen,* Whence

Sho was the worthilieste wighte that any wy mighte welde:
365 Hir gide was glorious and gaye, alle of girse grene;
Hir belle was of plonkete with birdes full baulde,
Botonede with besantes and bokellede full bene;
Hir faxe in fin perrye frette was in foulde —
The conterfelette in a kelle colourede full clene —
370 With a crowne of cristalle and of clere golde;
Hir courchefes were coriouse with many proude pin.
[Her fairhede was praised with prest and with knight;]
The brighte birdes and balde
Had note inoghe to behalde
375 One that freely to faulde,
And one that hende knighte.

That knighte in his coloures was armede full clene,
With his comly creste full clene to beholde;
His brenyes and his bacenett burneshet full bene,
380 With a bourdoure aboute alle of brinte golde;
His mailes was milk-whitte enclosede so clene,
His horse trappede with the same, als it was me taulde;
The shelde one his shuldir of silvere full shene,
With bare hevedes of blake, burely and baulde;
385 His horse withe sendale was teldede and trappede to the hele,
And [in] his chevarone beforne

364 *Sho,* She; *wy,* man; *welde,* rule over

365 *gide,* dress; *girse grene,* grass green

366 Her bell-shaped cloak was of white woolen cloth adorned with very bold birds.

367 *Botonede with besantes,* Buttoned with besants (gold coins); *bene,* neatly

368 Her hair was in plaits adorned with fine jewels.

369 *conterfelette in a kelle,* hair-net 371 *courchefes,* kerchiefs; *coriouse,* costly

372 *with,* by

373–76 The bright, bold maidens had not enough (*i.e.,* plenty) to do to look on that noble lady, and to embrace her, and on that courteous knight.

377 *coloures,* heraldic colors

379 *brenyes,* coats of mail; *bacenett,* light headpiece; *bene,* nicely

380 *brinte,* burnished 381 *enclosede so clene,* rivetted very neatly

382 *taulde,* told 384 With bare heads of black, stout and strong

385 *sendale,* silk; *teldede,* covered; *hele,* heel

386 *in,* MS *om.*; *chevarone,* head armor

Stode als ane unicorne,
Als so sharpe als any thorne,
[An andlas] of stele.

390 In stele was he stuffede, that steren was one stede,
Alle of sternes of golde that stekillede was one straye.
He and his gambesounns glomede als gledes
With graines of rubies that graithede were gaye,
And his shene shinbaudes, sharpe for to shrede,
395 [His poleines and his pelidodes that powdred wer to pay,
With a launce upon loft lovely in lede.
A faunt on a fair folower him folowed in fay;
The faunt was aferd for fray of that fare
He was wont not to se.
400 Nevere in the Round Table
Such game nor gle
Saw he nevere are.]

Arthure askede in hie, one herande tham alle:
"Whate woldest thou, wy, yif it were thy wille?
405 Telle me whate thou sekes and whedir that thou shalle,
And why thou stonies on thy stede and stondes so stille."

389 *An andlas,* A short, broad dagger, MS *And mailes*
390 *stuffede,* clad; *steren,* brave
391 All with stars of gold that were besprinkled all over
392 *gambesounns,* quilted doublet; *glomede als gledes,* gleamed like glowing coals
393 With small rubies that were gaily set out
394 *shinbaudes,* leg-armor; *shrede,* cut, slice
395–402 MS Thornton reads: *Thus with a lance appon lofte that lady gun he lede / A swayne one a fresone folowede hym in faye / He was seldome wounte / To see the tabille at his frounte / Swilke gammenes was he wonte / Full seldom to see.*
395 The key words in the line are corrupt. The sense seems to be: His knee-pieces were pleasantly powdered with peridots (a semi-precious stone).
396 *lovely in lede,* lovely in the land
397 *faunt,* youth; *folower,* accompanying horse
398 The youth was abashed for fear of that festivity. 402 *are,* before
403 Arthur asked loudly, in the hearing of them all
405 *whedir that thou shalle,* whither you shall (go) 406 *stonies,* sits astounded

He lifte upe his vesage fro the ventalle
And with a knightly contenance he carpes him till:
"Be thou kaisere or kinge, here I thee becalle
410 To finde me a freke to fighte one my fill,
For fightinge to fraiste I foundede fra hame."
The kinge carpede one heghte:
"Lighte and lende alle nighte,
If thou be curtaise knighte,
415 And telle me thy name."

"My name es Sir Galleroun, withoutten any gile,
The gretteste of Galowaye, of greves and of gilles,
Of Koninge, of Carrike, of Coningame, of Kille,
Of Lomonde, of Lenay, of Lowthyane hilles.
420 Thou hase wonnen thaim one werre with outtrageouse will,
And giffen tham Sir Gawayne, and that min herte grilles.
[He shal wringen his hondes and warie the while]
Or he welden my landes at min [unwilles].
By alle the welthe of this werlde, he shall tham never welde
425 Whills I my hede may bere,
Bot he win tham one werre
Bothe with shelde and with spere
Appone a fair felde!

"I will fighte one a felde, and therto make I my faithe,
430 With any freke one the foulde that frely es borne.

407 *vesage,* visage (possibly a mistake for visor); *ventalle,* ventaile (the moveable mouthpiece, below the visor)

409 *becalle,* call upon 410 *freke,* warrior; *one my fill,* to my fill

411 *fraiste,* seek; *foundede,* journeyed 413 Alight and stay all night.

417 *Galowaye,* Galway, an old Scottish kingdom; *greves and of gilles,* groves and glens

418 All are divisions of or places in Ayrshire, Scotland: *Koninge,* perhaps Cumnock; *Coningame,* Cunningham; *Kille,* Kyle.

419 *Lomonde,* in southwest Scotland; *Lenay,* Lennoxtown in Sterlingshire; *Lowthyane hilles,* the Lothian hills south of Edinburgh

421 *giffen tham,* given them to; *grilles,* torments 422 *warie,* curse

423 Before he possesses my lands at my displeasure

426 *Bot,* Unless; *one werre,* in war 430 *foulde,* earth; *frely,* nobly

To losse swilke a lordshipe me thinke it full laithe,
And ilke a leveande lede wolde laughe me to skorne."
"We aren here in the wode walkande one oure wathe;
We hunte at the herdes with hundes and with horne;
435 We aren one oure gamen; we ne hafe no gude graithe.
Bot yitt thou shalle be machede by middaye to-morne.
And forthy I rede thee, thou rathe mane, thou riste thee
alle the nighte."
Than Gawayne, gayeste of alle,
Ledes him oute of the haulle
440 Untill a paveleoune of paulle
That proudely was pighte.

Pighte was it proudely with purpure and paulle,
And dossours and queshens and bankoures full brighte;
Withinn was a chapelle, a chambir and ane haulle,
445 A chimneye with charecole to chauffen that knighte.
His stede was sone stabillede and lede to the stalle
And haye hendly hevede in hekkes one highte.
Sithen he braides up a burde and clathes gun calle,
Sanapes and salers, full semly to sighte,
450 Preketes and broketes and standertes betwene.
Than thay servede that knighte
And his worthy wighte

431 *swilke,* such; *laithe,* hard 432 *ilke a leveande lede,* each living person
433 *wathe,* hunting 435 *one oure gamen,* at our sport; *graithe,* equipment
436 *to-morne,* tomorrow
437 And therefore I counsel you, you rash man, (that) you rest yourself all the night.
440 *Untill,* Unto 441 *pighte,* adorned
442 *purpure and paulle,* purple and pall (rich cloth)
443 *dossours,* tapestries; *queshens,* cushions; *bankoures,* tapestried benches
445 *chauffen,* warm 447 *hekkes,* racks
448 Afterwards he sets up a table and calls for tablecloths.
449 *Sanapes,* Napkins; *salers,* salt-cellars
450 *Preketes,* Candles; *broketes,* candlesticks with small center spikes; *standertes,* large wax tapers
451 *Than,* Then
452 *wighte,* person (his lady)

With full riche dainteths dighte
In silvere full shene.

455 In silver sa semly thay serve tham of the beste,
With vernage in verres and couppes sa clene;
And thus thase gleterande gommes gladdes thaire gestes
With riche dainteths endorrede in dishes bedene.
When the ryalle renke was gone to his riste,
460 The kinge into concelle hase callede his knightes so kene.
Sayse: "Lukes nowe, ye lordings, oure lose be noghte loste!
Who shall enconter with yone knighte, nowe [cast] us betwene."
Thane saide Sir Gawayne: "He shall us noghte greve,
Here my trouthe I you plighte;
465 I shall feghte with yone knighte
In the defence of my righte,
My Lorde, with youre lefe!"

"I leve wele," quod the kinge; "thy lates are [light.]
[But I nold for no lordship se thyself lorn."]
470 "Late gaa," quod Sir Gawayne; "Gode [dele the right,]
If he scape scatheles [it were a grete scorn."]
In the dawinge of the [day the doghty were dight;]
Thaye herde matins [and masse erly by the morne.]
By that one [Plonton land a place was y-pight]
475 Whare never [freke of this fold had foght beforn.]
[They set listes on lengthe on that longe lande;
Two soppes atte demain
They broght to Sir Gawayn

456 *vernage,* sweet white wine; *verres,* glasses
457 *gleterande gommes,* glittering warriors; *gladdes,* entertain
458 *endorrede,* glazed with egg-yolk; *bedene,* in succession
459 *renke,* man 461 *lose,* honor 462 *cast,* cast lots among us, MS *lukes*
468 *leve wele,* readily allow; *thy lates are light,* your looks are unconcerned
469–82 Thornton MS damaged here. 469 *lorn,* lost
470 Forget about that . . . May God deliver the right 471 *scatheles,* uninjured
472 *dawinge,* dawning; *doghty,* brave (men)
474 By that time a place was prepared on Plonton land (perhaps Plumpton Park in Cumberland).
475 *freke of this fold,* man of this earth 477 Two strengthening sops

Forto comforte his brain –
480 The king dede comaunde.

The king dede comaunde to the Erl of Kent,
Curteisly in this cas, take tent to that knight.]
With riche daineteths that day he dinede in his tente,
With birdes baken in brede, of brinte golde brighte;
485 And sithen unto Dame Waynour full wiesely he wente
And lefte with hir in warde his worthily wighte.
And than thies hathells full hendely thaire horsses has hent
At the licence of the lorde that lordely gun lighte –
Alle bot thir berens, bouldeste of blode.
490 The kinges chaiere was sette
Aboune on a chasselett.
And many a gailiarde grett
For Gawayne the gude.

Gawayne and Galleron dightes thaire stedes;
495 Alle of gleterande golde, full gaye was thaire gere.
Twa lordes belife to thaire listes thaim ledes,
With many sergeauntes of mace – it was the manere.
The berens broches thaire blonkes to thaire sides bledes.
Aithire freke appon felde has fichede thaire spere;
500 Shaftes of shene wode thay sheverede in shides,
So jolily those gentill men justede one were,
Shaftes thay shever in shides full shene;
Sithen with brandes full brighte
Riche mailes thay righte.

482 *take tent to,* attend to
484 With birds baked in bread, on bright burnished gold (plates)
485 *sithen,* afterward
486 *in warde,* in safe-keeping; *wighte,* lady
487 *hathells,* noble knights; *hendely,* courteously; *hent,* taken
488 *licence,* permission; *gun lighte,* dismounted
489 *bot thir berens,* except these warriors 491 Above, on a platform
492 *gailiarde grett,* brave man wept 494 *dightes,* prepare
495 *gere,* equipment 496 *belife,* quickly 497 *sergeauntes of mace,* attendants
498 *broches,* spur; *blonkes,* steeds; *to,* until 499 *Aithire,* Each; *fichede,* fixed
500 *sheverede in shides,* shivered into splinters 501 *one were,* in war
503 *Sithen,* Afterward; *brandes,* swords 504 *righte,* rip

505 Thus enconterde the knighte
With Gawayne one grene.

Gawayne was graithely graithede one grene
With griffouns of golde engrelede full gaye,
Traifolede with traifoles and trewluffes betwene:
510 One a stirtande stede he strikes one straye.
[The tothir in] his turninge he talkes with tene:
["Why drawes thou] one dreghe and makes swilke delaye?"
[He swapped on the swithe] with a swerde kene;
[That greved Sir Gawayn to] his dede day,
515 [The dede of that doghty and his dintes] bedene.
[Fifty mailes and mo
The swerd swapped in two —
His kanell bone also —]
[And clef his] shelde shene.

520 [He clefe thurgh the cantell that covered the knight,
Thurgh shuldre and sheld a shaftmound and more;
And lothely that lord he laght up on hight,
And Gawayn grived gresily and groned ful sore:
"I shal reward thee with a route if I may rede right!"
525 He foloweth on that freke with a freshe fare:
Thurgh his blasing basnet that burnished was bright,
With a biting swerd thurgh him bare,
Thurgh the blasing basnet of that hende wight.
Than Galaron the gay —
530 Was no wondur in fay] —

506 *one grene,* on the green (or, clothed in green)
507 Gawain was readily clothed in green. 508 *engrelede,* indented
509 Ornamented with trefoils and true-love knots in between
510 *stirtande,* prancing; *strikes one straye,* lays about him
511–19 Thornton MS damaged. 511 *turninge,* tourneying; *tene,* annoyance
512 *Why drawes thou one dreghe,* Why do you draw aside
513 *swapped,* struck; *swithe:* probably a mistake for *swire,* neck
514 *dede,* death 515 *dintes bedene,* blows in succession
518 *kanell bone,* collarbone 519 *And clef his,* from MS Douce; *clef,* split
520 *cantell,* corner (of the shield) 521 *shaftmound,* hand breadth
522 *lothely,* loathsomely; *laght,* laughed 523 *gresily,* terribly
524 *route,* blow; *rede,* judge 525 *foloweth on,* rushed at; *fare,* onset
526 *blasing basnet,* flashing helmet 530 *fay,* faith

[The sturne strikes on stray
In stiropes strighte.]

[Sternely in his stiropes stifly he strikes
And waives at Sir Gawayn as he wer wood;
535 Than his lemman on loft sorowes and shrikes
Whan that bold berne so blenkes in his blood.
Lordes and ladies that the laike likes
Thonk God of his grace for Gawayn the good.
With a swappe of his swerd the tother at him strikes,
540 And stroke off the stedes heed with strengthe there he stood;
And than the fair stede foundred on fote.
Gawayn griuved in hert,
He was swithely smert;
Out of his stiropes he stert
545 From Gryselle the good.

"Now is gay Grisell gone that was so good;
He was the best body that evere bare knight.
By him that rufully ros and raght him on rood,
I shal venge him today, if I may aright!
550 Go fecche forth my frison, fairest on [fote;]
He wil stand in a stour in as mich stede.
No more for the good stede than a reshe rote —
But for dole of the dombe best that thus shold be dede —

531–32 From MS Douce. The brave man strikes (back) in succession erect in his stirrups.
534 And strikes at Sir Gawain as though he were mad
535 *lemman,* sweetheart 536 *blenkes,* blanches 537 *laike,* sport
540 *there,* where 541 *foundred,* stumbled 543 He was quickly stung.
548 *raght him,* stretched himself
550 *frison,* Friesland horse; *fote:* from MS Douce: Lambeth MS *food*
551 *stour,* fight; *in as mich stede,* in as much need
552–54 The sense of these lines is confused. If it is Gawain who is still speaking, the change of attitude toward his horse seems to result from his distinction between the loss of a horse, in itself, and the particular way in which this horse was lost: "(I care) no more for the loss of a good steed than for a rush root — or a bunch of monks — for I may get more. But I do grieve that a dumb beast should be killed in this way (thus)."
552 A verb like "I care" has probably been omitted; *reshe rote,* rush root
553 *dole of,* grief over

No more for no monkire for I may gete more!"
555 As he stode by his stede
That was good in eche nede,
He bethoght him of rede
And sighed sore.

He sighed for wo, Gawayn the wight,
560 And wendeth to his enemy that wounded was sore.
The tother withdrow him dervely for drede of the knight,
And boldily plis his stede on the bent bare.
"Thus may ye drive the day to the derk night;
The son is passed the mark of midday and more."
565 Within the listes on the laund ful lightly he light;
Toward the berne with a brond he busked ful yore.
Thus to bataill be they boun with brondes so bright.
Riche mailes were shred
With bright brondes y-bred;
570 Meny doghty dred,
So fersly they fight.

Thus they fight on her foot on her faire felde,
As frike as a lion that of fight fautes his fill;
Wisely thes wight-men her wepenes they weld.
575 Wite ye wele Sir Gawayn wantes no will;
He broched him with his brond undur the sheld,
Thurgh the waste he went that wounded him ill;
The swerd stint for no stuf, it was wel steled.
That other for that stroke stode stone still;
580 Thogh [he] were stonied that stound he striked ful sore

554 *monkire,* group of monks 557 *rede,* counsel 560 *wendeth,* goes
561 *dervely,* quickly 562 *plis,* drives; *bent bare,* bare plain 563 *drive,* spend
565 *light,* alights 566 *busked ful yore,* rushed quickly 567 *boun,* addressed
569 *y-bred,* drawn out 570 Many brave men are afraid. 572 *her,* their
573 *frike,* lusty; *fautes,* lacks 574 *wight-men,* brave men 575 *wantes,* lacks
576 *broched,* stabbed 578 *stint for no stuf,* stopped for no material
579 *for,* because of
580 *he,* from MS Douce, Lambeth MS *y*; *stonied that stound,* stunned at that moment; *striked,* struck

And gert Sir Gawayn
Thurgh ventaill and polain;
He went litil to have be slain –
He mayed him the more.

585 Hastily on helmes than thes hardy gan hewe;
They bete down berelles and bordures so bright;
Sheldes on shuldres that shene were to shewe,
That fretted were with fine gold, faileth in that fight.
Stones of grete strengthe they strinkil and strewe,
590 Stiff staples of stele striken down right.
Bernes banneth the time that bargain was brow,
So dolefully tho doghty with dintes were dight:
The dintes of tho doghty were doutous bedene.
Bothe Sir Lete and Sir Lake
595 Miche morning they make;
Gaynor gret for her sake
With her grey eyen.

Thus grette Dame Gaynor, that grete grefe was to sene,
For greef of Sir Gawayn that was grisly wounded.
600 The knight of corage was cruell and kene,
And with a stelen bronde striked that stound;
Alle the coste of the knight he cleveth down clene,
Thurgh riche mailes that ranke were and round.]
Swilke a touche at that time he taughte him in tene.

581 *gert,* struck 582 Through mouth-piece and knee-covering
583 He lacked little of being slain. 584 *mayed,* dismayed
585 *than thes hardy gan hewe,* then these brave men hewed
586 *berelles,* beryls: very hard, light bluish-green stones; *bordures,* edges
589 *strinkil,* scatter 590 *staples,* fastenings
591 *Bernes banneth,* Knights curse; *brow,* brewed
592 *tho,* those; *dight,* treated
593 *doutous,* fearful; *bedene:* here an expletive
594 *Lete,* King Lot, Gawain's father; *Lake,* father of Eric, a knight of the Round Table
596 *gret,* wept; *her,* their 600 The knight was valiant and keen of courage.
601 *stelen,* steel; *stound,* moment 602 *coste,* side 603 *ranke,* heavy
604 *touche,* stroke; *taughte him in tene,* gave him in wrath

605 He girdede Sir Galleron growelinge one grounde;
Galleron full grevousely granes on the grene,
And als wondede als he was,
Swiftly upe he rase
And folowde in faste on his faas
610 With a swerde shene.

Clenly that creuelle coverde him on highte,
And with a caste of the care in cautelle he strikes;
Full yerne he waittes Sir Gawayne the wighte,
Bot him limpede the werse, and that me wele likes.
615 He etillde with a slinge hafe slaine him with sleghte;
The swerde sleppes on slante and one the maile slides,
And Sir Gawayne by the colere clekes the knighte.
Than his lemane so loude scremes and skrikes,
Sho grete one Dame Gaynour with granes so grille,
620 And saide: "Lady, makles of mighte,
Hafe now mercy one yone knighte
That es so dulefully dighte,
Giffe it be thy will!"

Than wilfully Dame Waynour unto the kinge went;
625 Sho caughte off hir coronalle and knelede him till:
"Als thou erte roye ryalle and recheste of rent,
And I thin wife, wedded at min awen will,
Yone berens in yone batelle, that bledes one yone bent,

605 *girdede,* struck 606 *granes,* groans 609 And rushed quickly toward him
611 *creuelle,* valiant one; *coverde him,* recovered himself
612 *care:* probably a corrupt rendering of or shortening of *carhonde* (Ireland MS), left handed stroke; *cautelle,* craftiness
613 *Full yerne he waittes,* Full eagerly he watches
614 But worse happened to him, and that well pleases me.
615 He tried with a stroke to have slain him with cunning.
616 *sleppes on slante,* slips aslant 617 *clekes,* seizes 618 *lemane,* sweetheart
619 *Sho grete one,* She beseeched with tears; *grille,* tormented
620 *makles,* matchless 623 *Giffe,* If 624 *wilfully,* willingly
625 She took off her crown and kneeled to him.
626 *recheste of rent,* richest of possessions
627 *awen,* own 628 *bent,* plain

Thay are wery, I wisse, and wondede full ill;
630 Thurgh shene shildes thaire shuldirs are shent.
[The greves of Sir Gawayn do my hert grille;]
The granes of Sir Gawayne greves me full sare.
Wolde thou, lufly lorde,
Gare the knightes accorde,
635 It ware grete comforde
Till alle that here ware."

Bot than him spake Galleron to Gawayne the gude:
"I wende no wy in this werlde were halvendelle so wighte;
Here I make thee relese in my rentes, by the rode,
640 And before thiese ryalle resinge thee my righte!
And sithen I make thee manreden with a milde mode,
Als to mane in this medilerthe makles of mighte."
He talkes towarde the knighte one heghte there he stode;
He bedde that burely his brande that burneshede was brighte.
645 "Of renttes and reches I make thee relese."
Downne kneles that knighte,
And carpes thies wordes on highte.
The king stude uprighte
And commandes the pese.

650 The kinge commandes the pese and cries one highte,
And Gawaine was gudly and lefte for his sake.
And than to the listes the lordes leppes full lighte—
Sir Owaine Fitz-Uriene and Arrake, full rathe,

630 *shent,* wounded 631 *greves,* sufferings; *grille,* torment
632 *granes,* groans 634 Cause the knights to agree 636 To all that were here
637 *him spake Galleron,* Galleron himself spoke
638 *wende,* thought; *wy,* man; *halvendelle so wighte,* half so strong
639 Here I surrender my possessions to you, by the rood.
640 *thiese ryalle resinge,* these nobles resign
641 *make thee manreden,* do you homage
642 As to a man on this earth matchless of might
644 *bedde,* offered; *burely,* stout knight 647 *carpes,* speaks; *on highte,* aloud
649 *pese,* peace 651 *gudly,* noble; *lefte,* stopped
652 *leppes full lighte,* run quickly
653 Sir Ywain, son of Urien, and Eric (son of King Lake), very quickly

Marrake and Menegalle, that maste were of mighte –
655 Bathe thase travelde knightes trewly thay taghte.
Unnethes mighte those knightes stande uprighte;
Thay were forbett and forblede; thaire wedes wexe blake;
[The bernes were blody forbeten with brondes.]
Withoutten more lettinge
660 Was dighte there thiere semblinge
Before that comly kinge,
And helde upe thaire handes.

"I giffe to thee, Sir Gawayne," quode the kinge, "tresoure and golde,"
Glamorgane lanndes with greves so grene,
665 The wirshipe of Wales, to welde and to wolde,
With Griffouns castelle, kirnelde so clene,
And the Husters Haulle, to hafe and to holde,
Wayfurthe and Wakfelde, wallede I wene,
Twa baronrise in Burgoyne, with burghes so balde,
670 That are moted aboute and biggede full bene.
I shall endowe thee als a duke and dub thee with min hande,
With thy thou saughtill with yone gentill knighte
That es so hardy and wighte,
And relese him thy righte
675 And graunte him his lande."

654 *Marrake and Menegalle,* Marrok, one of Arthur's knights, and Menaduke, a kinsman of Lancelot

655 *travelde,* exhausted; *taghte,* took 656 *Unnethes,* Hardly

657 They were beaten to death and drained of blood, their clothes turned black.

659 *lettinge,* delay 660 Their meeting was prepared there.

664 *Glamorgane lanndes,* lands in Glamorganshire (Wales)

665 The honor of Wales, to wield and to hold

666 With Griffoun's Castle (possibly the Castle of Kirfre in south Scotland) so well battlemented

667 *Husters Haulle,* location uncertain

668 *Wayfurthe and Wakfelde,* uncertain locations

669 Two baronies in Burgundy with such strong towns

670 *biggede full bene,* built very well

672 *With thy,* Provided that; *saughtill,* become reconciled

"Now and here I giffe him," quod Gawayne, "withoutten any gile,
Alle the landes and the lithes fra Lowyke to Layre,
Commoke and Carrike, Conyghame and Kille,
Als the chevalrous knighte hase chalandchede als aiere,
680 The lebinge, the loupinge, the leveastre Ilee,
Bathe frithes and forestes, frely and faire,
[Undur our lordship to lende at thy will.
And to the Round Table make thy repeire:
I shal refeffe thee felefold in forestes so faire."]
685 Than the kinge and the quene
And alle the doghety bedene
Thorow the greves so grene
To Carlele thay caire.

The king to Carelele es comen with knighttes so kene,
690 To halde his Rounde Tabill one ryalle arraye.
Those knightes that were wondede full wathely, als I wene,
Surgeouns savede thaim, sothely to saye.
Bothe comforthede thaim than, the kinge and the quene.
Thay ware dubbede dukes bothe one a daye.
695 And ther Sir Galleron wedded his wife, that semly and shene,
With giftes and gersomms of Sir Gawayne the gaye.
And thus those hathells withhaldes that hende.
And when he was saved and sounde
Thay made him sworne to Sir Gawayne in that stounde,
700 And sithen a knighte of the Tabille Rounde,
Untill his lives ende.

677 *lithes,* tenements; *Lowyke,* possibly Locher Water in south Scotland; *Layre,* possibly Ayr, modified for alliterative purposes

678 See notes on ll. 418–19. 679 *chalandchede als aiere,* claimed as heir

680 Incomprehensible line 682 *lende,* dwell 683 *repeire,* visit

684 *refeffe,* invest again; *felefold,* many times 688 *caire,* ride

691 *wathely,* severely

693 Both the king and the queen comforted them then.

696 *gersomms of,* treasures from

697 And thus those nobles detain that courteous (knight).

700 *sithen,* afterward

Dame Gaynour garte besily write into the Weste,
To alle manere of religeous, to rede and to singe –
Pristes with processiouns – and [to pray they were prest
705 With masses a milion] to make hir meninge.
Dukes, erles, barouns, and beshoppes of the beste,
Thurghe all Ynglande sho garte make meninge.
And thus this ferlies befelle in a foreste
Undir an holte so bare at an hunttinge;
710 Swilke hunttinge in holtes shulde noghte ben hide.
Thus to the forestes thay fure,
Steren knighttes and sture,
And in the tim of Arthure
This *Auntir* betid.

715 This ferly befelle, full sothely to sayne,
In Yggillwode Foreste at the Ternwathelayne.

702 Dame Guinevere busily had (letters) written to the West.
704 *prest,* ready 705 *meninge,* remembrance
707 MS *Yglande*; *garte make,* caused to make 708 *ferlies,* marvels
709 *holte,* wood 711 *fure,* went 712 *sture,* strong 714 *Auntir,* Adventure
715 *Yggillwode,* Inglewood Forest in Cumberland near Tarn Wadling

21 *(Ca. 1330)*

SIR ORFEO

[We reden ofte and finde i-write,
As clerkes don us to wite,
The layes that ben of harping
Ben y-founde of frely thing:
5 Sum ben of wele and sum of wo,
And sum of joy and merthe also;
Sum of bourdes, and sum of ribaudy,
And sum ther ben of the feyre;
Sum of trechery and sum of gile,
10 And sum of happes that fallen by while;
Of alle thing that men may se,
Moost to love, forsothe, they be.
In Britain this layes arne y-writt,
Furst y-founde and forthe y-gete,
15 Of aventures that fallen by dayes,
Wherof Britouns made her layes.
When they might owher heren
Of aventures that ther weren,
They toke her harpes with game,
20 Maden layes, and yaf it name.
Of aventures that han befalle
I can sum telle, but nought all:
Herken, lordinges that ben trewe,
And I wol you telle of Sir Orphewe.]
25 Orfeo was a King,

(21) 1 *i-write,* written, MS indecipherable 2 *don us to wite,* inform us
4 *y-founde,* devised; *frely,* goodly 5 *wele,* prosperity
7 *bourdes,* jests; *ribaudy,* ribaldry 8 *feyre,* faery
10 *happes,* happenings; *by while,* from time to time
12 *moost to love,* most about love, MS *lowe*; *forsothe,* certainly
13 *Britain,* Brittany 14 First devised and then produced
15 *by dayes,* long ago 17 *owher,* anywhere 19 *her,* their; *with game,* merrily
20 *yaf,* gave 21 *aventures,* MS *avntures*

In Inglond an heighe lording,
A stalworth man and hardy bo;
Large and curteis he was also.
His fader was comen of King Pluto
30 And his moder of King Juno,
That sumtime were as godes y-hold
For aventours that thay dede and told.
[Orpheo most of ony thing
Lovede the gle of harping;
35 Siker was every gode harpure
Of him to have moche honour.
Himself loved forto harpe
And laide theron his wittes sharpe;
He lerned so, ther nothing was
40 A better harper in no plas.
In the world was never man born
That, onus Orpheo sat beforn
And he might of his harping her,
He shulde thinke that he wer
45 In one of the joys of Paradis,
Suche joy and melody in his harping is.]
This king sojournd in Traciens,
That was a cite of noble defens —
For Winchester was cleped tho
50 Traciens, withouten no.
The king hadde a quen of priis
That was y-cleped Dame Herodis,

26 *heighe,* high 27 *A,* MS *T*; *bo,* too 28 *Large,* Generous

29 Pluto apparently came to be regarded as the King of Faeryland. See Chaucer's "Merchant's Tale," l. 2227.

30 *King:* mistake for *Quen* (?) 32 *dede,* did 34 *gle,* pleasure 35 *Siker,* Sure

39 *nothing,* by no means 41 *In,* MS *om.* 42 Who, once (he) sat before Orfeo

43 *And,* If; *her,* hear 47 *Traciens,* Thrace 48 *cite,* city

49–50 Winchester was the early seat of the English kings.

49 *cleped,* called 50 *no,* denial 51 *of priis,* excellent

52 *Herodis,* Eurydice. For an account of this form of the name, see M. J. Donovan, "Herodis in the Auchinleck *Sir Orfeo,*" *Medium Aevum,* XXVII (1958), 162–65.

The fairest levedy, for the nones,
That might gon on body and bones,
55 Ful of love and of godenisse;
Ac no man may telle hir fairnise.
Befel so in the comessing of May,
When miry and hot is the day
And oway beth winter shours,
60 And every feld is ful of flours,
And blosme breme on every bough
Overal wexeth miry anough,
This ich quen, Dame Heurodis,
Tok to maidens of priis,
65 And went in an undrentide
To play by an orchard-side,
To se the floures sprede and spring,
And to here the fowles sing.
Thay sett hem down al thre
70 Under a fair impe-tre,
And wel sone this fair quene
Fel on slepe opon the grene.
The maidens durst hir nought awake,
Bot lete hir ligge and rest take.
75 So she slepe til after none,
That undertide was al y-done.
Ac, as sone as she gan awake,
She crid and lothly bere gan make.
She froted hir honden and hir fet,
80 And crached hir visage – it bled wete.

53 *levedy,* lady; *for the nones,* for the nonce (a metrical tag) 54 *gon,* walk
56 *Ac,* But 57 *Befel,* MS *Uifel*; *comessing,* beginning 59 *oway,* away
61 *breme,* glorious 62 *wexeth,* grows 63 *ich,* same 64 *to,* two
65 *undrentide,* mid-morning, near noon-time
66 *orchard-side,* edge of an orchard (or garden) 67 *spring,* sprout
69 *hem,* them 70 *impe-tre,* sapling, grafted tree; see Commentary, p. 384.
74 *ligge,* lie 76 So that the forenoon was quite passed
78 *lothly bere,* horrible outcry; *gan,* began
79 *froted,* wrung, tore at; *honden,* hands
80 *crached,* scratched; *it bled wete,* until it was wet with blood

Hir riche robe hie al torett,
And was reveid out of hir witt.
The two maidens hir beside
No durst with hir no leng abide,
85 Bot ourn to the palais ful right
And told bothe squier and knight
That her quen awede wold,
And bad hem go and hir athold.
Knightes urn and levedis also —
90 Damisels sexty and mo.
In the orchard to the quen hie come,
And her up in her armes nome,
And brought hir to bed atte last,
And held hir there fine fast.
95 Ac ever she held in o cry,
And wold up, and owy.
When Orfeo herd that tiding,
Never him nas wers for no thing.
He come with knightes tene
100 To chaumber, right befor the quene,
And beheld, and seid with grete pite,
"O, lef liif, what is te,
That ever yete hast ben so stille,
And now gredest wonder shille?
105 Thy body that was so white y-core
With thine nailes is al totore.
Allas! thy rode that was so red

[81] *hie,* she; *torett,* rent in pieces [82] *reveid,* drivèn
[84] *No durst,* Did not dare; *leng,* longer [85] *ourn,* ran; *ful right,* straightaway
[87] *her,* their; *awede,* go mad [88] *hem,* them; *athold,* restrain
[89] *urn,* ran; *levedis,* ladies
[90] Sixty (often a general number) young ladies and more [91] *hie,* they
[92] *her . . . her,* her . . . their; *nome,* took [94] *fine,* very
[95] *held,* persisted; *o,* one [96] *owy,* away
[98] He never felt worse for any other reason. [99] *tene,* ten [101] *pite,* pity
[102] O, beloved, what is the matter with you?
[104] *gredest,* cries out; *wonder shille,* marvellously shrilly
[105] *y-core,* an intensive rime tag [106] *totore,* torn to pieces
[107] *rode,* face

Is al wan, as thou were ded;
And also thine fingres smale
110 Beth al blody and al pale.
Allas! thy lovesom eyghen to
Loketh so man doth on his fo.
A! Dame, ich beseche mercy!
Lete ben al this reweful cry,
115 And tel me what thee is, and how,
And what thing may thee help now!"
Tho lay she stille atte last
And gan to wepe swithe fast,
And seid thus the king to:
120 "Allas, my lord, Sir Orfeo,
Sethen we first togider were,
Ones wroth never we nere;
Bot ever ich have y-loved thee
As my liif, and so thou me.
125 Ac now we mot delen ato —
Do thy best, for I mot go."
"Allas!" quath he, "Forlorn icham!
Whider wiltou go, and to wham?
Whider thou gost ichil with thee,
130 And whider I go thou shalt with me."
"Nay, nay, Sir, that nought nis!
Ichil thee telle all how it is.
As ich lay this undertide
And slepe under our orchard-side,
135 There come to me to fair knightes
Wele y-armed al to rightes,
And bad me comen an heighing

108 *as,* as if 111 *lovesom eyghen to,* two lovely eyes 112 *so,* as 113 *ich,* I
114 *Lete ben,* Stop 115 *what thee is,* what is the matter with you
117 *Tho,* Then 118 *gan,* began; *swithe,* very 121 *Sethen,* Since
122 We were never once angry. 125 But now we must separate.
126 *Do thy best,* Make the best of it. 127 *quath,* said; *icham,* I am
128 *wiltou,* will you; *wham,* whom 129 *ichil,* I will (go)
131 *nought nis,* is not possible 133 *undertide,* mid-morning
135 *to . . . to,* to . . . two 136 *to rightes,* properly 137 *an heighing,* in haste

And speke with her lord the king.
And ich answerd at wordes bold,
140 I no durst nought, no I nold.
Thay priked oyain as thay might drive.
Tho com her king also blive
With an hundred knightes and mo,
And damisels an hundred also,
145 Al on snowe-white stedes;
As white as milke were her wedes.
I no seighe never yete before
So fair creatours y-core.
The king hadde a crown on hed;
150 It nas of silver no of gold red,
Ac it was of a precious ston –
As bright as the sonne it shon.
And, as son as he to me cam,
Wold ich, nold ich, he me nam,
155 And made me with him ride
Opon a palfray by his side;
And brought me to his palais,
Wele atird in ich ways,
And shewed me castels and tours,
160 Rivers, forestes, frith with flours,
And his riche stedes ichon;
And sethen me brought oyain hom
Into our owhen orchard,
And said to me thus afterward,
165 'Loke, Dame, tomorwe thatou be
Right here under this impe-tre,
And than thou shalt with ous go,

139 *at,* with 140 *no,* MS *n*; I did not dare, nor I would not.
141 They galloped again as fast as they could go.
142 Then came their king just as quickly. 143 *mo,* more 145 *stedes,* steeds
147 *seighe,* saw 148 *y-core:* an intensive rime tag 150 *nas,* was not
154 Whether I would or no, he seized me. 158 Well equipped in every way
160 *frith,* a woodland 161 *stedes,* places; *ichon,* each one
162 *sethen,* afterwards; *oyain,* again 163 *owhen,* own 167 *ous,* us

And live with ous evermo;
And yif thou makest ous y-let,
170 Whar thou be, thou worst y-fet,
And totore thine limes al,
That nothing help thee no shal.
And they thou best so totorn
Yete thou worst with ous y-born.' "
175 When King Orfeo herd this cas,
"O, we!" quath he, "Allas! Allas!
Lever me were to lete my liif
Than thus to lese the quen my wiif!"
He asked conseil at ich man,
180 Ac no man him help no can.
Amorwe the undertide is come,
And Orfeo hath his armes y-nome,
And wele ten hundred knightes with him,
Ich y-armed, stout and grim;
185 And with the quen wenten he
Right unto that impe-tre.
Thay made sheltrom in ich a side,
And said thay wold there abide
And die ther, everichon,
190 Er the quen shuld fram hem gon.
Ac yete amiddes hem ful right
The quen was oway y-twight,
With fairy forth y-nome —
Men wist never wher she was become.
195 Tho was ther crying, wepe and wo;

169 And if you offer any resistance to us
170 *Whar,* Wherever; *worst y-fet,* shall be fetched
171 *totore,* torn to pieces; *limes,* limbs 173 *they,* though
174 *worst,* will be; *y-born,* carried off 175 *cas,* plight 176 *we,* woe
177 I would rather lose my life. 178 *lese,* lose 179 *at ich,* from each
180 *no can,* cannot 181 *Amorwe,* The next day 182 *y-nome,* taken
187 *sheltrom,* rank of armed men 190 *Er,* Before; *hem,* them
192 *oway y-twight,* snached away 193 *forth,* away; *y-nome,* taken
194 Men never knew what had become of her. 195 *wepe,* weeping

The king into his chaumber is go,
And oft swoned opon the ston,
And made swiche diol and swiche mon
That neighe his liif was y-spent –
200 Ther was non amendement.
He cleped togider his barouns,
Erls, lordes of renouns,
And when thay al y-comen were,
"Lordinges," he said, "Befor you here
205 Ich ordainy min heighe steward
To wite my kingdom afterward;
In my stede ben he shal
To kepe my londes overal.
For now ichave my quen y-lore,
210 The fairest levedy that ever was bore,
Never eft I nil no woman se.
Into wildernes ichil te,
And live ther evermore
With wilde bestes in holtes hore;
215 And when ye understond that I be spent,
Make you than a parlement,
And chese you a newe king.
Now doth your best with al my thing."
Tho was ther wepeing in the halle
220 And grete cry among hem alle;
Unnethe might old or yong
For wepeing speke a word with tong.
Thay kneled adown al y-fere
And prayd him, yif his wille were,
225 That he no shuld nought fram hem go.

197 *ston,* stone (floor) 198 *swiche,* such; *diol,* dole; *mon,* moan
199 *neighe,* nearly 200 *amendement,* help 201 *cleped,* called 206 *wite,* keep
207 He shall be in my place. 209 *ichave,* I have; *y-lore,* lost
211 *eft,* again; *nil,* will not 212 *ichil te,* I shall go. 214 *holtes hore,* grey woods
215 *spent,* dead 216 *you,* for yourselves 219 *Tho,* MS *Lo*
221 *Unnethe,* Scarcely 223 *y-fere,* together
224 *yif his wille were,* if it were his will

"Do way!" quath he, "It shal be so!"
Al his kingdom he forsoke;
Bot a sclavin on him he toke.
He no hadde kirtel no hode,
230 Shert, no nother gode,
Bot his harp he tok algate,
And dede him barfot out atte yate —
No man most with him go.
O, way! What ther was wepe and wo
235 When he that hadde ben king with crown
Went so pouerlich out of town!
Thurth wode and over heth
Into the wildernes he geth;
Nothing he fint that him is ais,
240 Bot ever he liveth in great malais.
He that hadde y-werd the fowe and griis,
And on bed the purper biis —
Now on hard hethe he lith;
With leves and gresse he him writh.
245 He that hadde had castels and tours,
River, forest, frith with flours —
Now they it comenci to snewe and frese,
This king mot make his bed in mese.
He that had y-had knightes of priis
250 Befor him kneland, and levedis —
Now seth he no thing that him liketh,
Bot wilde wormes by him striketh.
He that had y-had plente

226 *Do way,* Enough! 228 *sclavin,* pilgrim's mantle 229 *kirtel,* short coat
230 Shirt, nor any other belongings 231 *algate,* anyway
232 *dede him,* went; *yate,* gate 233 *most,* might 234 *way,* alas!
236 *pouerlich,* poorly 237 *Thurth,* Through; *heth,* heath 238 *geth,* goes
239 *fint,* finds; *him is ais,* gives him pleasure 240 *malais,* hardship
241 *y-werd,* worn; *fowe and griis,* colored and grey furs
242 *purper biis,* purple linen 244 *writh,* covers
247 *they,* though; *comenci,* commence 248 *mot,* must; *mese,* moss
249 *of priis,* excellent 250 *kneland,* kneeling; *levedis,* ladies
251 *seth,* sees; *liketh,* pleases 252 *wormes,* snakes; *striketh,* glide

Of mete and drink, of ich deinte –
255 Now may he al day digge and wrote
Er he finde his fille of rote.
In somer he liveth by wild frut
And berien bot gode lite;
In winter may he no thing finde
260 Bot rote, grases, and the rinde.
Al his body was oway dwine
For missais, and al tochine.
Lord, who may telle the sore
This king sufferd ten yere and more?
265 His here of his berd, blac and rowe,
To his girdel-stede was growe.
His harp, whereon was al his gle,
He hidde in an holwe tre;
And when the weder was clere and bright
270 He toke his harp to him wel right
And harped at his owhen wille.
Into alle the wode the soun gan shille,
That alle the wilde bestes that ther beth
For joye abouten him thay teth,
275 And alle the fowles that ther were
Come and sete on ich a brere
To here his harping a-fine,
So miche melody was therin;
And when he his harping lete wold,
280 No best by him abide nold.
He might se him besides,
Oft in hot undertides,
The king o fairy with his rout

255 *wrote,* root in the earth 258 And berries of but little worth
260 *rinde,* bark 261 *dwine,* wasted
262 *for missais,* because of hardship; *tochine,* scarred 263 *sore,* pain
265 *rowe,* shaggy 266 *girdel-stede,* waist 267 *gle,* pleasure
269 *weder,* weather 271 *at his owhen wille,* at his pleasure
272 *gan shille,* began to resound 274 *teth,* draw near
276 *ich a brere,* each briar 277 *a-fine,* to the end 279 *lete,* stop
280 *nold,* would not 281 *se him,* see for himself 283 *o,* of; *rout,* company

Com to hunt him al about
285 With dim cry and bloweing,
And houndes also with him berking;
Ac no best thay no nome,
No never he nist whider thay become.
And other while he might him se
290 As a gret host by him te,
Wele atourned, ten hundred knightes,
Ich y-armed to his rightes,
Of cuntenaunce stout and fers,
With many desplayd baners,
295 And ich his swerd y-drawe hold;
Ac never he nist whider thay wold.
And other while he seighe other thing,
Knightes and levedis com daunceing
In queint atire, gisely,
300 Queint pas and softly;
Tabours and trunpes yede hem by,
And al maner menstracy.
And on a day he seighe him beside
Sexty levedis on hors ride,
305 Gentil and jolif as brid on ris —
Nought o man amonges hem ther nis —
And ich a faucoun on hond bere,
And riden on haukin by o rivere.
Of game thay founde wel gode haunt,
310 Maulardes, hairoun, and cormeraunt;
The fowles of the water ariseth,

287 *nome,* took 288 *nist,* did not know; *become,* went
289 *him se,* see for himself 290 *te,* goes 291 *atourned,* equipped
292 *to his rightes,* properly 296 *wold,* were (going) 297 *seighe,* saw
299 *gisely,* skillfully 300 *Queint pas,* With skillful steps
301 Small drums and trumpets (*i.e.,* the players) went by.
302 *menstracy,* minstrelsy 303 *him beside,* near him
305 *brid on ris,* bird on a leafy spray 306 *nis,* is not
307 *ich,* each one; *faucoun,* falcon 308 *on haukin,* in hawking
309 *haunt,* resort, or plenty
310 Mallards, heron, and cormorant

The faucouns hem wele deviseth:
Ich faucoun his pray slough.
That seighe Orfeo, and lough:
315 "Parfay!" quath he, "Ther is fair game;
Thider ichil, by Godes name!
Ich was y-won swiche werk to se."
He aros and thider gan te.
To a levedy he was y-come,
320 Beheld, and hath wele undernome,
And seth by al thing that it is
His owhen quen, Dam Heurodis.
Yern he beheld hir, and she him eke,
Ac noither to other a word no speke.
325 For messais that she on him seigh,
That had ben so riche and so heighe,
The teres fel out of her eighe.
The other levedis this y-seighe
And maked hir oway to ride:
330 She most with him no lenger abide.
"Allas!" quath he, "Now me is wo!
Why nil deth now me slo?
Allas, wroche, that I no might
Die now after this sight!
335 Allas! Too long last my liif,
When I no daṛ nought with my wiif —
No hie to me — o word speke.
Allas! Why nil min hert breke?
Parfay!" quath he, "Tide wat betide,
340 Whiderso this levedis ride,
The selve way ichil streche —

312 *hem wele deviseth,* descry them easily 313 *slough,* slew
314 *lough,* laughed 316 *ichil,* I will (go). 317 *y-won,* accustomed
318 *gan te,* began to go 320 *wele undernome,* clearly recognized
321 *seth,* sees 323 *Yern,* Eagerly; *eḳe,* also 325 *messais,* suffering; *seigh,* saw
327 *eighe,* eyes 332 *nil,* will not; *slo,* slay 333 *wroche,* wretched one
337 *No hie to me,* Nor she to me; *o,* one
339 "By my faith," he said, "No matter what happens."
340 *Whiderso,* Wheresoever; *this,* these 341 The same way I will go.

Of liif no deth me no reche!"
His sclavain he dede on also spac,
And henge his harp opon his bac,
345 And had wel gode wil to gon;
He no spard noither stub no ston.
In at a roche the levedis rideth,
And he after, and nought abideth.
When he was in the roche y-go
350 Wele thre mile, other mo,
He com into a fair cuntray
As bright so sonne on somers day,
Smothe and plain and al grene;
Hille no dale nas ther non y-sene.
355 Amidde the lond a castel he sighe,
Riche and real and wonder heighe:
Al the utmast wal
Was clere and shine as cristal;
An hundred tours ther were about,
360 Degiselich, and bataild stout;
The butras com out of the diche,
Of rede gold y-arched riche;
The vousour was avowed al
Of ich maner divers aumal.
365 Within ther wer wide wones,
Al of precious stones;
The werst piler on to beholde
Was al of burnist gold.
Al that lond was ever light,
370 For when it shuld be therk and night

342 Of life nor death I do not care. 343 His pilgrim's cloak he put on quickly.
345 *wel,* MS *w* 346 He spared neither trunk nor stone (*i.e.,* nothing).
347 *roche,* rock 350 *other,* or 352 *so,* as
354 *nas ther non y-sene,* there was none seen 355 *sighe,* saw
356 *real,* royal 357 *utmast,* outermost
360 *Degiselich,* Wonderful; *bataild,* crenelated 361 *diche,* moat
362 *y-arched,* arched 363 *vousour,* vaulting; *avowed,* adorned
364 *aumal,* enamel 365 *wones,* halls 367 *werst,* worst, poorest
370 *therk,* dark

The riche stones light gonne
As bright as doth at none the sonne.
No man may telle, no thenche in thought,
The riche werk that ther was wrought;
375 By al thing him think that it is
The proude court of Paradis.
In this castel the levedis alight;
He wold in after, yif he might.
Orfeo knokketh atte gate;
380 The porter was redy therate,
And asked what he wold have y-do.
"Parfay!" quath he, "Icham a minstrel, lo!
To solas thy lord with my gle,
Yif his swete wille be."
385 The porter undede the yate anon
And lete him into the castel gon.
Than he gan behold about al
And seighe ful liggeand within the wal
Of folk that were thider y-brought,
390 And thought dede, and nare nought.
Sum stode withouten hade,
And sum non armes nade,
And sum thurth the body hadde wounde;
And sum lay wode, y-bounde,
395 And sum armed on hors sete;
And sum astrangled as thay ete,
And sum were in water adreint,
And sum with fire al forshreint.
Wives ther lay on child-bedde,
400 Sum ded and sum awedde.
And wonder fele ther lay besides

371 *stones,* stones'; *gonne,* began 373 *thenche in thought,* imagine
375 *him think,* it seems to him 381 *he wold have y-do,* he wanted
382 *Icham,* I am 383 *solas,* delight; *gle,* minstrelsy 384 *Yif . . . be,* If it is
385 *yate,* gate; *anon,* at once 388 *seighe,* saw; *liggeand,* lying
390 *dede,* dead; *nare nought,* were not 391 *hade,* head 392 *nade,* had not
393 *thurth,* through 394 *wode,* mad 397 *adreint,* drowned
398 *forshreint,* withered 400 *awedde,* gone mad 401 *wonder fele,* very many

Right as thay slepe her undertides.
Eche was thus in this warld y-nome,
With fairy thider y-come.
405 Ther he seighe his owhen wiif,
Dame Heurodis, his lef liif,
Slepe under an impe-tree;
By her clothes he knewe that it was he.
And when he hadde beholde this mervails alle
410 He went into the kinges halle.
Than seighe he ther a semly sight,
A tabernacle blisseful and bright:
Therin her maister-king sete,
And her quen, fair and swete —
415 Her crownes, her clothes shine so bright
That unnethe behold he hem might.
When he hadde beholden al that thing
He kneled adown befor the king:
"O Lord," he seid, "Yif it thy wille were,
420 My menstracy thou shust y-here."
The king answerd: "What man artou
That art hider y-comen now?
Ich, no non that is with me,
No sent never after thee.
425 Sethen that ich here regni gan
I no fond never so folehardy man
That hider to ous durst wende,
Bot that ichim wald off-sende."
"Lord," quath he, "Trowe ful wel,
430 I nam bot a pouer menstrel;
And, Sir, it is the maner of ous

402 *slepe,* slept (in); *her,* their 403 *y-nome,* taken 405 *seighe,* saw
406 *lef liif,* beloved, MS *liif liif* 407 *Slepe,* Sleeping 408 *he,* she
412 *tabernacle,* high seat under a canopy 413 *Therin,* Wherein
413, 14, 15 *her,* their 416 *unnethe,* scarcely; *hem,* them 420 *shust,* shouldst
421 *artou,* are you 423 I, nor none that is with me
425 Since that I began to reign here 427 *ous,* us; *durst wende,* dared come
428 Unless I would send for him 429 *Trowe ful wel,* Believe fully
430 *nam,* am not; *pouer,* poor

To seche many a lordes hous:
They we nought welcom no be,
Yete we mot proferi forth our gle."
435 Befor the king he sat adown
And tok his harp so miry of soun,
And tempreth his harp as he wele can,
And blisseful notes he ther gan,
That al that in the palais were
440 Com to him forto here,
And liggeth adown to his fete,
Hem thenketh his melody so swete.
The king herkneth and sitt ful stille;
To here his gle he hath gode wille.
445 Gode bourde he hadde of his gle;
The riche quen also hadde he.
When he hadde stint his harping,
Than seid to him the king:
"Menstrel, me liketh wele thy gle.
450 Now aske of me what it be,
Largelich ichil thee pay.
Now speke, and tou might asay."
"Sir," he seid, "Ich beseche thee
Thatou woldest yive me
455 That ich levedy, bright on ble,
That slepeth under the impe-tre."
"Nay!" quath the king, "That nought nere!
A sory couple of you it were,
For thou art lene, rowe, and blac,

432 *seche,* seek 433 *They,* Though 434 Yet we must offer our music
437 *tempreth,* tunes 438 *gan,* began 441 *liggeth,* lie
442 *Hem thenketh,* Seems to them 445 *bourde,* entertainment
446 *he,* she 447 *stint,* stopped
450 *aske,* MS *alke*; *what it be,* whatsoever it may be (Now ask anything of me)
451 *Largelich,* Generously; *ichil,* I will
452 *and tou might asay,* if you would like to try (me)
454 *Thatou,* That you; *yive,* give 455 *ich,* same; *ble,* complexion
457 *That nought nere,* That is not possible.
458 *of you it were,* you two would be 459 *rowe,* shaggy

460 And she is lovesum, withouten lac;
A lothlich thing it were, forthy,
To sen hir in thy compainy."
"O, Sir," he seid, "Gentil King!
Yete were it a wele fouler thing
465 To here a lesing of thy mouthe.
So, Sir, as ye seid nouthe
What ich wold aski have I shold,
And nedes thou most thy word hold."
The king seid, "Sethen it is so,
470 Take hir by the hond and go:
Of hir ichil thatou be blithe!"
He kneled adown and thonked him swithe.
His wiif he tok by the hond
And dede him swithe out of that lond,
475 And went him out of that thede;
Right as he come the way he yede.
So long he hath the way y-nome
To Winchester he is y-come,
That was his owhen cite —
480 Ac no man knewe that it was he.
No forther than the townes ende
For knoweleche no durst wende,
Bot with a begger, y-bilt ful narwe,
Ther he tok his herbarwe,
485 To him and to his owhen wiif,
As a minstrel of pouer liif,
And asked tidinges of that lond,
And who the kingdom held in hond.
The pouer begger in his cote

460 *lovesum,* lovely; *lac,* lack 461 *lothlich,* loathsome; *forthy,* therefore
464 *wele,* much 465 *lesing of,* lie from 466 *nouthe,* just now
469 *Sethen,* Since 471 I wish that you have joy of her. 472, 74 *swithe,* quickly
474 *dede him,* went 475 *thede,* country, region 476 *come,* came; *yede,* took
477 *y-nome,* taken 479 *cite,* city 480 *Ac,* But
482 For fear of recognition he dared not go
483 *y-bilt ful narwe,* housed in very close quarters 484 *herbarwe,* lodging
485 *To,* For 489 *cote,* cottage

490 Told him everich a grot:
How her quen was stole owy,
Ten yer gon, with fairy,
And how her king en exile yede,
Bot no man nist in wiche thede,
495 And how the steward the lond gan hold,
And other many thinges him told.
Amorwe, oyain none-tide,
He maked his wiif ther abide;
The beggers clothes he borwed anon
500 And heng his harp his rigge opon,
And went him into that cite
That men might him behold and se.
Erls and barouns bold,
Buryais and levedis him gun behold:
505 "Lo!" thay seid, "Swiche a man!
How long the here hongeth him opan!
Lo! How his berd hongeth to his kne!
He is y-clongen also a tre!"
And as he yede in the strete,
510 With his steward he gan mete,
And loude he sett on him a crye:
"Sir Steward!" he seid, "Mercy!
Icham an harpour of hethenisse:
Help me now in this destresse!"
515 The steward seid, "Com with me, come;
Of that ichave thou shalt have some.
Everich gode harpour is welcom me to
For my lordes love, Sir Orfeo."
In the castel the steward sat atte mete,

490 *everich a grot,* everything 491 *her,* their; *owy,* away
493 *her,* their; *yede,* went 494 But no man knew in what country
495 *gan hold,* held 497 On the next day, toward noon 500 *rigge,* back
504 *Buryais,* Citizens; *gun behold,* beheld 505 *Swiche,* What
506 *here,* hair; *opan,* upon 508 *y-clongen,* withered; *also,* as
509 *yede,* went 510 *gan mete,* met 511 *sett on him a crye,* cried out to him
513 *hethenisse,* pagan lands 516 *ichave,* I have
518 *For my lordes love,* For love of my lord 519 *mete,* food

520 And many lording was by him sete.
Ther were trompour and tabourers,
Harpours fele and crouders;
Miche melody thay maked alle.
And Orfeo sat stille in the halle
525 And herkneth; when thay ben al stille
He toke his harp and tempred shille.
The blissefulest notes he harped there
That ever any man y-herd with ere;
Ich man liked wele his gle.
530 The steward beheld and gan y-se,
And knewe the harp als blive:
"Menstrel!" he seid, "So mot thou thrive,
Where hadestou this harp, and how?
I pray that thou me telle now."
535 "Lord!" quath he, "In uncouthe thede,
Thurth a wildernes as I yede,
Ther I founde in a dale
With liouns a man totorn smale,
And wolves him frete with teth so sharp;
540 By him I fond this ich harp,
Wele ten yere it is y-go."
"O!" quath the steward, "Now me is wo!
That was my lord, Sir Orfeo!
Allas! wreche, what shal I do
545 That have swiche a lord y-lore?
A! way! that ich was y-bore,
That him was so hard grace y-yarked,

521 There were trumpeters and drummers. 522 *fele,* many; *crouders,* fiddlers
526 *tempred shille,* tuned (it) loudly 527 MS *blifulest*
530 *gan y-se,* began to see 531 *als blive,* quickly
532 *So mot thou thrive,* So may you prosper (an oath)
533 *hadestou,* did you get 535 *uncouthe thede,* unknown land
536 *Thurth,* Through; *yede,* went 538 *totorn smale,* torn to bits
539 *frete,* devoured 540 *ich,* same 541 *y-go,* ago
544 *wreche,* wretched one (the steward) 545 *y-lore,* lost
546 *A! way,* Oh! woe; *y-bore,* born
547 *grace,* fortune; *y-yarked,* ordained

And so vile deth y-marked!"
Adown he fel aswon to grounde;
550 His barouns him tok up in that stounde,
And telleth him how it geth:
"It nis no bot of mannes deth."
King Orfeo knewe wele by than
His steward was a trewe man
555 And loved him as he aught to do,
And stont up and seit thus: "Lo!
Steward, herkne now this thing!
Yif ich were Orfeo the king,
And hadde y-suffred ful yore
560 In wildernisse miche sore,
And hadde y-won my quen owy
Out of the lond of fairy,
And hadde y-brought the levedy hende
Right here to the townes ende,
565 And with a begger her inn y-nome,
And were myself hider y-come
Pouerlich to thee, thus stille,
Forto asay thy gode wille,
And ich founde thee thus trewe,
570 Thou no shust it never rewe,
Sikerlich for love or ay:
Thou shust be king after my day.
And yif thou of my deth hadest ben blithe
Thou shust have voided also swithe."
575 Tho al tho that therin sete
That it was King Orfeo underyete,

548 *y-marked,* appointed 549 *aswon,* in a swoon
550 *in that stounde,* in that moment 551 *geth,* goes
552 There is no cure for man's death. 553 *than,* then
556 *stont,* stands; *seit,* says 559 *ful yore,* for a very long time 560 *sore,* pain
561 *owy,* away 563 *hende,* gracious 565 *her inn y-nome,* her lodging taken
567 *stille,* secretly 568 *Forto asay,* In order to try
570 *shust,* shouldst; *rewe,* regret 571 Certainly, for love or money
573 *blithe,* glad 574 *voided,* been dismissed; *also swithe,* at once
575 *Tho,* Then; *tho,* those 576 *underyete,* perceived

And the steward him wele knewe;
Over and over the bord he threwe,
And fel adown to his fet.
580 So dede everich lord that ther sete,
And al thay seid at o crying,
"Ye beth our lord, Sir, and our king!"
Glad thay were of his live!
To chaumber thay ladde him als belive,
585 And bathed him and shaved his berd,
And tired him as a king apert;
And sethen, with gret processioun
Thay brought the quen into the town
With al maner menstracy.
590 Lord! ther was grete melody!
For joye thay wepe with her eighe
That hem so sounde y-comen seighe.
Now King Orfeo newe corownd is,
And his quen, Dame Heurodis,
595 And lived long afterward,
And sethen was king the steward.
  Harpours in Bretaine after than
Herd how this mervaile began,
And made herof a lay of gode likeing,
600 And nempned it after the king.
That lay *Orfeo* is y-hote;
Gode is the lay, swete is the note.
Thus com Sir Orfeo out of his care;
God graunt ous alle wele to fare! Amen!

578 He knocked over the table. 581 *seid at o crying,* cried together
583 *live,* being alive 584 *als belive,* at once 586 *tired,* dressed; *apert,* openly
587, 96 *sethen,* afterwards 591 *her eighe,* their eyes
592 *hem,* them; *sounde,* safe; *seighe,* saw 597 *Bretaine,* Brittany; *than,* then
599 *herof,* thereof; *of gode likeing,* well pleasing 600 *nempned,* named
601 *y-hote,* called 602 *note,* music

ALLEGORY AND VISION

ALLEGORY and dream vision are linked together, not because there is an absolutely necessary connection between them, but because in Middle English literature a vision or dream is so often the convention by which the poet moves from the natural into the allegorical world.

In discussing allegory it is necessary also to discuss symbolism, because these two literary modes so often appear together in Middle English poetry. Both are alike in presuming the existence of some immaterial reality beyond the reality of visible, concrete objects and literal events; but while symbolism presents this other reality through these visible objects and events, and is thus limited to what these are able to suggest, allegory begins with the immaterial reality and then invents visible objects and events to represent it.[1]

It is this priority of the immaterial concept rather than the nature of its visible equivalent that really distinguishes allegory from symbolism. Whereas symbolism cannot use the personified abstractions of allegory, allegory can use objects from the visible world to represent the immaterial reality with which it is concerned.

Neither the allegorical figures nor allegory itself should, however, be thought of as an attempt to be abstract rather than concrete. Rather, medieval allegory attempts to make religious and moral ideas as concrete as possible, as do the personifications of Mercy and Justice in *Piers Plowman,* or the even more vivid personifications of the Seven Deadly Sins earlier in the same poem. We are again reminded of the double sensibility — and the resulting tension — in much of the best Middle English poetry. The poet was usually interested in both the material and the immaterial worlds, and if commitment in one might sometimes seem to be at odds with commitment to the other, the allegorical and symbolic ways of seeing were reminders of how intimately

[1] Graham Hough, *A Preface to the Faerie Queene* (New York: W. W. Norton and Co., Inc., 1963), p. 102.

the two worlds were related to each other. The determination to make allegorical figures vividly concrete suggests a feeling that immaterial reality becomes compelling at least partly to the extent that it can be translated into (or discovered within) material equivalents. Similarly, the effectiveness of concrete symbols, like those in Dunbar's poem *Done is a battell on the dragon blak,* depends upon the continuing integrity of the symbol as an interesting and convincing material object, at the same time that it points beyond itself to another level of truth.

In his seminal *The Allegory of Love,*[2] C. S. Lewis suggested that the development of allegorical thought accompanied the movement from polytheism towards monotheism, as various divinities who had once existed independently came to be thought of as personified attributes of a single deity. It also accompanied the discovery that the really significant battles were those fought not on the familiar exterior battlegrounds but rather on the interior battleground within a man's self, where his passions struggle perpetually against each other for possession of his will. This change had begun among the Greeks themselves, but Christianity provided the most congenial atmosphere for such a change, with its emphasis upon a single god and upon the interior conflicts within fallen man as he struggles toward redemption. Allegory provided the method for objectifying these abstract forces and the interior theater of the human soul where the conflict was enacted. The *Psychomachia* of Prudentius (late 4th c.) is the first fully developed allegorical poem presenting this moral warfare. Later, after Chrétien de Troyes had explored the psychological processes of human love in his romances, allegory was used to personify these secular, amorous conflicts in the tremendously influential *Roman de la Rose* (mid 13th c.) begun by Guillaume de Lorris and finished by Jean de Meun.

At the same time allegory could be used for quite different purposes. Instead of objectifying an immaterial idea or activity, allegory could become a device for interpreting literature whose literal meaning was for some reason unacceptable. Classical writing whose pagan events and personages could not be believed might become credible

[2] C. S. Lewis, *The Allegory of Love* (Oxford: Oxford University Press, 1936), Ch. II.

and even significant once the literal surface was assumed to be an allegorical construct representing orthodox Christian truths. It was thus that Fulgentius (5–6th c.) interpreted Virgil, and it was in the same spirit that writers throughout the Middle Ages continued often to interpret all sorts of non-Christian literature. The same sort of allegorical interpretation could also be applied to events which at the literal level seem too trivial for serious concern but whose simplicity or literal attractiveness was a necessary first step in the progress to full understanding of some mysterious and difficult truth. Thus, when the common events of human and animal life are interpreted morally, the pleasure at their comic or even indecent nature becomes morally justified; even the quite respectable literal surface of Dante's famous progress through Hell, Purgatory, and Heaven was simply the basis for elaborate allegorical interpretations.

At this point, of course, allegory and symbolism again join hands, since both literal objects and allegorical figures appear within an allegorical narrative. And in the best medieval allegory, the same object may simultaneously be literal symbol and allegorical figure. In Henryson's *Testament* the figures who judge Cresseid represent simultaneously the classical gods, the medieval planets, and the psychological and physiological forces within human beings. Similarly in Charles d'Orleans' dream, Venus is simultaneously the classical goddess, the allegorical force of love, and a lady drawn from Charles's own courtly society. In *Piers Plowman,* Piers, Christ, and the allegorical figure of Light are constantly – and fruitfully – confounded. In Henryson's *Bludy Serk,* the intention is wholly allegorical, but the persons and events provide so exact a paradigm of a chivalric romance that the bare, unadorned outlines of Henryson's allegory are immediately enriched with all the associations which any listener could unconsciously supply from remembered details of conventional romance.

Although allegory is first of all a device for dealing with a particular mode of thought, this device almost becomes a genre when its typical characters, plot, and setting are manipulated within an extended narrative. Nevertheless, as Lewis points out in a slightly different connection,[3] it is not the complete allegories so much as the incidental

[3] *Allegory,* p. 86.

and briefer appearances of allegory within sermons, treatises, drama, and art that reveal the degree to which allegory was congenial to the medieval sensibility.

The dream as a means of entering the allegorical world seems obvious enough. The visions of saints had traditionally been preceded by a swoon or trance during which they passed out of the world of concrete reality. Similarly the dream removes the dreamer from the visible world, and it is natural that it should then conduct him to a vision of that more real world where the immaterial appears to take material shape and is endowed with even greater vividness and sharpness than the world he has left. Within the dream there are at least three ingredients which, together or separately, characterize much Middle English dream poetry. First is this appearance of allegorical figures and events, often within an idealized pastoral or woodland setting. Second is an actual prevision of the future, like that given to Charles or Cresseid. Third is the appearance of a guide — a parent or other grave and venerable person who declares the future, interprets the events in the dream, and gives sage advice, like Genius in Gower's poem. Perhaps the book which most stimulated Middle English dream literature was Macrobius' *Commentary on the Dream of Scipio* (late 4th–early 5th c.).[4]

The most familiar preludes to the dream leading to an allegorical vision are those appearing in the *Roman de la Rose* and in countless later poems, in which the lover, unable to sleep, wanders abroad in a lovely spring morning and falls asleep in a meadow filled with the fragrance of fresh flowers and the song of birds, often beside a running stream. The circumstances of the dream itself usually merge with this.

The poems included in this section suggest the variety with which allegory and the dream convention could be handled. Henryson's *Bludy Serk* is pure moral allegory, severe in its suppression of detail, although its spare outlines remain vividly precise. And in the poem the dream does not appear at all. Langland's poem is equally serious but spendthrift in its detail, including the whole range of medieval society and medieval sensibility, and combining almost at random

[4] *The Dream of Scipio (Somnium Scipionis)* originally was the closing part of Cicero's treatise *De re publica,* in which Scipio Africanus the Younger dreams that his famous father appears before him, to exhort him to shun fame and pursue virtue so as to win rewards in the afterlife.

its literal and allegorical figures. Gower's poem is both highly moral and highly entertaining, moving easily between human love and that higher love of which this is but a picture, and filling out its visionary and allegorical framework with tales which may contain no allegorical figures at all, and whose larger allegorical meanings often become almost submerged beneath the entertaining, literal surface of the tales. The dream of Charles d'Orleans is a conscious parody of the conventional love-dream, as craggy rocks and pounding seas replace for this despondent lover the usual quiet and idyllic scenes. In Henryson's *Testament,* not only does a bitterly cold winter evening replace the fragrant morning meadows, but then even in this interior scene, which could also lead to dreams — as it does in Chaucer's *Parlement of Foules* — the expected dream does not come. The story is revealed to us through direct wakeful narration, while the dream is held in reserve, to appear later, transformed, in the almost pathological trance and vision of Cresseid, which is the core of the poem.

22 *(ca. 1377)*

PIERS PLOWMAN

The Harrowing of Hell

B–TEXT, PASSUS XVIII

William Langland
(*ca.* 1330–*ca.* 1400)

Wolleward and wete shoed went I forth after,
As a reccheles renke that of no wo reccheth,
And yede forth like a lorel al my lif time
Til I wex wery of the worlde and wilned eft to slepe,
5 And lened me to a Lenten, and longe time I slepte.
And of Cristes Passioun — and penaunce the peple that ofraughte —
Rested me there, and rutte faste til *ramis palmarum;*
Of gerles and of *gloria laus*, gretly me dremed,
And how *osanna* by orgonye olde folke songen.
10 One semblable to the Samaritan, and somedel to Piers the Plowman,
Barfote on an asse bakke, botelees, cam prike

(22) *Passus,* a portion or division of a poem (Latin, a step)

1 *Wolleward,* with rough wool (instead of linen) against the skin; *wete shoed,* wet-shod

2 Like a careless man who is heedless of all pain and discomfort

3 *yede forth,* wandered about; *lorel,* tramp; *al,* all through

4–9 Until I grew weary of the world and wished again (*wilned eft*) to sleep, and rested until Lent (*lened me to a Lenten*), and slept for a long time. And from Christ's Passion Sunday — and the penance that extended to the people — I rested there, and snored away (*rutte faste*) until Palm Sunday (*ramis palmarum,* palm branches); of children (*gerles*) and *gloria laus* I dreamed much, and how the older men sang "Hosanna" with the organ. (*Gloria laus et honor* — Glory, praise, and honor — are the opening words of a processional hymn for Palm Sunday. As the procession reaches the church door, the choir divides; part, usually the boys, go inside to sing the verses of the hymn, while the rest, the men, stay outside to sing the refrain of which "Osanna" is a part.)

10 *semblable,* similar; *somedel,* somewhat (similar)

11 Barefoot, without boots, came riding on an ass's back

Withoute spores other spere; spakliche he loked,
As is the kinde of a knighte that cometh to be dubbed,
To geten hem gilte spores or galoshes y-couped.
15 Thanne was Faith in a fenestre, and cride: "*A, fili David!*"
As doth an Heraude of Armes whan auntrous cometh to justes;
Olde Juwes of Jerusalem for joye they songen;
Benedictus qui venit in nomine domini.
Thanne I frayned at Faith what al that fare bement,
And who sholde jouste in Jerusalem. "Jesus," he seide,
20 "And fecche that the Fende claimeth — Piers fruit the Plowman."
"Is Piers in this place?" quod I, and he preynte on me:
"This Jesus of his gentrice wole juste in Piers armes,
In his helme and his haberioun, *humana natura,*
That Crist be nought beknowe here for *consumatus Deus.*

12 *spores other spere,* spurs or spear; *spakliche,* eager 13 *kinde,* nature

14 *geten hem,* get for himself; *galoshes y-couped,* elegant shoes with a decorative pattern cut into them

15 *fenestre,* window; *A, fili David!,* Hosanna, son of David! (Matt. 21:9) This phrase and most of the Latin phrases that occur throughout this passus are taken from the various services of Holy Week, especially those on Palm Sunday, Good Friday, and Easter Day. They constantly remind the reader of the extent to which the dreamer's vision is prompted by details of the services themselves, as he remembers them or as they actually penetrate his dream.

16 *Heraude,* Herald; *auntrous,* an adventurous knight or squire; *justes,* jousts

17 *Juwes,* Jews; *songen,* sang; *Benedictus . . . ,* Blessed is he that cometh in the name of the Lord (Matt. 21:9. All Biblical ascriptions are to the Vulgate). Throughout this section, Life, Light, Truth are used ambivalently: as allegorical abstractions and as denominations for Christ, who personifies them all.

18 *frayned at,* enquired of; *fare bement,* commotion meant

19 *sholde jouste,* was to joust

20 And recover that which the Devil claims — the fruit (*i.e.,* soul) of Piers the Plowman

21 *quod,* said; *preynte on me,* looked sharply at me

22 *of his gentrice,* out of his noble nature; *juste,* joust

23 *haberioun,* coat of mail; *humana natura,* human nature

24 So that he may not be recognized here as God Almighty

25 In Piers paltok the Plowman this priker shal ride,
For no dinte shall him dere, as in *deitate patris*."
"Who shal juste with Jesus," quod I, "Juwes or Scribes?"
"Nay," quod he, "the foule Fende, and Fals Dome, and Deth.
Deth seyth he shal fordo and adown bringe
30 Al that liveth or loketh, in londe or in watere.
Lif seyth that he likthe, and leyth his lif to wedde
That, for al that Deth can do, within thre dayes
To walke and fecche fro the Fende Piers fruite the Plowman,
And legge it there him liketh, and Lucifer binde,
35 And forbete and adown bringe bale and Deth forevere –
O mors, ero mors tua!"
Thanne cam Pilatus with moche peple, *sedens pro tribunali,*
To se how doughtilich Deth sholde do, and deme her botheres righte.
The Juwes and the Justice ayeine Jesu they were,
And al her courte on him cride, "*Crucifige!*" sharpe.
40 Tho put him forth a pilour befor Pilat and seide:
"This Jesus of oure Jewes temple japed and dispised,
To fordone it on o day and in thre dayes after

[25] *paltok,* jacket; *priker,* horseman
[26] *dinte,* blow; *dere,* harm; *as in deitate patris,* in his divine nature
[28] *Fende,* Fiend; *Fals Dome,* False Judgment; *Deth,* Death
[29] Death says that he shall destroy and bring down [30] *loketh,* looks about
[31] *Lif,* Life, or Christ; *likthe,* lies; *leyth his lif to wedde,* pledges his life
[33] *fecche,* bring back; *Piers fruite the Plowman,* the fruit (*i.e.,* soul) of Piers Plowman
[34] And place it wherever he pleases, and bind Lucifer
[35] *forbete,* beat down; *bale,* sorrow; *bale and,* MS *om. and; O mors, ero mors tua,* Oh Death, I will be thy death! (Hosea 13:14)
[36] *cam,* came; *peple,* people; *sedens pro tribunali,* sitting before the judgment seat
[37] *doughtilich,* valiantly; *deme her botheres righte,* judge the rights of both of them (Death and Life)
[38] *Justice,* Judge; *ayeine,* against [39] *her,* their; *on,* against; *sharpe,* sharply
[40] Then a robber pushed himself forward before Pilate and said
[41] *japed,* made fun [42] *To fordone,* (promising) to destroy; *o,* one

Edefye it eft newe — here he stant that seide it —
And yit maken it as moche in al manere pointes,
45 Bothe as longe and as large by loft and by grounde!"
"*Crucifige!*" quod a cacchepolle, "I warante him a wicche!"
"*Tolle! tolle!*" quod another, and toke o kene thornes,
And began of kene thorne a gerelande to make,
And sette it sore on his hed, and seide in envye:
50 "Ave! Rabbi," quod that ribaude, and threw redes at him,
Nailled him with thre nailles, naked on the Rode,
And poisoun on a pole they put up to his lippes,
And bede him drinke his deth-ivel — his dayes were y-done.
"And yif that thou sotil be, help now thyselven!
55 If thou be Crist and Kinges sone, come downe off the Rode —
Thanne shul we leve that Lif thee loveth, and wil nought lete thee deie!"
"*Consummatum est!*" quod Crist, and comsed forto swowe;
Pitousliche and pale as a prisoun that deieth,
The Lorde of Lif and of Lighte tho leyed his eyen togideres.
60 The daye for drede withdrowe, and derke becam the sonne;
The wal wagged and clef, and al the worlde quaved.
Ded men for that dine come out of depe graves
And tolde why that tempest so longe time dured:

43 *Edefye,* Build; *eft,* again; *stant,* stands
44 And moreover make it as great in all details
45 *by loft and by grounde,* in height and breadth
46 *Crucifige,* MS *Crufige*; *cacchepolle,* officer; *warante him a wicche,* swear he's a sorcerer
47 *Tolle,* Away with him; *toke o,* took some; *kene,* sharp
48 *gerelande,* garland, crown 49 *sette it sore,* jammed it; *seide,* spoke
50 *Ave! Rabbi,* Hail! Rabbi (master or teacher); *ribaude,* villain; *threw redes,* thrust reeds
51 *Rode,* rood, cross 53 *bede,* bad; *deth-ivel,* death drink; *y-done,* finished
54 *sotil,* clever 55 *Kinges sone,* king's son 56 *leve,* believe
57 *Consummatum est,* It is finished (John 19:30); *comsed forto swowe,* began to swoon
58 *Pitousliche,* Piteously; *prisoun,* prisoner
59 *tho leyed his eyen togideres,* then closed his eyes 60 *daye,* daylight
61 *wagged and clef,* shook violently and split; *quaved,* quaked
62 *Ded,* Dead; *for that dine,* because of that din 63 *dured,* endured

"For a bitter bataille," the ded bodye saide,
65 "Lif and Deth in this derknesse, her one fordoth her other.
Shal no wighte wite witterly who shal have the maistrye
Er Sondey aboute sonne-risinge," and sank with that til erthe.
Some seide that he was Goddes Sone that so faire deide —
Vere filius dei erat iste, etc.;
And somme saide he was a wicche — "Good is that we assaye
70 Where he be ded or noughte ded, down er he be taken!"
Two theves also tholed deth that time
Uppon a crosse besides Crist — so was the commune lawe.
A cacchepole cam forth and craked bothe her legges,
And her armes after, of either of tho theves.
75 Ac was no boy so bolde Goddes body to touche,
For he was knighte and Kinges sone; Kinde foryaf that time
That non harlot were so hardy to leyne hande uppon him.
Ac there cam forth a knighte with a kene spere y-grounde,
Highte Longeus, as the lettre telleth, and longe had lore his sighte;
80 Befor Pilat and other peple in the place he hoved.
Maugre his many tethe he was made that time
To take the spere in his honde and justen with Jesus,

64 *the ded bodye,* one of the dead bodies
65 Life and Death (are waging) in this darkness, where one is destroying the other.
66 *wighte wite witterly,* man know for certain; *maistrye,* mastery
67 *Er,* Before; *Sondey,* Easter Sunday; *til,* into
68 *so faire deide,* died so nobly; *Vere filius . . . ,* Indeed, this was the son of God (Matt. 27:54).
69 *wicche,* sorcerer; *Good is that we assaye,* It would be a good idea to test
70 *Where,* Whether; *down er he be taken,* before he be taken down
71 *tholed,* suffered 73 *cacchepole,* officer; *her,* their 74 *either,* each; *tho,* those
75 *Ac,* But; *boy,* fellow 76 *Kinde foryaf that time,* Nature that time saw to it
77 *harlot,* rascal; *hardy,* bold; *leyne,* lay
78 *Ac,* But; *kene spere y-grounde,* spear ground sharp
79 *Highte Longeus,* Named Longinus; *lettre,* story; *lore,* lost
80 *hoved,* waited about
81 *Maugre his many tethe,* Despite his many protests
82 *justen with,* joust against

For alle they were unhardy that hoved on hors or stode,
To touche him or to taste him or take him down off Rode;
85 But this blinde bacheler thanne bar him thorough the herte.
The blode spronge down by the spere and unspered the knightes eyen.
Thanne fel the knighte upon knees and cried him mercy:
"Ayeine my wille it was, Lorde, to wounde you so sore!"
He seighed and saide, "Sore it me athinketh
90 For the dede that I have done! I do me in youre grace:
Have on me reuth, rightful Jesu!" and right with that he wept.
Thanne gan Faith felly the fals Juwes dispise,
Called hem caitives acursed forevere
For this foule vileinye: "Veniaunce to you alle!
95 To do the blinde bete him y-bounde – it was a boyes conseille.
Cursed caitive! knighthod was it nevere
To misdo a ded body by day or by nighte.
The gree yit hath he geten, for al his grete wounde;
For youre champioun chivaler, chief knight of you alle,
100 Yelt him recreaunt, renning right as Jesus wille!
For be this derkenesse y-do, his deth worth avenged.
And ye, lordeines, han y-lost, for Lif shal have the maistrye,
And youre fraunchise that fre was, fallen is in thraldome.
And ye, cherles, and youre children, chieve shal ye nevre,

83 For all the rest of them who hung around on horse or on foot were too timid
84 *taste,* test 85 *bacheler,* young knight; *bar,* pierced
86 *unspered,* unlocked; *eyen,* eyes 87 *cried him mercy,* begged forgiveness
88 *Ayeine,* Against 89 *seighed,* sighed; *athinketh,* distresses
90 *do me in,* put myself into 91 *reuth,* pity; *right,* immediately
92 *gan,* did; *felly,* fiercely; *fals,* false 93 *hem,* them
94 *vileinye,* villainy; *Veniaunce,* Vengeance
95 To make a blind (man) strike him (who is) bound – it was villain's counsel.
97 *misdo,* maltreat 98 *gree,* prize; *geten, for al,* gotten, in spite of
99 *chivaler,* chevalier
100 Is yielding himself as defeated, running (his course) exactly at Jesus' will
101 For once this darkness is over, his (Jesus') life will be avenged.
102 *lordeines, han y-lost,* rascals, have lost; *maistrye,* mastery
103 *fraunchise,* liberty; *in thraldome,* into slavery
104 *cherles,* villains; *chieve,* succeed

105 Ne have lordship in londe, ne no londe tilie,
But al bareine be, and usurye usen,
Which is lif that oure Lorde in alle lawes acurseth.
Now youre good dayes ar done, as Daniel prophecied:
Whan Crist cam, of her kingdom the crowne shulde cesse —
Cum veniat sanctus sanctorum, cessabit unxio vestra."
110 What for fere of this ferly and of the fals Juwes
I drowe me in that derkenesse to *decendit ad inferna.*
And there I sawe, sothely, *secundum scripturas*:
Out of the West-coste a wenche, as me thoughte,
Cam walkinge in the wey — to Helle-ward she loked.
115 Mercy hight that maide, a meke thinge withalle,
A ful benigne buirde and boxome of speche.
Her suster, as it semed, cam softly walking
Evene out of the Est, and Westward she loked —
A ful comely creature, Treuth she highte.
120 For the vertue that hir folwed, aferd was she nevere.
Whan this maidenes mette, Mercy and Treuth,
Either axed other of this grete wonder,
Of the dine and of the derknesse, and how the daye rowed,
And which a lighte and a leme lay befor Helle.
125 "Ich have ferly of this fare, in feith," seide Treuth,

105 Nor hold land in dominion, nor till any land
106 *bareine,* barren; *usurye usen,* practice usury 107 *lif,* way of life (*i.e.,* usury)
109 When Christ came, the crown of their kingdom shall cease; *of, cesse,* MS *om., from* MS Trinity; *Cum veniat . . . ,* When the Holy of Holies shall come, your anointing shall cease (see Dan. 9:24).
110 *What for fere of this ferly,* For fear of this marvel
111 *drowe me,* drew back; *decendit ad inferna,* descended into Hell
112 *sothely, secundum scripturas,* truly, according to the Scriptures
113 *coste,* regions; *wenche,* maiden; *as me thoughte,* as it seemed to me
114 *to Helle-ward,* towards Hell; *loked,* looked
115 *hight,* was called; *meke,* meek
116 *benigne buirde,* gentle maiden; *boxome,* cheerful 117 *suster,* sister.
120 *For,* Because of; *hir folwed,* followed her; *aferd,* afraid 121 *this,* these
122 *Either axed other,* Each asked the other
123 *dine,* din; *rowed,* dawned (with the coming of Christ into Hell)
124 *which a,* what sort of; *leme,* brightness
125 "I marvel at this business, in faith," said Truth.

"And am wending to wite what this wonder meneth."
"Have no merveille," quod Mercy; "Myrthe it betokneth.
A maiden that hatte Marye, and moder without feling
Of any kinnes creature, conceived thorw speche
130 And grace of the Holy Goste, wex grete with childe —
Withouten wem into this worlde she brought him.
And that my tale be trewe I take God to witnesse.
Sith this barn was bore ben thretty winter passed,
Which deide and deth tholed this day aboute midday.
135 And that is cause of this clips that closeth now the sonne,
In meninge that man shal fro merkenesse be drawe,
The while this lighte and this leme shal Lucifer ablende.
For patriarkes and prophetes han preched herof often,
That man shal man save thorw a maidenes helpe,
140 And that was tint thorw tre, tree shal it winne,
And that deth down broughte, deth shal releve."
"That thou tellest," quod Treuth, "is but a tale of waltrot,
For Adam and Eve and Abraham, with other
Patriarkes and prophetes that in peine liggen,
145 Leve thou nevere that yone lighte hem alofte bringe,
Ne have them out of Helle! Holde thy tonge, Mercy!
It is but a trufle that thou tellest; I, Treuth, wote the sothe.
For that is ones in Helle, out cometh it nevere;

126 *wending,* going; *wite,* learn; *meneth,* means
127 "Don't be amazed," said Mercy; "it signifies joy."
128 *hatte,* was called; *moder,* mother; *feling,* touch
129 *kinnes,* kind of; *thorw speche,* through the Word
130 *wex grete,* grew large 131 *Withouten wem,* Without stain
133 *barn,* child; *thretty,* thirty
134 *Which deide and deth tholed,* Who died and suffered death pangs
135 *clips,* eclipse 136 In token that man shall out of darkness be drawn
137 *The while,* While; *leme,* brightness; *ablende,* blind 139 *thorw,* through
140 And that one (Adam) who was lost through a tree (of knowledge), a tree (the cross) shall win back
141 *that,* that one whom; *releve,* raise up again
142 *That,* That which; *waltrot,* absurdity 144 *in peine liggen,* lie in pain
145 Don't ever believe that yonder light will raise them up. 146 *Ne,* Nor
147 *trufle,* nonsense; *wote the sothe,* know the truth (of the matter)
148 *that,* that which; *ones,* once

Job the prophete, patriarke, reproveth thy sawes:
Quia in inferno nulla est redempcio!"
150 Thanne Mercy ful mildly mouthed thise wordes:
"Thorw experience," quod she, "I hope they shal be saved.
For venim fordoth venim, and that I prove by resoun.
For of alle venimes, foulest is the scorpioun;
May no medcine helpe the place there he stingeth
155 Til he be ded and do therto — the ivel he destroyeth,
The first venimouste, thorw venim of himself.
So shal this deth fordo, I dar my lif legge,
Al that deth did furste, thorw the develles entisinge;
And right as thorw gile man was begiled,
160 So shal grace that began make a good sleighte —
Ars ut artem falleret."
"Now suffre we," seide Treuth; "I se, as me thinketh,
Out of the nippe of the North nought ful fer hennes,
Rightwisnesse come renning; reste we the while,
For he wote more than we — he was er we bothe."
165 "That is soth," seide Mercy, "And I se here by Southe
Where Pees cometh playinge, in Pacience y-clothed.
Love hath coveited hir longe — leve I none other

149 *reproveth thy sawes,* disproves thy sayings; *Quia . . . ,* He who shall go down to hell shall not come up (Job 7:9).

150 *Thanne,* Then 151 *Thorw,* Through; *hope,* expect that

152 *venim fordoth,* poison undoes 153 *scorpioun,* scorpion's

154 *there,* where 155 *do therto,* applied against the wound; *ivel,* evil

156 The first in poisonousness — through his own poison

157 *fordo,* undo; *dar,* dare; *legge,* wager

158 *furste,* in the beginning; *develles,* devil's

159 *right,* just

160 *began,* began (all things); *sleighte,* cunning trick; *Ars ut artem falleret,* Art shall be deceived through art (from third stanza of the hymn *"Pange lingua, gloriosi"*)

161 *suffre we,* let's wait patiently; *se,* see

162 *nippe,* nipping regions; *nought ful fer hennes,* not very far hence

163 Righteousness come running; let's wait until she comes

164 *he wote,* she knows; *he was er,* she existed before

165 *soth,* true; *by Southe,* from the south

166 Where Peace comes dancing along, clothed in Patience

167 Love has long desired her — I believe nothing else

But he sent hir some lettre what this lighte bemeneth
That overhoveth Helle thus; she us shal telle."
170 Whan Pees, in Pacience y-clothed, approched nere hem tweine,
Rightwisnesse hir reverenced for her riche clothing,
And preyed Pees to telle hir to what place she wolde,
And in her gay garnements whom she grete thoughte.
"My wille is to wende," quod she, "and welcome hem alle
175 That many day mighte I noughte se, for merkenesse of sinne –
Adam and Eve and other moo in Helle,
Moyses and many mo, Mercy shal have;
And I shal daunce therto – do thou so, sustre!
For Jesus justed wel, joye beginneth dawe –
Ad vesperum demorabitur fletus, et ad matutinum leticia.
180 Love, that is my lemman, suche lettres me sente,
That Mercy, my sustre, and I mankinde shulde save,
And that God hath forgiven and graunted me, Pees, and Mercy
To be mannes meinpernour for everemore after.
Lo! Here the patent!" quod Pees: "*in pace in idipsum* –
185 And that this dede shal dure – *dormiam et requiescam.*"
"What! Ravestou?" quod Rightwisnesse. "Or thou art right dronke!
Levestou that yonde lighte unlouke mighte Helle,

168 *But,* But that; *what,* (explaining) what; *bemeneth,* signifies
169 *overhoveth,* hovers over 170 *nere hem tweine,* near the two of them
171 *hir reverenced for,* showed respect to her because of
172 *hir,* her; *wolde,* wished (to go)
173 *garnements,* garments; *grete thoughte,* expected to greet
174 *wende,* go; *hem,* them
175 *many day,* for many days; *for merkenesse,* because of darkness
176 *moo,* more 177 *Moyses,* Moses; *mo,* more
178 *therto,* on this occasion; *sustre,* sister
179 *For,* Because; *justed,* jousted; *dawe,* to dawn; *Ad vesperum . . . ,* In the evening weeping shall have place: and in the morning gladness (Psalms 29:6).
180 *lemman,* lover 183 *mannes meinpernour,* man's bail.
184–85 "Lo! Hear the letter patent (legal pardon)!" said Peace: "In peace, in the selfsame (place) – And to make the deed endure – I will sleep and I will rest." (Psalms 4:9)
186 *Ravestou,* Are you raving; *right dronke,* completely drunk
187 *Levestou,* Do you believe; *unlouke mighte,* might unlock

And save mannes soule? Sustre, wene it nevre!
At the beginninge, God gaf the dome himselve:
190 That Adam and Eve and alle that hem suwed
Shulde deie downe righte and dwelle in pine after,
If that they touched a tre and the fruite eten.
Adam afterward, ayeines his defence,
Frette of that fruit and forsoke, as it were,
195 The love of oure Lorde and his lore bothe,
And folwed that the Fende taughte, and his felawes wille,
Ayeines resoun; I, Rightwisnesse, recorde thus with Treuth
That her peine be perpetuel, and no preyere hem helpe.
Forthy late hem chewe as they chose, and chide we nought,
sustres,
200 For it is botelees bale, the bite that they eten."
"And I shal preve," quod Pees, "her peine mote have ende,
And wo into wel mowe wende atte laste.
For had they wist of no wo, wel had they noughte knowen;
For no wighte wote what wel is, that nevere wo suffred,
205 Ne what is hote hunger, that had nevere defaute.
If no nighte ne were, no man, as I leve,
Shulde wite witterly what day is to mene;
Shulde nevere righte riche man that liveth in reste and ese
Wite what wo is, ne were the deth of kinde.
210 So God that began al of his good wille
Becam man of a maide, mankinde to save,
And suffred to be solde, to see the sorwe of deyinge,

188 *wene it nevre,* don't ever believe it 189 *gaf the dome,* gave the judgment
190 *hem suwed,* followed them
191 *deie downe righte,* surely die; *pine,* torment
193 *ayeines his defence,* against his prohibition 194 *Frette of,* Fed on
195 *lore,* teaching 196 *that,* that which; *Fende,* Devil; *felawes,* fellow's (Eve's)
198 *her peine,* their suffering; *hem,* them
199 Therefore let them chew as they chose, and let's not complain, sisters.
200 *botelees bale,* remediless evil; *eten,* ate
201 *I,* MS *om.,* from MS Trinity; *preve,* prove; *mote,* must
202 And woe must turn into joy at last. 203 *wist,* known
204 *wighte wote,* man knows 205 *hote,* sharp; *defaute,* lack (of food)
206 *leve,* believe 207 *wite witterly,* know for sure; *is to mene,* means
208 *righte,* very 209 Know what sorrow is, were it not for death
210 *of,* out of
212 *suffred to be solde,* allowed (himself) to be sold; *see,* experience

The which unknitteth al care and comsinge is of reste.
For til *modicum* mete with us, I may it wel avowe,
215 Wote no wighte, as I wene, what is inough to mene.
Forthy God of his goodnesse the firste gome, Adam,
Sette him in solace and in sovereigne mirthe,
And sith he suffred him sinne, sorwe to fele,
To wite what wel was, kindelich to knowe it.
220 And after, God auntred himself and toke Adames kinde,
To wite what he hath suffred in thre sondry places:
Bothe in Hevene and in erthe, and now til Helle he thinketh,
To wite what al wo is, that wote of al joye.
So it shal fare by this folke: her foly and her sinne
225 Shal lere hem what langour is, and lisse withouten ende.
Wote no wighte what werre is, there that Pees regneth,
Ne what is witterly wel, til 'weillowey' him teche."
Thanne was there a wighte with two brode eyen —
Boke highte that Beupere, a bolde man of speche.
230 "By Godes body!" quod this Boke, "I wil bere witnesse,
That tho this barne was y-bore there blased a sterre
That alle the wise of this worlde in o witte acordeden
That such a barne was borne in Bethleem Citee
That mannes soule sholde save and sinne destroye.
235 And alle the elements," quod the Boke, "herof bereth witnesse.
That he was God that al wroughte, the walkene firste shewed:

213 *comsinge,* beginning 214 *modicum,* scarcity
215 No man knows what "enough" means
216 *Forthy,* Therefore; *gome,* creature 217 *mirthe,* joy
218–19 And then he allowed him to sin, to experience sorrow, in order to understand what joy was, to know it by experience.
220 And afterward, God ventured himself and took on Adam's nature.
221 *wite,* know; *sondry,* different 222 *thinketh,* intends (to come)
223 *that,* he who 224 *fare by,* happen to; *her,* their
225 *lere hem,* teach them; *langour,* suffering; *lisse,* joy
226 *werre,* war; *there,* there where; *regneth,* reigns
227 *witterly wel,* truly joy; *weillowey,* alas! — *i.e.,* misery; *teche,* teaches
228 *brode eyen,* eyes wide open
229 *Boke highte that Beupere,* That Reverend Father was called Book
231 *tho,* when; *barne was y-bore,* child was born
232 *wise,* wise (men); *in o witte acordeden,* agreed in one opinion
234 *That,* Who
236 *al wroughte,* created everything; *walkene,* heavens

Tho that weren in Hevene token *stella comata*
And tendeden hir as a torche to reverence his birthe –
The lighte folwed the Lorde into the lowe erthe.
240 That water witnessed that he was God, for he went on it;
Peter the apostel parceived his gate,
And as he went on the water wel him knewe and seide:
Iube me venire ad te super aquas.
And lo! how the sonne gan louke her lighte in herself
Whan she seie him suffre that sonne and se made!
245 The erthe, for hevynesse that he wolde suffre,
Quaked as quikke thinge, and al bequasht the roche.
Lo! Helle mighte noughte holde, but opened tho God tholed,
And lete oute Simondes sones to seen him hange on Rode.
And now shal Lucifer leve it, though him loth thinke,
250 For *Gygas* the geaunt with a ginne engined
To breke and to bete down that ben ayeines Jesus.
And I, Boke, wil be brent, but Jesus rise to live
In alle mightes of man, and his moder gladye,
And conforte al his kinne and out of care bringe,

237 *Tho,* Those; *stella comata,* comet 238 *tendeden hir,* kindled it
239 *into,* down to 240 *went,* walked 241 *gate,* walking
242 *knewe,* recognized; *Iube me . . . ,* Bid me come to you upon the waters (Matt. 14:28).
243 *lo,* behold; *gan louke,* locked up; *in,* within
244 *seie,* saw; *se,* sea 245 *hevynesse,* sorrow
246 *quikke,* living; *al bequasht the roche,* shattered the rock to pieces
247 *holde,* hold together; *tho,* when; *tholed,* suffered
248 *Simondes sones,* Simeon's sons (In the Apocryphal Book of Nicodemus 12:21, Simeon's sons, Charinus and Lethius, are among those raised from the dead at the moment of Christ's death, and it is from their detailed account of the Harrowing of Hell that Langland ultimately derives much of his material.)
249 *leve,* believe; *him loth thinke,* he thinks it hateful
250 *Gygas,* Latin word for giant (*geaunt*); *ginne,* machine, contrivance; *engined,* contrived
251 *that ben ayeines,* whatever (gates) stand against (an allusion to Samson who, in carrying off the gates of Gaza, was considered a prototype of Christ breaking open the gates of Hell)
252 *brent, but,* burnt, unless
253 In all his human strength, and made his mother glad
254 *kinne,* kin; *bringe,* bring (them)

255 And al the Juwen joye unjoygnen and unlouken,
And but they reverencen his Rode and his resurexion
And beleve on a newe lawe, be lost lif and soule!"
"Suffre we," seide Treuth; "I here and se bothe
How a spirit speketh to Helle and bit unspere the yates –
Attollite portas, etc."
260 A voice, loude in that lighte, to Lucifer crieth;
"Princes of this place, unpinneth and unlouketh!
For here cometh with crowne that Kinge is of Glorye!"
Thanne siked Sathan, and seide to hem alle:
"Suche a lighte, ayeines oure leve, Lazar it fette;
265 Care and combraunce is comen to us alle!
If this Kinge come in, mankinde wil he fecche
And lede it ther him liketh, and lightlich me binde.
Patriarkes and prophetes han parled herof longe,
That such a lorde and a lighte shulde lede hem alle hennes."
270 "Listeneth!" quod Lucifer, "for I this Lorde knowe,
Bothe this Lorde and this lighte – is longe ago I knewe him.
May no Deth him dere, ne no develes queintise,
And where he wil is his waye! ac war him of the periles!
If he reve me my righte, he robbeth me by maistrye.

255 And disrupt and undo all the Jews' joy 256 *but,* unless
257 *be,* (let them) be
258 *Suffre we,* Let's wait; *here and se bothe,* both hear and see
259 *bit unspere the yates,* commands the gates to be unbarred; *Attollite portas, etc.,* Lift up (your) gates, (O ye princes, and be ye lifted up, O eternal gates. Psalms 23:7).
260 *Lucifer:* the difference here between Lucifer and Satan is not always clear, but seems generally to follow St. Jerome's distinction between Lucifer, the fallen angel, and Satan, the *spirit* of evil which was the consequence of that fall.
261 *unpinneth and unlouketh,* unpin and unbar 262 *that,* he that
263 *siked,* sighed; *hem,* them
264 Such a light, without our permission, fetched forth Lazarus.
265 *combraunce,* encumbrance
267 *ther him liketh,* wherever he please; *lightlich,* easily
268 *han parled herof longe,* have long spoken of this 269 *hennes,* hence
271 *is,* it was 272 *dere,* harm; *develes queintise,* devil's trick
273 And he will go wherever he will; but let him beware of the perils.
274 *reve me,* deprive me of; *maistrye,* force

275 For by right and by resoun, tho renkes that ben here –
Bodye and soule – ben mine, bothe gode and ille.
For himself seide, that Sire is of Hevene,
Yif Adam ete the apple, alle shulde deie
And dwelle with us develes – this thretinge he made.
280 And he that sothenesse is seide thise wordes.
And sithen I seised sevene hundreth wintre,
I leve that lawe nil naughte lete him the leest."
"That is sothe," seide Sathan, "but I me sore drede,
For thou gete hem with gile, and his gardine breke,
285 And in semblaunce of a serpent sat on the appeltre
And eggedest hem to ete – Eve by hirselve,
And toldest hir a tale – of tresoun were the wordes –
And so thou haddest hem oute and hider atte laste.
It is noughte graithely geten there gile is the rote."
290 "For God wil nought be begiled," quod Gobelyn, "ne bejaped;
We have no trewe title to hem, for thorwgh tresoun were
they dampned."
"Certes, I drede me," quod the Devel, "leste Treuth wil hem
fecche.
This thretty winter, as I wene, hath he gone and preched;
I have assailled him with sinne and sometime I asked
295 Where he were God or Goddess Sone – he gaf me shorte
answere.

275 *tho renkes that ben here,* those people who are here
277 For he that is Lord of Heaven said himself 278 *Yif,* If
279 *thretinge,* threat 280 *sothenesse is,* is Truth itself
281 *sithen,* since; *seised,* have been in possession; *wintre:* winters = years
282 I believe that the law will not allow him anything.
283 *sothe,* true; *I me sore drede,* I am terribly afraid
284 For you got them (Adam and Eve) with guile, and broke into his garden.
285 *semblaunce,* likeness 286 *eggedest hem,* egged them on
288 And thus you caused them to be banished and (brought) hither in the end.
289 *graithely geten,* securely won; *there,* where; *rote,* root
290 *Gobelyn,* Goblin; *ne bejaped,* nor tricked 291 *dampned,* damned
292 *Certes, I drede me,* Certainly I am afraid
293 *wene,* understand
295 *Where,* Whether

And thus hath he trolled forth this two and thretty winter.
And whan I seighe it was so sleping, I went
To warne Pilates wif what dones man was Jesus,
For Juwes hateden him and han done him to deth.
300 I wolde have lengthed his lif, for I leved yif he deied
That his soule wolde suffre no sinne in his sighte.
For the body, whil it on bones yede, aboute was evere
To save men fram sinne, yif hemself wolde.
And now I se where a soule cometh hiderward seillinge,
305 With glorye and with grete lighte; God it is, I wote wel!
I rede we flee," quod he, "faste alle hennes.
For us were better noughte be, than biden his sighte!
For thy lesinges, Lucifer, loste is al oure praye!
Firste thorw thee we fellen fro Hevene so heigh,
310 For we leved thy lesinges; y-lore we have Adam
And al oure lordeship, I leve, a londe and a water —
Nunc princeps huius mundi ejicietur foras."
Efte the lighte bad unlouke, and Lucifer answered:
"What Lorde artou?" quod Lucifer. "*Quis est iste?*"
"*Rex Glorie!*" the lighte sone seide,
315 "And Lorde of mighte and of maine and al manere vertues,
dominus virtutum!
Dukes of this dim place, anon undo this yates,

296 *trolled forth,* wandered forth
297 *seighe it was so sleping,* saw she was sleeping 298 *dones,* sort of
299 *hateden,* hated; *done,* put 300 *leved,* believed
301 That his soul would never endure the sight of sin (like ours)
302 For while his body was alive, it was ever busy.
303 *yif hemself wolde,* if they themselves were willing
304 *hiderward seillinge,* sailing hither
306 *rede,* advise that; *faste alle hennes,* quickly away! Everyone!
307 For it were better for us not to be at all, than to endure his look.
308 *For,* Because of; *lesinges,* lies; *praye,* prey
309 *thorw,* through. 310 *For we leved,* Because we believed; *y-lore,* lost
311 *lordeship,* dominion; *leve,* believe; *a,* on; *Nunc princeps . . . ,* Now shall the prince of this world be cast out (John 12:31).
312 *Efte,* Again; *bad unlouke,* commanded (them) to unbar (the gate)
313 *artou,* are you; *Quis est iste,* Who is this King . . . (Psalms 23:8)
314 *Rex Glorie,* The King of Glory; *sone,* immediately
315 *maine,* power; *al manere,* every; *dominus virtutum,* Lord of Powers
316 *anon,* quickly; *this yates,* these gates

That Crist may come in, the Kinges sone of Hevene!"
And with that breth Helle brake with Beliales barres,
For any wye or warde, wide opene the yates.
320 Patriarkes and prophetes, *populus in tenebris,*
Songen Seint Johanes songe, *Ecce! agnus dei!*
Lucyfer loke ne mighte, so lighte him ableinte.
And tho that oure Lorde loved, into his lighte he laughte,
And seide to Sathan, "Lo! here my soule to amendes
325 For alle sinneful soules, to save tho that ben worthy.
Mine they be, and of me: I may the bette hem claime.
Although resoun recorde, and right of myself,
That if they ete the apple alle shulde deie,
I behighte hem nought here, Helle forevere.
330 For the dede that they dede, thy deceite it made;
With gile thou hem gete againe al resoun.
For in my paleis, Paradis, in persone of an addre,
Falseliche thou fettest there thinge that I loved.
Thus, y-like a lusarde with a lady visage,
335 Thevelich thou me robbedest; the old lawe graunteth
That gilours be begiled and that is gode resoun:
Dentem pro dente, et oculum pro oculo.
Ergo, soule shal soule quite, and sinne to sinne wende,
And al that man hath misdo I, man, wil amende.

318–19 And with that word, Hell, together with Belial's bars, broke open, in spite of any warrior or guard, the gates wide open.
320 *populus in tenebris,* the people (that sat) in darkness (Matt. 4:16)
321 Sang St. John's song, Behold the Lamb of God (John 1:36).
322 *loke ne mighte,* might not look; *ableinte,* blinded
323 *tho,* those; *Lorde,* MS *om.,* from MS Trinity; *laughte,* caught up
324 *to amendes,* as ransom
326 *of,* derived from; *bette hem,* better them
327 Although reason set down, and directly from my authority
329 I did not condemn them to Hell forever.
330 *dede,* deed; *dede,* did; *made,* caused 331 *hem gete,* got them
332 *paleis,* palace; *persone,* form 333 *fettest,* snatched away
334 Thus, like a snake with a woman's face 335 *Thevelich,* Like a thief
336 *gilours,* tricksters; *Dentem pro dente . . . ,* Tooth for tooth, and eye for eye (Exod. 21:24)
337 *Ergo,* Therefore; *quite,* pay for; *wende,* turn against
338 *misdo,* misdone

Membre for membre by the olde lawe was amendes,
340 And lif for lif also, and by that lawe I claime it—
Adam and al his issue at my wille herafter.
And that Deth in hem fordid, my deth shal releve,
And bothe quikke and quite that queinte was thorw sinne.
And that grace gile destruye, good feith it asketh.
345 So leve it noughte, Lucifer, ayeine the lawe I fecche hem,
But by right and by resoun raunceoun here my liges:
Non veni soluere legem, sed adimplere.
Thou fettest mine in my place ayeines al resoun,
Falseliche and felounelich; gode faith me it taughte
To recovre hem thorw raunceoun and by no resoun elles,
350 So that with gile thou gete, thorw grace it is y-wone.
Thou, Lucifer, in liknesse of a luther addere
Getest by gile tho that God loved;
And I, in liknesse of a leode, that Lorde am of Hevene,
Graciouslich thy gile have quitte: go gile ayeine gile!
355 And as Adam and alle thorw a tre deiden,
Adam and alle thorwe a tree shal torne ayeine to live;
And gile is begiled, and in his gile fallen:
Et cecidit in foueam quam fecit.
Now beginneth thy gile ageine thee to tourne,
And my grace to growe ay gretter and wider.
360 The bitternesse that thou hast browe, brouke it thyselven;
That art Doctour of Deth, drinke that thou madest!
For I, that am Lorde of Lif—love is my drinke,
And for that drinke today I deide upon erthe—

339 *amendes,* amends 342 *that,* that which; *fordid,* destroyed; *releve,* restore
343 *quikke,* revive; *quite that queinte was,* acquit those who were destroyed
344 And that grace destroy guile, good faith requires it.
346 *raunceoun,* ransom; *liges,* subjects, liege men; *Non veni . . . ,* I am come not to destroy the law, but to fulfill (Matt. 5:17).
347 *fettest,* took away; *place,* domain
348 *felounelich,* feloniously; *me it taughte,* instructed me
350 *that,* that which; *y-wone,* won back 351 *luther,* treacherous
353 *leode,* man 354 *quitte,* requited 355 *deiden,* died 356 *torne,* return
357 *Et cecidit . . . ,* And he is fallen into the hole he made (Psalms 7:16).
359 *ay gretter,* ever greater 360 *browe,* brewed; *brouke,* enjoy
361 *that,* that which 363 *deide,* dead

I faughte so me threstes yet, for mannes soule sake.
365 May no drinke me moiste ne my thruste slake
Til the vendage falle in the vale of Josephath
That I drinke righte ripe must, *resureccio mortuorum;*
And thanne shal I come as a Kinge crowned with angeles,
And han out of Helle alle mennes soules.
370 Fendes and fendekines before me shulle stande
And be at my biddinge wheresoevre me liketh.
And to be merciable to man thanne, my kinde it asketh,
For we beth bretheren of blode, but noughte in baptesme alle.
Ac alle that beth mine hole, bretheren in blode and in baptesme,
375 Shal noughte be dampned to the deth that is withouten ende:
Tibi soli peccaui, etc.
It is nought used in erthe to hangen a feloun
Ofter than ones, though he were a tretour.
And yif the kinge of that kingedome come in that time
There the feloun thole sholde, deth or otherwise,
380 Lawe wolde he yeve him lif if he loked on him.
And I, that am Kinge of Kinges, shal come suche a time
There dome to the deth dampneth al wikked,
And yif lawe wil I loke on hem, it lithe in my grace

364 I fought so hard for the sake of man's soul that I am still thirsty.
365 *me moiste,* moisten me; *thruste,* thirst
366–67 Until vintage time come in the valley of Jehoshaphat (supposedly the site of the Last Judgment), that I must drink very ripe, the resurrection of the dead (Joel 3:12–13).
369 *han,* have 370 *Fendes and fendekines,* Devils and devilkins; *shulle,* shall
372 *kinde it asketh,* nature requires it
373 For we all be brothers in blood, though not in baptism.
374 *Ac,* But; *hole,* wholly
375 *Tibi soli peccaui, etc.,* To thee only have I sinned (Psalms 50:6).
376 *used,* customary; *feloun,* felon
377 *Ofter than ones,* More than once; *tretour,* traitor
379 *There,* Where; *thole sholde,* was supposed to suffer
380 The law is willing for the King to grant him his life, if he (so much as) looks at him.
381 *come suche,* come (at) such
382 Where judgment dooms to death all the wicked
383 *wil I,* lets me; *lithe,* lies

Whether they deie or deie noughte for that they deden ille.
385 Be it any thinge aboughte the boldenesse of her sinnes,
I may do mercy thorw rightwisnesse and alle my wordes trewe.
And though Holy Writ wil that I be wroke of hem that
deden ille —
Nullum malum inpunitum, etc.
They shul be clensed clereliche and washen of her sinnes
In my prisoun, Purgatorye, til *Parce* it hote,
390 And my mercy shal be shewed to manye of my bretheren,
For blode may suffre blode bothe hungry and acale,
Ac blode may nought se blode blede but him rewe."
(Audiui archana verba, que non licet homini loqui.)
"Ac my rightwisnesse and right shal reuelen al Helle,
And mercy al mankinde befor me in Hevene.
395 For I were an unkinde Kinge but I my kinde holpe,
And namelich at such a nede ther nedes helpe behoveth;
Non intres in iudicium cum seruo tuo.
Thus by lawe," quod oure Lorde, "lede I wil fro hennes
Tho that me loved and leved in my cominge.
And for thy lesinge, Lucifer, that thou lowe til Eve,
400 Thou shalt abye it bittre," and bonde him with cheines.
Astaroth and al the route hidden hem in hernes

384 *for that,* because; *deden ille,* did ill

385 So long as anything has atoned for the pride of their sins

387 *wil,* requires; *wroke of,* avenged against; *Nullum malum inpunitum, etc.,* No evil unpunished (Innocent III, *De Contemptu Mundi*).

388 *clereliche,* clearly; *washen,* washed

389 *til Parce it hote,* until "Spare!" is called out

391–92 A man may suffer his blood relations (to be) both hungry and cold, but may not see his kin bleed, without pitying (them); *Audiui archana . . . ,* I heard secret words which it is not granted to man to utter (II Cor. 12:4).

393 *Ac,* But; *reuelen,* rule over 394 *mercy,* mercy (shall rule over)

395 *unkinde,* unnatural; *but I my kinde holpe,* unless I help my kin

396 *namelich,* especially; *ther nedes helpe behoveth,* it is necessary to help; *Non intres . . . ,* And enter not into judgment with thy servant (Psalms 142:2).

398 *leved,* believed 399 *lesinge,* lie; *lowe,* told falsely; *til,* to

400 *abye,* pay for; *bonde,* bound; *cheines,* chains

401 Astaroth (the Phoenician moon-goddess — pagan divinities were often connected with the legions of Hell) and all the crowd (of devils) hid themselves in dark corners.

They dorste noughte loke on oure Lorde, the boldest of hem alle,
But leten him lede forth what him liked and lete what him liste.
Many hundreth of angeles harpeden and songen:
"Culpat caro, purgat caro; regnat deus dei caro."
405 Thanne piped Pees of poisye a note:
"Clarior est solito post maxima nebula phebus, post inimicitias, etc.
After sharpe shoures," quod Pees, "moste shene is the sonne,
In no weder warmer than after watery cloudes.
Ne no love lever, ne lever frendes,
Than after werre and wo, whan Love and Pees be maistres.
410 Was nevere werre in this worlde ne wikkednesse so kene,
That ne Love, and him luste, to laughinge ne broughte,
And Pees thorw Pacience alle perilles stopped."
"Trewes!" quod Treuth. "Thou tellest us soth, by Jesus!
Clippe we in covenaunt and uch of us kusse other."
415 "And lete no peple," quod Pees, "perceive that we chidde,
For inpossible is no thing to him that is almighty."
"Thou seist soth," seide Rightwisnesse, and reverentlich hir kiste,
Pees; and Pees here — *per secula seculorum:*
Misericordia et veritas obuiauerunt sibi, iusticia et pax osculate sunt.

402 *dorste,* dared
403 *leten,* let; *lete what him liste,* leave behind whomever he pleased
404 *harpeden,* harped; *Culpat caro . . . ,* The Flesh sins, the Flesh atones for sin; the Flesh of God reigns as God (from hymn *Aeterne rex altissime,* st. 4).
405 Then Peace piped a song of poetry: The sun is brighter after the heaviest cloud; love is brighter after unfriendliness (no known source).
406 *shoures,* showers; *shene,* bright 407 *weder,* weather
408 Nor no love dearer, nor friends dearer 409 *werre,* war; *maistres,* masters
411 That love, if he chose, didn't turn to laughter
413 *Trewes,* Truce; *soth,* truth
414 Let's embrace in agreement and each kiss the other.
415 *chidde,* quarreled
417–18 "You speak the truth," said Righteousness and reverently kissed her, Peace; and Peace (kissed) her — world without end. Mercy and truth have met each other; justice and peace have kissed (Psalms 84:11).

Treuth tromped tho and songe "*Te deum laudamus,*"
420 And thanne luted Love in a loude note,
Ecce quam bonum, et quam iocundum, etc.
Til the daye dawed this damaiseles daunced,
That men rongen to the resurexioun, and right with that
I waked,
And called Kitte my wif and Kalote my doughter:
"Ariseth and reverenceth Goddes ressurrexioun
425 And crepeth to the crosse on knees and kisseth it for a juwel!
For Goddes blissed body it bar for oure bote,
And it afereth the Fende, for suche is the mighte —
May no grisly gost glide there it shadweth!"

419 Truth then blew on a trumpet, and sang "Let us praise God."

420 *luted,* played on a lute; *Ecce . . . ,* Behold how good and how pleasant (it is for brethren to dwell together in unity. Psalms 132:1).

421 *dawed,* dawned; *this damaiseles,* these maidens

422 So that men rang (bells) to (celebrate) the resurrection, and immediately with that (sound) I awoke.

424 Arise, and do reverence to God's resurrection. 425 *for a juwel,* as a jewel

426 *bar,* bore; *bote,* advantage 427 *afereth,* terrifies

428 No horrid spirit may glide where it casts its shadow.

23 *(1392–93)*

CONFESSIO AMANTIS

Book I

John Gower
(*ca.* 1327-30–1408)

I may noght strecche up to the Hevene
Min hand, ne setten al in evene
This world, which evere is in balance:
It stant noght in my sufficance
5 So grete thinges to compasse.
Bot I mot lete it overpasse
And treten upon othre thinges.
Forthy the style of my writinges
Fro this day forth I thenke change,
10 And speke of thing is noght so strange
Which every kinde hath upon honde
And wherupon the world mot stonde
And hath don sithen it began
And shal, whil ther is any man.
15 And that is Love, of which I mene
To trete, as after shal be sene,
In which ther can no man him reule,
For Loves lawe is out of reule,

(23) *Confessio Amantis,* The Lover's Confession
1 *noght,* not 2 *in evene,* in even balance
3 *in balance,* in the scales, *i.e.,* in uncertainty
4 *stant,* stands; *sufficance,* power, sufficiency
5 *So,* Such; *compasse,* accomplish 6 *mot,* must 7 *treten upon,* deal with
8 *Forthy,* Therefore 9 *thenke,* intend (to)
10 *thing is,* (some)thing (which) is
11 *kinde,* race; *upon honde,* on hand, *i.e.,* to do with
12 *mot stonde,* must depend 13 *sithen,* since 16 *trete,* treat; *after,* hereafter
17 In which no man can rule himself 18 *out of,* beyond

That of too moche or of too lite
20 Wel nigh is every man to wite.
And natheles ther is no man
In al this world so wis that can
Of Love tempre the mesure,
Bot as it falth in aventure.
25 For wit ne strengthe may noght helpe,
And he which elles wolde him yelpe
Is rathest throwen under fote:
Ther can no wight therof do bote.
For yet was nevere such covine
30 That couthe ordeine a medicine
To thing which God in lawe of kinde
Hath set, for ther may no man finde
The righte salve of such a sor.
It hath and shal ben everemor
35 That Love is maister wher he wile;
Ther can no lif make other skile.
For wher as evere him lest to sette
Ther is no might which him may lette.
Bot what shal fallen ate laste,
40 The sothe can no wisdom caste
Bot as it falleth upon chance.
For if ther evere was balance
Which of Fortune stant governed,
I may wel lieve, as I am lerned,
45 That Love hath that balance on honde

19–20 That from (having) too much or too little, very nearly every man is to blame.
21 *natheles,* moreover 23 *tempre the mesure,* temper the degree, or measure
24 Except as chance falls out 25 *ne,* nor
26 And he who otherwise would boast 27 *rathest,* soonest; *fote,* foot
28 *wight,* man; *do bote,* offer help 29 *covine,* secret device or art
30 *couthe,* could; *ordeine,* prescribe 31 *kinde,* nature 33 *of,* for
35 *wher he wile,* wherever he will 36 *lif,* person; *skile,* case
37 For wherever it pleases him to attack 38 *lette,* hinder
39 *fallen ate laste,* happens in the end 40 *sothe,* truth (of it); *caste,* conjecture
41 *Bot,* Except 42 *balance,* scales 43 Which stands governed by Fortune
44 *lieve,* believe 45 *on honde,* in charge

Which wol no reson understonde,
For Love is blind and may noght se.
Forthy may no certeinete
Be set upon his jugement,
50 Bot as the whiel aboute went
He yifth his graces undeserved,
And fro that man which hath him served
Ful ofte he takth aweye his fees,
As he that pleyeth ate dees.
55 And therupon what shal befalle
He not, til that the chance falle,
Wher he shal lese or he shal winne.
And thus ful ofte men beginne
That if they wisten what it mente
60 They wolde change al here entente.
And forto proven it is so,
I am myselven on of tho
Which to this scole am underfonge
(For it is sithe go noght longe).
65 As forto speke of this matiere,
I may you telle, if ye woll hiere,
A wonder hap which me befell
That was to me bothe hard and fell,
Touchende of Love and his fortune,
70 The which me liketh to comune
And pleinly forto telle it oute
To hem that ben lovers aboute.
Fro point to point I wol declare
And writen of my woful care,

46 *wol,* will 48 *Forthy,* Therefore 50 *went,* goes 51 *yifth,* gives
52 *fro,* from 53 *fees,* wages 54 *ate dees,* at the dice 56 *not,* knows not
57 *Wher,* Whether; *lese,* lose 59 *That,* That which; *wisten,* knew
60 *wolde,* would; *al here entente,* all their purpose 61 *forto,* in order to
62 *on of tho,* one of those 63 Who are received into this school
64 *it, i.e.,* his acceptance into the school of Love
67 *wonder hap,* a wonderful occurrence 68 *fell,* cruel
69 *Touchende of,* Having to do with 70 Which I should like to communicate
72 *hem,* them; *aboute,* roundabout 74 *writen of,* write about

75 My wofull day, my wofull chance,
That men mowe take remembrance
Of that they shall hierafter rede.
For in good feith this wolde I rede:
That every man ensample take
80 Of wisdom which him is betake,
And that he wot of good aprise,
To teche it forth – for such emprise
Is forto preise; and therfore I
Woll write and shewe al openly
85 How Love and I togedre mette,
Wherof the world ensample fette
May after this, whan I am go,
Of thilke unsely jolif wo
Whos reule stant out of the weye –
90 Now glad, and now gladnesse aweye.
And yet it may noght be withstonde
For oght that men may understonde.
Upon the point that is befalle
Of Love, in which that I am falle,
95 I thenke telle my matiere.
Now herkne, who that wol it hiere,
Of my fortune how that it ferde.
This enderday, as I forthferde
To walke, as I you telle may –
100 And that was in the monthe of May
Whan every brid hath chose his make
And thenkth his merthes forto make

76 *mowe,* may 77 *Of that,* Of that (which); *rede,* read 78 *rede,* advise
79 *ensample,* example 80 *him is betake,* presented to him
81 And which he knows (to be) of sound teaching 82 *emprise,* enterprise
83 *forto preise,* to be praised 86 *fette,* take 87 *go,* gone
88–89 Of this same unhappy pleasant woe, whose rule is devious (or extraordinary)
90 *aweye,* gone 91 *withstonde,* withstood 92 *oght,* ought
93 *point,* matter; *is befalle,* befell 94 *falle,* fallen
95 I intend to tell my matter. 96 Now listen, whoever wants to hear it.
97 *ferde,* fared 98 *enderday,* recent day; *forthferde,* went forth
101 *brid,* bird; *make,* mate 102 And intends his joyful songs to make

Of love that he hath achieved
(Bot so was I nothing relieved,
105 For I was further fro my love
Than erthe is fro the Hevene above
As forto speke of eny sped) –
So wiste I me non other red,
Bot as it were a man forfare
110 Unto the wode I gan to fare –
Noght forto singe with the briddes –
For whanne I was the wode amiddes
I fond a swote grene pleine,
And ther I gan my wo compleigne,
115 Wishinge and wepinge al min one,
For other merthes made I none.
So hard me was that ilke throwe
That ofte sithes overthrowe
To grounde I was, withoute breth.
120 And evere I wishede after deth
Whanne I out of my peine awok,
And caste up many a pitous lok
Unto the Hevene, and seide thus:
"O thou Cupide, O thou Venus,
125 Thou God of Love and thou Goddesse,
Wher is pite? wher is meknesse?
Now doth me pleinly live or die,
For certes such a maladye
As I now have, and longe have hadd,
130 It mighte make a wisman madd
If that it sholde longe endure.
O Venus, Queene of Loves cure,

104 *Bot so,* But for all that 105 *fro,* from 107 *sped,* success
108 So I knew no other counsel
109–10 But, like a man worn out (with travel), into the woods I went.
112 *the wode amiddes,* in the middle of the woods
113 I found a sweet green meadow. 115 *al min one,* all alone
117 So cruel to me was that pang (or occasion)
118 *sithes,* times; *overthrowe,* overthrown 120 *after,* for
126 *pite,* pity; *meknesse,* gentleness 127 *doth,* make 128 *certes,* surely
130 *wisman,* MS *wismam* 132 *Loves,* Love's

Thou lif, thou lust, thou mannes hele,
Behold my cause and my querele,
135 And yif me som part of thy grace,
So that I may finde in this place
If thou be gracious or non."
And with that word I saugh anon
The King of Love and Queene bothe.
140 Bot he, that King, with yghen wrothe
His chiere aweyward fro me caste,
And forth he passede ate laste.
Bot natheles er he forth wente
A firy dart me thoghte he hente
145 And threw it thurgh min herte rote:
In him fond I non other bote,
For lenger list him noght to dwelle.
Bot she that is the source and welle
Of wel or wo that shal betide
150 To hem that loven, at that tide
Abod, bot forto tellen hiere,
She cast on me no goodly chiere.
Thus natheles to me she seide,
"What art thou, sone?" and I abreide
155 Right as a man doth out of slep,
And therof tok she right good kep
And bad me nothing ben adrad;
Bot for al that I was noght glad
For I ne saugh no cause why.

133–34 You, man's life, his joy, his salvation, behold my cause and my complaint (both terms also have legal and religious connotations).
135 *yif,* give 136 *finde,* find out 137 *If,* Whether
138 *saugh anon,* instantly saw 140 *yghen wrothe,* angry eyes
141–42 Turned his face away from me, and at last went away
143 *natheles,* nevertheless; *er,* before 144 It seemed to me he took a fiery dart.
145 *min herte rote,* my heart's core, or root 146 *bote,* help
147 For it pleased him to stay no longer. 148 *welle,* wellspring
149 *wel,* joy; *betide,* happen 150 *hem,* them; *tide,* season
151 *Abod,* Stayed; *hiere,* here 154 *What,* Who; *sone,* son; *abreide,* started
156–57 And she noticed that directly, and told me not to be afraid.
159 *no cause why,* no cause to be (glad)

160 And eft sheo asketh, what was I;
I seide, "A caitif that lith hiere.
What wolde ye, my Lady diere?
Shal I ben hol or elles die?"
She seide, "Tell thy maladye:
165 What is thy sor of which thou pleignest?
Ne hid it noght, for if thou feignest
I can do thee no medicine."
"Madame, I am a man of thine
That in thy court have longe served,
170 And aske that I have deserved:
Som wele after my longe wo."
And she began to loure tho
And seide, "Ther is manye of you
Faitours, and so may be that thou
175 Art right such on, and be feintise
Seist that thou hast me do servise."
And natheles she wiste wel
My world stod on another whiel,
Withouten eny faiterye.
180 Bot algate of my maladye
She bad me telle and seye hir trowthe.
"Madame, if ye wolde have rowthe,"
Quod I, "thanne wolde I telle you."
"Sey forth," quod she, "and tell me how;
185 Shew me thy seknesse everydiel."
"Madame, that can I do wel,
Be so my lif therto wol laste."

160 *eft,* again; *sheo,* she 161 *caitif,* wretch; *lith,* lies
162 What do you wish, my noble lady? 163 *hol,* whole
165 *sor,* sore; *pleignest,* complains 170 *aske that,* claim that (which)
171 *wele,* joy 172 *loure,* lower, frown; *tho,* then
174 *Faitours,* Feigners, Imposters; *so,* so (it)
175 Are just such a one, and by pretense
176 *seist,* says; *me do,* done me 177 *natheles,* yet; *wiste,* knew
178–79 My world (fortune) turned on another wheel, without any feigning.
180 *algate,* in any case 181 *seye hir trowthe,* tell her (the) truth
182 *rowthe,* pity 185 *seknesse everydiel,* every detail of your sickness
187 If my life will last long enough

With that hir lok on me she caste
And seide, "In aunter if thou live,
190 My will is ferst that thou be shrive;
And natheles how that it is
I wot myself, bot for al this
Unto my prest, which comth anon,
I woll thou telle it on and on,
195 Bothe all thy thoght and al thy werk.
O Genius, min oghne clerk,
Com forth, and hier this mannes shrifte,"
Quod Venus tho. And I uplifte
Min hefd with that, and gan beholde
200 The selve prest, which as she wolde
Was redy there, and sette him down
To hiere my confessioun.

188 *lok,* look, glance 189 And said: "If your life is in doubt"
190 *ferst,* first; *shrive,* shriven 192 *wot,* know; *for al this,* in spite of this
194 *woll,* desire that; *on and on,* point by point 195 *werk,* doings
196 *Genius:* appears as Priest of Nature in the *Romance of the Rose.* Here, he "represents the native moral instincts of mankind as setting bounds to the range of sexual passion." (*O.E.D.*); *oghne,* own
197 *shrifte,* confession 198 *Quod,* Said; *tho,* then
199 *hefd,* head; *gan beholde,* beheld 200 That very priest who, as she wished

The Tale of Florent

Book I

Genius My sone, and I thee rede this:
What so befalle of other weye,
That thou to loves heste obeye
Als ferr as thou it might suffise.
1400 For ofte sithe, in such a wise,
Obedience in love availeth
Wher al a mannes strengthe faileth.
Wherof, if that thee list to wite,
In a Cronique, as it is write,
1405 A gret ensample thou might finde
Which now is come to my minde.
Ther was whilom be dayes olde
A worthy knight, and as men tolde
He was nevoeu to th'emperour
1410 And of his court a courteour.
Wifles he was, Florent he highte;
He was a man that mochel mighte;
Of armes he was desirous,
Chivalerous, and amorous.
1415 And for the fame of worldes speche,
Strange aventures forto seche
He rod the Marches al aboute.

1396 *and* (refers syntactically to the preceding conversation, omitted here); *rede,* advise
1397 Whatever happens in other ways 1398 *heste,* behest, command
1399 As far as may be necessary for you 1400 *ofte sithe,* often; *wise,* manner
1403 *thee list to wite,* you wish to learn 1404 As it is written in a Chronicle
1405 *ensample,* example 1407 *whilom be,* once in 1409 *nevoeu,* nephew
1411 *Wifles,* Without a wife; *highte,* was called
1412 *mochel mighte,* might do much 1413 *desirous,* fond
1415 And for fame throughout the world
1417 *rod,* rode through; *Marches,* border territories

And fell a time as he was oute,
Fortune, which may every thred
1420 Tobreke and knette of mannes sped,
Shop, as this knight rod in a pas,
That he be strengthe take was;
And to a castell they him ladde
Wher that he fewe frendes hadde.
1425 For so it fell that ilke stounde
That he hath with a dedly wounde,
Feightende his oghne hondes, slain
Branchus, which to the capitain
Was sone and heir, wherof ben wrothe
1430 The fader and the moder bothe.
That knight Branchus was of his hond
The worthieste of al his lond,
And fain they wolden do vengance
Upon Florent, bot remembrance
1435 That they toke of his worthinesse
Of knighthod and of gentilesse,
And how he stod of cousinage
To th'emperour, made hem assuage
And dorsten noght slen him for fere;
1440 In gret desputeisoun they were
Among hemself, what was the beste.
Ther was a lady, the slygheste
Of alle that men knewe tho,
So old she mighte unethes go,
1445 And was grantdame unto the dede;

1418 *fell a time,* it happened 1419 *Fortune,* (that) Fortune
1420 Break and fasten together of man's prosperity
1421 *Shop,* Arranged; *pas,* pass 1422 That he was taken by force
1423 *ladde,* led 1425 *fell,* happened; *ilke stounde,* same occasion
1427 Fighting (with) his own hands, slain 1429 *wrothe,* angry
1431 *of his hond,* in his actions 1433 *fain,* willingly
1436 *gentilesse,* good breeding 1437 *cousinage,* kinship
1439 *dorsten,* durst; *slen,* slay; *fere,* fear 1440 *desputeisoun,* disputation
1441 Among themselves (about) what was the best (to do)
1442 *slygheste,* slyest 1443 *tho,* then 1444 *unethes go,* hardly walk
1445 *grantdame,* grandmother; *dede,* dead (man)

And she with that began to rede
And seide how she wol bringe him inne,
That she shal him to dethe winne
Al only of his oghne grant
1450 Thurgh strengthe of verray covenant,
Withoute blame of eny wight.
Anon she sende for this knight,
And of hire sone she alleide
The deth, and thus to him she seide:
1455 "Florent, how so thou be to wite
Of Branchus deth, men shal respite
As now to take vengement,
Be so thou stonde in juggement
Upon certein condicioun:
1460 That thou unto a questioun
Which I shal axe shalt answere;
And over this thou shalt ek swere
That if thou of the sothe faile
Ther shal non other thing availe
1465 That thou ne shalt thy deth receive.
And for men shal thee noght deceive,
That thou therof might ben avised,
Thou shalt have day and time assised
And leve saufly forto wende,
1470 Be so that at thy dayes ende
Thou come ayein with thin avis.
This knight, which worthy was and wis,

1446 *rede,* give counsel 1447 *bringe him inne,* catch him 1448 *winne,* bring
1449 Entirely through his own consent 1450 *verray,* true (*i.e.,* properly legal)
1452 *Anon,* Immediately; *sende,* sent 1453 *sone,* (grand)son; *alleide,* alleged
1455 *how so,* although; *to wite,* to blame 1456 *respite,* delay
1457 *As now,* For now; *vengement,* revenge 1458 *Be so,* So long as
1461 *axe,* ask 1462 *over,* beyond; *ek,* also 1463 *sothe,* true answer
1464–65 Nothing shall avail to save you from death. 1466 *for,* in order that
1467 *ben avised,* beware 1468 *assised,* appointed
1469 And permission to go in safety
1470 *Be so that,* So long as; *dayes ende,* end of your appointed time
1471 *avis,* opinion (as to the answer of the question)
1472 *worthy,* honorable; *wis,* prudent

This lady preyth that he may wite,
And have it under seales write,
1475 What questioun it sholde be
For which he shal in that degree
Stonde of his lif in jeupartye.
With that she feigneth compaignye
And seyth: "Florent, on love it hongeth,
1480 Al that to min axinge longeth:
What alle wommen most desire —
This wole I axe, and in th'empire
Wheras thou has most knowlechinge,
Tak conseil upon this axinge."
1485 Florent this thing hath undertake;
The day was set, the time take.
Under his seal he wrote his oth
In such a wise, and forth he goth
Hom to his emes court ayein,
1490 To whom his aventure plein
He tolde, of that him is befalle.
And upon that they weren alle,
The wiseste of the lond, asent;
Bot natheles of on assent
1495 They mighte noght acorde plat —
On seide this, anothre that.
After the disposicioun
Of naturel complexioun,
To som womman it is plesance

1473 *preyth,* requests; *wite,* know
1474 *under seales write,* written under seals, *i.e.,* a legally notarized document
1476 *in that degree,* according to that condition
1477 Stand in jeopardy of his life 1478 *compaignye,* friendliness
1479 *on love it hongeth,* it has to do with love
1480 *min axinge longeth,* concerns my question 1482 *th'empire,* the kingdom
1483 *knowlechinge,* recognition, praise 1486 *take,* noted 1488 *wise,* manner
1489 *emes,* uncle's; *ayein,* again 1490 *aventure,* marvel, chance
1493 *asent,* sent for 1494 *natheles,* nevertheless; *on,* one
1495 *acorde plat,* agree plainly 1496 *On,* One
1497–98 According to the disposition of bodily humors (*complexioun*) established by nature

1500 That to anothre is grevance;
Bot such a thing in special,
Which to hem alle in general
Is most plesant and most desired
Above alle othre and most conspired,
1505 Such o thing conne they noght finde
Be constellacion ne kinde.
And thus Florent withoute cure
Mot stonde upon his aventure,
And is al shape unto the lere
1510 As in defalte of his answere.
This knight hath levere forto die
Than breke his trowthe and forto lie
In place ther as he was swore,
And shapth him gon ayein therfore.
1515 Whan time cam he tok his leve,
That lengere wolde he noght beleve,
And preyth his em he be noght wroth,
For that is a point of his oth,
He seyth, that no man shal him wreke,
1520 Thogh afterward men hiere speke
That he par aventure deye.
And thus he wente forth his weye
Alone, as knight aventurous,
And in his thoght was curious
1525 To wite what was best to do.
And as he rod al one so
And cam nigh ther he wolde be,
In a forest under a tre

1501 *in special,* in particular 1502 *hem,* them 1504 *conspired,* agreed upon
1505 *o,* one 1506 By position of the stars or by natural signs
1507 *cure,* remedy
1508–9 Must accept his chance, and is all prepared to take the loss
1511 *levere forto,* rather 1512 *trowthe,* pledge
1514 And therefore prepared to return again 1516 *beleve,* remain
1517 *em,* uncle 1519 *wreke,* avenge 1520 *hiere speke,* hear (it) said
1521 That he die through mischance 1525 *wite,* know
1526 *al one so,* thus alone 1527 And came close to where he wished to be

He sigh wher sat a creature,
1530 A lothly wommannish figure,
That forto speke of fleisch and bon
So foul yit sigh he nevere non.
This knight behield hir redely,
And as he wolde have passed by
1535 She cleped him and bad abide;
And he his horse heved aside
Tho torneth, and to hire he rod,
And ther he hoveth and abod
To wite what she wolde mene.
1540 And she began him to bemene,
And seide: "Florent be thy name.
Thou hast on honde such a game
That, bot thou be the betre avised,
Thy deth is shapen and devised
1545 That al the world ne may thee save,
Bot if that thou my conseil have."
Florent, whan he this tale herde,
Unto this olde wight answerde,
And of hir conseil he hir preyde.
1550 And she ayein to him thus seide,
"Florent, if I for thee so shape
That thou thurgh me thy deth ascape
And take worshipe of thy dede,
What shal I have to my mede?"
1555 "What thing," quod he, "that thou wolt axe."
"I bidde nevere a betre taxe,"

1529 *sigh,* saw 1531 That, speaking of flesh and bone
1532 *sigh,* saw; *non,* no one 1533 *redely,* quickly
1535 *cleped,* called to; *bad abide,* bade him stay 1536 *horse heved,* horse's head
1537 *Tho,* Then 1538 *hoveth,* stopped; *abod,* stayed
1539 *wite,* know; *wolde mene,* intended 1540 *him to bemene,* to speak to him
1541 And said: "Your name is Florent."
1542 *on honde,* in hand; *game,* contest
1543 *bot,* unless; *betre avised,* better counseled 1544 *shapen,* arranged
1546 *Bot if,* Unless 1551 *shape,* arrange (matters)
1553 And receive honor for your deed 1554 *to my mede,* as my reward
1555 *What thing,* Whatsoever thing 1556 I ask no better arrangement.

Quod she, "Bot ferst, er thou be sped,
Thou shalt me leve such a wedd,
That I wol have thy trowthe in honde
1560 That thou shalt be min housebonde."
"Nay," seyth Florent, "that may noght be."
"Rid thanne forth thy wey," quod she,
"And if thou go withoute red,
Thou shalt be sekerliche ded."
1565 Florent behighte hire good inough
Of londe, of rente, of park, of plough,
Bot al that compteth she at noght.
Tho fell this knight in mochel thoght:
Now goth he forth, now comth ayein —
1570 He wot noght what is best to seyn;
And thoghte, as he rod to and fro,
That chese he mot on of the two;
Or forto take hire to his wif
Or elles forto lese his lif.
1575 And thanne he caste his avantage,
That she was of so gret an age
That she may live bot a while,
And thoghte put hire in an ile
Wher that no man hire sholde knowe
1580 Til she with deth were overthrowe.
And thus this yonge lusty knight
Unto this olde lothly wight
Tho seide: "If that non other chance
May make my deliverance,

1557 *sped,* helped 1558 *leve,* grant, leave; *wedd,* pledge
1559 *trowthe in honde,* word in hand 1563 *red,* counsel
1564 *sekerliche,* certainly 1565 *behighte,* promised; *good,* wealth
1566 *rente,* income from property; *park,* enclosed woodland; *plough,* plowed land
1567 *compteth,* accounts 1570 *wot,* knows; *seyn,* say
1572 *chese,* choose; *mot,* must; *on,* one 1573 *Or,* Either; *to,* as 1574 *lese,* lose
1575 *caste his avantage,* figured his advantage
1578 *thoghte put,* thought of putting; *ile,* island
1584 *make,* accomplish

1585 Bot only thilke same speche
Which, as thou seyst, thou shalt me teche,
Have hier min hond – I shal thee wedde."
And thus his trowthe he leyth to wedde.
With that she frounceth up the browe:
1590 "This covenant I wol allowe,"
She seyth; "if eny other thing
Bot that thou hast of my teching
Fro deth thy body may respite,
I woll thee of thy trowthe acquite,
1595 And elles be non other weye.
Now herkne me what I shal seye:
Whan thou art come into the place
Wher now they maken gret manace
And upon thy cominge abide,
1600 They wole anon the same tide
Oppose thee of thin answere.
I wot thou wolt nothing forbere
Of that thou wenest be thy beste;
And if thou might so finde reste,
1605 Wel is, for thanne is ther nomore.
And elles this shal be my lore:
That thou shalt seye upon this molde
That alle wommen lievest wolde
Be soverein of mannes love;
1610 For what womman is so above,
She hath, as who seyth, al hire wille,
And elles may she noght fulfille

1585 *thilke,* this same 1588 *leyth to wedde,* puts in pledge
1589 *frounceth,* wrinkles 1592 *that,* that (which)
1595 *elles,* otherwise; *be,* by 1598 *manace,* threatening
1600 *anon,* straightway; *tide,* time 1601 *Oppose,* Ask
1602 *wot,* know; *forbere,* leave out
1603–5 Of that (which) you think (to) be your best (answers); and if you might thus find relief, so much the better, for then is there no more (to pay).
1606 *elles,* otherwise; *lore,* advice 1607 *molde,* earth
1608 *lievest wolde,* above everything else want to (be)
1610 *what,* whatever; *so,* thus 1611 *as who seyth,* as they say

What thing hir were lievest have.
With this answere thou shalt save
1615 Thyself, and otherwise noght.
And whan thou hast thin ende wroght,
Com hier ayein — thou shalt me finde;
And let nothing out of thy minde."
He goth him forth with hevy chiere,
1620 As he that not in what manere
He may this worldes joye atteigne:
For if he deie, he hath a peine,
And if he live, he mot him binde
To such on which of alle kinde
1625 Of wommen is th'unsemilieste.
Thus wot he noght what is the beste.
Bot be him lief or be him loth,
Unto the castell forth he goth
His full answere forto yive,
1630 Or forto deie or forto live.
Forth with his conseil cam the lord;
The thinges stoden of record;
He sende up for the lady sone,
And forth she cam, that olde mone.
1635 In presence of the remenant
The strengthe of al the covenant
Tho was reherced openly,
And to Florent she bad forthy
That he shal tellen his avis,
1640 As he that woot what is the pris.

1613 Whatever thing she wishes most to have
1616 *thin ende wroght,* accomplished your purpose
1618 And don't forget anything 1619 *chiere,* expression, heart
1620 *not,* knows not 1623 *mot,* must 1624 *on,* a one; *kinde,* race
1625 *th'unsemilieste,* the most unattractive 1627 But like it or not
1629 *yive,* give 1630 *Or,* Either 1631 *conseil,* council
1632 *thinges,* matters; *stoden,* stood 1633 *sone,* quickly 1634 *mone,* crone
1635 *remenant,* rest (of them) 1636 *strengthe,* legal authority
1638 *forthy,* therefore 1639 *avis,* opinion 1640 *woot,* knows; *pris,* prize

Florent seyth al that evere he couthe,
Bot such word cam ther non to mouthe
That he for yifte or for beheste
Mighte eny wise his deth areste.
1645 And thus he taryeth longe and late
Til that this lady bad algate
That he shal for the dom final
Yif his answere in special
Of that she hadde him ferst opposed.
1650 And thanne he hath trewly supposed
That he him may of nothing yelpe
Bot if so be tho wordes helpe,
Whiche as the womman hath him taught,
Wherof he hath an hope caught
1655 That he shal be excused so,
And tolde out plein his wille tho.
And whan that this matrone herde
The manere how this knight answerde,
She seide: "Ha! treson! wo thee be
1660 That hast thus told the privite
Which alle wommen most desire!
I wolde that thou were afire!"
Bot natheles in such a plit
Florent of his answere is quit.
1665 And tho began his sorwe newe,
For he mot gon, or ben untrewe,
To hire which his trowthe hadde.
Bot he, which alle shame dradde,

1641 *couthe,* knew 1643 *yifte,* gift; *beheste,* promise 1644 *areste,* hold back
1645 And thus he delays for a long time
1646 *bad algate,* commanded in any case 1647 *dom,* judgment
1648 *in special,* in particular
1649 To that (question which) she had first posed to him
1650 *supposed,* believed 1651 *yelpe,* boast 1652 *Bot if so be,* Unless; *tho,* those
1654 *hath an hope caught,* took hope 1655 *excused so,* let off thus
1656 *wille,* pleasure 1659 *Wo thee be,* Woe to you 1660 *privite,* secret
1663 *plit,* manner 1665 *sorwe,* sorrow; *newe,* anew
1667 *trowthe,* troth, oath 1668 *which,* who; *dradde,* dreaded

Goth forth in stede of his penance,
1670 And takth the fortune of his chance
As he that was with trowthe affaited.
  This olde wight him hath awaited
In place wher as he hire lefte;
Florent his wofull heved uplefte
1675 And sigh this vecke where she sat,
Which was the lothlieste what
That evere man caste on his ighe:
Hire nase bass, hire browes highe,
Hire ighen smale and depe set;
1680 Hire chekes ben with teres wet
And rivelen as an emty skin,
Hangende down unto the chin;
Hire lippes shrunken ben for age —
Ther was no grace in the visage;
1685 Hir front was nargh, hir lockes hore —
She loketh forth as doth a More;
Hire necke is short, hir shuldres courbe,
That mighte a mannes lust destourbe;
Hire body gret and nothing smal —
1690 And shortly to descrive hire al,
She hath no lith withoute a lak.
Bot, lich unto the wollesak,
She proferth hire unto this knight
And bad him, as he hath behight,

1669 *in stede of,* into the place of
1671 *with trowthe affaited,* bound to an oath
1674 *heved uplefte,* head uplifted 1675 *sigh,* saw; *vecke,* hag
1676 *what,* thing 1677 *Caste on his ighe,* Cast his eye upon
1678 *nase bass,* flat nose 1679 *ighen,* eyes; *depe,* deep 1680 *ben,* were
1681 *rivelen,* wrinkled; *skin,* wine skin
1685 Her forehead was narrow, her locks hoar.
1686 She keeps watch like a Moor. 1687 *courbe,* bent
1688 (In a way) that might dampen a man's ardor
1689 *gret,* large; *and nothing small,* and not at all small (a tag)
1690 And briefly to describe her altogether 1691 *lith,* limb; *lak,* fault
1692 But (shaped) like a sack of wool 1693 *proferth hire,* offers herself
1694 *behight,* promised

1695 So as she hath ben his warant,
That he hire holde covenant,
And be the bridel she him seseth.
Bot Godd wot how that she him pleseth
Of suche wordes as she spekth!
1700 Him thenkth wel nigh his herte brekth
For sorwe that he may noght fle,
Bot if he wolde untrewe be.
Loke how a sek man for his hele
Takth baldemoine with canele,
1705 And with the myrre takth the sucre,
Right upon such a maner lucre
Stant Florent, as in this diete:
He drinkth the bitre with the swete,
He medleth sorwe with likinge,
1710 And liveth, as who seyth, deyinge.
His youthe shal be cast aweye
Upon such on which, as the weye,
Is old and lothly overal.
Bot nede he mot that nede shal.
1715 He wolde algate his trowthe holde
As every knight therto is holde,
What happ so evere him is befalle.
Thogh she be the fouleste of alle,
Yit to th'onour of wommanhiede

[1695] *So as,* So (long) as, since; *warant,* protector, security
[1696] That he hold his agreement with her [1697] *be,* by; *seseth,* seizes
[1698] *wot,* knows [1699] *Of,* With; *spekth,* speaks
[1700] It seems to him that his heart almost breaks.
[1702] Unless he were willing to be untrue (to his oath)
[1703–5] Look how a sick man for his health takes gentian (*baldemoine*) with cinnamon (*canele*), and with the myrrh takes the sugar (*i.e.,* sweetens a bitter medicine).
[1706] In just such a kind of advantage [1707] *Stant,* Stands
[1709] *medleth,* mixes; *likinge,* pleasure
[1710] *as who seyth,* so to speak; *deyinge,* dying
[1712] Upon such a one that, like the whey [1713] *lothly,* ugly
[1714] But needs he must whom necessity compels [1715] *algate,* in any event
[1716] *holde,* held, faithful [1717] *happ,* chance
[1719] *th'onour,* the honor; *wommanhiede,* womankind

1720 Him thoghte he sholde taken hied;
So that for pure gentilesse,
As he hire couthe best adresce,
In ragges as she was totore,
He set hire on his hors tofore,
1725 And forth he takth his weye softe —
No wonder thogh he siketh ofte.
Bot as an owle fleth be night
Out of alle othre briddes sighte,
Right so this knight on dayes brode
1730 In clos him hield and shop his rode
On nightes time, til the tide
That he cam there he wolde abide.
And prively withoute noise
He bringth this foule grete coise
1735 To his castell in such a wise
That no man mighte hire shappe avise
Til she into the chambre cam,
Wher he his prive conseil nam
Of suche men as he most troste,
1740 And tolde hem that he nedes moste
This beste wedde to his wif,
For elles hadde he lost his lif.
The prive wommen were asent,
That sholden ben of his assent.
1745 Hire ragges they anon off drawe

1720 It seemed to him he should take heed. 1721 *gentilesse,* knightly breeding
1722–23 Arranging her as best he could — seeing that she was in tattered rags
1724 *tofore,* before him 1725 *softe,* at a slow pace 1726 *siketh,* sighs
1727 *fleth be,* flies by 1728 Out of sight of all other birds
1729 *on dayes brode,* in broad daylight
1730 Kept himself concealed and arranged his journey 1731 *tide,* time
1732 *cam there,* came to where 1733 *prively,* privately
1734 *foule grete coise,* great ugly monster 1735 *wise,* manner
1736 *hire shappe avise,* see her appearance
1738 (and 1743) *prive,* private; *nam,* took 1739 *troste,* trusted
1740 *hem,* them; *nedes moste,* must needs (*i.e.,* is obliged to) 1741 *beste,* beast
1743 *asent,* sent for 1744 *sholden,* should; *assent,* will, accord
1745 *anon,* quickly

And, as it was that time lawe,
She hadde bath, she hadde reste,
And was arrayed to the beste.
Bot with no craft of combes brode
1750 They mighte hire hore lockes shode,
And she ne wolde noght be shore
For no conseil, and they therfore,
With such atir as tho was used,
Ordeinen that it was excused,
1755 And hid so crafteliche aboute,
That no man mighte sen hem oute.
Bot when she was fulliche arrayed
And hire atir was al assayed,
Tho was she foulere on to see,
1760 Bot yit it may non other be —
They were wedded in the night.
So wo begon was nevere knight
As he was thanne of mariage.
And she began to pleye and rage,
1765 As who seyth, I am wel inough;
Bot he therof nothing ne lough,
For she tok thanne chiere on honde
And clepeth him hire housebonde,
And seyth, "My lord, go we to bedde,
1770 For I to that entente wedde,
That thou shalt be my worldes blisse,"

1746 *that time lawe,* the law (or custom) at that time
1748 *to the beste,* as well as possible
1749–50 But with no art of broad combs were they able to separate her hoary locks.
1751 *shore,* shorn 1752 *For no conseil,* In spite of any advice
1753 *atir,* attire; *tho,* then 1754 Decided that it (combing) was (to be) omitted
1755 *hid,* concealed (the hairs) 1756 *sen hem oute,* see them (sticking) out
1757 *fulliche,* fully 1758 *assayed,* assessed
1760 But yet there was nothing else to be done 1763 *thanne,* then
1764 *rage,* make sport 1765 Like (one) who says, "I am well enough off."
1766 *nothing ne lough,* didn't laugh at all 1767 For she then began to be merry
1768 *clepeth,* called 1769 *go we,* let's go
1770 Because I married for that purpose 1771 *worldes,* world's

And profreth him with that to kisse,
As she a lusty lady were.
His body mighte wel be there,
1775 Bot as of thoght and of memoire
His herte was in purgatoire.
Bot yit for strengthe of matrimoine
He mighte make non essoine
That he ne mot algates plye
1780 To gon to bedde of compaignye.
And whan they were abedde naked,
Withoute slep he was awaked:
He torneth on that other side
For that he wolde hise yghen hide
1785 Fro lokinge on the fole wight—
The chambre was al full of light,
The courtins were of cendal thinne.
This newe brid which lay withinne,
Thogh it be noght with his acord,
1790 In armes she beclipte hire lord
And preyde, as he was torned fro,
He wolde him torne ayeinward tho,
"For now," she seyth, "we ben bothe on."
And he lay stille as eny ston,
1795 Bot evere in on she spak and preyde,
And bad him thenke on that he seide
Whan that he tok hire be the hond.
He herde and understod the bond,
How he was set to his penance,
1800 And as it were a man in trance

1772 And with that offers to kiss him 1773 *As,* As though; *lusty,* handsome
1775 But as for imagination and memory 1776 *purgatoire,* purgatory
1777 But yet, on account of the legal rights of matrimony 1778 *essoine,* excuse
1779 But that he must in any case comply 1780 *of compaignye,* for company
1782 *awaked,* kept awake 1783 *torneth,* turns 1784 *yghen,* eyes
1785 *fole,* foul 1787 *cendal,* sendal, silk 1788 *brid,* bride
1790 *beclipte,* embraced 1791 *fro,* away 1792 *ayeinward,* toward her
1793 *on,* one 1794 *ston,* stone 1795 *evere in on,* incessantly
1796 And bade him remember what he said 1800 *as it,* as though he

He torneth him al sodeinly —
And sigh a lady lay him by
Of eightetiene winter age,
Which was the faireste of visage
1805 That evere in al this world he sigh.
And as he wolde have take hire nigh,
She put hire hand and be his leve
Besoghte him that he wolde leve,
And seyth that forto winne or lese
1810 He mot on of two thinges chese:
Wher he wol have hire such on night,
Or elles upon dayes light,
For he shal noght have bothe two.
And he began to sorwe tho
1815 In many a wise, and caste his thoght,
Bot for al that yit couthe he noght
Devise himself which was the beste.
And she that wolde his hertes reste
Preyth that he sholde chese algate,
1820 Til ate laste, longe and late,
He seide: "O ye, my lives hele,
Sey what you list in my querele;
I not what answere I shal yive,
Bot evere whil that I may live
1825 I wol that ye be my maistresse,
For I can noght myselve gesse
Which is the beste unto my chois.

1801 *sodeinly,* suddenly 1802, 1805 *sigh,* saw 1803 Eighteen years old
1806 And as he was about to pull her close 1807 *be,* by; *leve,* leave
1808 *Besoghte,* Besought; *leve,* desist 1809 *lese,* lose
1810 *on,* one; *chese,* choose
1811 *Wher,* Whether; *such on night,* such (a beautiful girl) at night
1812 *upon,* during 1814 *to sorwe tho,* to sorrow then
1815 And cast his thoughts in many directions 1816 *couthe,* could
1817 *Devise himself,* Determine 1818 And she who wished for his heart's ease
1819 *algate,* in any event 1820 *longe and late,* after delaying
1821 *lives hele,* life's health 1822 *Sey,* Say; *list,* please; *querele,* case
1823 *not,* know not; *yive,* give 1825 *wol,* will

Thus grante I you min hole vois:
Ches for ous bothen, I you preye,
1830 And what as evere that ye seye,
Right as ye wole, so wol I."
"My lord," she seide, "grant mercy.
For of this word that ye now seyn,
That ye have mad me soverein,
1835 My destine is overpassed,
That nevere hierafter shal be lassed
My beaute, which that I now have,
Til I be take into my grave.
Bot night and day as I am now
1840 I shal alwey be such to you.
The kinges doughter of Cizile
I am, and fell bot sithe awhile,
As I was with my fader late,
That my stepmoder, for an hate
1845 Which toward me she hath begonne,
Forshop me til I hadde wonne
The love and sovereinete
Of what knight that in his degre
Alle othre passeth of good name;
1850 And as men seyn ye ben the same —
The dede proeveth it is so —
Thus am I youres evermo."
Tho was plesance and joye inough;
Echon with other pleyde and lough.
1855 They live longe and wel they ferde,

1828 *min hole vois,* my whole voice (in a legal sense)
1829 *Ches,* Choose; *ous,* us 1830 *what as evere,* whatever 1831 *wole,* will
1832 *grant mercy,* thank you 1833 *of,* by means of 1835 *overpassed,* fulfilled
1836 *That,* (With the result) that; *lassed,* lost
1841–42 I am the daughter of the King of Sicily, and it happened a little while ago.
1843 *late,* lately 1846 *Forshop,* Transformed; *til,* until the time that
1848 *what,* whatever; *degre,* manner 1850 *the same,* the very one
1851 *dede,* deed 1853 *inough,* enough
1854 *Echon,* Each one; *lough,* laughed
1855 *live,* lived; *ferde,* fared

And clerkes that this chance herde
They writen it in evidence
To teche how that obedience
May wel fortune a man to love
1860 And sette him in his lust above,
As it befell unto this knight.
Forthy, my sone, if thou do right
Thou shalt unto thy love obeye
And folwe hir will be alle weye.
Lover Min holy fader, so I wile;
For ye have told me such a skile
Of this ensample now tofore,
That I shal evermo therfore
Hierafterward min observance
1870 To love and to his obeissance
The betre kepe.

1856 *chance,* adventure 1859 *fortune,* ordain 1860 *lust,* joy
1862 *Forthy,* Therefore; *sone,* son 1864 And follow her will in everything
1866 *skile,* reasonable (story) 1867 *Of,* Through; *now tofore,* just now
1870 *to his obeissance,* obedience to him

24 (*Ca. 1490?*)

THE TESTAMENT OF CRESSEID

Robert Henryson
(fl. 1460–1505)

Ane doolye sessoun to ane cairfull dite
Suld correspond and be equivalent.
Richt sa it wes when I began to write
This tragedye — the wedder richt fervent,
5 When Aries in middis of the Lent
Shouris of haill can fra the North discend,
That scantlye fra the cauld I micht defend.

Yit nevertheles within mine oratur
I stude when Titan had his bemis bricht
10 Withdrawin down and silit under cure,
And fair Venus, the beutye of the nicht,
Uprais and set unto the West full richt
Hir goldin face, in oppositioun
Of God Phebus direct discending down.

15 Throwout the glas hir bemis brast sa fair

(24) 1 A doleful season to a sorrowful poem 2 *Suld,* Should
3 *sa,* so; *wes,* was 4 *wedder richt fervent,* weather very bitter
5–7 When Aries (the constellation of the Ram), in the middle of Lent, caused (*can*) showers of hail to blow in out of the North so that scarcely might I protect myself from the cold (The astrological details suggest April 11.)
8 *oratur,* private chapel
9 *stude,* stood; *Titan,* the Sun; *bemis bricht,* bright beams
10 *silit under cure,* hidden under cover
11 *Venus,* the planet that appears as the evening star; *nicht,* night
12 *Uprais,* Rose up; *full richt,* very plainly
14 *Phebus,* Phoebus Apollo, god of the Sun (Astronomically, Venus and the sun are never in opposition, east to west. *Oppositioun* should be understood generally as a contrast between the setting of one and the rising of the other.)
15 *glas,* window glass; *brast sa,* burst so

That I micht se on everye side me by
That northin wind had purifyit the air
And shed the mistye cloudis fra the sky;
The froist freisit, the blastis bitterly
20 Fra Pole Artick come whisling loud and shill,
And causit me remufe aganis my will.

For I traistit that Venus, Luifis Quene,
To whome sumtime I hecht obedience,
My faidit hart of lufe sho wald mak grene;
25 And therupon with humbill reverence
I thocht to pray hir hie magnificence,
Bot for greit cald as than I lattit was,
And in my chalmer to the fire can pas.

Thocht lufe be hait, yit in ane man of age
30 It kendillis nocht sa sone as in youtheid,
Of whome the blude is flowing in ane rage,
And in the auld the curage doif and deid –
Of whilk the fire outward is best remeid;
To help be phisike whair that nature faillit
35 I am expert, for baith I have assailit.

I mend the fire and beikit me about,
Than tuik ane drink my spreitis to comfort,

16 *micht se,* might see; *me by,* around me 18 *shed,* driven; *fra,* from
19 *froist freisit,* frost froze 20 *shill,* shrill 21 *remufe,* withdraw
22 *traistit,* hoped; *Luifis,* Love's 23 *sumtime,* at one time; *hecht,* vowed
24 She would make my faded heart green with love.
26 *thocht,* thought; *hir hie,* her high
27 But because of the great cold I was prevented at that time.
28 *in,* into; *chalmer,* chamber; *can,* did 29 *Thocht,* Though; *hait,* hot
30 It kindles not so soon as in youth. 31 *blude,* blood; *rage,* passion
32 And in the old, the spirits (are) dull and dead
33 *Of whilk,* For whom; *outward,* exterior, *i.e.,* in the fireplace; *remeid,* remedy
34 *be phisike,* by medical prescription; *faillit,* fails 35 *baith,* both; *assailit,* tried
36 *mend,* poked up; *beikit,* warmed
37 *tuik,* took; *spreitis,* spirits

And armit me weill fra the cauld thairout.
To cut the winter nicht and mak it short
40 I tuik ane quair — and left all uther sport —
Writtin be worthye Chaucer glorious
Of fair Creisseid and worthye Troylus.

And thair I fand, efter that Diomeid
Ressavit had that Lady bricht of hew,
45 How Troylus neir out of wit abraid
And weipit soir with visage paill of hew,
For whilk wanhope his teiris can renew,
Whill Esperus rejoisit him agane:
Thus while in joy he levit, while in pane.

50 Of hir behest he had greit comforting,
Traisting to Troy that sho suld mak retour,
Whilk he desirit maist of eirdly thing
Forwhy sho was his only paramour.
Bot when he saw passit baith day and hour
55 Of hir ganecome, than sorrow can oppres
His wofull hart in cair and hevines.

Of his distres me neidis nocht reheirs,
For worthye Chauceir in the samin buik

38 *armit me weill,* protected myself well
40 *quair,* book; *uther sport,* other pastimes 41 *be,* by
43 *fand,* found; *efter,* after
44 *Ressavit had,* Had received; *bricht of hew,* bright of hue
45 *neir,* nearly; *abraid,* started 46 *weipit soir,* wept bitterly
47 *whilk wanhope,* which despair; *teiris can,* tears did
48 Until Hope cheered him up again (For a discussion of Esperus as both Hope and the Evening Star see Charles Elliott, "Two Notes on Henryson's 'Testament of Cresseid,'" *JEGP,* LIV (April, 1955), 241–47.)
49 *while,* for a while; *levit,* lived; *pane,* pain
50 He took great comfort from her promise.
51 *Traisting,* Trusting; *mak retour,* return
52 *Whilk,* Which; *maist,* most; *eirdly,* earthly
53 *Forwhy sho,* Because she; *paramour,* mistress 54 *passit,* pass
55 *ganecome,* return; *than,* then; *can,* did
57 I do not need to rehearse his distress. 58 *samin buik,* same book

In gudelye termis and in joly veirs
60 Compilit hes his cairis, wha will luik.
To brek my sleip ane uther quair I tuik,
In whilk I fand the fatall destenye
Of fair Cresseid, that endit wretchitlye.

Wha wait gif all that Chauceir wrait was trew?
65 Nor I wait nocht gif this narratioun
Be authoreist, or fenyeit of the new
Be sum poeit throw his inventioun,
Maid to report the lamentatioun
And wofull end of this lustye Creisseid,
70 And what distres sho thoillit, and what deid.

When Diomeid had all his appetite –
And mair – fulfillit of this fair Ladye,
Upon ane uther he set his haill delite,
And send to hir ane Libell of Repudye,
75 And hir excludit fra his companye.
Than desolait sho walkit up and down,
And sum men sayis, into the Court Commoun.

O fair Creisseid, the flour and *A per se*
Of Troy and Grece, how was thou fortunait!
80 To change in filth all thy feminitye

59 *gudelye,* goodly; *veirs,* verse
60 Has compiled his cares for whoever wants to look
61 *brek,* break; *quair,* book (This second book is not known and may be simply a fictitious source.)
62 *fand,* found 63 *that endit,* who ended
64 *Wha wait gif,* Who knows whether; *wrait,* wrote
65 *wait nocht,* knows not 66 Be authoritative, or made up new
67 *Be,* By; *throw,* through 69 *lustye,* lively, merry, beautiful
70 *sho thoillit,* she suffered; *what deid,* what sort of death
72 *mair,* more; *of,* on 73 *uther,* other (lady); *haill,* whole
74 *hir,* her (Cresseid); *Libell of Repudye,* Bill of Divorce 76 *sho,* she
77 *into the Court Commoun,* became a prostitute – a common (available to all) courtesan
78 *flour,* flower; *A per se,* peerless one 79 *fortunait,* treated by fortune
80 *in,* into

And be with fleshelye lust sa maculait,
And go amang the Greikis air and lait
Sa giglotlike, takand thy foull plesance!
I have pietye thou suld fall sic mischance.

85 Yit nevertheless whatever men deme or say
In scornefull langage of thy brukkilnes,
I sall excuse, als far furth as I may,
Thy womanheid, thy wisdome and fairnes,
The whilk Fortoun hes put to sic distres
90 As hir pleisit, and nathing throw the gilt
Of thee, throw wickit langage to be spilt.

This fair Lady, in this wise destitute
Of all comfort and consolatioun,
Richt privelye but fellowship, on fute,
95 Disagisit, passit far out of the town
Ane mile or twa, unto ane mansioun
Beildit full gay, whair hir father Calchas
Whilk than amang the Greikis dwelland was.

When he hir saw, the caus he can inquire
100 Of hir cumming. Sho said, siching full soir:
"Fra Diomeid had gottin his desire,
He wox werye and wald of me no moir."

81 *maculait,* spotted 82 *Greikis air and lait,* Greeks early and late
83 *giglotlike,* wantonly; *takand,* taking; *plesance,* pleasure
84 *pietye,* pity; *fall,* receive; *sic,* such 85 *deme,* judge 86 *brukkilnes,* frailty
87 *excuse,* defend; *als far furth,* as far 88 *womanheid,* womanhood
89 *The whilk,* Which (Charteris, *quhik*); *hes,* has; *sic,* such
90 As pleased her, and not at all through the guilt
91 *wickit langage,* slanderous tongues; *spilt,* ruined 92 *wise,* manner
94 Very secretly, without companions, on foot
95 *Disagisit,* Disguised; *passit,* travelled 96 *twa,* two; *mansioun,* house
97 *Beildit full gay,* Decorated very handsomely
98 *Whilk,* Who; *dwelland,* dwelling 99 *can,* did
100 *cumming,* coming; *siching full soir,* sighing very sorrowfully
101 *Fra,* From the time that
102 He grew tired of me and wanted nothing more to do with me.

Quod Calchas, "Douchter, weip thou not thairfoir;
Peraventure all cummis for the best.
105 Welcum to me! Thou art full deir ane gest."

This auld Calchas, efter the law was tho,
Wes keiper of the Tempill, as ane Preist,
In whilk Venus and hir sone Cupido
War honourit; and his chalmer was thame neist,
110 To whilk Cresseid, with baill aneuch in breist,
Usit to pas, hir prayeris forto say.
Whill at the last, upon ane solempne day,

As custome was, the pepill far and neir,
Befoir the none unto the Tempill went
115 With sacrifice, devoit in thair maneir.
Bot still Cresseid, hevye in hir intent,
Into the Kirk wald not hirself present,
For giving of the pepill ony deming
Of hir expuls fra Diomeid the King,

120 Bot past into ane secreit orature
Whair sho micht weip hir wofull desteny.
Behind hir bak sho cloisit fast the dure
And on hir kneis bair fell down in hy;
Upon Venus and Cupide angerly

103 *Quod,* Said; *Douchter,* Daughter; *weip,* weep 104 *Peraventure,* Perhaps
105 *gest,* guest 106 *auld,* old; *efter,* as; *tho,* then 107 *Wes keiper,* Was keeper
108 *whilk,* which; *sone,* son
109 Were worshiped; and his own room was next to them
110 *baill aneuch in breist,* trouble enough in (her) breast
112 *Whill,* Until; *solempne,* festival 113 *pepill,* people
114 *Befoir the none,* Before noon 115 *devoit,* devout; *maneir,* manner
116 *hevye in hir intent,* heavy in her thought
117 *Kirk,* Church; *wald,* would 118 For (fear of) giving the people any hint
119 *expuls fra,* rejection from 120 *past,* passed; *secreit orature,* secret chapel
121 *Whair sho micht weip,* Where she might weep
122 *cloisit,* closed; *dure,* door
123 *kneis bair,* bare knees; *in hy,* in haste
124 *Upon,* Against

125 Sho cryit out, and said on this same wise:
"Allace that ever I maid you sacrifice!

"Ye gave me anis ane devine responsaill
That I suld be the flour of luif in Troy;
Now am I maid ane unworthye outwaill,
130 And all in cair translaitit is my joy.
Wha sall me gide? What sall me now convoy,
Sen I fra Diomeid and nobill Troylus
Am clene excludit as abject odious?

"O fals Cupide, is nane to wite bot thou,
135 And thy Mother, of lufe the blind Goddes!
Ye causit me alwayis understand and trow
The seid of lufe was sawin in my face,
And ay grew grene throw your supplye and grace.
Bot now, allace, that seid with froist is slane,
140 And I fra luifferis left and all forlane."

When this was said, down in ane extasye,
Ravishit in spreit, intill ane dreame sho fell,
And be apperance hard, whair sho did ly,
Cupide the King ringand ane silver bell
145 Whilk men micht heir fra Hevin unto Hell,

125 *on this same wise,* in words to this effect 126 *Allace,* Alas; *maid,* did
127 *anis,* once; *responsaill,* response 128 *suld,* should; *luif,* love
129 *maid,* made; *outwaill,* outcast 130 *in cair translaitit,* changed into sorrow
131 Who shall guide me? Who shall now accompany me 132 *Sen,* Since
133 Am completely excluded, as an odious object
134 *is nane to wite bot,* no one is to blame except
135 *lufe,* love (The attribution of blindness to Venus is unusual; ordinarily only her son, Cupid, is thought to be blind.)
136 You always caused me to understand and believe that
137 *seid,* seed; *sawin,* sowed 138 *ay,* ever; *supplye,* assistance
139 *froist,* frost; *slane,* killed
140 And I abandoned by lovers and all forsaken 141 *extasye,* swoon
142–43 Her spirits spent, she fell into a dream, and seemed to hear, where she lay
144 *ringand,* ringing 145 *heir,* hear

At whais sound befoir Cupide appeiris
The sevin Planetis, discending fra thair Spheiris,

Whilk hes power of all thing generabill,
To reull and steir be thair greit influence
150 Wedder and wind and coursis variabill.
And first of all Saturne gave his sentence,
Whilk gave to Cupide litill reverence.
Bot as ane busteous churle on his maneir
Come crabitlye with auster luik and cheir.

155 His face fronsit, his lire was like the leid,
His teith chatterit, and cheverit with the chin,
His ene droupit, how sonkin in his heid,
Out of his nois the meldrop fast can rin,
With lippis bla and cheikis leine and thin;
160 The iceshoklis that fra his hair down hang
Was wonder greit, and as ane speir als lang.

Atouir his belt his liart lokkis lay
Felterit unfair, ouirfret with froistis hoir;
His garmound and his giis full gay of gray —
165 His widderit weid — fra him the wind out woir.

146 *whais,* whose; *appeiris,* appear
147 *Spheiris:* the spherical plane in the heavens over which the planets move in their orbits
148 Who have power over all created things 149 *reull,* rule; *steir,* steer; *be,* by
150 *Wedder,* Weather; *coursis,* events 151 *sentence,* pronouncement
152 *Whilk,* Who
153–54 But like a rough fellow in his manner came in ill-humor with a stern expression and appearance
155 *fronsit,* wrinkled (Charteris, *frosnit,* frozen ?); *lire,* skin; *leid,* lead
156 *cheverit,* shook 157 His eyes drooped, sunk hollowly in his head.
158 *nois,* nose; *meldrop,* drops of mucous; *can rin,* ran
159 *bla,* pale; *cheikis leine,* lean cheeks 160 *iceshoklis,* icicles
161 Were marvelously huge and long as a spear
162 *Atouir,* Down to; *liart lokkis lay,* grizzled locks hung
163–65 Matted untidily and overspread with hoarfrost. His very handsome outer garments of grey (*giis* and *garmound* are probably synonymous) (and) his faded clothes were blown out from him by the wind.

Ane busteous bow within his hand he boir,
Under his girdill, ane flashe of felloun flanis
Fedderit with ice and heidit with hailstanis.

Than Juppiter, richt fair and amiabill,
170 God of the starnis in the firmament
And nureis to all thing generabill,
Fra his father, Saturne, far different,
With burelye face and browis bricht and brent,
Upon his heid ane garland wonder gay
175 Of flouris fair, as it had bene in May.

His voice was cleir, as cristall wer his ene,
As goldin wire sa glitterand was his hair;
His garmound and his giis full gay of grene,
With goldin listis gilt on everye gair;
180 Ane burelye brand about his midill bair;
In his richt hand he had ane groundin speir,
Of his father the wraith fra us to weir.

Nixt efter him come Mars, the God of ire,
Of strife, debait, and all dissensioun —
185 To chide and fecht, als feirs as ony fire —
In hard harnes, heumound, and habirgeoun;
And on his hanche ane roustye, fell fachioun;

166 *busteous,* stout; *boir,* bore

167–68 Under his belt (he bore) a quiver of cruel arrows, feathered with ice and headed with hailstones.

169 *Than,* Then 170 *starnis,* stars 171 And nourisher of all created things

173 *burelye,* ruggedly handsome; *bricht and brent,* fair and smooth

174 *heid,* head; *wonder,* wonderfully 175 *bene,* been

176 *ene,* eyes 177 *sa glitterand,* just as shining

178 His garments (are) a very handsome green; *gay,* Charteris *om.*

179 *listis,* borders; *gair,* seam 180 *burelye brand,* stout sword; *bair,* bore

181 *groundin speir,* sharply honed spear

182 To defend us from his father's (Saturn's) wrath

185 *fecht,* fight; *als feirs,* as fierce; *ony,* any

186–87 In hard armor, helmet, and coat of mail, and on his hip, a rusty (*i.e.,* blood-stained), cruel hooked sword

And in his hand he had ane roustye sword;
Writhing his face with mony angrye word,

190 Shaikande his sword, befoir Cupide he come
With reid visage and grislye, glowrand ene,
And at his mouth ane bullar stude of fome,
Like to an bair whetting his tuskis kene –
Richt tuilyeour-like, but temperance in tene.
195 Ane horne he blew with mony bosteous brag,
Whilk all this warld with weir hes maid to wag.

Than fair Phebus, lanterne and lamp of licht
Of man and beist, baith frute and flourishing,
Tender nureis and banisher of nicht,
200 And of the warld causing, be his moving
And Influence, life in all eirdlye thing,
Without comfort of whome, of force to nocht
Must all ga die that in this warld is wrocht.

As king royall he raid upon his chair
205 The whilk Phaeton gidit sumtime upricht.
The brichtnes of his face when it was bair
Nane micht behald for peirsing of his sicht.
This goldin cart with firye bemis bricht
Four yokkit steidis full different of hew,
210 But bait or tiring throw the spheiris drew.

190 *Shaikande,* Brandishing 191 With red and horrible face, glowering eyes
192 *bullar stude of fome,* stood a bubble of foam 193 *bair,* boar
194 *tuilyeour-like,* like a bully; *but,* without; *tene,* wrath
195 *mony bosteous brag,* many a noisy blast
196 Which has made all this world to shake with war 197 *licht,* light
198 For man and beast, both fruit and flower 199 *nureis,* nourisher
200 *be,* by 201 *eirdlye,* earthly
202–3 Without whose comfort, everything that is in this world must necessarily (*of force*) die to nothing
204 *raid,* rode; *chair,* chariot 205 Which Phaeton, assuredly, once drove
206 *bair,* bare 207 None might behold for (fear of) blinding his sight
208 *firye bemis,* fiery beams 209 *yokkit steidis,* yoked steeds
210 Drew through the spheres without stopping or tiring

The first was soir with mane als reid as rois,
Callit Eoye into the Orient;
The secund steid to name hecht Ethios,
Whitlye and paill and sum deill ascendent;
215 The thrid Peros, richt hait and richt fervent;
The feird was blak, callit Philologye,
Whilk rollis Phebus down into the sey.

Venus was thair present, that Goddes gay,
Hir sonnis querrell forto defend, and mak
220 Hir awin complaint, cled in ane nice array —
The ane half grene, the uther half sabill blak;
White hair as gold kemmit and shed abak —
Bot in hir face semit greit variance,
Whiles perfite treuth, and whiles inconstance.

225 Under smiling sho was dissimulait,
Provocative, with blenkis amorous,
And suddanely changit and alterait,
Angrye as ony serpent vennemous,
Richt pungitive with wordis odious.
230 Thus variant sho was, wha list tak keip,
With ane eye lauch, and with the uther weip,

211 *soir,* roan; *reid,* red; *rois,* rose
212 *Callit,* Called (The names of the first three horses correspond to the names in Ovid's *Metamorphosis,* ii, 153–55: Eöus, Æthon, and Pyröeis. For a discussion of "Philologye," see Elliott, *JEGP,* LIV (April, 1955), 247–54); *into,* in
213 *hecht,* was called
214 *Whitlye,* Whitish; *sum deill ascendent,* somewhat inclined to mount upward
215 *richt hait,* very hot; *fervent,* fiery 217 *sey,* sea
218 *gay,* Charteris *om.* 219 *querrell,* case
220 *awin,* own; *cled,* clad; *nice,* subtle 221 *The ane half,* The one half
222 White hair like gold combed and parted backward 223 *semit,* seemed
224 Now perfect fidelity, and now inconstancy 225 *dissimulait,* deceitful
226 *blenkis,* glances 228 *ony,* any 229 *Richt pungitive,* Very stinging
230 *wha list tak keip,* whoever took the trouble to notice
231 *lauch,* would laugh; *weip,* would weep

In taikning that all fleshelye paramour,
Whilk Venus hes in reull and governance,
Is sumtime sweit, sumtime bitter and sour,
235 Richt unstabill and full of variance,
Mingit with cairfull joy and fals plesance,
Now hait, now cauld, now bliith, now full of wo,
Now grene as leif, now widderit and ago.

With buik in hand than come Mercurius,
240 Richt eloquent and full of Rethorye,
With polite termis and delicious,
With pen and ink to report al reddye,
Setting sangis and singand merilye;
His hude was reid, heklit atouir his croun,
245 Like to ane poeit of the auld fassoun.

Boxis he bair with fine electuairis,
And sugerit syropis for digestioun,
Spicis belangand to the Pothecairis,
With mony hailsum sweit confectioun;
250 Doctour in Physick cled in ane skarlot gown,
And furrit weill – as sic ane aucht to be –
Honest and gude, and not ane word culd lie.

Nixt efter him come Lady Cynthia,

232 *taikning,* token; *paramour,* love 233 *hes,* has; *reull,* rule
236 *Mingit,* Mixed; *cairfull,* sorrowful; *plesance,* delight 237 *hait,* hot
238 *widderit and ago,* withered and gone 239 *buik,* book
240 *Rethorye,* rhetorical art 241 With artful and delicious phrases
242 *reddye,* ready 243 *Setting sangis,* Composing songs; *singand,* singing
244–45 His hood was red with a fringed edge around the crown, like that of a poet in the old style.
246 *bair,* bore; *electuairis,* sweet medical pastes
247 *sugerit syropis,* sweetened syrups
248 *belangand,* belonging; *Pothecairis,* Druggists
249 *hailsum,* wholesome; *sweit,* sweet 250 *Physick,* Medicine
251 And well trimmed with fur, as such a one ought to be
252 *gude,* good; *culd,* could

The last of all, and swiftest in hir Spheir,
255 Of colour blak, buskit with hornis twa,
And in the nicht sho listis best appeir.
Haw as the leid, of colour nathing cleir,
For all hir licht sho borrowis at hir brother
Titan, for of hirself sho hes nane uther.

260 Hir gise was gray and full of spottis blak,
And on hir breist ane churle, paintit full evin,
Beirand ane bunche of thornis on his bak,
Whilk for his thift micht clim na nar the Hevin.
Thus when thay gadderit war, thir Goddes sevin,
265 Mercurius thay cheisit with ane assent
To be Foirspeikar in the Parliament.

Wha had bene thair and liken for to heir
His facound toung and termis exquisite,
Of Rethorick the prettick he micht leir —
270 In breif sermone ane pregnant sentence write.
Befoir Cupide veiling his cap alite,
Speiris the caus of that vocatioun;
And he anone shew his intentioun.

"Lo!" quod Cupide, "wha will blaspheme the name

255 *buskit,* adorned; *twa,* two 256 *sho listis best appeir,* she likes best to appear
257 Dull colored as lead, of color not at all bright 258 *at,* from 260 *gise,* dress
261–63 And on her breast, painted very precisely, (was) a peasant, bearing a bundle of thorns on his back, who because of his theft might climb no closer to Heaven. (According to folk legend, the man in the moon is a peasant who has been banished there for stealing thorns.)
264 *gadderit war,* were gathered; *thir,* these 265 *cheisit,* chose
266 *Foirspeikar,* Spokesman 267 *Wha,* Whoever; *liken for,* took the trouble
268 *facound,* eloquent; *termis exquisite,* choice phrases
269–70 He might learn the practice of Rhetoric — (to) write a pregnant thought in a brief statement.
271 *veiling,* doffing; *alite,* slightly
272 *Speiris,* (Mercury) enquires; *vocatioun,* convocation
273 And he (Cupid) at once set forth his case
274 *wha,* whoever

275 Of his awin God, outher in word or deid,
To all Goddis he dois baith lak and shame,
And suld have bitter panis to his meid.
I say this by yone wretchit Cresseid,
The whilk throw me was sumtime flour of lufe,
280 Me and my mother starklye can reprufe,

"Saying, of hir greit infelicitye
I was the caus, and my mother Venus –
Ane blind Goddes hir cald, that micht not se,
With sclander and defame injurious.
285 Thus hir leving unclene and lecherous
Sho wald returne on me and my mother,
To whome I shew my grace abone all uther.

"And sen ye ar all sevin deificait,
Participant of devine sapience,
290 This greit injurye done to our hie estait
Me think with pane we suld mak recompence;
Was never to Goddes done sic violence.
As weill for you as for myself I say;
Thairfoir ga help to revenge, I you pray."

295 Mercurius to Cupide gave answeir
And said: "Shir King, my counsall is that ye
Refer you to the hiest planeit heir,
And tak to him the lawest of degre,
The pane of Cresseid forto modifye –

275 *awin*, own; *outher*, either; *or*, Charteris *in*
276 *dois baith lak*, does both disparagement 277 *to his meid*, as his reward
278 *by*, with reference 279 *The whilk*, Who; *sumtime*, once
280 *starklye can reprufe*, sharply reproved
283 *hir cald*, called her; *se*, see 284 *sclander*, slander; *defame*, defamation
285 *leving*, way of life 286 *returne*, blame 287 *shew*, showed
288 *sen*, since; *deificait*, deified 289 Participating in divine wisdom
290 *hie estait*, high position 291 *pane*, punishment 292 *sic*, such
293 *weill*, much 294 *ga help*, it is incumbent on you to help
296 *Shir*, Sir 298 *to*, with; *lawest*, lowest 299 *modifye*, assess

300 As God Saturne, with him tak Cynthia."
"I am content," quod he, "to tak thay twa."

Than thus proceidit Saturne and the Mone,
When thay the mater ripelye had degest:
For the dispite to Cupide sho had done
305 And to Venus, oppin and manifest,
In all hir life with pane to be opprest
And torment sair, with siknes incurabill,
And to all lovers be abhominabill.

This duleful sentence Saturne tuik on hand
310 And passit down whair cairfull Cresseid lay,
And on hir heid he laid ane frostye wand;
Than lawfullye on this wise can he say:
"Thy greit fairnes and all thy beutye gay,
Thy wantoun blude, and eik thy goldin hair,
315 Heir I exclude fra thee for evermair.

"I change thy mirth into melancholy,
Whilk is the mother of all pensivenes;
Thy moisture and thy heit in cald and dry;
Thine insolence, thy play, and wantones
320 To greit diseis; thy pomp and thy riches
In mortall neid; and greit penuritye
Thou suffer sall, and as ane beggar die."

303 *ripelye had degest,* carefully had considered 304 *dispite,* outrage
305 *oppin,* open 307 *sair,* sore; *seiknes,* sickness
309 *duleful,* grievous; *tuik on hand,* undertook to administer
310 *cairfull,* sorrowful 312 Then lawfully, in this manner he said
314 *wantoun blude,* lively (or lecherous) blood; *eik,* also
315 *Heir,* Here; *exclude fra,* deprive
318 *heit,* heat; *in,* into (a reference to qualities associated with the four humors: moisture and heat were associated with the sanguine humor, cold and dry with the melancholy humor)
319 Thy licentiousness, thy playfulness (either amorous or innocent), and wantonness (wilfulness or lecherousness)
320 *diseis,* discomfort 321 *In,* Into; *neid,* need

O cruell Saturne, fraward and angrye,
Hard is thy dome and too malitious!
325 On fair Cresseid why hes thou na mercy,
Whilk was sa sweit, gentill, and amorous?
Withdraw thy sentence and be gracious,
As thou was never – sa shawis thou thy deid:
Ane wraikfull sentence gevin on fair Cresseid.

330 Than Cynthia, when Saturne past away,
Out of hir sait discendit down belive
And red ane bill on Cresseid whair sho lay,
Contening this sentence diffinitive:
"Fra heit of bodye I thee now deprive,
335 And to thy seiknes sall be na recure,
But in dolour thy dayis to indure.

"Thy cristall ene minglit with blude I mak,
Thy voice sa cleir, unplesand, hoir and hace,
Thy lustye lire ouirspred with spottis blak,
340 And lumpis haw appeirand in thy face.
Whair thou cummis, ilk man sall fle the place:
This sall thou go begging fra hous to hous
With cop and clapper like ane lazarous."

This doolye dreame, this uglye visioun
345 Brocht to ane end, Cresseid fra it awoik,
And all that Court and convocatioun

323 *fraward,* perverse 324 *dome,* judgment 325 *hes thou na,* have you no
328 *shawis,* demonstrates; *deid,* deed 329 *wraikfull,* vengeful
330 *Than,* Then 331 *sait,* seat; *belive,* quickly 332 *red,* read
333 *diffinitive,* final 335 *recure,* recovery 336 *dolour,* grief
337 *ene,* eyes; *minglit with blude,* bloodshot
338 *unplesand, hoir and hace,* unpleasing, rough and hoarse
339 *lustye lire,* fresh complexion 340 *haw,* livid; *appeirand,* appearing
341 *Whair,* Wherever; *ilk,* every 342 *This,* Thus
343 With begging bowl and clapping dish (a dish with a wooden cover that was rattled to warn others away) like a leper
344 *doolye,* doleful 345 *Brocht,* Brought

Vanishit away. Than rais sho up and tuik
Ane poleist glas and hir shaddow culd luik;
And when sho saw hir face sa deformait,
350 Gif sho in hart was wa aneuch, God wait!

Weiping full sair, "Lo! what it is," quod she,
"With fraward langage for to mufe and steir
Our craibit Goddis, and sa is sene on me!
My blaspheming now have I bocht full deir!
355 All eirdlye joy and mirth I set areir.
Allace this day! allace this wofull tide,
When I began with my Goddis forto chide!"

Be this was said ane child come fra the hall
To warne Cresseid the supper was reddy,
360 First knokkit at the dure and sine culd call:
"Madame, your father biddis you cum in hy.
He hes mervell sa lang on grouf ye ly,
And sayis your prayers bene too lang sum deill—
The Goddis wait all your intent full weill."

365 Quod sho: "Fair child, ga to my father deir,
And pray him cum to speik with me anone."
And sa he did and said: "Douchter, what cheir?"
"Allace," quod sho, "Father, my mirth is gone!"
"How sa?" quod he. And sho can all expone

347 *rais sho up,* she rose up
348 A polished glass (mirror) and examined her reflection
350 God knows if she was heart-broken enough
351 *sair,* bitterly; *what,* thus
352 *fraward,* perverse; *mufe and steir,* upset and disturb
353 *craibit,* ill-natured; *sa,* so, such 354 *bocht,* bought
355 *eirdlye,* earthly; *areir,* behind (me) 356 *tide,* time 357 *with,* against
358 *Be,* By (the time) 359 *warne,* advise
360 *sine culd call,* then called 361 *in hy,* in haste
362–63 He marvels that you lie prostrate so long, and says your prayers are too long by a good deal.
364 *wait,* know; *intent,* thoughts 366 *anone,* quickly
367 *what cheir,* how are you 369 *can all expone,* explained everything

370 As I have tauld – the vengeance and the wraik
For hir trespas Cupide on hir culd tak.

He luikit on hir uglye lipper face,
The whilk befor was white as lillye flour;
Wringand his handis oftimes he said, allace
375 That he had levit to se that wofull hour!
For he knew weill that thair was na succour
To hir seiknes, and that doublit his pane.
Thus was thair cair aneuch betwix thame twane.

When thay togidder murnit had full lang,
380 Quod Cresseid: "Father, I wald not be kend;
Thairfoir in secreit wise ye let me gang
Unto yone Hospitall at the townis end.
And thidder sum meit, for Cheritye, me send
To leif upon, for all my mirth in this eird
385 Is fra me gane – sic is my wickit weird!"

Than in ane mantill and ane bawer hat,
With cop and clapper, wonder prively,
He opnit ane secreit yet and out thairat
Convoyit hir, that na man suld espy,
390 Unto ane village half ane mile thairby,
Deliverit hir in at the Spittaill Hous
And dailye sent hir part of his almous.

370 *wraik*, punishment 371 *culd tak*, took
372 *luikit*, looked; *lipper*, leprous 375 *levit*, lived 377 *doublit*, doubled
378 *aneuch*, enough; *twane*, twain
379 *togidder murnit had*, had grieved together
380 *wald not be kend*, don't want to be recognized
381 Therefore, let me go secretly. 382 *yone*, yonder; *end*, edge
383 *thidder*, thither; *meit*, food 384 *leif*, live; *eird*, earth
385 *gane*, gone; *sic*, such; *wickit weird*, wicked fate
386 *mantill*, cloak; *bawer*, beaver 387 *wonder prively*, very secretly
388 *opnit*, opened; *yet*, gate; *thairat*, thereat
389 *convoyit*, conducted; *that*, so that 390 *thairby*, away
391 *Spittaill Hous*, Hospital
392 *almous*, alms (which he, as a priest, would receive)

Sum knew her weill, and sum had na knawledge
Of hir becaus sho was sa deformait,
395 With bilis blak ouirspred in hir visage
And hir fair colour faidit and alterait.
Yit thay presumit, for hir hie regrait
And still murning, sho was of nobill kin.
With better will thairfoir they tuik hir in.

400 The day passit and Phebus went to rest;
The cloudis blak ouirwhelmit all the sky.
God wait gif Cresseid was ane sorrowfull gest,
Seing that uncouth fair and harbery!
But meit or drink sho dressit hir to ly
405 In ane dark corner of the hous allone,
And on this wise, weiping, sho maid her mone.

The Complaint of Cresseid

"O sop of sorrow, sonkin into cair!
O cative Creisseid, for now and evermair
Gane is thy joy and all thy mirth in eird;
410 Of all bliithnes now art thou blaiknit bair.
Thair is na salve may saif thee of thy sair:
Fell is thy Fortoun, wickit is thy weird,
Thy blis is baneist, and thy baill on breird;

393 *had na knawledge,* did not recognize 395 *bilis,* boils 396 *alterait,* altered
397 Yet they supposed, because of her loud lamenting 398 *still,* continual
402 *wait,* knows; *gest,* guest 403 Seeing that rough food and lodging
404 *But meit,* Without food; *dressit hir,* proceeded
406 And weeping in this way she made her complaint.
407 *sop,* a piece of bread steeped in liquid; *sonkin into,* soaked in
408 *cative,* wretched 409 *eird,* earth
410 *bliithnes,* joy; *blaiknit bair,* dark and destitute
411 *saif,* heal 412 *Fell,* Cruel; *weird,* fate
413 *baneist,* banished; *baill on breird,* grief is sprouting

Under the eirth God gif I gravin wer,
415 Whair nane of Grece nor yit of Troy micht heird!

"Whair is thy chalmer wantounlye besene
With burely bed and bankouris browderit bene?
Spicis and wine to thy collatioun,
The coupis all of gold and silver shene,
420 The sweit meitis servit in plaittis clene,
With saipheron sals of ane gud sessoun,
Thy gay garmentis with mony gudely gown,
Thy plesand lawn pinnit with goldin prene —
All is areir, thy greit royall renown!

425 "Whair is thy garding with thir greissis gay
And freshe flouris, whilk the Quene Floray
Had paintit plesandly in everye pane,
Whair thou was wont full merilye in May
To walk and tak the dew be it was day,
430 And heir the merle and mawis mony ane,
With Ladyis fair in carrolling to gane,
And se the royall rinkis in thair array,
In garmentis gay garnishit on everye grane?

"Thy greit triumphand fame and hie honour,

414 *God gif I gravin wer,* Would to God that I were buried
415 *nane,* none; *micht heird,* could have heard
416–17 Where is thy chamber, luxuriously furnished — with handsome bed and beautifully embroidered coverlets?
418 *to,* to go with; *collatioun,* meal 419 *coupis,* cups; *shene,* bright
420 *sweit meitis,* sweet foods; *plaittis,* plates
421 With saffron sauce well seasoned 422 *mony gudely,* many a goodly
423 Thy pleasing fine linen pinned with golden brooch 424 *areir,* past
425 *garding,* garden; *thir greissis,* these grasses
426 *Floray,* Flora (Goddess of spring and of flowers)
427 *paintit,* painted with various colors; *pane,* flower bed 429 *be,* before
430 And hear many a blackbird and thrush
431 *in carrolling to gane,* to go a-caroling (both singing and dancing)
432 *rinkis,* knights 433 In gay garments decorated with every color
434 *triumphand,* triumphant

435 Whair thou was callit of eirdlye wichtis flour –
All is decayit, thy weird is welterit so:
Thy hie estait is turnit in darknes dour.
This lipper ludge tak for thy burelye bowr,
And for thy bed tak now ane bunche of stro;
440 For waillit wine and meitis thou had tho,
Tak moulit breid, peirrye, and ceder sour –
Bot cop and clapper, now is all ago.

"My cleir voice and courtlye carrolling,
Whair I was wont with Ladyes forto sing,
445 Is rauk as ruik, full hiddeous, hoir and hace;
My plesand port all utheris precelling –
Of lustines I was hald maist conding –
Now is deformit; the figour of my face,
To luik on it na leid now liking hes;
450 Soupit in site, I say with sair siching,
Ludgeit amang the lipper leid, allace!

"O Ladyis fair of Troy and Grece, attend
My miserye, whilk nane may comprehend:
My frivoll Fortoun, my infelicitye,
455 My greit mischeif, whilk na man can amend.
Be war in time – approchis neir the end –
And in your mind ane mirrour mak of me:

435 *of eirdlye wichtis flour,* the flower of earthly creatures
436 *weird is welterit,* fate is reversed 437 *in,* into
438 Take this leper house for thy handsome bower. 439 *stro,* straw
440 *waillit,* choice; *tho,* then
441 Take mouldy bread, pear juice (often fermented) and sour cider (It has been pointed out that this diet was not only penurious, but was in Henryson's day considered medically appropriate for leprosy.)
442 *Bot,* Except for 445 Is raucous as a crow, very hideous, rough and hoarse
446 *port,* bearing; *precelling,* excelling
447 *lustines,* beauty; *maist conding,* most excellent 448 *figour,* appearance
449 To look on it no person now takes pleasure.
450 Drowned in sorrow, I speak with bitter sighing.
451 *Ludgeit,* Lodged; *leid,* folk 454 *frivoll,* fickle
455 *mischeif,* misfortune 456 *war,* ware

As I am now, peradventure that ye,
For all your micht, may cum to that same end,
460 Or ellis war, gif ony war may be.

"Nocht is your fairnes bot ane faiding flour;
Nocht is your famous laud and hie honour
Bot wind inflat in uther mennis eiris;
Your roising reid to rotting shall retour.
465 Exempill mak of me in your memour,
Whilk of sic thingis wofull witnes beiris.
All welth in eird away as wind it weiris:
Be war thairfoir – approchis neir the hour;
Fortoun is fikkill when sho beginnis and steiris."

470 Thus chidand with hir dreryе destenye,
Weiping sho woik the nicht fra end to end.
Bot all in vane: hir dule, hir cairfull cry
Micht not remeid, nor yit hir murning mend.
Ane lipper Lady rais and till hir wend
475 And said: "Why spurnis thou aganis the wall
To sla thyself, and mend nathing at all?

"Sen thy weiping doubillis bot thy wo,
I counsall thee mak vertew of ane neid –
To leir to clap thy clapper to and fro,
480 And leir efter the law of lipper leid."
Thair was na buit, bot furth with thame sho yeid

458 *peradventure,* perhaps 459 *micht,* power 460 *war,* worse; *gif,* if
462 *laud,* praise 463 *inflat in,* blown into; *eiris,* ears 464 *roising reid,* rosy red
465 *memour,* memory 466 Who bears woeful witness to such things
467 *weiris,* wastes away 469 *beginnis and steiris,* begins to work
470 *chidand with,* complaining aloud against
471 *woik the nicht,* lay awake the whole night 472 *dule,* grief
473 *remeid,* help; *mend,* mend (her fortune)
474 *rais,* rose; *till her wend,* went to her
475 *spurnis thou,* do you hurl (yourself)
476 *sla,* slay 477 *doubillis bot,* only doubles
478 *vertew of ane neid,* virtue out of necessity 479 *leir,* learn
480 *leir efter,* learn (to live) according to; *leid,* folk, Charteris *leir*
481 *buit,* help; *yeid,* went

Fra place to place, whill cauld and hounger sair
Compellit hir to be ane rank beggair.

That samin time, of Troy the Garnisoun,
485 Whilk had to Chiftane worthye Troylus,
Throw jeopardye of weir had strikken down
Knichtis of Grece in number mervellous;
With greit triumphe and laude victorious
Agane to Troy richt royallye they raid
490 The way whair Cresseid with the lipper baid.

Seing that companye, thay come all with ane stevin;
Thay gaif ane cry, and shuik coppis gude speid;
Said: "Worthye Lordis, for Goddis lufe of Hevin,
To us lipper part of your almous deid!"
495 Than to thair cry nobill Troylus tuik heid;
Having pietye, neir by the place can pas
Whair Cresseid sat, not witting what sho was.

Than upon him sho cest up baith hir ene,
And with ane blenk it come into his thocht
500 That he sumtime hir face befoir had sene.
Bot sho was in sic plie he knew hir nocht;
Yit than hir luik into his mind it brocht
The sweit visage and amorous blenking
Of fair Cresseid, sumtime his awin darling.

482 *whill,* until
483 *rank beggair,* foul beggar (Lepers were not necessarily beggars; hence this is an additional fall from fortune.)
484 *samin,* same; *Garnisoun,* Garrison 485 *to,* as a
486 *jeopardye of weir,* fortune of war 488 *laude,* praise
489 *Agane,* Back again, Charteris repeats *richt*; *raid,* rode 490 *baid,* stayed
491 *come,* come together; *stevin,* accord
492 *shuik,* shook; *gude speid,* vigorously
494 *lipper,* leper (folk); *almous deid,* alms gift 495 *heid,* heed
496 *can pas,* passed 497 *witting what sho,* knowing who she
498 *ene,* eyes 499 *blenk,* glance 501 *sic plie,* such plight
502 *than,* then 503 *blenking,* glances 504 *awin,* own

505 Na wonder was, suppois in mind that he
Tuik hir figure sa sone — and lo now why:
The idole of ane thing in cace may be
Sa deip imprentit in the fantasy
That it deludis the wittis outwardly,
510 And sa appeiris in forme and like estait
Within the mind as it was figurait.

Ane spark of lufe than till his hart culd spring
And kendlit all his bodye in ane fire;
With hait fewir ane sweit and trimbling
515 Him tuik whill he was reddye to expire;
To beir his sheild his breist began to tire;
Within ane while he changit mony hew,
And nevertheless not ane aneuther knew.

For knichtlye pietye and memoriall
520 Of fair Cresseid, ane girdill can he tak,
Ane purs of gold, and mony gay jowall,
And in the skirt of Cresseid down can swak;
Than raid away and not ane word spak,
Pensive in hart whill he come to the town,
525 And for greit care oft siis almaist fell down.

The lipper folk to Cresseid than can draw

505–6 It was no wonder, although he received her impression into his mind so quickly — and do you know why?

507 *idole,* image; *in cace,* in a (particular) case

508 *deip imprentit,* deeply imprinted; *fantasy,* imagination

510–11 *sa appeiris,* so appears; *figurait,* imagined (*i.e.,* the remembered image — of Cresseid when she was fair — is so strong that it blots out, is superimposed on, the external object — Cresseid's leprous face — that he is looking at)

512 *lufe,* love; *than till,* then to; *culd spring,* sprang

514 *hait fewir,* hot fever; *sweit,* sweat 515 *tuik,* seized; *whill,* until

516 *beir,* bear 517 Within a short time he changed color many times.

518 *not ane aneuther knew,* neither knew the other

520 *girdill can he tak,* belt he took

521 Charteris repeats this line; *jowall,* jewel 522 *can swak,* threw

524 *whill,* until 525 *care,* sorrow; *oft siis,* often 526 *can draw,* drew close

To se the equall distributioun
Of the almous; bot when the gold thay saw,
Ilk ane to uther prevelye can rown
530 And said: "Yone Lord hes mair affectioun,
However it be, unto yone lazarous
Than to us all — we knaw be his almous."

"What Lord is yone," quod sho, "— have ye na feill —
Hes done to us so greit humanitye?"
535 "Yes," quod a lipper man, "I knaw him weill;
Shir Troylus it is, gentill and fre."
When Cresseid understude that it was he,
Stiffer than steill thair stert ane bitter stound
Throwout hir hart, and fell down to the ground;

540 When sho ouircome, with siching sair and sad,
With mony cairfull cry and cald, "Ochane!
Now is my breist with stormye stoundis stad,
Wrappit in wo, ane wretch full will of wane!"
Than swounit sho oft or sho culd refrane,
545 And ever in hir swouning cryit sho thus:
"O fals Cresseid and trew knicht Troylus!

"Thy lufe, thy lautye, and thy gentilnes,
I countit small in my prosperitye,
Sa elevait I was in wantones

529 Each one to other privately whispered.
531 *However it be,* For whatever reason; *lazarous,* leprous one
532 *be,* by 533 *feill,* knowledge 534 *Hes,* (Who) has
536 *gentill and fre,* courteous and generous
538 *steill,* steel; *stert,* sprang; *stound,* pang 539 *fell,* (she) fell
540 *ouircome,* revived; *siching,* sighing
541 *cairfull,* full of care; *cald Ochane,* called out, "Ochone" (Gaelic cry of grief)
542 *stad,* beset 543 *full will of wane,* completely at my wit's end
544 Then she swooned often, before she was able to recover.
547 *lautye,* loyalty 548 *countit small,* valued slightly
549–50 So carried away I was in heedless pleasure and climbed so high on the (Fortune's) unstable wheel.

550 And clam upon the fickill wheill sa hie.
All faith and lufe I promissit to thee
Was in the self fickill and frivolous –
O fals Cresseid and trew knicht Troylus!

"For lufe of me thou keipt gude continence,
555 Honest and chaist in conversatioun.
Of all wemen protectour and defence
Thou was, and helpit thair opinioun;
My mind in fleshelye foull affectioun
Was inclinit to lustis lecherous –
560 Fy fals Cresseid, O trew knicht Troylus!

"Lovers be war and tak gude heid about
Whome that ye lufe, for whome ye suffer paine;
I lat you wit thair is richt few thairout
Whome ye may traist to have trew lufe agane –
565 Preif when ye will, your labour is in vaine.
Thairfoir I reid ye tak thame as ye find,
For thay ar sad as widdercock in wind.

"Becaus I knaw the greit unstabilnes,
Brukkill as glas, into myself, I say –
570 Traisting in uther als greit unfaithfulness,
Als unconstant, and als untrew of fay –
'Thocht sum be trew, I wait richt few ar thay:
Wha findis treuth lat him his Lady ruse!'
Nane but myself as now I will accuse."

551 *All,* All (the) 552 *the self,* in itself
554 *gude continence,* good chastity 555 *chaist,* pure
557 *helpit thair opinioun,* advanced their good reputation 561 *heid,* heed
563 *lat you wit,* let you know
564 From whom you may hope to have true love in return
565 *Preif,* Test (my statement) 566 *reid,* advise
567 *sad,* firm, reliable; *widdercock,* weathervane
569 *Brukkill,* Fragile; *into,* within; *say,* speak (this)
570 *Traisting,* Expecting (to find); *uther,* others
571 *untrew of fay,* false of faith 572 *Thocht,* Though; *wait,* know
573 *Wha,* Whoever; *ruse,* praise 574 *as now,* now

575 When this was said, with paper sho sat down,
And on this maneir maid hir Testament:
"Heir I beteiche my corps and carioun
With wormis and with taidis to be rent.
My cop and clapper and mine ornament
580 And all my gold, the lipper folk sall have
When I am deid, to burye me in grave.

"This royall ring, set with this rubye reid,
Whilk Troylus in drowrye to me send,
To him agane I leif it when I am deid
585 To mak my cairfull deid unto him kend.
Thus I conclude shortlye, and mak ane end:
My spreit I leif to Diane whair sho dwellis,
To walk with hir in waist woddis and wellis.

"O Diomeid, thou hes baith broche and belt
590 Whilk Troylus gave me in takning
Of his trew lufe," and with that word sho swelt.
And sone ane lipper man tuik off the ring,
Sine buryit hir withouttin tarying.
To Troylus furthwith the ring he bair
595 And of Cresseid the deith he can declair.

When he had hard hir greit infirmitye,
Hir legacye and lamentatioun,
And how sho endit in sic povertye,
He swelt for wo and fell down in ane swoun —
600 For greit sorrow his hart to brist was boun,

576 *on,* in 577 Here I bequeath my dead body 578 *taidis,* toads
579 *ornament,* jewels 583 *in drowrye,* as love-token; *send,* sent
585 To make my sorrowful death known to him 586 *shortlye,* briefly
587 *spreit,* spirit; *Diane,* Diana, goddess of chastity and of the chase; *whair,* wherever
588 *waist,* desolate; *wellis,* fountains 590 *takning,* token 591 *swelt,* died
592 *sone,* immediately 593 *Sine,* Then 595 And told of Cresseid's death
596 *hard,* heard about 599 *swelt,* fainted
600 *to brist was boun,* was ready to break

Siching full sadlye said: "I can no moir —
Sho was untrew and wo is me thairfoir."

Sum said he maid ane tomb of merbell gray,
And wrait hir name and superscriptioun,
605 And laid it one hir grave whair that sho lay
In goldin letteris, conteining this ressoun:
"Lo, fair Ladyis, Cresseid of Troyis town,
Sumtime countit the flour of womanheid,
Under this stane, lait lipper, lyis deid."

610 Now, worthye Wemen, in this ballet short
Made for your worship and instructioun,
Of cheritye I monishe and exhort:
Ming not your lufe with fals deceptioun.
Beir in your mind this short conclusioun
615 Of fair Cresseid, as I have said befoir;
Sen sho is deid, I speik of hir no moir.

601 *can,* can do, say 603 *merbell,* marble
604 *wrait,* wrote 606 *ressoun,* legend 608 *Sumtime countit,* Once accounted
609 *lait,* more recently 610 *ballet,* poem
611 *worship,* honor 612 *monishe,* admonish 613 *Ming,* Mix
614 *short conclusioun,* untimely end 616 *Sen,* Since

25

THE BLUDY SERK

Robert Henryson
(fl. 1460–1505)

This hindir yeir I hard betald
Thair was a worthy king;
Dukis, erlis, and barronis bald
He had at his bidding.
5 The lord was anceane and ald,
And sexty yeiris couth ring;
He had a dochter fair to fald,
A lusty lady ying.

Of all fairheid sho bur the flour,
10 And eik hir faderis air,
Of lusty laitis and he honour,
Meik bot and debonair.
Sho winnit in a bigly bour,
On fold wes none so fair;
15 Princis luvit hir paramour
In cuntreis our allwhair.

Thair dwelt a lit beside the king
A foull giane of ane;

(25) *The Bludy Serk,* The Bloody Shirt [1] This recent year I heard (it) told
[3] *bald,* bold [5] *anceane,* ancient [6] *couth ring,* did reign
[7] *fald,* embrace [8] A handsome young lady
[9] Of all fairness she bore the flower (took the prize). [10] *eik,* also; *air,* heir
[11] With cheerful looks and high honor [12] *Meik bot,* Both meek
[13] She dwelt in a pleasant bower. [14] *fold,* earth [15] *paramour,* amorously
[16] *our allwhair,* everywhere [17] *a lit beside,* nearby
[18] An exceedingly foul giant

Stollin he hes the lady ying,
20 Away with hir is gane,
And cest hir in his dungering,
Whair licht sho micht se nane;
Hunger and cauld and grit thristing
Sho fand into hir wame.
25 He wes the laithliest on to luk
That on the ground micht gang;
His nailis wes lik ane Hellis cruk,
Thairwith five quarteris lang.
Thair wes nane that he ourtuk,
30 In richt or yit in wrang,
Bot all in shondir he thame shuke,
The giane wes so strang.

He held the lady day and nicht
Within his deip dungeoun;
35 He wald nocht gif of hir a sicht,
For gold nor yit ransoun,
Bot gife the king micht get a knicht
To fecht with his persoun,
To fecht with him both day and nicht
40 Whill ane wer dungin down.

The king gart seik baith fer and neir,
Beth be se and land,
Of ony knicht gife he micht heir
Wald fecht with that giand.
45 A worthy prince that had no peir

21 *dungering,* dungeon 22 Where she might see no light
23 *cauld,* cold; *grit thristing,* great thirst 24 She felt in her stomach
25 He was the most loathsome to look at. 26 *micht gang,* might walk
27 *Hellis cruk,* hook of Hell
28 And in addition five quarter-yards (45 inches) long 29 *ourtuk,* overtook
30 *richt,* right; *wrang,* wrong 31 *shondir,* sunder 37 *Bot gife,* Unless
38 To fight with him in person 40 Until one were beaten down
41 *gart seik,* caused a search to be made 42 *Beth be se,* Both by sea
43 If he might hear of any knight 44 *Wald,* Would 45 *peir,* peer

Hes tane the deid on hand,
For the luve of the lady cleir,
And held full trew cunnand.

That prince come proudly to the town
50 Of that giane to heir,
And faucht with him his awin persoun,
And tuke him presoneir
And cest him in his awin dungeoun
Allane withouttin feir,
55 With hunger, cauld, and confusioun,
As full weill worthy weir;

Sine brak the bour, had hame the bricht
Unto hir fadir deir.
Sa evill wondit was the knicht
60 That he behuvit to de;
Unlusum was his likame dicht,
His sark was all bludy;
In all the warld was thair a wicht
So peteous forto sy?

65 The lady murnit and maid grit mone
With all hir mekle micht:
"I luvit nevir lufe bot one
That dulfully now is dicht;
God sen my life wer fra me tone

[46] Has taken the task in hand [47] *cleir,* fair
[48] And held all true knowledge (or covenant) [50] *heir,* hear
[51] *faucht,* fought; *awin,* own [54] *feir,* companion
[56] As was very well deserved
[57] Then broke open the room (and) took home the bright one
[59] *Sa evill wondit,* So badly wounded [60] *behuvit to de,* was doomed to die
[61] Unlovely was his body adorned. [63] *wicht,* creature [64] So piteous to see
[65] *murnit,* mourned; *mone,* moan [66] *mekle micht,* great might
[67] *lufe,* lover [68] *dulfully,* dolefully; *dicht,* put to death
[69] *God sen,* would God; *fra me tone,* from me taken

70 Or I had sene yone sicht,
Or ellis in begging evir to gone
Furth with yone curtas knicht!"

He said: "Fair lady, now mone I
De, trestly ye me trow;
75 Tak ye my sark that is bludy
And hing it forrow you;
First think on it and sine on me
When men cumis you to wow."
The lady said, "Be Mary fre,
80 Thairto I mak a vow!"

When that sho lukit to the serk
Sho thocht on the persoun,
And prayit for him with all hir harte
That lousd hir of bandoun,
85 Whair sho was wont to sit full merk
In that deip dungeoun.
And evir whill sho wes in quert,
That was hir a lessoun.

Sa weill the lady luvit the knicht
90 That no man wald sho tak:
Sa suld we do our God of micht
That did all for us mak,
Whilk fullely to deid wes dicht
For sinfull manis saik;
95 Sa suld we do both day and nicht
With prayaris to Him mak.

70 *Or,* Before 72 *Furth,* Forth; *curtas,* courteous 73 *mone,* must
74 Die, truly believe me 76 *hing,* hang; *forrow,* before 77 *sine,* then
78 *wow,* woo 79 *Be,* By; *fre,* noble 81 *lukit to,* looked on
82 *thocht on,* thought of 84 That freed her from bondage
85 *merk,* in darkness 87 *in quert,* alive 88 *hir,* to her 91 *do,* do for
92–93 Who did make everything for us, who foully to death was done

Moralitas

This king is lik the Trinitye,
Baith in Hevin and heir;
The manis saule to the lady,
100 The giane to Lucefeir,
The knicht to Christ that deit on tre
And coft our sinnis deir,
The pit to Hell with panis fell,
The sin to the woweir.

105 The lady was wowd, bot sho said nay
With men that wald hir wed;
Sa suld we writh all sin away
That in our breistis bred.
I pray to Jesu Christ verrey,
110 For us His blud that bled,
To be our help on Domisday,
Whair lawis ar straitly led.

The saule is Godis dochtir deir
And eik His handewerk,
115 That was betrasit with Lucifeir
Wha sittis in Hell full merk,
Borrowit with Christis angell cleir—
Hend men, will ye nocht herk?
For His lufe that bocht us deir,
120 Think on the bludy serk.

Moralitas, Moral
98 *heir*, here 101 *deit on tre*, died on cross 102 *coft*, ransomed
103 *pit*, dungeon; *panis fell*, cruel torments 104 *woweir*, wooer
106 *With*, To 107 *writh*, turn 108 *breistis*, breasts; *bred*, springs up
109 *verrey*, true 110 That bled his blood for us
112 Where laws are strictly applied 113 *dochtir*, daughter
115 *betrasit with*, betrayed by 116 *merk*, dark
117 *Borrowit with*, Redeemed by 118 *Hend*, Gentle; *nocht herk*, not listen
119 *bocht*, bought; *deir*, dearly

26 *(Ca. 1500)*

AMANG THIR FREIRIS WITHIN ANE CLOISTER

William Dunbar
(*ca.* 1460–*ca.* 1513)

Amang thir freiris within ane cloister
I enterit in ane oritorye,
And knelit down with ane *Pater Noster*
Befoir the michty King of glorye,
5 Haveing his passioun in memorye;
Sin to his mother I did incline,
Hir halsing with ane *Gaude Flore*;
And sudandlye I sleipit sine.

Methocht Judas with mony ane Jow
10 Tuik blissit Jesu our salvatour
And shot him furth with mony ane show,
With shamefull wourdis of dishonour;
And lik ane theif or ane tratour
Thay leid that hevinlye Prince most hie
15 With manassing attour messour,
O mankind for the luif of thee.

Falslye condamnit befoir ane Juge,
Thay spittit in his visage fair,
And as liounis with awfull ruge
20 In ire thay hurlit him heir and thair,

(26) 1 Among these friars within a cloister
2 *oritorye,* chapel 3 *Pater Noster,* Our Father (which art in Heaven, *etc.*)
6 *Sin,* Then 7 Greeting her with a *Gaude Flore* (a hymn to the Virgin)
8 *sine,* then 9 *Methocht,* It seemed to me; *Jow,* Jew
11 *shot,* pushed; *show,* shove 15 With threatening beyond measure
16 *luif,* love 19 *ruge,* roaring

And gaif him mony buffat sair,
That it wes sorrow forto se;
Of all his claithis thay tirvit him bair,
O mankind for the luif of thee.

25 Thay terandis, to revenge thair tein,
For scorne thay cled him into whit,
And hid his blythfull glorious ene,
To se wham angellis had delit.
Dispitouslye sin did him smit,
30 Saying, "Gif sone of God thou be,
Wha straik thee now, thou tell us tit" —
O mankind for the luf of thee.

In tene thay tirvit him agane,
And till ane pillar thay him band
35 Whill blude birst out at everye vane.
Thay scurgit him baith fut and hand:
At everye straik ran furth ane strand
Whilk micht have ransonit warldis thre.
He baid in stour whill he micht stand,
40 O mankind for the luif of thee.

Nixt all in purpir thay him cled,
And sine with thornis sharp and kene
His saikles blude agane thay shed,
Persing his heid with pikis grene;
45 Unneis with lif he micht sustene
That crowne, on thrungin with crueltye,
Whill flude of blude blindit his ene,
O mankind for the luif of thee.

21 *sair,* sore 23 *claithis,* clothes; *tirvit,* stripped
25 *Thay terandis,* Those villains; *tein,* anger 28 *wham,* which 30 *Gif,* If
31 Tell us quickly who struck thee now. 33 *tene,* anger 35 *Whill,* Until
37 *straik,* blow; *strand,* stream (of blood) 39 *baid in stour,* endured the assault
41 *purpir,* purple 43 *saikles,* innocent 44 *pikis,* thorns
45 *Unneis,* Scarcely 46 *on thrungin,* crushed on

Ane croce that wes baith large and lang
50 To beir thay gaif this blissit Lord;
Sin fullelye, as theif to hang,
Thay harlit him furth with raip and corde;
With bluid and sweit was all deflorde
His face, the fude of angellis fre;
55 His feit with stanis was revin and scorde,
O mankind for the luif of thee.

Agane thay tirvit him bak and sid
Als brim as ony baris woid;
The claith that claif to his cleir sid
60 Thay raif away with ruggis rude,
Whill fersly followit fleshe and blude
That it was pietye forto se:
Na kind of torment he ganestude,
O mankind for the luif of thee.

65 Onto the crose of breid and lenth,
To gar his limmis langar wax,
Thay straitit him with all thair strenth,
Whill to the rude thay gart him rax,
Sin tyit him on with greit irne takkis;
70 And him all nakit on the tre,
Thay raissit on loft be houris sax,
O mankind for the lufe of thee.

When he was bendit so on breid
Whill all his vanis brist and brak,
75 To gar his cruell pane exceid

51 *fullelye*, foully 52 *harlit*, dragged; *raip*, rope 53 *deflorde*, disfigured
54 *fude*, food 55 *revin*, torn; *scorde*, cut 58 As fierce as a mad bear
59 *claith*, cloth; *claif*, clung; *cleir*, beautiful 60 *raif*, tore; *ruggis*, tugs
63 *ganestude*, opposed 65 *breid*, breadth
66 To force his limbs to grow longer 67 *straitit*, stretched
68 *rude*, cross; *gart*, forced; *rax*, to stretch 69 *irne takkis*, iron nails
71 *sax*, six 72 *of*, MS *om.* 73 *bendit so on breid*, stretched to such an extent
74 *brist*, burst 75 To make his cruel pain unbearable

Thay leit him fall down with ane swak,
Whill cors and corps all did crak;
Agane thay rasit him on hie,
Reddye mair turmentis forto mak,
80 O mankind for the luif of thee.

Betwix two theiffis the spreit he gaif
Onto the Fader most of micht;
The erde did trimmill, the stanis claif,
The sone obscurit of his licht,
85 The day wox dirk as ony nicht,
Deid bodyis rais in the cite:
Goddis deir sone all thus was dicht,
O mankind for the luif of thee.

In weir that he wes yit on lif
90 Thay rane ane rude speir in his side,
And did his precious body riff
Whill blude and watter did furth glide.
Thus Jesus with his woundis wide
Ane martirdome sufferit forto de,
95 And tholit to be crucifyid,
O mankind for the luif of thee.

Methocht Compassioun, vode of feiris,
Than straik at me with mony ane stound;
And for Contrition, bathit in teiris,
100 My visage all in watter drownit;
And Reuth into my eir ay rownde,
"For shame, allace! behald, man, how
Beft is with mony ane wound
Thy blissit Salvatour Jesu."

76 *swak,* jolt 81 *spreit,* spirit 83 *claif,* split 86 *rais,* rose
87 *dicht,* treated 89 *weir,* doubt 90 *rude,* rough 91 *riff,* tear 94 *de,* die
95 *tholit,* suffered 97 *vode,* destitute; *feiris,* companions
98 *stound,* sudden pain 99 *for,* because of
101 *Reuth,* Pity; *rownde,* whispered 103 *Beft,* Beaten

105 Than rudelye come Remembrance
Ay rugging me withouttin rest,
Whilk crose and nailis sharp, scurge and lance,
And bludy crowne befoir me cest;
Than Pane with Passioun me opprest,
110 And evir did Petye on me pow,
Saying, "Behald how Jowis hes drest
Thy blissit Salvatour Christ Jesu."

With greiting glaid be than come Grace
With wourdis sweit saying to me,
115 "Ordane for him ane resting place
That is so werye wrocht for thee,
That short within thir dayis thre
Shall law undir thy lintell bow,
And in thy hous shall herbrit be—
120 Thy blissit Salvatour Christ Jesu."

Than swith Contritioun wes on steir
And did eftir Confessioun rin,
And Conscience me accusit heir
And cest out mony cankerit sin;
125 To ris Repentence did begin
And out at the yettis did show;
Pennance did walk the house within,
Biding our Salvatour Christ Jesu.

Grace become gid and governour
130 To keip the house in sicker stait,
Ay reddy till our Salvatour
Whill that he come air or lait;

106 *rugging,* tugging 107 *Whilk,* Which 109 *Than,* Then 110 *pow,* pull
113 *be than,* then 116 *wrocht,* brought about 117 *thir,* these
119 *herbrit,* harbored 121 *swith,* quickly; *on steir,* astir 122 *rin,* run
124 *cankerit sin,* cankered sins 126 *yettis,* gates; *show,* shove
128 *Biding,* Praying to, waiting for 129 *gid,* guide 130 *sicker,* secure
131 *Ay reddy till,* Always ready for 132 *air,* early

Repentence ay with cheikis wait
No Pane nor Pennence did eschew
135 The house within evir to debait,
Onlye for luif of sweit Jesu.

For grit terrour of Christis deid
The erde did trimmill whair I lay,
Whairthrow I waiknit in that steid
140 With spreit halflingis in effray.
Than wrait I all without delay,
Richt heir as I have shawin to you,
What me befell on Gud Friday
Befoir the crose of sweit Jesu.

133 *wait,* wet 135 *debait,* protect 137 *deid,* death
138 The earth trembled where I lay. 139 *steid,* place
140 With spirit partly in alarm 141 *wrait,* wrote

27 *(1415–40)*

THE NEW LADY

Charles d'Orleans
(1394–1465)

Now felle me, when this Jubile thus was made,
Not coude I ellis but wandir up and downe
4640 Musing in my waking dremes sad;
Min idill thought so besy gan me roune
That alle the hertes dwelling in a towne
Ne had no no so small to doon as I,
For in No Care thus lived I, wot ye why.

4645 Seing I nadde as lady nor maistres
As laboure noon me left nas, soth to say,
Without it were to here evensong and masse
And for the soule of my swethert to pray;
Which esy liif I ledde this many day,
4650 Without it were that sum oon, he or she,
Wolde me complaine of ther adversite

And pray me that I wolde suche labour take
Of ther complaintes, as they to me tolde,

(27) 4638 *felle me,* befell to me; *Jubile,* Jubilee — his collection of roundels, written to accompany a banquet of song and dance for all lovers, and which immediately precedes this section on the new lady

4639 *ellis,* else 4640 *dremes,* dreams

4641 My idle thoughts so busily whispered to me. 4642 *hertes,* hearts

4643 Had not so little to do as I

4644 *No Care,* Indifference (see Commentary); *wot ye why,* you know why

4645 *nadde as,* had neither; *maistres,* mistress

4646 So there was no labor left for me, truth to say. 4647 *Without,* Unless

4649 *liif,* life 4650 Unless it happened that someone, he or she

4651 *Wolde,* Would; *me,* to me 4653 *Of,* Concerning

In a roundell or balade them to make.
4655 This, for I was so moche to love beholde
In my fer afore past dayes olde,
Ther nas to love so simpill serving wight
But that I faine wolde plese hem, if I might.

As now but lat that on me ded requere
4660 Forto bewaile Fortunes stabilnes,
And tolde me all the case of his matere;
And I, that faine wolde doon hem all gladnes,
Had tane on me right so the bisines
And took me so min enke and papir to.
4665 And for because me thought it best to do,

Forth by mysilf thus went I me alone
Toward the see, where nigh my biding was,
To I come to an high huge rokke of stone
That to beholde hit glemshed bright as glas,
4670 Where as I fonde a benche of mosse and gras
So moche y-growe and eek so verry soft
That it was liik a carpet, as me thought,

Where as anoon that down mysilf I sat
And gan me muse to maken this complaint,
4675 Sin it must nede be doon, as wot you what,

4654 *In,* Into; *roundell or balade:* popular lyric verse forms in both French and English (see Introduction to Lyric Poetry)
4655 *This, for,* Thus, because; *beholde,* indebted
4656–57 In my long before past days of old, there was not so simple a servant of love.
4658 *plese hem,* please him
4659 As now only recently a certain one required me 4660 *Forto,* To
4661 *the case of his matere,* the substance of his case
4663 *tane on me,* taken on myself, undertaken; *bisines,* business
4664 And therefore took to me my ink and paper 4665 *for because,* because
4667 Towards the sea, near which was my dwelling
4668 *To,* Until; *rokke,* cliff 4669 *hit glemshed,* it glittered 4670 *benche,* bank
4671 *moche y-growe,* much (thickly) grown; *eek,* also 4672 *liik,* like
4673 *anoon,* immediately 4675 Since it must needs be done, don't you know

And that I can not make it ovir quaint.
But nevirtheles these were my wordes faint
I for him seide, and gan my papir sprede
And wrote right thus, if so ye list to rede.

4680 O thou Fortune that causest pepill plaine
Upon thy chaunge and mutabilite,
Did I thee so I blamed wrong, certaine,
For stabill yet herto as finde I thee,
Withouten chaunge forto prevailen me;
4685 But whereas first thou fond me in simplesse,
Thou holdest me in min adversite,
So that I may bewaile thy stabilnes.

And yet full many holde opinioun
As that thou shulde now hurt and now amende,
4690 And gladly, als of thy condicioun,
A simpill wight in honure to ascende
And most in weele, as don him downe descende.
But I may well contrary, lo, witnes,
For of my wrecched liif I finde noon ende,
4695 So that I may bewaile thy stabilnes.

For well I se how ricches ascendeth,
And all folke bisy him to plese and yeve;
Whereas the simpill wight descendeth,

4676 *that,* (since) that; *make it ovir quaint,* be too particular 4677 *faint,* weak
4678 *seide,* said; *gan . . . sprede,* spread out 4679 *list to rede,* please to read
4680 *pepill plaine,* people to complain
4682 *Did I thee so,* If I did so to thee; *certaine,* certainly
4683 *yet herto as,* as up to this moment 4684 *forto prevailen,* that might profit
4685 *simplesse,* foolishness, simpleness 4688 And yet, very many believe
4689 *amende,* make reparation
4690–92 And readily, in keeping with your nature, (cause) a simple creature to rise in honor and (be) in greatest bliss, as to cause him to sink (in fortune)
4693 *contrary, lo, witnes,* bear witness, lo, to the contrary
4696 *ricches ascendeth,* wealth prospers
4697 *him:* the wealthy man; *yeve,* give (gifts, services, etc.)

Of alle lothed, and noon him lust releve.
4700 Among which on am I, in suche mischef
Ordained love; but too moche bisynes
Thou hast me geve my lady to acheve,
So that I may bewaile thy stabilnes

Thorugh which I winne more maugre, oft, then love
4705 By my too bisy demening;
And yet God wot, that sitt above,
I most desire of any erthely thing
To doon all that as were to hir plesing;
But of reudenes thou gevest me such larges
4710 That thank to pike me wanteth the konning,
So that I may bewaile thy stabilnes.

Alas, Fortune, now were me wondir wise;
Sett me in wey my lady forto plese,
And if that I have tane too high emprise
4715 I pardoun axe, and that thou not displese,
But turne thy whele my langour to apese
And of my smert to shape me sum redresse,
For yet thou baitest me in noyouslesse,
So that I may bewaile thy stabilnes.

4699 Loathed by all, and no one wants to help him

4700–02 Among which I am one, ordained to love within such adversity; but thou hast given me too much trouble to obtain my lady.

4704 *maugre,* ill-will; *then,* than 4705 *bisy demening,* diligent conduct

4706 *wot,* knows; *sitt,* acts 4708 To do everything that would please her

4709 *reudenes,* harshness; *larges,* largess, abundance

4710 So that to win thanks I lack the skill

4712 *were,* support; *wondir wise,* very skillfully

4713 Set me in the way to please my lady

4714 *tane,* taken; *emprise,* undertaking

4715 *axe,* ask; *and,* and (ask); *displese,* cause (me) displeasure

4716 *langour,* suffering; *apese,* lighten

4717 And prepare me some redress for my pain

4718 For still you cause me 1) to be harassed with annoyance (if *noyouslesse* is misprint for noyousnesse); 2) to be fed in noxious pastures (if *noyouslesse* = noyous lese)

4720 For my dull reudenes hath no governaunce,
Thorugh my demening, hir to doon plesere;
And yet, God wot, as that I have pusshaunce,
I sett min hert, my will, and my desere
Hir forto serve, but all too gret am hir
4725 I willed have, thorugh fonned wilfulnes.
But me prevaileth werring nor prayere,
So that I may bewaile thy stabilnes.

Now fare well, Fortune, with thy stedfast face,
For as I finde, right so I write of thee.
4730 And in my refrait, though I thee manace,
Thou oughtest not, me thenke, displesed be
Though I say trouthe as that thou dost to me,
Bot evir truse and reue on my distres
That I endure in suche adversite,
4735 So that I may bewaile thy stedfastnes.

And when that I had made this poor bill,
So hevy gan min eye liddes way
That even therwith into a slepe I fill;
And all be hit that sum folkes say
4740 To truste on dremes nis but trifill play,
Yet oon may mete the dreme wel in his sevin
As aftirward that shall befalle him evin.

Unto record I take min autour this,

4720 *governaunce,* mode of behavior 4721 Through my conduct, to please her
4722 *wot,* knows; *as,* to the extent; *pusshaunce,* power
4724 *gret am* (an?) *hir,* great a payment 4725 *fonned,* infatuated
4726 But neither struggle nor plea profits me.
4730 *refrait,* refrain; *manace,* threaten 4731 *me thenke,* it seems to me
4732 *as that,* about what
4733 But always make a truce and take pity on my distress 4736 *bill,* document
4737 *gan,* began; *way,* to weigh 4738 *fill,* fell 4739 *all be hit that,* although
4740 To trust dreams is nothing but foolishness.
4741 *oon,* one; *mete,* dream; *wel,* clearly; *sevin,* sleep
4742 *evin,* exactly 4743 For the record I take my authority thus

Of him that wrote the straunge avisioun,
4745 Which called was the preudent Macrobius,
How it befill unto King Sipioun.
So nis hit no, to min opinioun,
Filly noon to take onto thim hid,
Forwhy I thinke it thus, so God me spede:

4750 That hit doth to the body signify
What aftirward as shulde unto him falle —
All othir trust I holde it fantesy —
If so that oon coude well remembre all.
But to my tale, as this, retourne I shall:
4755 That as I lay and slepte thus on the rokke
That on the cleef upon the banke outstokke,

Ovir the see where that the roring wawes
Did overcast the gravell here and there,
As that I slepe, in sweven I saw this —
4760 A lady naked all thing save hir here,
And on her hed liik as a crowne she were
Of doufes white, and many a thousand paire
Hie over hir gan fletter in the aire;

About hir wast a kercher of plesaunce,

4744 *avisioun*, vision
4745 *Which*, Who; *preudent*, wise; *Macrobius:* Latin writer of the late fourth century A.D. whose commentary on Cicero, *Somnium Scipionis* (*Dream of Scipio*), was immensely influential on medieval notions about dreams. Chaucer refers often to the work.
4746 *Sipioun*, Scipio
4747–48 So it is not, in my opinion, any folly to pay attention to them.
4749 *Forwhy*, Because; *me spede*, give me success 4750 *hit*, it; *body*, person
4752–53 All other sources of foreknowledge I hold to be fanciful — if only one could remember everything (that he learned from dreams.)
4754 *as this*, for now 4755 *rokke*, rock
4756 *cleef*, cliff; *banke*, seashore; *outstokke*, jutted out 4757 *wawes*, waves
4758 *overcast the gravell*, broke over the pebbly beach
4759 *sweven*, dream 4760 A lady totally naked except for her hair
4761 *liik as*, something like a; *were*, wore 4762 *doufes*, doves
4763 *Hie*, High; *gan fletter*, fluttered
4764 *wast*, waist; *kercher of plesaunce*, scarf of transparently thin material

4765 And on hir hond an owle I sigh sitting.
Upon the wawes, out more suffisaunce
Me thought afer, she came to me fleting,
And verily it semed me waking,
And went me downe unto the bank a pace
4770 To undirstonde of hir what that she was.

When she came nere, than gan I to hir say,
"Good thrift, Madame, to youre streight sides taine.
But whidir wandre ye this wersom way?
Have I no service might be to you faine?
4775 Me thinke this watir is unto you paine —
Ne nis hit?" "No, no! noon nis hit, iwis!"
Coth she; and as I shope me hir to kis,

She waifed me and loked passing straunge,
"What! nis," quod she, "as purse is of an ay!"
4780 And even forbashed hir coloure gan to chaunge.
"Knowe ye not me?" "No." "Yes!" "Nay, certes, nay."
"No, ye wil not se poore folk now-a-day!

4765 *hond,* hand; *sigh,* saw. Doves are traditionally associated with Venus; the owl belongs to Pallas Athene, and its association here with Venus is both unusual and comic.

4766–68 Upon the waves, without any other support, so it seemed to me from this distance, she came floating toward me; and, truly, I seemed to wake up.

4769 *a pace,* quickly 4770 To learn from her who she was

4771 *than,* then; *gan . . . say,* said

4772 *thrift,* fortune (a conventional greeting); *taine,* twain, two

4773 *wersom,* wearisome 4774 *might,* (that) might; *faine,* pleasing

4775 *paine,* discomfort 4776 "Isn't it?" "No, no! Truly, not at all!"

4777 *Coth,* Said; *shope me,* got ready

4778 *waifed,* avoided; *passing straunge,* exceedingly annoyed

4779 The sense of this expression, which also appears in an earlier roundel (*Jubilee,* 88), is not clear. *Purse* can mean a pouch or wallet, or the membrane surrounding the egg (*ay*). *Nis* (nice) can mean foolish, wanton, strange, slothful, reserved (modest, shy). The phrase "to make it nice" — to display reserve, seems most appropriate here, even though the NED does not record it before 1530. The line would then mean: "What! (Be) reserved or careful, as a wallet is of the egg (carried inside)!"

4780 *even forbashed,* quite abashed

4782 *se,* look at, acknowledge; *now-a-day,* nowadays

Who is hit who that oft hath bete your hound?"
For which I stood so mased in that stound

4785 That I not coude oon sely word abreide;
For sene I had hir, how I niste not where.
To that eft sone she this unto me seide:
"Charlis," quod she, "I thanke youre devoure
That ye shal make suche as my folkes are,
4790 And but so were that ye shulde be aquit,
Iwis, I might wel say I were to wite."

When that I herde hir calle me by my name,
And that I wel had loked on hir face,
Min hert in me hit quoke for verry shame,
4795 For wel I wiste that Venus then hit was,
And seide, "Madame, I putt me to youre gras,
And pardone me, as of youre gret nobles,
That I forgat you of my simplesse."

"You pardone what? What nedeth this," quod she,
4800 Youre mendes is as passing light to make.
But how lede ye youre liif, good — lete us se."
"As an Ancre, Madame, in clothes blake."

4783 *hit,* it; *bete your hound,* beaten your hound (apparently some personal, private reference)

4784–86 Because of which (remark) I stood so dumbfounded at that moment that I could not utter a single word; for I had seen her, though (*how* an error for *thow*?) I knew not where.

4787 *To that eft sone,* Immediately after that

4788–90 "Charles," she said, "I thank you for your service" (perhaps a reference to the lover's complaint he has just written) "that you shall perform for such as are my servants, and unless you were repaid"

4791 *Iwis,* Truly; *wite,* blame 4793 *that,* (when) that

4794 *hit quoke,* it quaked; *verry,* real 4795 *wiste,* knew 4796 *gras,* grace

4797 *as of,* out of; *nobles,* nobleness 4798 *of,* because of

4799 *You pardone what,* Pardon you for what?

4800 *mendes,* amends; *as passing light,* easy enough

4801 *lede,* lead; *good,* my good man 4802 *Ancre,* Anchorite, hermit

"So thinketh me ye have professioun take,
Or ellis ye cast to fonde sum ordir newe,
4805 For strike ye are from Rosett out and blewe."

"A trouthe, ye say me soth, so sett me wel!
For as for blew, I clothe therin min hert;
And alltha rosett is y-entirmelle,
I kepe therin my pouer thought covert,
4810 Alle suche as esy arne — not suche as smert,
For in tawny I leye alle them aside —
And to my deth in blak mysilf I bide."

"Why so?" quod she, "Dwell ye not in No Care?"
"Soth! dwelle I so liik as a mased man
4815 That hath a biding and wot not where,
For though I whilom fer from Sorow ran,
Yet wol he, lo, for ought that evir I can,
Be with me to and to, wil I or no,
And as my frend thus cherishe I my fo."

4820 "But how is it? how cometh he to you so?
Ye dwelle a sondir fer!" "Nay, sothely, nere!
For when me happeth here or there to go,
And thenke that yondir, lo, my lady dere

4803 So, it appears to me that you have taken religious orders.
4804 *cast to fonde,* are trying to found
4805 For you have abandoned rose and blue (in the color of your dress: blue was the traditional color of true love).
4806 In faith, you say truly, so help me!
4808 *alltha,* although; *y-entirmelle,* intermingled (with it)
4809 *pouer,* poor; *covert,* hidden
4810 *suche,* such (thoughts); *esy arne,* are pleasant; *smert,* smart
4811 *tawny,* tawny colors; *leye,* lay 4812 *to,* until; *bide,* continue (to dress)
4813 *No Care,* Indifference (see l. 4644 above)
4814 True! I dwell like a stupefied man. 4815 *biding,* dwelling; *wot,* knows
4816 *whilom,* formerly; *fer,* far 4817 *wol,* will; *can,* can do
4818 Be with me side by side whether I want it or not. 4819 *fo,* foe
4821 *a sondir fer,* far apart; *nere,* near together 4822 *me happeth,* I happen

Gaf me this word, or made me suche a chere,
4825 And aundir herde I hir so swetely sing,
And in this chambre led I hir daunsing;

"In yondir baine so se I hir all naked,
And this and that I sawe hir youndir worche,
Here I fond hir slepe, and yondir waked,
4830 And in this window pleyde we at the lorche,
And from this staire I lad hir to the chirche,
And by the way this tale I to hir tolde,
And here she gaf me, lo, this ring of gold;

"And there at Post and Piler did she play
4835 And so I first my love unto hir tolde,
And there, aferd, she start fro me away;
And with this word she made min hert too bold,
And with this word, allas, she made me cold,
And yondir sigh I hir this resoun write,
4840 And here I baste hir faire round pappes white;

"In suche a towre also I sigh hir last,
And yet wel more a thousand thoughtes mo,
How in that bed the liif eek from hir past —
Thus ay newly aquaint I me with woo
4845 To that to chirche he doth me forto goo
And for hir soule upon my knees pray.
Lo, thus my lives time I drive away.

4824 *Gaf,* Gave; *chere,* welcome 4825 *aundir,* yonder; *herde,* heard
4827 *baine,* bath; *se,* saw 4828 *worche,* do
4829 *slepe,* asleep, sleepy; *waked,* awakened
4830 *lorche,* a kind of backgammon 4832 *by,* along
4834 *Post and Piler,* a game of tag (see note to l. 5203)
4835 *so,* thus (in these circumstances, while we were playing)
4836 And there, fearful, she started back from me.
4839 *sigh,* saw; *resoun,* statement 4840 *baste,* kissed; *pappes,* breasts
4842 And still more than a thousand other memories
4843 *eek,* also; *past,* went 4844 *ay,* perpetually
4845 Until he (sorrow) makes me go to church.
4847 *lives,* life's; *drive away,* spend

"For charge nave I of thing to me beleft
Of good nor harme, more then I telle you this.
4850 And as for yet, I care no thing of theft,
For thorugh the deth my thoughtes riche I mis,
That stede of hit the walles bare I kis,
Or ellis a glove or smokke I from hir stale,
Which was the shitht of hir I loved and shall.

4855 "Unto this painfull, ded professioun
My hert and I are swore unto my last,
Withouten chaunge or newe opinioun,
But this service to kepe me to stedfast:
Ay to remembre on my joyes past.
4860 And I that so must doon, that wold I lere —
Where that I dwelle from woo then fer, or nere?

"Thus have I told you my poore ancre liif,
And what professioun that I am to bounde;
How thenke ye, lo — nis hit contemplatiif?"
4865 "No, certis." "Why?" "Ye do youresilf confound."
"Why, wherof serve I now but bete the ground
As that I goo? Ellis helpe I unto nought."
"Ye, fy!" quod she; "nay — chaunge ye muste that thought!

"Remembre must ye that ye ar a man,

4848 I don't care about anything that is left to me. 4849 *harme,* ill; *this,* thus
4850–52 And as for a gate, I don't worry about theft, for through the death (of her) I lack my thought's treasure (his lady), so that instead of it (her) I kiss the bare walls.
4853 *smokke,* smock (which); *stale,* stole 4854 *shitht,* sheath, covering
4855 *ded,* dead; *professioun,* religious vow
4858 But to keep myself steadfastly at this devotion
4860–61 And I who must do so would like to know this — whether I dwell then far from woe, or near?
4862 *ancre,* hermit-like 4863 *to bounde,* bound to 4864 *nis hit,* isn't it
4865 *certis,* certainly (not); *youresilf confound,* mix yourself up
4866 *serve I,* am I good for; *bete,* beat
4867 As I walk; otherwise, I'm good for nothing 4868 *Ye, fy,* Yes, fie (on you)

4870 And have of nature, als, youre limes goode;
So ought ye kindely, thenk me, spend it than,
Or ellis ye were too moche to blame, by the roode,
Though that youre hert so trewly stonde — or stode —
Youre lady to. O what — now she is goo —
4875 What vaileth here to stroy youresilf in woo?

"Ye may as wel chese you a lady newe,
And for hir soule as daily forto pray
And ben in hert to hir as verry trewe,
As wilfully to doon youresilf to day,
4880 And forto spende in vaine youre time away.
For though ye take a lady in youre arme,
God wot, as now hit doth hir litill harme."

"Alas, Madame," seide I, "that ye shulde say!
Durst I yet speke so foul a word as this?
4885 For ben she ded, min hert must serve hir ay
As I have swore, and so shall doon, iwis,
For in good trouthe ellis did I fer amis.
Allas, Madame, speke me therof no more!
The more ye speke the more me greveth sore.

4890 "And where ye say that I shulde ben a man —
A wrecche am I, an off-cast creature;
For who is she that joy of me wolde han
That am forfaded so in my figure?
Certis, to wrappe me in a sepulture

4870 *als,* also; *limes goode,* limbs sound
4871 So ought you naturally, it seems to me, to spend it (your life) then
4872 *ellis,* else; *by the roode,* by the cross (a mild oath)
4873 *Though that,* Even though; *stode,* stood 4874 *goo,* gone
4875 *vaileth,* availeth; *stroy,* destroy 4876 *chese you,* choose for yourself
4879 *doon,* make; *day,* die 4882 *wot,* knows; *hir,* her (the former lady)
4883 *say,* say (so) 4884 *speke,* speak
4885 *ben she ded,* though she be dead; *ay,* always 4886 *doon, iwis,* do, surely
4887 *fer,* act 4889 *me greveth,* it grieves me 4892 *han,* have
4893 *forfaded,* faded; *figure,* face, appearance
4894 *Certis,* Certainly; *sepulture,* tomb

4895 Me sitteth bet, as wisly God me save,
Then in min armes a newe lady have!"

"Now by my soth, that were a worthy toy —
So preve ye well ye are not worth at all!
What nede I, lo, to paint or make it coy
4900 And in this case youresilf so shame ye shall
And me, and alle my folke in generall?
For alle may say my service is too badde,
That ye nave lust to serve me as ye had.

"And more, therin ye do youre lady shame:
4905 For all the world wol thinke hit, verily,
And she had ben as folk hath gen hir name
Ye wolde have tane anothir hastily:
But they wil say ye doon it for a sy,
And clakke of hir a full ungoodly clause —
4910 Thus shall ye doon hir shame without a cause."

"Allas, Madame! as wisly finde I blis
As me were loth to shame it you or youres,
And most of alle my lady dere, iwis;
But I se deth so creuelly devoures
4915 Suche folkes faire, and in cheef of ther flowres,
That as me think hit is a chois in vaine
To chesen that on shall not long attaine.

4895 Suits me better, so help me God 4896 *Then,* Than 4897 *toy,* trick
4898 Thus you prove that you aren't worth anything at all.
4899 *paint,* pretend; *make it coy,* speak with reserve
4900 If in this matter you intend to shame yourself so 4902 *badde,* bad
4903 *That ye nave lust,* So that you have no wish 4904 *more,* moreover
4905 *hit, verily,* it truly 4906 If she had been as (worthy) as people said
4907 *tane,* taken 4908 *sy,* spot or stain (in her)
4909 *clakke of,* chatter about; *clause,* gossip
4911–12 Alas, Madame! as surely as I hope to find bliss am I reluctant to shame you or yours.
4913 *iwis,* truly 4915 *cheef of ther flowres,* their finest bloom
4916 *me think,* it seems to me
4917 To choose that which one shall not keep for long

"For chase I me a lady, lo, this day,
(As well I wot that shal me not betide)
4920 Yet shulde I drede the deth of hir alway,
To thinke how yong and faire my lady dide.
Thus gif I shulde my service newe provide,
Then brought I me in sorow dubbil fold:
As first to thinke upon my dayes old,

4925 "And then againe upon my service deue,
How were me best to sett my governaunce
To get the favour of my lady newe —
So hard it is in taking acqueintaunce.
For that which is unto sum oon plesaunce
4930 Anothir will, parcas, ben with hit wroth:
The craft of love is straunge who to hit goth.

"For some they joy hem in a port al straunge,
And othir some in gladsom demening;
And some wil thinke he useth fillith of chaunge,
4935 And some will deme this word is flatering.
Thus newe to lere were I in my giding,
For all knew I my lady verry wel,
Anothir newe, I knowe hir nevir a del."

"O what!" quod she, "Ye make a gret perail
4940 To love! me thinke ye nede not don hit so,

4918 *chase I me,* if I chose for myself
4919 Though well I know that won't happen 4920 *drede,* fear
4921 *dide,* died 4922 *gif,* if 4923 *brought I me,* I would bring myself
4925 *deue,* due 4926 *sett my governaunce,* arrange my conduct
4928 *taking,* making 4929 *sum oon,* someone
4930 *parcas,* perchance; *wroth,* angry
4931 *who to hit goth,* for whoever sets himself to learn it
4933 *gladsom demening,* friendly behavior
4934 *he,* a man; *fillith of chaunge,* abundance (?) of fickleness
4936 Thus I would have to learn all over again how to conduct myself.
4937 *all,* although
4938 *Anothir newe,* Some other new (lady); *del,* bit
4939 "O nonsense!" she said. "You make it out to be a great danger"

For if ye cast in love prevaile
Spare not to speke, spede ye so, or no.
Parde, noon wol become youre foo
For youre good will, this ben ye seure —
4945 Hit were too moche ageine nature.

"And where ye care for youre havour —
Where ye shulde ben mery or sad —
Loke wher ye cast stonde in favour
And who that most in prais is had
4950 With hir, where he loke glom or glad:
Folow the same, if that ye can,
And hard it is but ye plese hir than.

"And where ye wolde as have mor dred of deth,
Had ye a lady, for hir then yoursilf,
4955 Parde, deth in youthe not alle a sleth:
Some may ye se that live four score and twelfe,
And by that houre were time for thee to delve.
So fy! for shame! ye ought to trust the best —
Of every dout to sett youre hert at rest.

4960 "And where ye cast alway from love withdrawe,
A feith! I trowe youre labour vaileth not —
For when ye se that that ye nevir saw,

4941–42 For if you expect to succeed in love, don't be reluctant to speak (it) out, whether you succeed by doing this, or not.
4943 *Parde,* By God 4944 On account of your good will, be sure of this
4945 *Hit,* It; *ageine,* against
4946 And where you are worried about your behavior 4947 *Where,* Whether
4948 *Loke wher ye cast,* Look where you hope
4949 *prais is had,* is held in esteem 4950 *where,* whether; *glom,* gleems
4952 And it will be strange if you don't then please her.
4953 *wolde as have,* expect to have 4954 *then,* than (for)
4955 By God, death slays not everyone in youth.
4957 And at that age it were time to dig a grave.
4958 *fy,* fie; *trust,* hope for 4960 *cast,* propose to
4961 In faith, I believe your attempt (to withdraw) won't succeed.
4962 *that that,* that which

It may wel happe you thinke ye never thought."
And as I threw min eye therwith aloft,
4965 Me thought I saw descending in the aire
A chare of gold so verry riche and faire

That forto se hit nas no wondir lite —
The ricches of the stones therupon —
Whiche drawen was with two large stedes white,
4970 And, as me thought, on wheles foure it ran;
About it als I sigh full many on
That did hir paine to put it forth and shove.
And in this chaire ther sat a Quene above,

That forto say you how she ware hir gere,
4975 Hit was y-doon hardly, at point devise.
And if that I shall say you what she were —
But, verry God, me thought it passing nise!
All though it riche were of a wondir prise,
For evirmore the coloure gan to chaunge.
4980 So semed me hir surcot verry straunge,

For the body was couched thorugh and thorugh
As evirmore a saphir and a balaise,
That to beholde it, as I tolde you now,
So as the plaites up and down araise,
4985 So did diverse the heue in sondry wise;

4963 *happe,* happen; *thinke,* think (that which) 4966 *chare,* chariot

4967–68 That it was no small wonder to see the richness of the precious stones upon it. (The following description of Fortune is perhaps the most elaborate in Middle English literature.)

4969 *stedes,* steeds 4971 *als I sigh,* also I saw; *on,* a one

4972 *hir paine,* their best effort 4974 *say,* tell; *ware hir gere,* wore her apparel

4975 It was done (worn) boldly, to the point of perfection. 4976 *were,* wore

4977 But, true God, it seemed to me remarkably curious!

4978 *wondir prise,* great value 4979 *For evirmore,* Continually

4980 *surcot,* outer garment

4981–82 For the bodice was embroidered throughout with, alternately, a sapphire and a ruby.

4983 *to beholde,* in looking at 4984 *So as,* As; *plaites,* pleats; *araise,* rose

4985 So did the color change in various ways.

For though on wey the safir shewed bleu,
This way the balise geveth a purpil heu.

And as the surcot forgoth in substaunce
Of ermin, and is poudred round about,
4990 So was it wrought with fin pinche and plesaunce,
And in the stede of poudring all without,
As I beheld, right wel persaive I mought
How it was sett ful thikke with laughing eyene,
But many moo that wepte I might aspyen.

4995 Upon the whiche she ware a mantell large –
That many fold was fested with a lace,
Because only hit bare so gret a charge –
Of which the coloure blak nor grene it nas,
But most liik to a rainbow heue it was,
5000 Forwhy the silkes were so verry straunge
That ay from bleu to reed or grene they chaunge,

Of which the tisseu ran in cloude-werk,
And as they brak now there and here,
Some with raine and tempest loked derk,
5005 And out of othir smote sonne bemes clere,
And othir some were worst in a manere

4986 *on wey,* one way
4988 *forgoth in substaunce,* substantially excels (other coats)
4989 *Of,* With; *poudred,* sprinkled with small decorations
4990–91 So (also) was it decorated with fine pleating and fine linen, and in place of small decorations sprinkled over the surface
4992 *persaive I mought,* I might perceive 4993 *eyene,* eyes
4994 *moo,* more 4995 *Upon the whiche,* Over which; *ware,* wore
4996–97 That many times over was fastened with a lace (or braid), because it alone bore so great a weight
4998 *nas,* was not 5000 *Forwhy,* Because 5001 *ay,* continually; *reed,* red
5002 Whose rich cloth was worked into patterns resembling clouds
5003 *brak,* broke (into the cloth) 5005 *smote,* burst
5006–8 Some others were wrought (*worst* = *worcht*?) in the shape of moons, some just at the full, very curiously (wrought), some at the wane, some increasing after the new moon. (In the MS the words *some . . . straunge* in l. 5007 have been erased and replaced, in the margin, by *weche that wroʒt wer in a rang*: which were fashioned in a row.)

Of moones, some at ful, right vary straunge,
Some at a wane, some cresing after chaunge.

A bordir had this mantell eek theron
5010 That praty was and riche in verry dede,
For made it was a brere of gold that ron
Now here and there, with roses whit and reede
Upon the which, and leves as they sprede,
Some loose, some fast they sett were ful of ston,
5015 And that of perles passing many oon.

The lining of hit was with nedill wrought
So plain, so thikke, so smothe, so pratily,
With litill, litill flowres soft:
The soven and the daïsy,
5020 But most of pancy might I spy.
About hir nek also she ware
A serpe — the fasson to declare,

Hit wrought was full of broken bales
Of dise; and as they fillen out
5025 By linkes and so downe avales,
To se them how they werle about,
Hit wondir was, withouten dout —
Why, they turned so many chaunses,
And that so ful of verriaunces!

5009 *eek,* also 5010 *praty,* pretty; *in verry dede,* indeed
5011 *a brere,* (into) a brier; *ron,* ran 5012 *reede,* red 5013 *sprede,* opened up
5014 They were thickly set with precious stones — some hanging loose, some tightly attached.
5015 That is, with exceedingly many pearls
5016 *hit,* it (the mantle); *with nedill wrought,* worked with a needle
5017 So simply, so profusely, so smoothly, so prettily 5019 *soven,* forget-me-not
5020 But mostly I noticed pansies. 5021 *ware,* wore
5021–22 About her neck she also wore a collar: to tell about its fashion
5023–29 It was completely worked through with broken pairs of dice; and as they fell out and hung down on loose strings, to see them, how they whirled about, was a great wonder without doubt — why, they turned so many chances (falls of the dice in Hazard), and these so full of changes!

5030 Hir crowne was made with wawes nise
And sett ful of carbonkil ston,
The reising up with flowre-de-lise.
Her heer also so bright it shon
That it was hard to loke it on,
5035 Which spredde hir shuldres all abrod
And all the chaire in which she rood.

Hir visage was eek wel y-made,
But then sumwhile she loured sore,
And even as soune she loked glad.
5040 And in hir hond a whell she bore,
And gan to turne it evirmore,
That berel was, me thought, or glas;
And this was wreten in compas:

"I shal raine, I raine, I have rained";
5045 And "I out-raine," was wreten last of al —
On which that many folkes hem constrained
To gete aloft that sone downe from hit fall,
And wolde clime that might no thing at all;
And othir some they sat up passing hy,
5050 Among the which that on I might aspy,

So inly faire, so full of goodlines,

5030 *wawes nise,* with ingenious waves
5031 *carbonkil ston,* carbuncle stones, MS *son*
5032 *reising up,* raised part of the crown; *flowre-de-lise,* fleur-de-lys
5033 *heer,* hair 5035 Which spread out all over her shoulders
5036 *chaire,* chariot; *rood,* rode 5037 *y-made,* formed
5038 *sumwhile,* for a while 5039 And (then) just like the sun she looked glad
5041 *gan to turne,* turned 5042 *berel was,* was made of beryl
5043 *wreten in compas,* written around the circumference
5044 *raine,* reign 5045 *out-raine,* out-reign (everything else)
5046 *which, i.e.,* the wheel; *hem constrained,* tried hard
5047 *that sone,* who immediately
5048 And wanted to climb who were unable to do it at all
5049 And some others sat very high up (on the wheel)
5050 *on,* one 5051 *inly,* thoroughly

So wel enseured bothe of port and chere,
That this bethought me, lo, doutles
How that it was min owen self lady dere,
5055 And ay the more, the more she came me nere.
"Allas," quod I, "but liveth my lady yet?
Nis she not she, that I se yonder sitt?"

So that I stood so mased and for-mad
That I not coud but stele to gase hir on,
5060 To Venus saw how sore I was bestad,
And to me seide: "Where loke ye, doty fon?"
But my hering so fer was fro me gon
That I not herde nor wiste what that she seide,
To she me shook so that I with-abraide,

5065 And with a sigh I seide hir thus: "Allas!
O faire Madame, now be min helpe or never,
For Jesu wot I stond now in the cas
That certis, swete, the deth were to me lever
Then that I shulde from hir as now dissever,
5070 Which is my lady, hie on yondir whel!"
"Ye, wo is me," quod she, "for youre seek heel!

"I trowe that ye have spide a mase,
Or ye have tane sum sodeine swevene —

5052 *enseured,* assured; *port and chere,* bearing and appearance
5053 That this occurred to me, lo, doubtless
5054 *owen self lady dere,* own dear lady herself
5055 And the closer she (the Queen) came to me, the more I believed it.
5057 *Nis she not she,* Isn't it she? 5058 *mased and for-mad,* dazed and frantic
5059 Could do nothing but gaze at her silently 5060 *To,* Until; *bestad,* beset
5061 *doty fon,* silly fool 5063 *she,* MS *I*
5064 *To,* Until; *with-abraide,* started back
5068 *certis, swete,* surely, sweet one; *lever,* preferable
5069–70 Than that I should now separate from her, who is my lady, high up on yonder wheel
5071 *for youre seek heel,* on account of your ill health
5072–73 I think that you have seen a mirage, or you have fallen into a sudden dream.

For wheron ist, good, that ye gase?"
5075 "A Quene," quod I — "I can not nemene
Hir name — that cometh downe from Hevene,
And in hir hond she hath a whill
Wheron I see my lady well.

"I pray you turne about — not hastily,
5080 But as it were who seith for othir thing —
And loke where so that ye can ought aspy
What that she is, or gesse, to youre seming."
"No more," quod she, and lete downe fall a ring
To pike a countenaunce, so wot ye what,
5085 And turned as it had ben bout for that,

And so began to cast hir eye aside,
Of which look for shame therwith she blosht.
"A Seint Antone! But turne you — hide, hide, hide!
Allas, that ther nar ny of hir sum bosh!"
5090 "But wherof, la, this fer, Madame? O toush!
By verry God, ye are too ferfull oon!"
"Ye, ye, my sone, I wolde some were agoon,

"For trowe ye that they wol not thinke amis
That finde as this no more but ye and I?"
5095 "Why — gef they doo, what can they think on this?
Outt-septe my lady, clene I them defy."
"Ye? Baw! my sheele-straw in youre ey!

5074 *ist, good,* is it, good man 5075 *nemene,* name
5080–82 But like someone who is looking for something else — and look to see whether you can possibly discover, or guess, who she is, in your judgment.
5084 To make a pretext, don't you know 5085 *as,* as if; *bout,* only
5087 *blosht,* blushed 5088 *A Seint Antone,* By Saint Anthony!
5089 Alas that there isn't some bush nearby 5090 *fer,* fear; *toush,* tush
5091 *too ferfull oon,* too fearful a one
5092 Yes, yes, my son, I wish someone were gone.
5093 *trowe ye,* do you believe 5094 *That,* Who; *as this,* at the moment
5095 *gef,* if 5096 Except for my lady, I defy them completely.
5097 Yes? Bah! You're not awake to the danger! (Exact meaning uncertain, but there is a seventeenth century expression — that one's eyes draw straws — to indicate drowsiness.)

For though ye men in such case litill care,
It sitteth well we wimmen to ben ware!

5100 "Yond same is Fortune. How knowe ye hir not?"
"O no, Madame!" "Why yes!" "By God, now, now
I am — I am right wel on hir bethought!
She stale with deth my lady — wot ye how —
Which yondir sitt. By God! I make a vow:
5105 Micht I hir reche, anoon I shulde hir slee!"
"Yee — nar ye holde? Ye are too perlous bee!

"Now, good, graunt us letter of youre pese.
But is hitt ains youre lady that ther sit?"
"O yee!" "O nay, no nist!" "O yes, doutles!"
5110 "O trouthe me thinke ye ought wel borow wit,
For out of drede, wot ye, hit is not hit —
All be she faire and wel unto hir liik."
"A ye, my frend — can ye suche motes piik?"

"I have aspide ye marchaunt at the faire —
5115 Ye lust not on a simpil market see,
That cast you to engros up such a paire
As that your lady was — this semeth me —
And now this same, which lakketh no beute.

5099 It is fitting that we women be cautious! 5100 *How,* Why
5102 I do — I recall her very clearly.
5103 *stale,* stole; *wot ye how,* you know how 5104 *Which,* Who
5105 *reche,* reach; *anoon,* at once; *slee,* slay
5106–07 Well, are you not gracious? You are becoming too mischievous! Now, my good man, give us assurance of your peaceful behavior.
5108 *hitt,* it; *ains youre,* your former, MS *aind*
5109 *no nist,* no it's not; *doutles,* surely 5110 *O trouthe,* In truth
5111–13 For without doubt, you know, it is not she, although she be fair and very much like her. "Ah yes (she is), my friend," (replies Charles). "Can you pick out such small points (as would distinguish them)?"
5114–18 I have watched you shop at the fair — you don't care to look at a humble (cheap) market, who hope to buy up such a pair as your lady was — it seems to me — and now this one, who lacks no beauty.

Ye wold ben dited, sothely, were this knowe,
5120 As for a regrater of the faire, I trowe.

"I wend that ye wold nevir bye nor selle
Suche litill ware, but ye it had forswore;
But now ye nave not, so me thinketh well,
Of which Fortune thank I, not you, therfore.
5125 And if your hert be sett on hir so sore,
Spede if ye can — I cast you not prevaile
Forwhy ye have eschewed my counsaile.

"And nevirtheles I seide it for the best,
As have I joy, more for youre ese then min.
5130 For, as me thought, hit more were for your rest
A lady chese then thus yoursilf forpine —
As that I tolde you now right wel a fin:
When ye had sene, parcas, ye nevir saw,
It might wel happe you finde a bon to gnaw.

5135 "And how is now? what cast you? love or no?
It is not she, I put you out of drede,
So whethir wil ye — love or lete hir go?"
"Allas, Lady, what is me best do rede;
I am so smiten with hir goodlihede

5119 *dited,* indicted; *sothely,* truly; *knowe,* known
5120 As a monopolizer of the fair, I believe 5121 *wend,* thought
5122 Such trifling ware, but (thought that) you had forsworn it
5123 *nave not,* have not (done so)
5124 For which I thank Fortune, not you, therefore
5126 *Spede,* Succeed; *cast,* predict; *not,* (will) not
5127 *Forwhy,* Because 5128 *for the best,* with the best intentions
5129 *As have I joy,* As I hope to have bliss (a mild oath); *ese,* ease
5130–34 For, as I thought, it would do you more good to choose a lady than to pine away — as I told you now to very good effect: when you had seen, perchance, (that which) you never saw, it might well happen that you would find a bone to gnaw on.
5135 *is,* is (it); *cast you,* do you propose
5136 *she, i.e.,* your former lady; *drede,* doubt 5137 *whethir,* which of the two
5138 *me,* for me; *rede,* advise 5139 *goodlihede,* goodliness

5140 That, next my lady, but I love hir best
I am not liik to sett min hert at rest.

"And ner it no that she is hir so liik,
Not shulde I love hir — nor noon living —
The which sight doth my dedly hert aqueke,
5145 That, sin that deth made carfull departing
Betwene me and my lady, saw I thing
Thorugh which I felt on only joy at al,
Nor yet, out this, I wot I nevir shal.

"For levir were me serve hir, lo, for nought
5150 Then to ben king of al this world so round;
If so were onis that she might knowe my thought,
I nolde no more desire upon the ground —
And without you, that may it not be found.
Thus redles in my wery gost I stond:
5155 Save liif and deth, I put it in youre hond.

"Have I doon messe, then ax I you pardoun;
Have I my deth desert, then let me dy;
Beth not my foo, o welaway, so soun!
If I offended have, I mercy cry,

5140 *next,* next to; *but,* unless

5142 And were it not that she is so like her (the former lady)

5143 *noon,* no one

5144–45 Whose sight sets my deathlike heart aquiver, for the reason that, since death caused a sorrowful separation

5146 *thing,* nothing 5147 *on only,* one single 5148 *out,* except for

5149 *levir were me,* I would rather

5151–52 If only she might once know my intention, I would desire nothing more on earth.

5153 *be found,* be achieved

5154 *redles,* without counsel; *wery gost,* weary spirit

5155 Can be read either: Except for life and death, I put matters in your hands; or: Save (my) life and protect (me) from death — I put it in your hands.

5156 *messe,* amiss; *ax,* ask 5157 *desert,* deserved

5158 *Beth,* Be; *foo,* foe; *welaway,* exclamation of despair; *soun,* soon

5160 And as ye lust me now this mater gy,
I me content in all thing moche or lesse:
What may I more then axe you foryefnesse?"

"Then all forgeve — I am not so creuell
To you, as ye to serve me were all straunge —
5165 So that hensforth youre hert in every dell
Ye geve it hir, and never forto chaunge.
And for any wheel reneth so gret a raunge
That it is hard for you to come hir to,
Then shall I telle you how that ye shal do:

5170 "Hange hir upon my kercher of plesaunce,
And I shal bringe thee up to hir aloft."
"Madame, I shall obey your ordinaunce."
"Nay, yet abide, my frend — I am bethought:
As for Fortune, I will ye sle hir nought —
5175 That shal ye promis me yet or ye go."
"Madame, all this it nedeth not, no, no!

"For all the world, I graunt unto hem pese —
Save only deth, that slew my lady dere.
Therof ye must me pardone, lo, doutlese;
5180 For him to love, I can in no manere,
Though that I lived here a thousand yere."
"Nay, sothely, lo, ye resoun have in that.
But honge now on my kercher, wot ye what!"

5160 And however you please to guide this matter for me
5161 *me content,* content myself; *moche or lesse,* more or less, great or small
5162 What more may I do than ask you (for) forgiveness?
5163 *all forgeve,* all is forgiven 5164 *straunge,* diffident
5165 *So that,* So long as; *dell,* part
5167 And because any wheel turns through so great an arc
5168 *hir to,* to her 5170 *hir,* here; *kercher of plesaunce,* scarf of fine linen
5173 Nay, my friend, wait a moment — I call (something) to mind.
5174 *sle,* slay 5175 *or,* before 5176 *it nedeth not,* is unnecessary
5177 *hem,* them 5178 Except for Death, who slew my dear lady
5179 *pardone,* excuse 5183 *wot ye what,* look sharp

And so dredles hir kercher thus I took,
5185 And, as me thought, she bare up me so hie
That even for fere to falle therwith I quok,
And gan "O Lady Venus, mercy!" cry
So loude that it awook me verily,
And fond mysilf wheras I was downe laid;
5190 And in min hond, as I from slepe abreid,

Yet se I wel a gret pese of plesaunce,
The which I took and in my bosum put
So forto kepe it in remembraunce.
And for because that I nedes mut
5195 Muse on my dreem, I sett me up afoot,
And so gan wandre in my thoughtes sade
To that I come undir a grene-wood shade

Upon a launde — the gras soft, smothe, and faire,
That liking gret hit was me to behold.
5200 And homward thus as I gan me repaire,
I fond a company, some yong, some olde,
That gan eche othir fast in armes hold,
For at the Post and Piler did they play;
And all were gentil folkes, dar I say,

5205 As ladies and ther wimmen many oon,
With many a squier and many a knight,
Among the whiche min eyen spide anoon
The selfe lady, by verry God of might,
That I se Fortune bere so high on hight.

5184 *dredles,* fearlessly 5186 *quok,* shook
5187 *gan . . . cry,* cried 5190 *abreid,* started up
5191 *se,* saw; *pese,* piece; *plesaunce,* fine linen 5194 *nedes mut,* must
5196 *sade,* sober, serious 5197 *To that,* Until 5198 *launde,* glade
5199 That it was a great pleasure for me to behold 5200 *gan me repaire,* went
5201 *fond,* found 5202 *gan . . . hold,* held
5203 *Post and Piler:* a game like prisoner's base, in which the object was to seize a member of the opposing team while he was running from pillar to post
5205 *ther,* their 5208 *selfe,* very same; *verry,* true 5209 *se,* saw; *hight,* height

5210 But how me than? Had I more joy or woo?
Now, certis, wel I can not telle you, noo!

For joyful was I on hir to beholde
Because she was so liik my lady swete;
But me to queint — not durst I be so bold
5215 Nad be the dreem that I did of hir mete,
That Venus had hir helpe to me behight
As I have to you told what that she said,
For which that I tho the lesse me dismayd.

Now was ther on had knowen me tofore
5220 That me aspide, and I not how,
And in his corse he fel and had fortore
His hose, at which full many of hem lough.
"Now laughe," seide he, "for some han pleyd inough!"
Which to me spake, "I thank you, frend, my fal,
5225 For nad ye be, I had hit not at al.

"But nevirtheles ye ar welcome, parde.
So now gef rome — take here a pleyer in!
For he shal pley his pagaunt now for me,
Though that his chekes be but passing thin.
5230 Set forth! let se how faire ye can beginne!"
"Nay, good Cosine," seide I, "therof no more.
Seintt Ive, ye shall see that min hose is tore!"

5210 But how did I feel then? Had I more joy or woe? 5211 *noo,* no
5214 *me to queint,* to become acquainted, introduce myself
5215 *Nad be,* Had it not been for; *mete,* dream 5216 *behight,* promised
5218 Because of which I was then less dismayed
5219 *on had,* one who had; *tofore,* before 5220 *not,* know not
5221 *corse,* course; *fortore,* badly torn
5222 *hem,* them; *lough,* laughed 5223 *han,* have
5224–25 Who (then) spoke to me, "I thank you, my friend, for my fall, for had you not been there, I would not have fallen at all."
5227 *gef rome,* make room 5228 *pagaunt,* role 5229 *passing,* exceedingly
5231 *Cosine,* a term of affection, not necessarily of kinship
5232 "By St. Ive, you shall see to it that my stockings are torn!"

By hond he hent me so, and to the place
He drew me in. "Is ther noon othir bote?"
5235 Seide I. "Noo, no, ye get no bettir grace."
Quod I: "Then must I to that nedes mote!"
And so to renne I gan to make a foot;
And wel I wot I ran not long about,
Or that I on had touched of the rout.

5240 And as the corse thus drove me here and there,
Unto my lady newe so streight I went
With gastful hert that quoke for verry fere
How me were best to uttir min entent.
Yet at the last on this poore posse I bent,
5245 When that ther stood no mo but she and I:
"A questioun wold I axe of you, Lady."

"Of me?" quod she, "now, good, what thing is that?"
"It is not small, Madame, I you enseure.
I put a case: if so min hert it sat
5250 To you in love, above eche creature —
Told I it you, wold ye it so discever
And make of it a scoffe or yet a play,
In which, percas, my liif so might it way?"

"God helpe me, nay! Why, wat erthely wight
5255 That loved me unto min honour evir,
Sothely me thinke I did him gret unright
Without the more he were unto me lever.

5233 *hent,* seized 5234 *bote,* help
5236 Said I, "Then I must do what must be done." 5237 *renne,* run
5239 Before I had tagged one of the crowd 5241 *so streight,* thus directly
5242 *gastful,* timid; *fere,* fear 5244 *posse I bent,* post (?) I leaned
5247 *good,* good man 5248 *enseure,* assure
5249 I put a case: suppose that my heart were directed 5251 *discever,* reveal
5252 *play,* joke 5253 *percas,* perchance; *way,* oppress, *i.e.* destroy
5254 *wat,* whatever
5255–60 That loved me always honorably, truly I think I did him great injustice unless he became even dearer to me. Moreover, let her who wishes to be scornful scoff on, for I never will, for I know better what is proper for me to do in such a case — if I didn't, I would have but little wit.

Eek who wil scorne, scoffe on, for I will never,
For bett I wot in suche case how me set
5260 To doon — and ellis I had but litill witt."

"Mercy, Madame, for I stond in the case
That bothe my liif and deth doth on you hong,
For certis, swete, but ye have on me grace,
As for my deth I must it nedes fong.
5265 I can not say that I have loved you long,
But well I wott I love you so, my dere,
That bothe ye are my joy and paine in fere.

"My paine are ye only for fere and drede
The which I have to plaine you of my greef;
5270 And then my joy — that is youre goodlihede
Forto behold, and shall while that I live.
Ther nis no more, but from this time do preve
In any thing where that I be youre man,
And if ye othir finde, so sle me than.

5275 "This is hit all that I of you desere,
That as youre gostly childe ye wold me take
And ye to ben my faire shrift-fadir dere,
To here the poore confessioun that I make,
And that ye not my simpilnes forsake —
5280 For half so moche I dar not to you say
As that I wolde, and these folk were away.

"Eek not I eft from this time how aquaint
Without the helpe of you, min owne swet-hert.

5261 *Mercy,* Thank you 5262 *hong,* hang 5263 *but,* unless
5264 *fong,* receive 5267 *in fere,* together 5268 *for,* because of the
5269 *The which,* Which; *plaine you,* complain to you 5270 *goodlihede,* beauty
5271 *shall,* shall (continue to be) 5272 *do preve,* make proof
5274 *sle,* slay; *than,* then 5276 *gostly,* spiritual
5277 *shrift-fadir dere,* dear confessor
5279 *simpilnes forsake,* despise my simpleness 5281 *and,* if
5282–83 Also I don't know how after this moment to become further acquainted with you without your help, my own sweetheart.

Allas! Be war! youre coloure ginnes faint!
5285 Pinne up youre kercher, kepe youre face covert!
Ye mow say how the sonne hit doth you smert."
"By my good soth, I holde you nise," quod she,
And did right so, and sins seide to me:

"I trowe wel ye have my reude haver sene,
5290 The which ye praise so clein out mesure.
Gramercy you therof, and not youre eyene,
For which ny me they finde no such figure
To cause you of so gret a paine endure.
But many suche as ye in wordes dy,
5295 That passing hard ther graffes ar to spy.

"Also, to lett you speke — that may I not,
And when ye lust, so say me what ye wol;
But forto love, it cometh not in my thought,
Save only on which pleseth me at full,
5300 Nor I cast not to me noon othir pull.
But in all that ye love in good entent,
I thank you. But wist I ye othir ment,

"God helpe me so, I shulde you then eschew.
But then, I gesse ye wolde min honour more."
5305 "Now dredles, lo, Madame, that is yet treu,
For lever nad I ben to liif y-bore

5284 *Be war,* Be careful; *ginnes faint,* grows pale
5286 You may say that the sun troubles you.
5287 *holde you nise,* find you discreet 5288 *sins,* then
5289 *reude haver,* inexperienced behavior
5290 *clein out mesure,* immoderately
5291–95 For that I thank you, not your eyes, because they would not find around me any such face as to cause you to suffer so great distress. But many such as you die in words (only) — it's very hard to locate their graves.
5293 *cause,* MS *sawse* 5296 *lett you speke,* prevent you from speaking
5297 *lust,* please 5299 *on,* one; *at full,* completely
5300–02 Nor do I propose to attract to myself any other sort of person. But to the extent that you love with good intentions, I thank you. But if I knew that you intended otherwise
5304 But then, I rather think that you are more interested in my honor.
5305 *dredles,* certainly 5306 For rather had I not been born

Then that I shulde, for any gref or soore,
Wil ye more fer then ye may goodly graunt
Unto me, wrecche — durste I say, youre servaunt?

5310 "But wold God ye knew min hert eche deel.
Can ye not rede?" "Ye so, so," quod she.
"O what, dere hert, though fer from you I dwel,
Yet wil ye graunt me writ to you, parde —
And not disdaine you on hit forto see —
5315 And send me so of hit sum word againe,
If that I shulde desire you such a paine?"

The raket cometh. "I graunt hit you. Writ on."
And so anothir came and afore hir stood,
For which that I must nedes ben agoon;
5320 Yet nevirtheles me thought it did me good
That she so moche knew of min hert, by the rood.
And so we ran a corse or two, no more,
Or that we must depart, unto my sore.

For Crepusculus, that reveth day his light,
5325 Gan in the West his cloudy mantel shake;
And for because I fasted, lo, that night,
From oon to oon of them my leve I take.
But Lord, so that min hert began to quake,
When that I take shulde of my lady leve,

5307 *Then,* Than; *gref or soore,* grief or pain
5308 Wish you to go further than you may honorably grant
5310 *eche deel,* every bit 5311 *rede,* read; *Ye so, so,* Yes, yes 5312 *fer,* far
5313 *graunt me,* allow me to 5314 And not disdain to read it
5315 *againe,* in reply 5316 If I should ask you to take such trouble
5317 *The raket cometh,* The noisy crowd approached
5319 So that I had to leave (Here the game seems to involve groups of a fixed number arranged in a large circle with the members of each group standing one behind the other as in our child's game of three-deep. Whenever a player attaches himself to the front of a group, thus increasing its number, the back player must run off — as Charles is now obliged to do.)
5323 *Or that,* Before; *unto my sore,* to my sorrow
5324 For dusk, that steals the light (from) day
5326 *fasted:* part of his ceremonial grief for his dead lady
5327 I took my leave of them one by one. 5328 *so that,* how
5329 When I came to take leave of my lady

5330 And for nothing it wold me not beleve.

She blushed reed to see how that I ferde,
For as I kist, I seide, "Now welcome sorow!"
"Ye made me gast," quod she, "I shrimpe your berd;
But may ye not abide here to tomorow?"
5335 "A Madame, no – farewel, Seint John to borow!"
"By Holy God, I trowe bet that ye may;
Ellis come and se us, lo, sum othir day."

"Madame, a trouthe, I thanke youre Ladyship;
It may me happe to se you here this weke."
5340 Thus did I so depart the feleship
And gan me forth to my poor logging peke.
But all that night min hert did rore and seke,
For nought me nist as what was best to do –
To speke or writ – when next I came hir to.

5345 But nevirtheles to this purpos I fell,
That when I might, for fere of forgeting,
By mouth I wolde my mater to hir tell;
And lak of space, to take it by writing –
For which that thus began my new serving,
5350 When that I fond my times of laisere,
As seweth next, if it lust you to here.

5330 *me not beleve,* not stop (trembling) 5331 *ferde,* fared, acted
5333 *gast,* terrified; *shrimpe your berd,* cut your beard, *i.e.,* a statement of defiance or derision (?)
5334 *to,* till 5335 *Seint John to borow,* as St. John is my witness
5336 By Holy God, I think that you could 5337 *Ellis,* Otherwise
5338 *a trouthe,* in truth 5339 *happe,* chance; *weke,* week
5340 *feleship,* company 5341 *peke,* slink 5342 *rore and seke,* howl and sigh
5343 *nought me nist,* I didn't know
5346 *for fere of forgeting,* for fear that she would forget (if he waited long enough to write)
5348–49 And if there were lack of time (to speak), to take the matter up in writing – because of which resolution my new service began.
5350 *fond,* found; *laisere,* leisure
5351 *seweth,* follows; *lust,* please; *here,* hear (An incomplete series of 36 ballades follows, broken off by Charles's release from his long imprisonment.)

BEAST LITERATURE

Beast literature was enormously popular in the Middle Ages, perhaps because it could so easily combine teaching with entertainment. One influence was the group of fables attributed to Aesop, which were known to the Middle Ages through the poetic Latin versions of Phædrus (1st c. A.D.) and Avianus (4th–5th c. A.D.) and through a prose version of Phædrus known as the *Fables of Romulus.* A second influence was the *Physiologus,* or *Bestiary,* deriving ultimately from a 4th century Greek text but familiar to the Middle Ages chiefly through a Latin version written by the abbot Theobaldus (11th c.) and through various later vernacular versions.

The *Fables* of Aesop provided simple stories which treated animals anthropomorphically and which were constructed both to entertain and to illustrate specific moral lessons. The *Bestiaries* told no story but rather interpreted the characteristics and habits of animals — birds, beasts, reptiles, and various fabulous creatures — to show how they illustrate some Christian event or belief, as the owl's shunning of daylight symbolizes the Jews who rejected the light of Christ, or as the panther, who sleeps for three days after a full meal and then wakes with a belch of marvelous sweetness, symbolizes Christ, who after a full life died for three days, and then rose from the dead with a great noise and breathing forth sweetness.[1]

Both of these forms of animal literature readily departed from the literal truth about animal nature and habits. The bestiaries included fabulous creatures like the unicorn and the manticore and fabulous detail and legend about real animals. The beast fables, for their part, were not always faithful to the natural character of the animals they included: the wolf, for instance, is usually stupid and obtuse in the stories, though he is hardly so in nature. Sometimes these fictions were

[1] T. H. White, *The Bestiary* (New York: G. P. Putnam's Sons, 1954), pp. 14–17, 133–34.

due to real ignorance, but more often they derived from a willingness to include any details, true or imaginary, which would contribute to moral or spiritual edification. The candid anthropomorphism of the beast tales makes this immediately clear; it is not always so clear in the bestiaries, which have often been thought by later readers to be honest but misguided attempts at strict scientific descriptions, when in fact their first purpose was to offer reliable spiritual guidance, not reliable natural history.

It is possible to distinguish several different kinds of medieval beast literature: the bestiary itself, the beast epic, beast tale, beast fable, and beast debate. Although there is not a rich Middle English supply of all these kinds, there are examples of each, except for the beast epic, and these probably represent a much larger body of beast literature now lost. There is a Middle English bestiary (early-mid 13th c.); three beast tales — *The Fox and the Wolf* (mid 13th c.), *The False Fox* (mid 13th c.), Chaucer's *Nun's Priest's Tale*; numerous beast fables both standing alone and embedded in other works, before the collections of Lydgate, Henryson, and Caxton in the fifteenth century; and at least three beast debates — *The Owl and the Nightingale* (early 13th c.), *The Thrush and the Nightingale* (late 13th c.), *The Cuckoo and the Nightingale* (late 14th–early 15th c.). In all of its forms this kind of literature draws much of its strength from the medieval belief in a universe of created things which are arranged in an orderly series of parallel, interrelated hierarchies. The world of animals stands just below, and parallels, the world of men. Since its relationships are like those among men they can provide lessons about human conduct; but since it stands lower in the cosmic hierarchy it can also remind men to shun that part of themselves which they share with the beasts as they embrace and perfect those qualities which they share with the angelic ranks above them.

Beast Epic

Although beast stories in general were popular throughout medieval Europe, the beast epic itself was apparently the product of only one limited area. All the extant versions of the Reynard the Fox material come from western France, northern Germany, or the Low Countries; and one story from Aesop — the fox's suggestion that the wolf be flayed so that the sick lion could be wrapped in his skin — seems to be the core episode in them all, appearing in even the shortest and becoming a high point in the longest. The medieval beast epic thus appears to be the conscious elaboration and expansion of a single story popular in one region rather than a gathering together of different stories from many different areas, since it seems unlikely that different writers at different times and places should have independently chosen the same core episode — particularly since it was an episode not included in the versions of Aesop available to the Middle Ages and therefore, perhaps, available only through oral transmission.[2]

The earliest version of the beast-epic is the *Ecbasis Captivi* (early 10th c.), an undistinguished Latin poem which still uses the generic names of the animals but which includes the core episode of the healing of the lion and also associates the wolf with false monks, thus looking forward to his frequent later appearance as a monk or friar, as in Henryson's fable. The use of special animal names first occurs in an anecdote told by Guibert of Nogent (1112) in which the wolf is called Ysengrimus, though not in connection with any particular story. The first fully developed cycle of beast stories is the Latin poem *Ysengrimus* (1148) by Nivard of Ghent. This poem was the main source for the Old French *Roman de Renart* (late 12th c.) which in its turn was the source of the Middle High German *Reinhart Fuchs* (late 12th c.) and a Middle Dutch version (mid 13th c.).

Nivard's *Ysengrimus* is the only one of these collections which can be called an epic in any structural sense. In proper classical tradition it begins *in medias res,* includes a later narrative which fills in earlier events, and is generally organized into a tight, unified whole. The later, vernacular versions are simply collections of stories, in most of which Reynard is the central figure but which are not arranged in any significant order. Moreover, while Nivard's poem had emphasized the tragic fall and death of the wolf, Ysengrimus, through his greed and ignorance, the *Roman* and later versions shift attention from the wolf to the fox, from the failure to the triumph of vice. The loss of epic structure allows these so-called "epics" to be broken up into separate tales that can stand alone, like the Middle English *Fox and the Wolf,*

[2] This account is indebted to W. T. H. Jackson, *The Literature of the Middle Ages* (New York: Columbia University Press, 1960), pp. 329–30.

a version of one of the episodes in the *Roman*. The shift to the fox as central figure allows a shift from tragedy to comedy and a consequent reversal in the moral allegory. While the frustrations and defeats of Ysengrimus had revealed the triumph of orthodox morality, within which the greedy and stupid must pay for their sins, the escapes of Reynard suggest a more realistic — if scandalous — morality in which the wicked succeed, as long as they are clever enough to turn their vices to good account.

The *Roman de Renart* and the separate beast tales that it fostered actually present a double morality — orthodox in the defeats of the wolf, now a secondary character, and pragmatic in the triumphs of the fox. And a medieval audience could enjoy both, simultaneously reassured by the triumph of orthodox morality in the just sufferings of the wolf and delighted by the flaunting of morality in the audacious escapes of the fox. The possibilities for satire were thus enlarged. Animal literature had always provided a good vehicle for satire, since animal characters effectively concealed any real persons or events being criticized, and since animal society was similar enough to ensure identification between animal actors and human audience, yet different enough to allow the objective judgment which satire demands, and remote enough to transform crude farce and immorality into amusement. But in its developed form, its satire cut many ways — satirizing authority for being corrupt and indifferent, or for being virtuous but ineffective, or for being efficient but wicked; satirizing the pretensions of the nobility as they appear in courtly romance; satirizing the vulgarity and coarseness of the lower classes as they appear in *fabliau*.

Beast Tale

The Fox and the Wolf is an illustration of this later tradition. It is a version of one of the stories that make up the *Roman de Renart,* but it can stand quite independently. In itself it is no beast epic, and since the author provides no explicit moral, neither is it a beast fable, but simply a beast tale. There is an implied moral, to be sure, as in most medieval literature, but in the tradition of the *Roman* it has little to do with the triumph of virtue over vice. As we see them, the fox and the wolf are equally wicked — it is not virtue but cleverness that allows one to triumph over the other.

Beast Fable

Robert Henryson's beast fable of *The Fox's Confession* not only provides the explicit moral interpretation characteristic of the fable, but goes behind the traditions of the *Roman* back to the severer moral tone of earlier tradition. Even Nivard's *Ysengrimus* had been unusual in including the death of the wolf at the end, an episode which occurs in no other version. But the death of the fox in Henryson is even more startling. Henryson's probable source tells of a wolf, rather than a fox, who irreverently burlesques the eucharist as he "transforms" flesh into fish; and if Henryson wished to add death to sharpen the morality he had only to add the death of a wolf, for which he had precedent in Nivard and which was in any case appropriate to the wolf's traditional stupidity. But Henryson apparently wished to give to his fable the terribly bitter thrust that only the unexpected death of the clever fox would provide — and he accordingly changed characters, even though he was then obliged to improvise a new fox for the related tale that follows.

Beast Debate

In the beast debate, of which *The Thrush and the Nightingale* is a distinguished Middle English example, the poet relies especially on the traditions of the bestiary, choosing the disputants at least partly on the basis of characteristics and habits assigned to them in these collections of animal descriptions and legend. The nightingale of the bestiaries, for instance, has already been changed from the tragic Philomela of classical myth to Lucina, the light-bringer, who heralds the new day with her song and who is especially associated with childbirth and tender, solicitous motherhood, characteristics which are appropriate on both literal and figurative levels to her role in *The Thrush and the Nightingale*. The thrush is not usually described in the bestiaries, but it too, especially the mavis or song-thrush, is a sweet singer, second only to the nightingale and therefore a worthy opponent. Its different point of view can be attributed to its sex (its remarks about experience with women suggests that it is a male, while the nightingale is traditionally female), and the association of his song with the clear light of day is appropriate to the clear, anti-sentimental cynicism of his arguments.

28 *(13th c.)*

THE THRUSH AND THE NIGHTINGALE

Somer is comen with love to towne,
With blostme and with brides roune
    The note of hasel springeth;
The dewes darkneth in the dale.
5 For longing of the nighttegale
    This foweles murye singeth.

Hic herde a strif betweies two,
That on of wele, that other of wo,
    Betwene two i-fere:
10 That on hereth wimmen that hoe beth hende;
That other hem wole with mighte shende —
    That strif ye mowen i-here.

The nightingale is on by nome
That wol shilden hem from shome;
15   Of scathe hoe wole hem skere.
The threstelcok hem kepeth ay —

(28) [1] *Somer,* Summer

[2] *blostme,* blossom; *brides roune,* birds' song (ll. 1–2 also open a familiar ME lyric.)

[3] The song rises out of the hazel bush (or, the hazel nut is growing).

[4] *dewes,* dews; *darkneth,* darken

[5–6] Because of the desire of the nightingale these birds sing merrily.

[7] *Hic,* I; *strif,* dispute; *betweies,* between

[8] One of them (in defense) of joy, the other, of sorrow [9] *i-fere,* together

[10–11] One praises women, (saying) that they are kind; the other wishes with vigor to put them to shame.

[12] *mowen i-here,* may hear [13] *on by nome,* the name of the one

[14] *shilden hem,* shield them; *shome,* shame

[15] *scathe,* blame; *hoe,* she; *skere,* free

[16] The thrush ever opposes them.

He seyth by nighte and eke by day
 That hi beth fendes i-fere,

For hi beswiketh euchan mon
20 That mest beleveth hem ouppon.
 They hi ben milde of chere,
Hoe beth fikele and fals to fonde,
Hoe wercheth wo in euchan londe:
 Hit were betere that hi nere!

[*Nightingale*] 25 "Hit is shome to blame levedy,
For hi beth hende of corteisy;
 Ich rede that thou lete!
Ne wes nevere bruche so strong
I-broke with righte ne with wrong,
30 That mon ne mighte bete.

"Hi gladieth hem that beth wrothe,
Bothe the heye and the lowe;
 Mid gome hi cunne hem grete.
This world nere nout yif wimen nere;
35 I-maked hoe wes to mones fere —
 Nis no thing also swete."

[17] *seyth,* says; *eke,* also
[18–20] That they are devils together, for they deceive each man who most believes in them.
[21] *They,* Though; *ben,* be; *chere,* appearance
[22] They be fickle and false to the test [23] *wercheth wo,* cause woe
[24] *Hit,* It; *nere,* never were (born or made)
[25] *shome,* (a) shame; *levedy,* (the) lady
[26] *hende,* gracious [27] *Ich rede,* I advise; *lete,* cease
[28–30] Nor was never any offense (or sin) so violent, justly or unjustly committed, that one might not make amends. (MS Auchinleck's *wimmen* serves the argument better than MS Digby's *mon.*)
[31] *Hi gladieth,* They gladden or reconcile; *wrothe,* angry
[32] *heye,* high (noble); *lowe,* lowly
[33–36] They know how to greet (entertain, divert) them with games. This world were nothing, were it not for women; she was created to be as man's companion — there is nothing so sweet.

[*Thrush*] "I ne may wimen herien nohut,
For hi beth swikele and false of thohut,
Also ich am ounderstonde.
40 Hi beth feire and bright on heue —
Here thout is fals and ountreue!
Ful yare ich have hem fonde.

"Alisaundre the King meneth of hem —
In the world nes non so crafty mon,
45 Ne non so riche of londe.
I take witnesse of monye and fele
That riche weren of worldes wele:
Muche wes hem the shonde!"

[*Nightingale*] The nightingale hoe wes wroth:
50 "Fowel, me thinketh thou art me loth
Sweche tales forto showe!
Among a thousent levedies i-tolde
Ther nis non wickede, I holde,
Ther hi sitteth on rowe.

55 "Hi beth of herte meke and milde,
Hemself hi cunne from shome shilde
Withinne bowres wowe,
And swettoust thing in armes to wre,

[37] I cannot praise women. [38] *swikele,* treacherous; *thohut,* thought, intention
[39] As I am informed [40] *feire,* fair; *heue,* appearance [41] *Here,* Their
[42] For a long time I have found them (to be so).
[43] Alexander the King complains of them (Candace outwits Alexander in the ME poem, "King Alexander").
[44] In (all) the world is no man so skillful. [46] *monye and fele,* many and many
[47] *weren,* were; *worldes wele,* worldly wealth
[48] Much was the shame to them.
[50–51] Fowl, I think you are hateful to me, to reveal such tales.
[52] *thousent,* thousand; *i-tolde,* counted up
[54] *Ther,* There where; *on rowe,* in a row [55] *herte,* heart; *meke,* meek
[56–57] They are able to protect themselves from shame inside the walls of a bower.
[58] *swettoust,* sweetest; *wre,* embrace

The mon that holdeth hem in gle.
60 Fowel, wy ne art thou hit i-knowe?"

[*Thrush*] "Gentil fowel, seyst thou hit me?
Ich habbe with hem in bowre i-be —
I haved al mine wille.
Hi willeth for a luitel mede
65 Don a sunfoul derne dede,
Here soule forto spille.

"Fowel, me thinketh thou art les!
They thou be milde and softe of pes,
Thou seyst thine wille.
70 I take witnesse of Adam,
That wes oure furste man,
That fonde hem wicke and ille."

[*Nightingale*] "Threstelcok, thou art wod,
Other thou const too luitel goed,
75 This wimmen forto shende!
Hit is the swetteste driwerye,
And mest hoe counnen of curteisye —
Nis nothing also hende.

"The mest murthe that mon haveth here?
80 Wenne hoe is maked to his fere,

59–60 (For) the man who embraces them with joy. Bird, why don't you confess it?
61 *me,* to me 62 *habbe,* have; *i-be,* been 63 *wille,* desire
64 *willeth,* are willing; *luitel mede,* little reward, bribe
65 (To) do a sinful secret deed 66 *Here,* Their; *spille,* destroy
67 *les,* false 68 *They,* Though; *softe of pes,* easy going
69 *seyst,* sayest; *wille,* desire (*i.e.,* what you wish) 71 *furste,* first
72 Who found them wicked and evil, *wicke,* MS *wicle* 73 *wod,* mad
74–78 Or you know too little good, to shame these women. It is the sweetest love-making, and most (of all) they understand about courtesy. There is nothing altogether so gracious.
79–80 (What is) the greatest pleasure that men have here? When she is made his companion (*fere* can mean wife or mistress).

In armes forto wende.
Hit is shome to blame levedy!
For hem thou shalt gon sory —
Of londe ich wille thee sende!"

[*Thrush*] 85 "Nighttingale, thou havest wrong!
Wolt thou me senden of this lond
For ich holde with the rightte?
I take witnesse of Sire Wawain,
That Jesu Crist yaf might and main
90 And strengthe forto fightte:

"So wide so he hevede i-gon,
Treue ne founde he nevere non,
By daye ne by nightte.
Fowel, for thy false mouth
95 Thy sawe shal ben wide couth —
I rede thee fle with mightte!"

[*Nightingale*] "Ich habbe leve to ben here
In orchard and in erbere,

81 *wende,* enfold 83 *For hem,* Because of them; *gon,* become
84 *Of,* Out of 85 *havest,* are, will be 87 *For,* Because
88 *Wawain,* Gawain (In chronicle and romance before the fifteenth century, Gawain was the preeminent knight of Arthur's court and was famous especially for his courtesy and general knowledge of love and women: see *Romance of the Rose,* 2206–2212, Chaucer's "Squire's Tale," l. 95.)
89 *yaf,* gave 91–92 As widely as he had traveled, he never found a true one.
95 *sawe,* saying; *wide couth,* known widely
96 I advise you to flee with (all your) strength.
97 *leve,* a right (Other editors have contended that the Nightingale's speech begins at l. 94, rather than at l. 97. We find no reason to change the rhetorical pattern of the speeches in the poem, *i.e.,* two complete stanzas for each bird's speech. At the end of his speech (ll. 94–96) the Thrush has asked the Nightingale to get out, in response to the Nightingale's threat (l. 84); and the Nightingale's rejoinder, "I have a right to be here," is perfectly appropriate. Also the direct address of the other as "fowel" in the fourth line of the second stanza of each speech occurs often enough — ll. 94, 106, 112, 154, 178 — to constitute a recurring rhetorical pattern.)
98 *erbere,* arbor

Mine songes forto singe!
100 Herd I nevere by no levedy
Bote hendinese and curteisy,
And joye hi gunnen me bringe.

"Of muchele murthe hi telleth me —
Fere, al so I telle thee,
105 Hi livieth in longinge.
Fowel, thou sitest on hasel bou,
Thou lastest hem, thou havest wou —
Thy word shal wide springe!"

[*Thrush*] "Hit springeth wide, wel ich wot —
110 Thou tel hit him that hit not!
This sawes ne beth nout newe.
Fowel, herkne to my sawe!
Ich wile thee telle of here lawe —
Thou ne kepest nout hem i-knowe.

115 "Thenk on Costantines Quene —
Foul wel hire semede fow and grene —
How sore hit gon hire reue!
Hoe fedde a crupel in hire bour

100 *by,* about 101 *Bote hendinese,* But graciousness
102 And joy they brought to men. 103 *muchele,* much
104 *Fere,* Friend; *al so,* just as
105 (And how) they live in longing, *longinge,* MS *longinginge*
106 *bou,* bough 107 *lastest,* vilify; *havest wou,* art wrong
108 *wide springe,* spread abroad 109 *wot,* know
110–11 Tell it to somebody who doesn't know it! These sayings are not new.
112 *herkne,* listen 113 *here lawe,* their custom
114 You do not bother to understand them.
115 *Thenk on,* Remember. There is a whole class of medieval stories telling of queens who loved an inferior; the detail of a cripple derives from the Orient through Ireland; see Stith Thompson, *Motif-Index of Folk Literature,* Bloomington, Indiana, 1935, V, pp. 278–79: T-232)
116–17 Full well she liked green and various colors (rich apparel) — how bitterly she regretted it.
118 *fedde,* fed; *crupel,* cripple; *bour,* bower

And helede him with covertour:
120 Loke war wimmen ben treue!"

[*Nightingale*] "Threstelcok, thou havest wrong,
Also I sugge one my song,
And that men witeth wide!
Hi beth brighttore ounder shawe
125 Then the day wenne hit dawe
In longe someres tide.

"Come thou hevere in here londe,
Hi shulen don thee in prisoun stronge,
And ther thou shalt abide.
130 The lesinges that thou havest maked —
Ther thou shalt hem forsake,
And shome thee shal betide!"

[*Thrush*] "Nighttingale, thou seyst thine wille;
Thou seyst that wimmen shulen me spille —
135 Datheit wo hit wolde!
In Holy Bok hit is i-founde,
Hi bringeth mony mon to grounde
That proude weren and bolde.

"Thenk oupon Saunsum the stronge,
140 How muchel is wif him dude to wronge —
Ich wot that hoe him solde!
Hit is that worste hord of pris

119 And healed him with a coverlet, *i.e.,* in bed
120 See whether women are true! 122 Just as I say in my song
123 *witeth wide,* know everywhere 124 They are brighter beneath the grove.
125 *Then,* Than; *wenne,* when; *dawe,* dawns 127 *hevere,* ever; *here,* their
128 *shulen don,* shall put 130 *lesinges,* lies 131 *forsake,* renounce
132 *shome,* shame; *betide,* befall 134 *spille,* destroy
135 A curse on (him) who wishes it!
137 They bring many men to ground (to grief).
140 How much his wife did to wrong him! 141 *wot,* know
142–44 It (She) is the worst precious hoard that Jesus created in Paradise to be held as a treasure (with a possible pun on *hoard / whored*)!

That Jesu makede in Parais
In tresour forto holde!"

[*Nightingale*] 145 Tho seide the nighttingale:
"Fowel, wel redy is thy tale;
Herkne to my lore!
Hit is flour that lasteth longe,
And mest i-herd in every londe,
150 And lovelich ounder gore.

"In the worlde nis non so goed leche,
So milde of thoute, so feir of speche,
To hele monnes sore.
Fowel, thou revest al my thohut,
155 Thou dost evele, ne geineth thee nohut—
Ne do thou so nammore!"

[*Thrush*] "Nightingale, thou art ounwis
On hem to leggen so muchel pris—
Thy mede shal ben lene.
160 Among on houndret ne beth five,
Nouther of maidnes ne of wive,
That holdeth hem al clene,

"That hi ne wercheth wo in londe,
Other bringeth men to shonde,
165 And that is wel i-seene.

145 *Tho,* Then 146 Bird, you're quick to answer. 147 *lore,* counsel
148 *Hit,* It 149 *mest i-herd,* most praised
150 And lovely under garments (a common tag)
151 In (all) the world there is no doctor so good 153 *hele,* heal; *sore,* pain
154 *revest,* take away (*i.e.,* drive me out of my wits)
155 *geineth,* gain; *nohut,* naught 156 Don't do so anymore!
157 *ounwis,* foolish 158 *leggen,* lay; *muchel pris,* great excellence
159 *mede,* reward; *lene,* slender 160 Among one hundred there are not five.
161 *Nouther,* Neither; *maidnes,* maidens 162 That keep themselves all pure
163 *wercheth wo,* bring about woe 164 *Other,* Or; *shonde,* harm
165 *i-seene,* seen

And they we sitten therfore to striven,
Bothe of maidnes and of wive,
    Soth ne seyst thou ene."

[*Nightingale*] "O fowel, thy mouth thee haveth i-shend!
170 Thoru wam wes al this world i-wend?
    Of a maide meke and milde!
Of hire sprong that holy bern
That boren wes in Bedlehem,
    And temeth al that is wilde.

175 "Hoe ne weste of sunne ne of shame —
Marie wes ire righte name,
    Crist hire i-shilde!
Fowel, for thy false sawe
Forbedd I thee this wode shawe;
180   Thou fare into the filde!"

[*Thrush*] "Nighttingale, I wes woed,
Other I couthe too luitel goed,
    With thee forto strive.
I suge that ich am overcome
185 Thoru hire that bar that holy sone
    That soffrede wundes five.

166 And though we are sitting (here) to debate about that
168 Truth you say not once.
169 *thee haveth i-shend,* has put you to shame
170 *Thoru wam,* Through whom; *i-wend,* changed
172 From her sprung that holy child
173 *boren,* born; *Bedlehem,* Bethlehem (This spelling accounts for the word *bedlam,* derived from its appearance in the name of a London hospital — St. Mary of Bethlehem — which was an asylum for the insane.)
174 *temeth,* tames 175 *ne weste,* knew not; *sunne,* sin
176 *ire righte,* her proper 177 Christ shield her! 178 *sawe,* saying
179 I forbid you this forest grove. 180 *fare,* go; *filde,* field 181 *woed,* mad
182 Or I knew too little good 184 *suge,* say; *ich am,* I am
185–86 Through her that bore that holy son who suffered five wounds (One of the mystical associations of the number 5 was the five wounds of Christ — nail wounds in the four extremities, and the spear wound in the side.)

"Hi swerie by his holy name
Ne shal I nevere suggen shame
By maidnes ne by wive.
190 Hout of this londe will I te,
Ne rech I nevere weder I fle —
Away ich wille drive!"

187 *Hi swerie,* I swear 189 *By,* About 190 *Hout,* Out; *te,* go
191 *rech,* care; *weder,* whether 192 *drive,* hasten

29 *(13th c.)*

THE FOX AND THE WOLF

A vox gon out of the wode go,
Afingret so that him wes wo;
He nes nevere in none wise
Afingret erour half so swithe.
5 He ne hoeld nouther wey ne strete,
For him wes loth men to mete;
Him were levere meten one hen
Then half an oundred wimmen!
He strok swithe overal
10 So that he ofsei ane wal;
Withinne the walle wes on hous —
The vox wes thider swithe vous,
For he thohute his hounger aquenche,
Other mid mete other mid drunche.
15 Abouten he beheld wel yerne.
Tho eroust begon the vox to erne
Al fort he come to one walle;
And som therof wes afalle,
And wes the wal overal tobroke,
20 And on yat ther wes i-loke.
At the furmeste bruche that he fond

(29) [1–2] A fox went out of the woods, so hungry that he was in distress.
[3] *nes nevere,* was never; *none wise,* no way [4] *erour,* before; *swithe,* sharply
[5] He kept to neither path nor highway.
[6] *him wes loth,* he was loath; *mete,* meet [7] He preferred to meet one hen.
[8] *oundred,* hundred
[9–10] He went along quickly in every direction until he caught sight of a wall.
[11] *wes,* was; *on,* a [12] The fox was very eager (to go) thither.
[13] *thohute,* thought; *aquenche,* to satisfy [14] Either with food or with drink
[15] He looked around very eagerly. [16] *Tho eroust,* Then first; *erne,* run
[17] *Al fort,* Until [18] *afalle,* fallen down
[19] *overal tobroke,* everywhere broken to pieces
[20] *on yat,* a gate; *i-loke,* locked [21] *furmeste bruche,* first breach

He lep in, and over he wond.
Tho he wes inne, smere he lou,
And therof he hadde gome inou —
25 For he com in withouten leve
Bothen of hayward and of reve.
   On hous ther wes, the dore wes ope;
Hennen weren therinne i-crope
Five — that maketh anne flok —
30 And mid hem sat on cok.
The cok him wes flowen on hey,
And two hennen him seten ney.
"Vox!" quad the cok, "wat dest thou thare?
Go hom! Crist thee yeve care!
35 Houre hennen thou dest ofte shome."
"Be stille, ich hote, a Godes nome!"
Quath the vox. "Sire Chauntecler,
Thou fle adown and com me ner.
I nabbe don her nout bote goed —
40 I have leten thine hennen blod;
Hi weren seke ounder the ribe,
That hi ne mightte non lenger libe

22 *lep,* leaped; *wond,* went   23 When he was in, scornfully he laughed.
24 *gome inou,* plenty of enjoyment   25 *leve,* leave
26 Either of hedgekeeper or reve (bailiff)   27 *On,* A
28–29 Five hens had crept in there together — that makes a flock.
30 *mid hem,* with them
31 The cock had flown aloft. (There is probably a gap here, during which the fox has killed three hens while the cock flies aloft with the remaining two; see esp. ll. 55, 68.)
32 *him seten ney,* sat near him
33 "Fox," said the cock, "what are you doing there?"
34 *thee yeve care,* give you sorrow   35 You often do our hens dishonor.
36 Be still, I command (you), in God's name.
37 *Quath,* Said; *Sire Chauntecler,* Sir Chantecleer (Clear Singer), generic name for the cock
38 *fly,* fly; *com me ner,* approach me   39 I have done here nothing but good.
40 *leten,* let, drawn; *hennen blod,* hens' blood (To let blood was a common medical remedy for almost any ill and also a means of preserving good health.)
41–43 They were sick under the rib, so that they might no longer live unless the blood in their veins were drawn (out).

Bote here heddre were i-take —
That I do for almes sake.
45 Ich have hem leten eddre-blod,
And thee, Chauntecler, hit wolde don goed!
Thou havest that ilke ounder the splen —
Thou nestes nevere dayes ten,
For thine lif-dayes beth al ago
50 Bote thou by mine rede do.
I do thee lete blod ounder the brest,
Other sone axe after the prest."
"Go wey!" quod the cok, "wo thee bego!
Thou havest don oure kunne wo —
55 Go mid than that thou havest nouthe.
Acoursed be thou of Godes mouthe!
For were I adown, by Godes nome,
Ich mighte ben siker of othre shome.
Ac weste hit houre cellerer
60 That thou were i-comen her,
He wolde sone after thee yonge
Mid pikes and stones and staves stronge —
Alle thine bones he wolde tobreke.
Thene we weren wel awreke!"
65 He wes stille ne spak namore,

44 *almes,* charity's 45 I have let the blood in their veins.

46 And, Chantecleer, it would do you good.

47 *ilke,* same (sickness); *splen,* spleen (whose secretions were thought to purify the blood)

48 You will never live in the nest (survive) ten days (or, you haven't copulated for ten days).

49 *beth al ago,* are all over 50 Unless you act according to my advice

51–52 I will have you bled under the breast, or immediately send for the priest.

53 "Get out," said the cock, "may misery fall upon you!" 54 *kunne,* kindred

55 *mid than that,* with that which; *nouthe,* now 56 *Acoursed,* Acurst; *of,* by

57 *Godes nome,* God's name

58 *ben siker,* be sure; *othre shome,* additional harm

59 But if our steward knew of it 61 *sone,* immediately; *yonge,* go

63 *tobreke,* break to pieces

64 Then we would be well avenged!

65 *ne,* nor; *namore,* no more

Ac he werth athurst wel sore;
The thurst him dede more wo
Then hevede rather his hounger do.
Overal he ede and sohute:
70 On aventure, his wiit him brohute
To one putte wes water inne,
That wes i-maked mid grete ginne.
Two boketes ther he founde:
That other wende to the grounde,
75 That wen me shulde that on opwinde
That other wolde adown winde.
He ne hounderstod nout of the ginne;
He nom that boket and lop therinne,
For he hopede inou to drinke.
80 This boket beginneth to sinke;
Too late the vox wes bethout
Tho he wes in the ginne i-brout.
Inou he gon him bethenche,
Ac hit ne halp mid none wrenche:
85 Adown he moste, he wes therinne —
I-caut he wes mid swikele ginne.
Hit mighte han i-ben wel his wille
To lete that boket hongi stille.
Wat mith serewe and mid drede,
90 Al his thurst him over-hede.

66 *Ac,* But; *werth,* became 67 *dede,* caused
68 Than his hunger had done earlier
69 *ede,* went; *sohute,* searched, MS *sohbte*
70–71 By chance, his wit brought him to a well with water in it.
72 *mid,* with; *ginne,* ingenuity 73 *boketes,* buckets
74–76 The second one went to the bottom, so that when a man should wind that one up, the other would wind down.
77 He didn't understand the contrivance at all. 78 *nom,* took; *lop,* leapt
79 *inou,* enough, very much 81 *wes bethout,* took thought
82 When he was brought into the contrivance
83–85 He thought a great deal, but no trick helped — down he must, (once) he was therein.
86 *I-caut,* Caught; *swikele,* treacherous 87 *han i-ben wel,* well have been
88 *hongi stille,* hang quietly 89 What with sorrow and fear
90 *him over-hede,* left him

Al thus he com to the grounde,
And water inou ther he founde.
Tho he fond water, yerne he dronk —
Him thoute that water there stonk,
95 For hit wes toyeines his wille!
"Wo worthe," quath the vox, "lust and wille
That ne con meth to his mete!
Yef ich nevede to muchel i-ete,
This ilke shome neddi nouthe,
100 Nedde lust i-ben of mine mouthe.
Him is wo in euche londe
That is thef mid his honde.
Ich am i-caut mid swikele ginne,
Other soum devel me broute herinne.
105 I was woned to ben wiis,
Ac now of me i-don hit hiis!"
The vox wep and reuliche began.
Ther com a wolf gon, after than,
Out oı the depe wode blive,
110 For he wes afingret swithe.
Nothing he ne founde in al the nighte
Wermide his honger aquenche mightte.
He com to the putte, thene vox i-herde —
He him knew wel by his rerde,
115 For hit wes his neighebore
And his gossip of children bore.

91 *Al thus,* Just so 92 *inou,* enough 93 *Tho,* Then; *yerne,* eagerly
94 *Him thoute,* It seemed to him; *stonk,* stank 95 *toyeines,* against
96–100 "A curse," said the fox, "on appetite and desire that knows no moderation in its food! If I hadn't eaten too much, this very shameful thing need not (have happened), had there not been appetite in my mouth."
101 *euche,* every 102 *thef,* thief 104 *Other soum devel,* Or some devil
105 *woned,* accustomed, wont; *wiis,* wise 106 But now it's all over with me!
107 The fox wept and behaved piteously. 108 *com . . . gon,* came; *than,* that
109 *depe,* deep; *blive,* swiftly 110 *afingret swithe,* very hungry
112 *Wermide,* Wherewith; *aquenche,* be satisfied
113 *putte,* well; *thene vox i-herde,* heard the fox 114 *rerde,* voice
115 *hit,* it (he)
116 And his co-sponsor at the baptism of children born (to them)

Adown by the putte he sat.
Quod the wolf, "Wat may ben that
That ich in the putte i-here?
120 Hertou Cristine, other my fere?
Say me soth, ne gabbe thou me nout:
Wo haveth thee in the putte i-brout?"
The vox hine i-knew wel for his kun;
And tho eroust com wiit to him,
125 For he thoute mid sommne ginne
Himself houpbringe, thene wolf therinne.
Quod the vox: "Wo is now there?
Ich wene hit is Sigrim that ich here."
"That is soth," the wolf sede,
130 "Ac wat art thou, so God thee rede?"
"A!" quod the vox, "Ich wille thee telle:
On alpi word ich lie nelle.
Ich am Reneward, thy frend;
And yif ich thine come hevede i-wend,
135 Ich hedde so i-bede for thee
That thou sholdest comen to me."
"Mid thee?" quod the wolf, "Warto?

118 *Wat,* Who 119 *i-here,* hear

120 Are you a Christian (*i.e.,* one of the friars), or my companion?

121 *Say,* MS *May*; *soth,* the truth; *gabbe,* deceive

122 *Wo haveth,* Who has

123 The fox readily recognized him as his kin (probably a reference to the father-godfather relationship just mentioned, though in other versions of the fable the two were sometimes related as uncle-nephew, as were many of the other creatures who appeared in the tale).

124 And only then came an idea to him.

125 *mid sommne ginne,* with some trick

126 To bring himself up, the wolf (down) in 127 *Wo,* Who

128 *wene,* believe; *Sigrim:* derived from Ysengrin, the name of the wolf in the French *Roman de Renart*

130 *wat,* who; *rede,* help (an oath) 132 A single word I shall not lie.

133 *Reneward:* derived from Renart, the name of the fox in the French *Roman de Renart*; *frend,* friend, or kinsman

134–36 And if I had known of your coming, I should have waited for you so that you could have come with me.

137 *Mid,* With; *Warto,* Where to? or To what purpose?

Wat shulde ich ine the putte do?"
Quod the vox, "Thou art ounwiis –
140 Her is the blisse of Paradiis!
Her ich may evere wel fare
Withouten pine, withouten care;
Her is mete, her is drinke;
Her is blisse withouten swinke;
145 Her nis hounger nevermo,
Ne non other kunnes wo –
Of alle gode her is inou!"
Mid thilke wordes the wolf lou.
"Art thou ded, so God thee rede,
150 Other of the worlde?" the wolf sede.
Quod the wolf: "Wenne storve thou?
And wat dest thou there now?
Ne beth nout yet thre dayes ago
That thou, and thy wif also,
155 And thine children, smale and grete,
Alle togedere mid me hete!"
"That is soth," quod the vox;
"Gode thonk, now hit is thus
That ich am to Criste wend!
160 Not hit non of mine frend;
I nolde for al the worldes goed
Ben ine the worlde, ther ich hem fond.
Wat shuld ich ine the worlde go,
Ther nis bote care and wo,
165 And livie in fulthe and in sunne?

138 *Wat,* What 139 *ounwiis,* foolish 140 *Her,* Here 142 *pine,* suffering
144 *swinke,* toil 145 *nis,* is not; *nevermo,* nevermore 146 *kunnes,* kinds of
147 *gode,* good things; *inou,* plenty
148 *Mid thilke,* With (at) these same; *lou,* laughed 149 *ded,* dead
150 *Other of,* Or out of; *sede,* said 151 *Wenne storve thou,* When did you die?
152 *dest thou,* are you doing 153 It is not yet three days ago 156 *hete,* ate
158 *Gode thonk,* thanks to God; *hit,* it 159 *wend,* gone
160 None of my friends (or kinsmen) know of it.
161 I would not for all the world's treasure
162 *ther ich hem fond,* where I found them 163 *Wat,* Why
164 *nis bote,* is nothing but 165 *fulthe,* wickedness; *sunne,* sin

Ac her beth joyes fele cunne —
Her beth bothe shep and get!"
The wolf haveth hounger swithe gret
For he nedde yare i-ete,
170 And tho he herde speken of mete
He wolde bletheliche ben thare.
"A!" quod the wolf, "gode ifere,
Mony goed mel thou havest me benome!
Let me adown to thee come,
175 And al ich wole thee foryeve."
"Ye!" quod the vox, "were thou i-shrive,
And sunnen hevedest al forsake,
And to clene lif i-take,
Ich wolde so bidde for thee
180 That thou sholdest comen to me."
"To wom shuld ich," the wolf seide,
"Ben i-knowe of mine misdede?
Her is nothing alive
That me couthe her now shrive.
185 Thou havest ben ofte min ifere;
Woltou now my shrift i-here,
And al my liif I shal thee telle?"
"Nay!" quod the vox, "I nelle!"
"Neltou?" quod the wolf, "Thin ore!
190 Ich am afingret swithe sore —
Ich wot tonight ich worthe ded,

166 But here are joys of many kinds. 167 *shep and get,* sheep and goats
168 *swithe,* very
169–70 For he had not eaten for a long time, and when he heard food spoken of
171 *bletheliche,* gladly 172 *ifere,* friend
173 *goed mel,* a good meal; *me benome,* taken from me
175 *al,* all; *foryeve,* forgive
176 *were thou i-shrive,* if you were shriven (absolved after confession)
177–78 And had altogether forsaken (your) sins, and adopted a pure life
179 *bidde,* pray 181 *wom,* whom 182 *Ben i-knowe of,* Confess
184 *Her,* Here 185 *ifere,* companion 186 *Woltou,* Will you 187 *And,* If
188 *nelle,* will not 189 *Neltou,* Won't you? *Thin ore,* Have pity!
190 I am very bitterly hungry. 191 *wot,* know; *worthe,* shall be

Bote thou do me somne reed.
For Cristes love, be my prest!"
The wolf bey adown his brest
195 And gon to siken harde and stronge.
"Woltou," quod the vox, "shrift ounderfonge;
Tel thine sunnen, on and on,
That ther beleve never on?"
"Sone," quad the wolf, "wel i-faye!
200 Ich habbe ben qued al my lif-daye;
Ich habbe widewene cors —
Therfore ich fare the wors.
A thousent shep ich habbe abiten,
And mo, yef hi weren i-writen —
205 Ac hit me ofthinketh sore.
Maister, shal I tellen more?"
"Ye!" quad the vox, "al thou most sugge,
Other elleswer thou most abugge."
"Gossip," quod the wolf, "foryef hit me —
210 Ich habbe ofte sehid qued by thee!
Men seide that thou on thine live
Mis-ferdest mid mine wive.
Ich thee aperseivede one stounde,
And in bedde togedere ou founde;
215 Ich wes ofte ou ful ney
And in bedde togedere ou sey.
Ich wende, also othre doth,
That ich i-seie were soth —

192 Unless you give me some counsel 193 *prest,* priest 194 *bey,* bowed
195 *gon,* began; *siken,* sigh 196 *ounderfonge,* undertake
197 *on and on,* one and all 198 *That,* Until; *beleve,* remains; *on,* one
199 *Sone,* At once; *wel i-faye,* very gladly, MS *j-fare* 200 *qued,* wicked
201 I have widows' curse. 202 *wors,* worse 203 *abiten,* bitten to death
204–5 And more, if they were written down — but I regret it sorely.
207 *sugge,* say 208 Or elsewhere (in Hell) you must atone for it.
209 *foryef hit me,* forgive me for it 210 *sehid qued by thee,* spoken evil of you
211 *on thine live,* during your life 212 *Mis-ferdest,* Misbehaved
213 *aperseivede one stounde,* observed on one occasion 214 *ou,* you
215 *ou ful ney,* very near you 216 *ou sey,* you saw
217–18 I believed, as others do, that (what) I saw was true.

And therfore thou were me loth.
220 Gode gossip, ne be thou nohut wroth!"
"Wuolf!" quad the vox him tho,
"Al that thou havest herbefore i-do —
In thohut, in speche, and in dede,
In euche otheres cunnes quede —
225 Ich thee foryeve at thisse nede."
"Crist thee foryelde!" the wolf seide;
"Now ich am in clene live,
Ne recche ich of childe ne of wive!
Ac sey me wat I shal do
230 And ow ich may comen thee to."
Tho quod the vox: "Ich wille thee lere:
I-siist thou a boket hongi there?
Ther is a bruche of Hevene blisse!
Lep therinne, mid iwisse,
235 And thou shalt come to me sone."
Quod the wolf: "That is light to done!"
He lep in and way sumdel —
That weste the vox ful wel! —
The wolf gon sinke, the vox arise.
240 Tho gon the wolf sore agrise!
Tho he com amidde the putte,
The wolf thene vox opward mette.
"Gossip," quod the wolf, "wat now?

219 *loth*, hateful 220 Good kinsman, don't be angry!
221 *him tho*, to him then 222 *herbefore i-do*, done before now
224 In every other kind of evil 225 *at thisse nede*, in this difficult hour
226 *foryelde*, reward
227–28 Now (that) I am cleansed, I care not for (the curses of) child nor of wife!
229 But tell me what I ought to do; *Ac*, MS *At* 230 *ow*, how
231 *lere*, instruct 232 *I-siist*, Do you see; *hongi*, hanging (to hang)
233 *bruche of*, opening into 234 *mid iwisse*, confidently
236 *light to done*, easy to do
237 *way sumdel*, dropped down somewhat
238 *weste*, knew
240–42 Then the wolf began to shudder exceedingly! When he came to the middle of the well, the wolf met the fox (on his way) upward.

Wat havest thou i-munt? weder wolt thou?"
245 "Weder ich wille," the vox sede;
"Ich wille oup, so God me rede!
And now go down with thy meel –
Thy beyete worth wel smal!
Ac ich am therof glad and blithe
250 That thou art nomen in clene live.
Thy soule-knul ich wile do ringe,
And masse for thine soule singe!"
The wrecche benethe nothing ne vind
Bote cold water, and hounger him bind.
255 To colde gistninge he wes i-bede –
Vroggen haveth his dou i-knede!
The wolf in the putte stod,
Afingret so that he wes wod.
Inou he cursede that thider him broute!
260 The vox therof luitel route.

The put him wes the house ney
Ther freren woneden, swithe sley.
Tho that hit com to the time
That hoe shulden arisen, prime,
265 Forto suggen here houssong,
O frere ther wes among

244–46 "What do you have in mind? Where are you going?" "Where I please," said the fox. "I want to go up, so God save me!"

247 *with thy meel,* toward your meal 248 May your profit be very small.

249 *Ac,* MS *At* 250 *nomen in,* brought into

251 Your death knell I will have rung. 252 *singe,* sung

253 *nothing ne vind,* found nothing 254 *him bind,* oppressed him

255 *gistninge,* feast; *i-bede,* invited 256 Frogs have kneaded his dough.

258 *wod,* crazy 259 *Inou,* Much; *that,* the one who

260 The fox cared little for that.

261–62 The well was near the house where lived very shrewd friars.

263 *Tho that hit,* When it

264 When they should arise, prime (early morning); *prime,* MS *.jme* (= *.Ime*)

265 *suggen,* say, chant; *houssong,* matins

266 *O,* one; *among,* among (them)

Of here slep hem shulde awecche,
Wen hoe shulden thidere recche.
He seide: "Ariseth, on and on,
270 And cometh to houssong hevereuchon!"
This ilke frere heite Ailmer;
He wes hoere maister curtiler.
He wes hofthurst swithe stronge:
Right amidward here houssonge
275 Al hone to the putte he hede,
For he wende bete his nede.
He com to the putte and drow —
And the wolf wes hevy inou!
The frere mid al his maine tey
280 So longe that he thene wolf i-sei.
For he sei thene wolf ther sitte,
He gradde, "The Devel is in the putte!"

To the putte hi gonnen gon,
Alle mid pikes and staves and ston,
285 Euch mon mid that he hedde.
Wo wes him that wepne nedde!
Hi comen to the putte, thene wolf opdrowe;
Tho hede the wreche fomen inoue
That weren egre him to slete
290 Mid grete houndes, and to bete!
Wel and wrothe he wes i-swonge —

267–68 (Who) should awaken them from their sleep, when they should go thither (to chapel)
269 *on and on,* one and all 270 *hevereuchon,* everyone 271 *heite,* was called
272 He was their master gardener. 273 *hofthurst,* thirsty
274 *amidward,* in the middle of 275 *hone,* alone; *hede,* went
276 *wende bete,* thought to satisfy 277 *drow,* drew
279 *maine tey,* might pulled 280 So long that he saw the wolf
281 *For,* Because; *sei thene,* saw the 282 *gradde,* cried out
283 *hi gonnen gon,* they went 285 *that,* that which
286 *wepne nedde,* was without a weapon 287 *Hi,* They
288 Then the wretch had enemies enough. 289 *egre,* eager; *slete,* bait
290 *bete,* beat 291 *wrothe,* cruelly; *i-swonge,* beaten

Mid staves and speres he wes i-stounge.
The vox bicharde him, mid iwisse,
For he ne fond none cunnes blisse
295 Ne hof dintes foryevenesse.

292 *speres,* spears; *i-stounge,* stabbed
293 *bicharde,* tricked; *mid iwisse,* certainly
294–95 For he found no bliss of any sort, nor of (his) blows any remission (forgiveness).

30

THE FOX'S CONFESSION

The Taill how this foirsaid Tod maid
his Confessioun to Freir Wolf Waitskaith

Robert Henryson
(fl. 1460–1505)

Leif we this wedow glaid, I you assure,
Of Chantecleir mair blith than I can tell,
And speik we of the subtell aventure
And destenye that to this foxe befell,
5 Whilk durst na mair with waiting intermell
Als lang as leme or licht wes of the day,
Bot bidand nicht, full still lurkand he lay

Whill that Thetes, the Goddis of the flude,
Phebus had callit to the harberye,
10 And Hesperous put up his cluddye hude,
Shawand his lustye visage in the sky.

(30) *Tod,* Fox; *Waitskaith,* One lying in wait to do harm

1–2 We leave this widow happy, I assure you, more happy over Chauntecleer than I can say. (Henryson has just told a version of the Cock and the Fox, the story told by Chaucer's Nun's Priest.)

3 *speik,* speak; *subtell aventure,* strange chance (see gloss l. 36)

4 *destenye,* fate (see gloss l. 36)

5–6 Who dared meddle no more with hunting, as long as there was a beam of daylight

7 *Bot bidand nicht,* But awaiting night; *lurkand,* crouching.

8 *Whill that,* Until; *Thetes,* Thetis, one of the Nereids, MS *om.,* from MS Bannatyne; *flude,* sea

9 Had called Phoebus (God of the Sun) to shelter

10 *Hesperous,* Hesperus, the Evening Star; *cluddye hude,* misty hood

11 *Shawand,* Showing; *lustye,* fair

Than Lawrence luikit up, whair he culd ly,
And cest his hand upoun his ee on hicht,
Merye and glaid that cummit wes the nicht.

15 Out of the wod into ane hill he went,
Whair he micht se the twinkling sterris cleir,
And all the planeitis of the firmament,
Thair cours and eik thair moving in the spheir,
Sum retrograde and sum stationeir,
20 And of the zodiake in what degre
Thay wer ilk ane — as Lowrence leirnit me.

Than Saturne auld wes enterit in Capricorne,
And Juppiter movit in Sagittarye,
And Mars up in the Rammis heid was borne,
25 And Phebus in the Lioun furth can carye;
Venus, the Crab, the Mone was in Aquarye;

12 Then Lowrence (folk name for the fox, possibly from *lowrie* — one that lurks) looked up, where he lay.

13 *cest,* cast; *ee,* eyes; *on hicht,* aloft 14 *cummit wes,* was come

15 *ane,* a 16 *micht se,* might see; *sterris cleir,* bright stars

18 *eik* also; *spheir,* sphere (It was believed that all of the seven planets, which included the sun and moon, were carried on hollow, transparent, concentric spheres, whose different movements accounted for the planets' different speeds and courses through the sky. An outer, eighth sphere held the so-called fixed stars, arranged in figures (Lion, Crab, *etc.*) — the constellations of the Zodiac. Each sphere was tuned to a different musical note, all notes together sounding a celestial harmony or music of the spheres. The Earth was fixed, motionless and silent, at the dead center of this celestial axis.)

19 *Sum retrograde,* some (apparently) moving backwards

20–21 And in what degree of the Zodiac they were, each one, as Lowrence taught me (The Zodiac is that band of the sky, about 8° on either side of the sun's path, which contains all the movements of the planets. As a planet, moving in its own sphere, passed in front of the moving background constellations of fixed stars, it entered the "house" of a particular zodiacal sign; its position within this house determined its "degree.")

22 *auld,* old 23 *in Sagittarye,* into Sagittarius 24 *Rammis heid,* Ram's head

25 *furth can carye,* made (his) way forward

26 *was in Aquarye,* was in Aquarius (The verb serves Venus as well as the Moon.)

Mercurius, the god of eloquence,
Into the Virgine maid his residence.

But astrolab, quadrant, and almanak,
30 (Teichit of nature be instructioun),
The moving of the Hevin this tod can tak —
What influence and constellatioun
Was like to fall upoun the eirth adown.
And to himself he said, withouttin mair:
35 "Weill worth my father that send me to the lair!

"My destenye and eik my weird I ken,
My aventure is cleirlye to me kend;
With mischeif mingit is my mortale men,
My misleving the soner bot gif I mend:

[28] *Into,* In; *maid,* made

[29] *But astrolab,* Without astrolabe (an instrument for observing astronomical positions)

[30] Taught by instruction of nature

[31] *tod,* fox, MS *om.,* from Bassandyne ed. (1571); *tak,* calculate

[32] *constellatioun,* stellar effects [33] *like,* likely

[34] *withouttin mair,* without more ado

[35] A blessing on my father who sent this instruction (revealed by the various planetary conjunctions) to me.

[36] *eik my weird I ken,* also my fate I know (Within Boethian philosophy, which influenced Henryson as it had influenced Chaucer, these various forces can be defined in this way. *Providence* is God's total plan; *Destiny* (*Fate, Weird*) administers this plan through such various agencies as divine spirits, good and evil angels, Nature, celestial influences; *Fortune,* personified as a blind goddess whirling men capriciously up and down on her wheel, is actually the complex interaction on any man of the various destinal forces affecting him; *Aventure* (*Hap, Chance*) is that particular set of events which happen to a given man: seen from his point of view they are completely haphazard; seen from God's point of view, they have been meted out by *Fortune* precisely as *Destiny* has dictated, as it administers through its various agencies God's own *Providence.* From Walter Clyde Curry, *Chaucer and the Mediaeval Sciences,* rev. ed. (New York: Barnes and Noble, 1960), pp. 155–58; 242–45.)

[37] *aventure,* lot; *kend,* made known

[38] *mingit,* mingled; *men,* methods (or way of life)

[39–40] Unless I quickly amend my mis-living: a shameful end is the reward of sin.

40 It is rewaird of sin ane shamefull end.
Thairfoir I will ga seik sum confessour,
And shriiff me clene of my sinnis to this hour.

"Allace!" quod he, "richt waryit ar we thevis!
Our lifis set ilk nicht in aventure;
45 Our cursit craft full mony man mischevis;
Forever we steill and ever ar like pure;
In dreid and shame our dayis we indure —
Sine 'Widdye-nek' and 'Crak-raip' callit als,
And till oure hire hangit up be the hals."

50 Accusand this his cankerit conscience,
Into ane craig he cest about his ee;
Sa saw he cumand ane litill than frome thence
Ane worthye Doctour in Divinitye:
Freir Wolf Waitskaith, in science wonder slye
55 To preich and pray, wes new cummit fra the closter,
With beidis in hand, sayand his *Pater Noster.*

Seand this wolf, this wilye tratour tod
On kneis fell, with hude into his nek.
"Welcome, my father, gostliest under God!"

41 *ga seik,* go seek 42 *shriiff,* shrive
43 "Alas," said he, "properly cursed are we thieves!"
44–45 Our lives sit each night in hazard; our cursed profession (or guile) injures many a man.
46 *steill,* steal; *ar like,* pretend to be 47 *dreid,* dread
48–49 Then, too, we are also called "Withy-neck" and "Crack-rope," and, for our wages, are hanged up by the neck. (The names are appropriate to men who seem marked for hanging: the halter was made of willow-twigs, or withies.)
50 (With) his cankered conscience thus accusing (him)
51 *Into ane craig,* Toward a crag; *ee,* eye
52 (As he did) so, he saw approaching, a little way off
54 Friar Wolf Waitskaith, wonderfully skilled in learning (This name recurs in Caxton's *Reynard,* and the role recurs in another of Henryson's Fables.)
55 *preich,* preach; *new commit fra the closter,* recently come from the cloister
56 *beidis,* beads; *sayand,* saying; *Pater Noster,* Lord's Prayer (lit. Our Father . . .)
57 *Seand,* Seeing; *wilye tratour tod,* wily, treacherous fox
58 *hude into,* hood (pushed back) about 59 *gostliest,* most spiritual

60 Quod he, with mony binge and mony bek.
"Ha!" quod the wolf, "Shir Tod, for what effek
Mak ye sic feir? Rise up! Put on your hude!"
"Father," quod he, "I haif grit caus to dude.

"Ye ar mirrour, lanterne, and sicker way
65 Suld gide sic sempill folk as me to grace.
Your bair feit, and your russat cowle of gray,
Your lene cheik, your paill, pietious face,
Shawis to me your perfite halienes.
For weill war him that anis in his life
70 Had hap to you his sinnis forto shrive."

"Na, selye Lawrence!" quod the wolf, and leuch.
"It plesis me that ye ar penitent."
"Of reif and stouth, shir, I can tell aneuch
That causis me full sair forto repent.
75 Bot, Father, bide still heir upoun the bent,
I you beseik, and heir me to declair
My conscience that prikkis me sa sair."

"Weill," quod the wolf, "sit down upon thy kne."
And he down, bairheid, sat full humilly
80 And sine began with "Benedicitie!"
When I this say, I drew ane litill by,
For it effeiris nouther to heir nor spy

60 *mony binge,* much cringing; *bek,* bowing 61 *Shir,* Sir; *effek,* purpose
62 *sic feir,* such fear (or carrying on) 63 *haif grit,* have great; *dude,* do (so)
64 *Ye ar,* You are; *sicker way,* sure means
65 (Which) should guide such simple folk as me to grace
66 *feit,* feet; *russat cowle,* rusty cowl 67 *lene cheik,* lean cheek
68 *Shawis,* Shows; *perfite halienes,* perfect holiness 69 *weill,* well; *anis,* once
70 *hap,* the good luck; *forto shrive,* to confess
71 *selye,* poor, foolish; *leuch,* laughed
73 *reif and stouth,* theft and robbery; *aneuch,* enough (*i.e.,* plenty)
74 *sair,* bitterly 75 *bide,* abide; *heir,* here; *bent,* heath
76 *beseik,* beseech; *heir,* hear 77 *prikkis,* pricks
78 *Weill,* Well; *upon,* MS *om.,* from Bassandyne ed.
79 *bairheid,* bareheaded; *humilly,* humbly
80 *sine,* then; *Benedicitie,* Bless me! (a customary opening for Confession)
81 *say,* saw; *by,* aside 82 *effeiris,* is proper

Nor to revele thing said under that seill.
Unto the tod this-gait the wolf couth kneill.

85 "Art thou contreit and sorye in thy spreit
For thy traspas?" "Na shir! I can not dude;
Me think that hennis ar sa honye-sweit,
And lambes fleshe that new ar lattin blude,
Forto repent my minde can not conclude
90 Bot of this thing — that I haif slane sa few!"
"Weill," quod the wolf, "in faith, thou art ane shrew!

"Sen thou can not forthink thy wickitnes,
Will thou forbeir in time to cum, and mend?"
"And I forbeir, how shall I leif, allace,
95 Haifand na uther craft me to defend?
Neid causis me to steill whairever I wend.
I eshame to thig; I can not wirk, ye wait;
Yit wald I fane pretend to gentill stait."

"Weill," quod the wolf, "thou wantis pointis twa
100 Belangand to perfite Confessioun.

83 *revele,* reveal; *seill,* seal (of confession)
84 *this-gait,* in this fashion; *couth kneill,* kneeled 85 *spreit,* soul, spirit
86 *dude,* do so 87 It seems to me that hens are so honey-sweet.
88 *new ar lattin blude,* recently are killed (lit. bled) 90 *Bot of,* Except for
91 *shrew,* wicked fellow 92 *Sen,* Since; *forthink,* repent
93 *forbeir,* desist; *mend,* improve 94 *And,* If; *leif,* live
95 Having no other trade (craft) to support me 96 *Neid,* Need; *wend,* go
97–98 I am ashamed to beg; I cannot work, you know (work is beneath him); yet would I gladly aspire to noble estate.
99 *wantis,* lacks
100 *Belangand,* Belonging. Perfect penance comprises three parts: 1) *Contrition* — or true sorrow for the sin; 2) *Confession* — admission of the sin; 3) *Satisfaction* — payment of a temporal punishment. Lawrence confesses, but feels no contrition and undertakes only a trivial punishment. But since the question of satisfaction has not yet come up, and since his confession has apparently been forthright, the two parts may refer to the two parts of contrition: sorrow for what has been done (*forthink*) and determination not to continue (*forbeir*).

To the thrid part of Penitence let us ga:
Will thou tak pane for thy transgressioun?"
"Na shir! considder my complexioun,
Selye and waik, and of my nature tender,
105 Lo – will ye se? – I am baith lene and sklender.

"Yit nevertheles I wald – swa it war licht,
Short, and not grevand to my tendernes –
Tak pairt of pane, fulfill it gif I micht,
To set my selye saule in way of grace."
110 "Thou shall," quod he, "forbeir fleshe untill Pace
To tame this corps, that cursit carioun,
And heir I reik thee full remissioun."

"I grant thairto, swa ye will gif me leif
To eit puddingis, or laip ane litill blude,
115 Or heid or feit or panchis let me preif
In cace na fleshe unto my fude I fall."
"I gif thee leif to gust thy mouth with all
Twiis in the oulk, for neid may haif na law."
"God yeild you shir, for that text weill I knaw."

120 When this wes said, the wolf his wayis went.
The foxe on fute he fuir unto the flude –
To fang him fishe haillelye wes his intent.

101 *ga,* go 102 *tak pane,* accept punishment 103 *complexioun,* constitution
104 *Selye and waik,* Poor and weak
105 *se,* look (at me); *lene and sklender,* lean and undernourished
106 *wald,* would; *swa,* if; *licht,* easy 107 *grevand,* injurious
108 Undertake something of punishment, if I might carry it through
109 *selye saule,* poor soul 110 *forbeir,* give up; *Pace,* Easter
111 *corps,* body; *cursit carioun,* cursed flesh 112 *heir,* here; *reik,* grant
113 I agree to that, if you will give me leave. 114 *eit,* eat; *laip,* lap
115–16 Or let me taste (*preif*) head or feet or stomachs, in case I come by no meat for my food.
117 I give you leave to taste these things.
118 *oulk,* week; *neid,* need; *haif,* have 119 *yeild,* reward; *knaw,* understand
121 *fute,* foot; *fuir,* went; *flude,* sea
122 *fang him,* catch; *haillelye,* entirely

Bot when he saw the watter and wallis woude,
Astonist all still into ane stair he stude
125 And said, "Better that I had biddin at hame
Nor bene ane fishar, in the devillis name!

"Now man I scraip my meit out of the sand,
And I haif nouther boittis, net, nor bait."
As he was thus for falt of meit murnand,
130 Lurkand about his leving forto lait,
Under ane tre he saw ane trip of gait;
Than wes he blithe, and in ane heuch him hid,
And fra the gait he stall ane litill kid.

Sine, over the heuch unto the see he hyis,
135 And tuik the kid be the hornis twane,
And in the watter outher twiis or thriis
He doukit him, and till him can he sayne:
"Ga down Shir Kid, cum up Shir Salmond agane!"
Whill he wes deid; sine to the land him drewch,
140 And of that new-maid salmond eit aneuch.

Thus finelye fillit with young tender meit,
Unto ane derne for dreid he him addrest,
Under ane busk, whair that the sone can beit —
To beik his breist and bellye he thocht best.

[123] *wallis woude,* wild waves [124] Astonished, he stood still in amazement.
[125] *biddin,* stayed; *hame,* home [126] *bene,* been; *fishar,* fisherman
[127] *man,* must; *meit,* food [128] *boittis,* boats; MS *nor net bait*
[129] *falt,* lack; *murnand,* complaining [130] Skulking about to seek his living
[131] *tre,* tree; *trip of gait,* small flock of goats
[132] *blithe,* happy; *heuch,* steep glen, or ravine [133] *stall,* stole
[134] *Sine,* Then; *hyis,* hurries [135] *tuik,* took; *be,* by; *twane,* twain
[136] *outher twiis or thriis,* either twice or thrice
[137] He ducked him, and said to him
[138] *Ga,* Go; *Salmond,* Salmon; *agane,* once more
[139] *Whill,* Until; *drewch,* drew [140] *eit aneuch,* ate enough (plenty)
[141] *finelye fillit,* completely filled
[142] Into a secret hiding place for fear he went.
[143] *busk,* bush; *can beit,* beat down [144] *beik,* warm

145 And rekleslye he said whair he did rest,
Straikand his wame aganis the sonis heit:
"Upoun this wame set war ane bolt full meit!"

When this wes said, the keipare of the gait,
Cairfull in hart his kid wes stollen away,
150 On everye side full warlye couth he wait,
Whill at the last he saw whair Lawrence lay.
Ane bow he bent, ane flane with fedderis gray
He haillit to the heid, and or he steird,
The fox he prikkit fast unto the eird.

155 "Now," quod the foxe, "Allace and wallaway!
Gorrit I am and may no ferther gang;
Me think na man may speik ane worde in play,
Bot now-on-dayis in eirnist it is tane!"
He harlit him, and out he drew his flane,
160 And for his kid, and uther violence,
He tuik his skin and maid ane recompence.

Moralitas

This suddane deith and unprovisit end
Of this fals tod, without provisioun,
Exempill is exhortand folk to mend
165 For dreid of sic ane like confusioun;
For mony now hes gude professioun

146–47 Stretching his belly against the sun's heat: "This belly would make a perfect target for an arrow."
149 *Cairfull,* Full of sorrow 150 Looked very carefully on every side
151 *Whill,* Until 152 *flane,* arrow; *fedderis,* feathers
153 *haillit,* pullet; *or he steird,* before he stirred
154 *prikkit,* pinned; *eird,* earth 155 *wallaway,* an expression of grief
156 *Gorrit,* Pierced through, gored; *gang,* go 157 *Me think na,* It seems no
158 *tane,* taken 159 *harlit,* dragged away 160 *uther,* other
161 *recompence,* atonement *Moralitas,* Moral
162 *deith,* death; *unprovisit,* unforeseen 165 For fear of a similar end
166 *hes,* has; *gude professioun,* good outward appearance (of virtue)

Yit not repentis, nor for thair sinnis greit,
Becaus thay think thair lustye life sa sweit.

Sum bene also, throw consuetude and rite,
170 Vincust be carnale sensualitye;
Suppois thay be as for the time contreit,
Can not forbeir, nor fra thair sinnis fle;
Use drawis nature sa in propertye
Of beist and man, that neidlingis thay mon do
175 As thay of lang time hes bene hantit to.

Bewar, gude folk, and feir this suddane shot
Whilk smitis sair, withoutin resistence.
Attend wiselye, and in your hartis be note:
Aganis deith may na man mak defence;
180 Ceis of your sin, remord your conscience,
Obay unto your God, and ye shall wend
Efter your deith to blis withoutin end.

167 *not,* nothing; *greit,* grieves 168 *lustye,* pleasant
169 Some also be, through custom and practice 170 *Vincust,* Vanquished
172 *forbeir,* abstain; *fle,* fly 173 Habit so dominates the properties of nature.
174 *beist,* beast; *neidlingis,* necessarily; *mon,* must
175 *of lang,* for a long; *hantit,* accustomed 176 *shot,* blow
177 *Whilk,* Which; *sair,* grievously 178 *note,* watchful
180 *Ceis of,* Cease; *remord,* have remorse in 181 *wend,* go

FABLIAU AND BURLESQUE

A *fabliau* is a verse tale, often anonymous, realistic in character and action, written not to instruct but to amuse. Its structure is usually sure and economical, often involving an outrageously contrived plot based on incredible trickery and deception. Its characters are usually ordinary people who engage in lively, colloquial dialogue and indulge in broad humor, often sexual or scatological.

The *fabliau* was popular in France from the late twelfth to the mid-fourteenth century. The genre probably proceeded to England from France sometime in the thirteenth century. A French background for the genre in English is suggested by the occurrence of *Dame Sirith,* the earliest English *fabliau* (late 13th c.), in a MS, Digby 86, which contains pieces both in French (among them several *fabliaux*) and in English, perhaps compiled by an Anglo-Norman scribe. Because we have a *fabliau* from the late thirteenth century and because the genre is mentioned in an Oxford University prohibition in 1292, we can presume that the form was established in England by that time.

Not many examples of the form have survived in English. *Dame Sirith* is, in fact, the only *fabliau* before Chaucer's seven *fabliaux* in the *Canterbury Tales* (Miller's, Reeve's, Friar's, Summoner's, Merchant's, and Shipman's Tales, and the Cook's fragment). Several more survive from the fifteenth century, among them *The Wright's Chaste Wife, The Tale of the Lady Prioress and Her Suitors,* and *The Friars of Berwick.*

Recent critics[1] have suggested that the origins of the *fabliau* may be in the fable. If so, the *fabliau* has moved some distance from the explicit moral strictures and serious intentions of the fable. Yet, *Dame Sirith* for all its comedy contains implicit moral condemnations of women

[1] D. D. R. Owen and Ronald C. Johnston, ed., *Fabliaux* (Oxford: Blackwell, 1957); and Thomas B. W. Reid, *Twelve Fabliaux* (Manchester: University of Manchester Press, 1958).

and lust. Another recent critic,[2] who agrees with this origin of the *fabliau* in fable, also believes that the *fabliau* is a courtly genre composed primarily for the amusement of the upper classes, and that, in its burlesque of courtly romance and courtly erotic intrigue, *fabliau* is *un genre burlesque.*

If we understand by burlesque a grotesque imitation, intended to provoke laughter, of the manner and spirit of a serious work, then we can see that a spirit of burlesque prevails in many genres in Middle English. In the drama perhaps the best example is *The Second Shepherd's Play,* in which the serious action, Christ's Nativity, is preceded by a burlesque nativity. In the lyric, *As I went on Yule Day,* another burlesque of the Nativity is suggested in the "illegitimate" pregnancy of Alysoun. Delight in burlesque may be related to the presentation of Joseph in some medieval texts as a foolish old cuckold. Beast literature of whatever type is full of burlesque, like the burlesque of the confessional in *The Fox and the Wolf.*

The supposition that there may have been in later medieval Europe an aristocratic and courtly literature of burlesque, within which the *fabliau* was an important genre, is interesting. If Chaucer's *Canterbury Tales* are a compendium of late fourteenth-century English courtly literary entertainment, then the presence of seven *fabliaux* in that work reminds us that his aristocratic audience liked a *fabliau* as well as anything. And it is perhaps evidence of this popularity that Chaucer chose for himself the "Tale of Sir Thopas," a burlesque of the courtly romance. Nor does the courtly popularity of burlesque and *fabliau* end with Chaucer, for the fifteenth-century burlesque included here, *The Tournament of Tottenham,* may be such a work (see p. 429). Dunbar, the Scottish court poet of the late fifteenth century, supplies further evidence of the continuance of an aristocratic taste for literary burlesque — witness the mockery of the dream-vision in *Lucina Shining in Silence of the Night* and of the *chanson d'aventure* in *The Treatise of the Two Married Women and the Widow.*

[2] Per NyKrog, *Les Fabliaux* (Copenhagen, 1957).

31 (*13th c.*)

DAME SIRITH

[*Narrator*] As I com by an waye,
Hof on ich herde saye —
  Ful mody mon and proud.
Wis he wes of lore,
5 And gouthlich under gore,
  And clothed in fair shroud.

To lovien he begon
On wedded wimmon;
  Therof he hevede wrong.
10 His herte hire wes al on
That reste nevede he non,
  The love wes so strong.

Wel yerne he him bethoute
How he hire gete moute
15 In any kunnes wise.
That befel on an day
The loverd wend away
  Hon his marchaundise.

He wente him to then inne
20 Ther hoe wonede inne

(31) [1] *com by an waye,* came along the highway
[2] Of one I heard tell [3] *Ful mody mon,* very high-spirited man
[4] *Wis,* Wise; *wes,* was; *lore,* learning [5] And handsome in his clothes
[6] *shroud,* garment [7] *lovien,* love [8] *On,* One, a; *wimmon,* woman
[9] *hevede,* had (was in the) [10] His heart was completely (set) on her.
[11] So that he had no rest [12] *wes,* was [13] Very eagerly he considered
[14] *gete moute,* might get [15] *kunnes wise,* kind of way [16] *That,* It
[17] *loverd,* husband; *wend,* went [18] On his business
[19] *then inne,* the house [20] Wherein she dwelt

(That wes riche won!)
And com into then halle
Ther hoe wes shrud with palle,
And thus he begon:

[*Clerk*] 25 "God almightten be herinne!"
[*Wife*] "Welcome, so ich ever bide wenne!"
Quod this wif.
"His hit thy wille, com and site —
And wat is thy wille let me wite,
30 My leve lif.

"By houre Loverd, Hevene-King,
If I may don anything
That thee is lef,
Thou mightt finden me ful fre —
35 Fol blethely will I don for thee
Withhouten gref."

[*Clerk*] "Dame, God thee foryelde!
Bote on that thou me nout bemelde
Ne make thee wroth,
40 Min hernde will I to thee bede.
Bote wrathen thee for any dede
Were me loth."

[*Wife*] "Nay, iwis, Wilekin!

21 *won,* dwelling 22 *then,* the 23 Where she was dressed in rich cloth
25 May God Almighty be herein!
26 Welcome, as I ever hope for happiness (a mild oath) 27 *Quod,* Said
28 *His hit,* If it is; *site,* sit down
29–30 And let me know what is your will, my dear.
31 *houre Loverd,* our Lord 32 *don,* do
33 That is pleasing to you 34 *finden,* find; *fre,* generous
35–36 Very willingly will I perform for you, without grudging.
37 *foryelde,* reward 38 Providing only that you not inform on me
39 *Ne,* Nor 40 *Min hernde,* My errand (business); *bede,* announce
41–42 But I would be loth for you to get angry over anything done.
43–48 Nay, surely not, Wilekin, of nothing whatever that is mine, though you desire it, will I be ungenerous. Neither do I know anything about meanness nor do I intend to learn.

For nothing that ever is min,
45 Thau thou hit yirne,
Houncurteis ne will I be.
Ne con I nout on vilte,
Ne nout I nelle lerne.

"Thou mait sayen al thine wille,
50 And I shal herknen — and sitten stille —
That thou have told.
And if that thou me tellest skil,
I shal don after thy wil —
That be thou bold.

55 "And thau thou saye me any shame,
Ne shal I thee nouight blame
For thy sawe."
[*Clerk*] "Now ich have wonne leve,
Yif that I me shulde greve
60 Hit were hounlawe.

"Certes, Dame, thou seyst as hende,
And I shal setten spel on ende
And tellen thee al —
Wat ich wolde and wy ich com;
65 Ne con ich sayen non falsdom,
Ne non I ne shal.

"Ich habbe i-loved thee mony yer,
Thau ich nabbe nout ben her

49 *mait*, may 50 *herknen*, listen 51 *That*, Until
52 *skil*, something reasonable 53 *don after*, do according to
54 Be sure of that. 55 *thau*, though 56 *nouight*, nought
57 *sawe*, words 58 *ich*, I; *leve*, permission
59–62 If I should complain, that would be wrong. Certainly, Dame, you speak like a courteous (person), and I shall come to the point.
64–66 What I wanted and why I came; neither do I know how to tell lies, nor shall I tell any.
67–68 I have loved you many a year, though I have not been here.

My love to showe.
70 Wile thy loverd is in towne,
Ne may no mon with thee holden roune
With no thewe.

"Yurstenday ich herde saye,
As ich wende by the waye,
75 Of oure sire:
Me tolde me that he was gon
To the Feire of Botolfston
In Lincolnshire.

"And for ich weste that he wes houte,
80 Tharfore ich am i-gon aboute
To speken with thee.
Him burth to liken wel his lif
That mightte welde secc a wif
In privite.

85 "Dame, if hit is thy wille,
Both dernelike and stille
Ich wille thee love."
[*Wife*] "That wold I don for non thing,
By houre Loverd, Hevene-King,
90 That ous is bove!

"Ich habe my loverd that is my spouse,
That maiden broute me to house

70 *Wile,* While 71 *mon,* man; *roune,* private conversation
72 *thewe,* propriety
73–75 Yesterday, as I went along the highway, I heard our master spoken of.
76 *Me,* Men 77 *Feire,* Fair; *Botolfston,* Boston
79 And because I knew that he was away from home
80 *i-gon aboute,* taken steps
82–84 He who might privately possess such a wife ought to be well pleased with his life.
86 Both secretly and silently 88 *wold,* would; *don,* do; *thing,* MS *þin*
90 *ous,* us; *bove,* above 91 *habe,* have
92–93 Who brought me (as a) maiden to (his) house, with great honor

Mid menske inou.
He loveth me and ich him wel;
95 Oure love is also treue as stel,
Withhouten wou.

"Thau he be from hom on his hernde,
Ich were ounsely if ich lernede
To ben on hore.
100 That ne shal nevere be
That I shal don selk falsete
On bedde, ne on flore.

"Nevermore his lif-wile,
Thau he were on hondred mile
105 Beyende Rome,
For nothing ne shuld I take
Mon on erthe to ben my make
Ar his hom-come."

[*Clerk*] "Dame, Dame, torn thy mod!
110 Thy curteisy wes ever god,
And yet shal be:
For the Loverd that ous haveth wrout
Amend thy mod, and torn thy thout,
And reu on me!"

[*Wife*] 115 "We! we! oldest thou me a fol?
So ich ever mote biden Yol,
Thou art ounwis!

95 *also treue as stel,* just as true as steel 96 *wou,* evil 98 *ounsely,* wicked
99 *on hore,* a whore 101 *selk,* such 102 *flore,* floor
103 Never (during) his lifetime 104 *on,* a 105 *Beyende,* Beyond
106–8 I wouldn't for anything take (a) man in the earth to be my lover before his home-coming.
109 *torn thy mod,* change your mind 110 *curteisy,* graciousness; *god,* good
112 *ous haveth wrout,* hath made us 113 *thout,* thought 114 *reu,* take pity
115–16 Oh! Oh! do you take me for a fool? As I ever hope to see another Christmas
117 *ounwis,* foolish

My thout ne shalt thou never wende.
My loverd is curteis mon and hende,
120 And mon of pris;

"And ich am wif bothe god and treue —
Treuer womon ne may no mon knowe
Then ich am.
Thilke time ne shal never betide
125 That mon for wowing ne thoru prude
Shal do me sham!"

[*Clerk*] "Swete lemmon, mercy!
Shame ne vilany
Ne bede I thee non,
130 Bote derne love I thee bede —
As mon that wolde of love spede
And finde won."

[*Wife*] "So bide ich evere mete other drinke,
Her thou lesest al thy swinke.
135 Thou might gon hom, leve brother,
For wille ich thee love, ne non other,
Bote my wedde houssebonde —
To tellen hit thee ne wille ich wonde."
[*Clerk*] "Certes, Dame, that me forthinketh!
140 And wo is the mon that muchel swinketh

118 *wende,* alter 119 *mon,* man; *hende,* gracious 120 *pris,* worth
124 *Thilke,* That same; *betide,* happen
125 That (a) man through soliciting or through pride 126 *sham,* shame
127 Sweet mistress, mercy! *lemmon,* MS *lenmon* 129 I ask of you none
130 *Bote,* But; *derne,* secret 132 *finde,* MS *fide*
131–32 Like a man who wants to prosper in love and find plenty. (*Won* also means dwelling place; surely both meanings are intended.)
133–35 As ever I hope to have food and drink, here you lose all your labor. You can go home, dear brother.
136 A negative seems to be missing in the first clause. 137 *Bote,* Except
138 *wonde,* hesitate
139 *that me forthinketh,* I am sorry to hear it.
140 *wo,* woe; *that,* MS *þa*; *muchel swinketh,* greatly labors

And at the laste leseth his sped!
To maken menes his him ned.
By me I saye, ful iwis,
That love the love that I shal mis.
145 An, Dame, have now godneday!
And thilke Loverd that al welde may
Leve that thy thout so tourne
That ich for thee no leng ne mourne."

[*Narrator*] Drerymod he wente away,
150 And thoute bothe night and day
Hire al forto wende.
A frend him radde forto fare —
And leven al his muchele care —
To Dame Sirith the hende.

155 Thider he wente him anon
So swithe so he mightte gon —
No mon he n'i-mette;
Ful he wes of tene and treye.
Mid wordes milde and eke sleye
160 Faire he hire grette:
[*Clerk*] "God thee i-blessi, Dame Sirith!
Ich am i-com to speken thee with,
For ful muchele nede.
And ich may have help of thee,
165 Thou shalt have, that thou shalt se,

141 *leseth,* loses; *sped,* success
142–44 It is necessary for him to employ an intermediary. Concerning myself I speak, quite certainly, who loves the love that I shall lack.
145 *An,* And 146 *thilke,* that same; *welde,* control 147 *Leve,* Grant
148 *ich,* MS *ihc*; *leng,* longer; *ne mourne,* mourn
149 *Drerymod,* Downhearted 150 *thoute,* planned
151 (How to) change her (mind) entirely 152 *radde,* advised; *fare,* go
153 *leven,* leave behind; *muchele,* great 154 *hende,* clever
155–56 Thither he went directly as quickly as he might go. 157 *n'i-mette,* met
158 *tene and treye,* grief and affliction 159 *Mid,* With; *eke sleye,* also crafty
160 He greeted her pleasantly. 161 *i-blessi,* bless 164 *And,* If
165 *se,* see

Ful riche mede."
[*Woman*] "Welcomen art thou, leve sone!
And if ich may other cone
In eny wise for thee do,
170 I shal strengthen me therto.
Forthy, leve sone, tel thou me
Wat thou woldest I dude for thee."
[*Clerk*] "Bote, leve nelde! Ful evele I fare!
I lede my lif with tene and care.

175 "With muchel hounsele ich lede my lif,
And that is for on swete wif
That heightte Margeri.
Ich have i-loved hire mony day,
And of hire love hoe seyth me nay:
180 Hider ich com forthy.

"Bote if hoe wende hire mod,
For serewe mon ich wakese wod
Other miselve quelle.
Ich hevede i-thout myself to slo;
185 Forth then radde a frend me go
To thee my serewe telle.

"He saide me, withhouten faille,
That thou me couthest helpe and vaile,
And bringen me of wo,

166 *mede,* reward 167 *leve sone,* dear son 168 *may other cone,* may or can
169 In any way act in your behalf 170 *strengthen me,* exert myself
171 *Forthy,* Therefore 172 *Wat,* What; *dude,* did
173 Remedy, dear old lady! I fare very wickedly. 174 *tene,* grief
175 *hounsele,* misery 176 *for on,* because of one 177 *heightte,* is named
178 *mony,* many a 179 *hoe seyth me nay,* she refuses me 180 *Hider,* Hither
181–83 Unless she changes her mind, for sorrow I must go mad, or kill myself.
184 *hevede i-thout,* had thought; *slo,* slay 185 *Forth,* MS *For*
185–86 When a friend advised me to go out to tell you my sorrow
187 *saide,* told
188 *couthest,* could; *vaile,* assist
189 *of,* out of

190 Thoru thine crafftes and thine dedes.
And ich wile yeve thee riche mede,
With that hit be so."

[*Woman*] "Benedicite be herinne!
Her havest thou, sone, mikel senne.
195 Loverd, for his swete nome,
Lete thee therfore haven no shome!
Thou servest affter Godes grome
Wen thou seyst on me silk blame.
For ich am old and sek and lame —
200 Seknesse haveth maked me ful tame.
Blesse thee! blesse thee! leve knave,
Leste thou mesaventer have,
For this lesing that is founden
Oppon me, that am harde i-bonden!
205 Ich am on holy wimon —
On wicchecrafft nout I ne con,
Bote with gode men almesdede
Ilke day my lif I fede,
And bidde my *Paternoster* and my Crede,
210 That Goed hem helpe at hore nede
That helpen me my life to lede,
And leve that hem mote wel spede —
His lif and his soule worthe i-shend

190 *crafftes,* tricks 191 *yeve,* give; *mede,* reward 192 *With,* If
193–94 God bless us! In this matter, son, you have great sin.
195 *nome,* name 196 *Lete,* Let; *shome,* shame
197–98 You deserve God's anger when you speak against me such accusation.
199 *sek,* sick 201 *leve knave,* dear boy 202 *mesaventer,* misadventure
203–4 Because of this lie that is invented about me, who am hard pressed
205 *on,* a
206–7 Of witchcraft I know nothing — but (or, only) with good men's alms-gifts
208 *Ilke,* Each; *fede,* feed
209 And pray the Lord's Prayer (*Paternoster*) and my Creed
210 *Goed,* God; *hem,* them (*i.e.,* the *gode men* of l. 207); *hore,* their
211 *That,* Who
212–14 And grant that they may prosper well — may his life and soul be destroyed who hath sent you to me on this errand!

That thee to me this hernde haveth send!
215 And leve me to ben i-wreken
On him this shome me haveth speken!"

[*Clerk*] "Leve nelde, belef al this!
Me thinketh that thou art onwis.
The mon that me to thee taute,
220 He weste that thou hous couthest saute.
Help, Dame Sirith, if thou maut,
To make me with the sweting saut,
And ich wille geve thee gift ful stark –
Mony a pound and mony a mark,
225 Warme pilche and warme shon –
With that min hernde be wel don.
Of muchel godlec might thou yelpe,
If hit be so that thou me helpe."
[*Woman*] "Ligh me nout, Wilekin, by thy leute.
230 Is hit thin hernest thou tellest me?
Lovest thou wel Dame Margeri?"
[*Clerk*] "Ye, nelde, witerly
Ich hire love! Hit mot me spille
Bote ich gete hire to my wille!"
[*Woman*] 235 "Wat God, Wilekin, me reueth thy scathe –
Houre Loverd sende thee help rathe!

215 *leve,* grant; *i-wreken,* avenged 216 *him,* him who; *me,* of me
217 *belef,* leave 218 It seems that you are unskillful; *that,* MS *þa*
219 *taute,* directed 220 He knew that you could reconcile us.
221 *maut,* might 222 *sweting saut,* mistress reconciled
223 *ful stark,* very large 224 A *mark* is worth two thirds of a *pound.*
225 *pilche,* fur coat; *shon,* shoes 226 *With that,* If
227 Of much goodness might you boast
229 Don't lie to me, Wilekin, by your loyalty.
230 *thin hernest,* your real intention
232–34 Yes, old one, truly I love her! It may kill me unless I win her to my desire.
235 God knows, Wilekin, I pity your suffering.
236 *Houre,* Our; *rathe,* quickly

"Weste hic hit mighhte ben forholen,
Me wolde thunche wel folen
Thy wille forto fullen.
240 Make me siker with word on honde
That thou wolt helen, and I wile fonde
If ich may hire tellen.

"For al the world ne wold I nout
That ich were to Chapitre i-brout
245 For none selke werkes.
My juggement were sone i-given
To ben with shome somer-driven
With prestes and with clarkes."

[*Clerk*] "Iwis, nelde, ne wold I
250 That thou hevedest vilany
Ne shame for my goed.
Her I thee my trouthe plightte:
Ich shal helen by my mightte,
By the holy roed!"

[*Woman*] 255 "Welcome, Wilekin, hiderward!

237–39 If I knew it might be concealed, I would think myself well employed to fulfill your desires.

240 Make me sure with a hand shake. (See B. D. H. Miller, " 'Word in Hand'; A Problem in 'Dame Sirith,' " *Notes and Queries* CCVIII (1963), 51–54, 90–92, 123–27.)

241 *helen*, keep silent or secret; *fonde*, try

242 *tellen*, persuade 243 *ne wold I nout*, I do not wish

244–48 That I were brought to Chapter (before an ecclesiastical court) for any such dealings. Judgment against me would soon be given – to be driven with shame on a pack horse (through the streets) – by both priests and clerks. (Chaucer's *Friar's Tale* ll. 1301–11 gives further evidence of this jurisdiction by ecclesiastical courts over bawdry and witchcraft, both of which are involved in Dame Sirith's fears.)

249 *Iwis*, Surely 251 *for my goed*, on account of my good fortune

252–53 Here I pledge you my truth: I shall keep silent to my best ability.

254 *roed*, rood, cross 255 *hiderward*, to this place

Her havest i-maked a foreward
  That thee may ful wel like.
Thou maight blesse thilke sith,
For thou maight make thee ful blith;
260 Thar thou namore sike.

"To goder-hele ever come thou hider,
For sone will I gange thider
  And maken hire hounderstonde;
I shal kenne hire sulke a lore
265 That hoe shal lovien thee mikel more
  Then any mon in londe."

[*Clerk*] "Also hav I Godes grith,
Wel havest thou said, Dame Sirith!
  And goder-hele shal ben thin!
270 Have her twenty shiling:
This ich yeve thee to meding,
  To buggen thee shep and swin."

[*Woman*] "So ich evere brouke hous other flet,
Neren never pones beter beset
275 Then thes shulen ben!
For I shal don a juperty
And a ferly maistry,
  That thou shalt ful wel sen.

256–57 Here have you made a bargain that may very well please you.
258 *maight,* may; *thilke sith,* the particular occasion
260 *Thar,* Need; *sike,* sigh 261 *To goder-hele,* To (thy) good fortune
262 *sone,* immediately; *gange,* go 263 *hounderstonde,* understand
264 *kenne,* teach; *sulke a lore,* such a lesson 265 *hoe,* she
267 As I (hope to) have God's peace 270 *her,* here
271–72 This I give you as a reward, to buy yourself sheep and swine.
273–75 As I ever (hope to) enjoy house or floor, never were pence better employed than these shall be!
276 *don,* do; *juperty,* exploit
277 And a wonderful feat
278 *sen,* see

"Pepir now shal thou eten;
280 This mustart shal ben thy mete,
And gar thin eyen to rene.
I shal make a lesing
Of thin heye-renning —
Ich wot wel wer and wenne."

[*Clerk*] 285 "Wat! now const thou no god!
Me thinketh that thou are wod!
Yevest thou the welpe mustard?"
[*Woman*] "Be stille, boinard!
I shal mit this ilke gin
290 Gar hire love to ben al thin.
Ne shal ich never have reste ne ro
Til ich have told how thou shalt do —
Abid me her til min hom-come."
[*Clerk*] "Yus, by the somer blome!
295 Hethen null I ben benomen
Til thou be ayein comen."

[*Narrator*] Dame Sirith begon to go
As a wrecche that is wo,
That hoe com hire to then inne
300 Ther this gode wif wes inne.
Tho hoe to the dore com,
Swithe reuliche hoe begon:

279 *Pepir,* Pepper, MS *Pepis*; *eten,* eat (Lines 279–84 are spoken to her dog)
280 *mustart,* mustard; *mete,* food 281 And make your eyes to run (water)
282 *lesing,* lying tale 283 *heye-renning,* running of the eyes
284 I know well where and when. 285 What! Now you are unwise!
286 *wod,* crazy 287 Are you giving mustard to the puppy? *thou,* MS *þo*
288 *boinard,* fool
289–90 I shall with this very device cause her love to be all yours.
291 *ro,* peace 293 Wait for me here until my return home.
294 *somer blome,* summer flowers 295 Hence shall I not be removed.
296 *ayein comen,* returned 297 *begon to go,* traveled along
298 *wo,* full of woe 299 Until she came to the house
300 *Ther,* Where; *inne,* in 301 *Tho,* When 302 Very pitifully she began

[*Woman*] "Loverd!" hoe seyth, "wo is holde wives,
That in poverte ledeth ay lives!
305 Not no mon so muchel of pine
As poure wif that falleth in nausine!
That may ilke mon by me wite,
For may I nouther gange ne site —
Ded wold I ben ful fain.
310 Hounger and thurst me haveth ney slain —
Ich ne may mine limes onwold
For mikel hounger and thurst and cold.
Warto liveth selke a wrecche?
Wy nul Goed my soule fecche?"

[*Wife*] 315 "Sely wif, God thee hounbinde!
Today wille I thee mete finde
For love of Goed.
Ich have reuthe of thy wo,
For evele i-clothed I se thee go
320 And evele i-shoed.

"Com herin — Ich wile thee fede."
[*Woman*] "Goed almightten do thee mede,
And the Loverd that wes on rode i-don,
And faste fourty dayes to non,
325 And Hevene and erthe haveth to welde,
As thilke Loverd thee foryelde!"

303 *holde,* old 304 *ledeth ay,* leads always (their)
305 No man knows so much about sorrow
306 *nausine,* distress, hardship, MS *ausine*
307 *ilke,* each; *by me wite,* know through me
308–9 For I may neither walk nor sit — I would very gladly be dead.
310 *ney,* nigh, almost 311 *limes onwold,* limbs control
313 *Warto,* To what purpose; *selke,* such
314 *Wy nul,* Why won't; *fecche,* fetch 315 *Sely,* Poor; *hounbinde,* deliver
316 *mete,* food 318 *reuthe,* pity 319 *evele,* badly 320 *i-shoed,* shod
322 *do thee mede,* reward you 323 *wes on rode i-don,* was put on the cross
324 *to non,* until noon, or the ninth hour (3:00 P.M. See Brian Miller, "Two Notes on *Dame Sirith,*" *Medium Aevum,* XXVIII (1958), 180–83.)
325 *haveth to welde,* controls 326 May this same Lord reward you.

[*Wife*] "Have her fles and eke bred,
And make thee glad — hit is my red!
And have her the coppe with the drinke —
330 Goed do thee mede for thy swinke."
Thenne spac that holde wif
(Crist awarie hire lif!):
[*Woman*] "Alas, alas, that ever I live!
Al the sunne ich wolde forgive
335 The mon that smite off min heved —
Ich wolde my lif me were bereved!"
[*Wife*] "Sely wif, what eilleth thee?"
[*Woman*] "Bote ethe may I sory be!
Ich hevede a douter feir and fre,
340 Feiror ne mightte no mon se.
Hoe hevede a curteis hossebonde,
Freour mon mightte no mon fonde.
My douter lovede him al too wel —
Forthy mak I sory del.
345 Oppon a day he was out wend,
And tharthoru wes my douter shend.
He hede on ernde out of towne,
And com a mody clark with crowne;
To my douter his love beed,
350 And hoe nolde nout folewe his red:
He ne mightte his wille have
For nothing he mightte crave.

327 *fles,* flesh, meat; *eke,* also 328 *red,* counsel 329 *coppe with,* cup containing
330 May God reward you for your labors. 332 Christ curse her life!
334–35 All the sin I would forgive (to) the man who (would) smite off my head.
336 *me were bereved,* were taken from me 337 *eilleth,* ails
338 *Bote ethe,* But well 339 I had a daughter, fair and gracious.
341 *Hoe,* She 342 *Freour,* More generous, gracious
344 Therefore I make sorrowful complaint. 345 *was out wend,* went out
346 *tharthoru,* through that; *shend,* ruined 347 *hede,* had; *ernde,* errand
348 And there came a high-spirited clerk with a tonsure.
349 *beed,* offered, announced
350 *folewe his red,* follow his advice
352 No matter how he begged

Thenne begon the clerk to wiche,
And shop my douter til a biche.
355 This is my douter that ich of speke –
For del of hire min herte breke.
Loke how hire heyen greten!
On hire cheken the teres meten!
Forthy, Dame, were hit no wonder
360 Thau min herte burste assunder.
A, wose-ever is yong houssewif,
Ha loveth ful luitel hire lif,
And eny clerk of love hire bede,
Bote hoe grante and lete him spede!"
[*Wife*] 365 "A! Loverd Crist, wat may I thenne do?
This enderday com a clark me to
And bed me love on his manere,
And ich him nolde nout i-here.
Ich trouve he wolle me forshape!
370 How troustou, nelde, ich mowe ascape?"
[*Woman*] "God almightten be thin help
That thou ne be nouther bicche ne welp!
Leve dame, if eny clerk
Bedeth thee that love-werk,
375 Ich rede that thou grante his bone
And becom his lefmon sone.
And if that thou so ne dost,
A worse red thou ounderfost."

353 *wiche,* practice witchcraft 354 *shop,* transformed; *til a biche,* to a bitch
356 *del,* grief 357 *heyen greten,* eyes weep
358 On her cheeks the tears flow together! 360 *Thau,* Though
361 Ah, whosoever is (a) young housewife 362 *Ha,* She; *luitel,* little
363 *And,* If; *bede,* asks 364 Unless she consent and let him succeed!
365 *wat,* what; *I,* MS *om.* 366 *enderday,* other day
367 *on his manere,* in his way 368 And I would not listen to him.
369 *trouve,* believe; *forshape,* transform
370 How do you think, old woman, that I may escape?
372 *ne be,* not become 374 *love-werk,* love-play
375 *rede,* advise; *bone,* request
376 *lefmon sone,* mistress immediately
378 *red,* counsel; *ounderfost,* undertakes

[*Wife*] "Loverd Crist, that me is wo,
380 That the clark me hede fro
Ar he me hevede bewonne!
Me were levere then any fe
That he hevede enes leyen by me,
And efftsones begunne!

385 "Evermore, nelde, ich wille be thin
With that thou feche me Willekin,
The clark of wam I telle.
Giftes will I geve thee
That thou maight ever the betere be,
390 By Godes howne belle!"

[*Woman*] "Sothliche, my swete dame,
And if I may withhoute blame,
Fain ich wille fonde;
And if ich may with him mete
395 By eny wey other by strete,
Nout ne will I wonde.

"Have godday, Dame, forth will I go."
[*Wife*] "Allegate loke that thou do so
As ich thee bad.
400 Bote that thou me Wilekin bringe,
Ne may I never lawe ne singe
Ne be glad."

379–84 Lord Christ, I am sorry that the clerk went away before he had won me! I would rather than any money (I would give anything) that he had once lain with me and immediately begun (to make love).
385 *thin,* thine 386 *With that,* If; *feche,* fetch
387 *wam,* whom 389 *betere,* better
390 By God's own bell (rung during the Mass) (See Miller, *Medium Aevum,* XXVIII (1958), 183–88.)
391 *Sothliche,* Truly 393 *Fain,* Eagerly; *fonde,* try 394 *mete,* meet
395–96 By any highway or by street, I'll not hesitate at all (to do what you ask).
397 *godday,* good day 398 *Allegate loke,* In any event see
399 *bad,* asked 400 *Bote that,* Unless 401 *I,* MS *om.*; *lawe,* laugh

[*Woman*] "Iwis, Dame, if I may,
Ich wille bringen him yet today
405 By mine mightte."
Hoe wente hire to hire inne,
Ther hoe founde Wilekinne,
By houre Drightte!

"Swete Wilekin, be thou nout dred,
410 For of thin hernde ich have wel sped.
Swithe com forth thider with me,
For hoe haveth send affter thee.
Iwis now maight thou ben above
For thou havest grantise of hire love!"
[*Clerk*] 415 "God thee foryelde, leve nelde,
That Hevene and erthe haveth to welde!"

[*Narrator*] This mody mon begon to gon
With Sirith to his levemon
In thilke stounde.
420 Dame Sirith begon to telle
And swor by Godes owene belle
Hoe hevede him founde.

[*Woman*] "Dame, so have ich Wilekin sout,
For now have ich him i-brout!"
[*Wife*] 425 "Welcome, Wilekin, swete thing!
Thou art welcomere then the king!

"Wilekin the swete,
My love I thee behete,
To don al thine wille.

405 By my power 406 She went to her house 407 *hoe,* she 408 By our Lord!
409 *dred,* afraid 410 *hernde,* MS *herde* 411 *Swithe,* Quickly; *forth,* MS *for.*
413 *ben above,* be in heaven (succeed) 414 *grantise,* consent
415 God reward you, dear old woman. 416 *welde,* rule
417 This lusty man set out. 418 *levemon,* loved one 419 At that very moment
423 *so,* so (in the way that you asked); *sout,* sought
426 *then,* than 428 *thee behete,* promise to you

430 Turnd ich have my thout,
For I ne wolde nout
That thou thee shuldest spille."

[*Clerk*] "Dame, so ich evere bide noen,
And ich am redy and i-boen
435 To don al that thou saye.
Nelde, par ma fay,
Thou most gange away,
Wile ich and hoe shulen playe!"

[*Woman*] "Goddot, so I wille,
440 And loke that thou hire tille
And strek out hire thes!
God yeve thee muchel care
Yeif that thou hire spare
The wile thou mid hire bes!

445 "And wose is onwis,
And for no pris
Ne con geten his levemon,
I shal, for my mede,
Garen him to spede,
450 For ful wel I con!"

432 That you should kill yourself
433 Dame, as I ever hope to see noon (or the ninth hour, the hour of the first meal in monasteries — hence a very welcome moment)
434 *i-boen,* prepared 436 *par ma fay,* by my faith
438 *Wile,* While; *shulen,* shall 439 *Goddot,* God knows
440–41 And see to it that you plough her, and spread out her thighs!
442 *yeve,* give; *care,* sorrow 443 *Yeif that,* If 444 While you are with her!
445 *wose,* whosoever; *onwis,* unskillful 446 *pris,* price 448 *mede,* reward
449 *Garen,* Cause 450 *con,* know how

32 *(Ca. 1400–40)*

THE TOURNAMENT OF TOTTENHAM

Of all thes kene conquerours to carpe it were kinde;
Of fele feghting folk ferly we finde:
The Turnament of Totenham have we in minde.
It were harme sich hardynes were holden behinde,
5 In story as we rede,
Of Hawkyn, of Herry,
Of Tomkyn, of Terry,
Of them that were [dughty]
And stalworth in dede.

10 It befel in Totenham on a dere day
Ther was mad a shurting be the hiway.
Theder com al the men of the contray –
Of Hyssyltoun, of Hygate, and of Hakenay –
And all the swete [swinkers]:
15 Ther hopped Hawkyn,
Ther daunsed Dawkyn,
Ther trumped Tomkyn;
And all were treue drinkers

(32) 1 *thes kene,* these fierce; *carpe,* tell; *kinde,* natural
2 *fele feghting,* many fighting; *ferly,* marvels
3 *Totenham:* Tottenham lies about 5 miles north of the City of London. Now an undistinguishable part of the metropolitan area, it was in the 15th century a quite separate village.
4 It were a shame if such boldness were concealed. 5 *rede,* read
8 *dughty,* brave 9 *stalworth,* stalwart; *dede,* deed
10 *dere,* memorable 11 *mad,* made; *shurting be,* festival by
12 *Theder com,* Thither came; *contray,* region
13 Of Islington, of Highgate, and of Hackney (all, like Tottenham, separate parishes north of the City)
14 *swete swinkers,* sweet workingmen
16 *daunsed,* danced
17 *trumped,* trumpeted
18 *treue,* true

Til the day was gon and Evin-song past,
20 That thay shuld rekin ther scot and ther contes cast.
Perkyn the potter into the [prees] past,
And said, "Rondol the refe, a doghter thou hast –
Tyb, the dere;
Therfor wit wold I
25 Which of all this bachelery
Were best worthy
To wed hur to his fere."

Up stirt thes gadelinges with ther long staves,
And said, "Randal the refe, lo! this lad raves!
30 Baldely amang us thy dughter he craves,
And we er richer men [then] he, and more god haves
Of catell and corn."
Then said Perkyn, "To Tybbe I have hight
That I shal be alway redy in my right,
35 If that it shuld be this day sevenight
Or ellis yet tomorn."

Then said Randolfe the refe, "Ever be he waryed
That about this carping lenger wold be taried!
I wold not that my doghter that sho were miscaried,
40 But at hur most worship I wold sho were maried.
Therfor a turnament shal begin

19 *Evin-song,* Evensong, evening prayers
20 So that they were obliged to reckon their bill and total up their accounts
21 *prees past,* crowd passed 22 *refe,* reve, bailiff; *doghter,* daughter
23 *dere,* precious one 24 Therefore I would (like to) know
25 *bachelery,* young unmarried men, company of knights
27 To wed her as his wife 28 *stirt,* started; *gadelinges,* good fellows
30 *Baldely amang,* Boldly among 31 *er,* are; *god haves,* possessions have
32 Of property and grain 33 *hight,* promised
34 *in my right,* to defend my rights 35 *this day sevenight,* a week from today
36 Or else tomorrow; *ellis,* MS *ell* 37 *waryed,* cursed
38 Who would be delayed (any) longer over this haggling; *taried,* MS *atryed*
39 I would not (wish) that my daughter were misplaced
40 *at hur most worship,* to her greatest honor; *sho,* she

This day sevenight,
With a flail forto fight;
And [he] that is of most might
45 Shall brouke hur with winne.

"Whoso beres him best in the turnament,
Him shall be granted the gre, be the camon assent,
Forto winne my doghter with [dughtynesse] of dent,
And Coppeld, my brode-henne, was broght out of Kent,
50 And my donned cowe.
[For] no spens wil I spare,
For no catell wil I care;
He shal have my gray mare,
And my spotted sowe!"

55 Ther was many bold lad ther bodies to bede.
Than thay toke thair leve and homward thay yede;
And all the woke afterward thay graithed ther wede,
Till it come to the day that thay suld do ther dede.
Thay armed ham in mattes;
60 Thay set on ther nolles –
Forto kepe ther polles –
Gode blake [bolles],
For batring of battes.

Thay sowed tham in shepe skinnes for thay suld not brest;
65 Ilkon toke a blak hat insted of a crest,

43 To be fought with a flail 45 *brouke,* enjoy; *winne,* pleasure
46 *Whoso beres him,* Whosoever bears himself
47 *Him,* (to) him; *gre,* prize; *be,* by 48 *dughtynesse of dent,* boldness of blow
49 *brode-henne,* brood-hen; *was,* (which) was 50 *donned,* brown
51 *spens,* expense 52 *catell,* possessions 55 *to bede,* (ready) to offer
56 *Than,* Then; *yede,* went
57 *woke,* week; *graithed ther wede,* prepared their gear 58 *suld,* should
59 *ham,* themselves; *mattes,* mats 60 *nolles,* heads
61–63 To protect their crowns, good black bowls, for (protection against) battering of bats
64 *sowed tham in,* sewed themselves into; *for,* so that; *brest,* burst
65 *Ilkon,* Each one; *crest:* the decoration on top of a helmet

A harow brod as a fanne aboune on ther brest,
And a flail in ther hande forto [fight] prest.
  Furth gon thay fare.
  Ther was kid mekil fors
70 Who shuld best fend his cors;
  He that had no gode hors,
  He gat him a mare.

Sich another gadring have I not sene oft!
When all the gret cumpany com ridand to the croft,
75 Tyb on a gray mare was set upon loft
On a sek ful of sedes, for sho shuld sit soft,
  And led hur to the [gappe];
  For cryeng of al the men,
  Forther wold not Tyb then
80 Til she had hur gud brode-hen
  Set in hur lap.

A gay girdil Tyb had on, borwed for the nones,
And a garland on hur hed ful of rounde bones,
And a broche on her brest ful of safer stones,
85 With the holy rode tokening was wroten for the nones —
  No catel was ther spared!
  When joly Gyb saw hure thare,
  He gird so his gray mere
  [That] she lete a faucon-fare
90 At the rereward.

66 *harow,* some sort of wickerwork frame (see George F. Jones, "The Tournaments of Tottenham and Lappenhausen," *PMLA,* LXLI (Dec. 1951), p. 1138); *fanne:* a wicker shield used in mock combat; *aboune,* above
67 *prest,* ready 68 Forth they went. 69 There was displayed much prowess
70 *fend,* protect; *cors,* body 73 *gadring,* gathering
74 *com ridand,* came riding; *croft,* field 75 *upon loft,* aloft
76 *sek,* sack; *sedes,* seeds; *for,* so that 77 *gappe,* opening in the hedge
78 *For cryeng,* Because of the shouting 79 *Forther,* Further 80 *hur,* her
82 A gay belt Tyb had on, borrowed for the nonce. 83 *bones,* bobbins
84 *broche,* brooch; *safer,* sapphire
85 While a representation of the Holy Cross was inscribed as well (?)
86 *catel,* goods 88 *gird,* struck 89–90 That she let a fart at the rear

"I vow to God," quod Herry, "I shal not lefe behende!
May I mete with Bernard on Bayard the blinde!
Ich man kepe him out of my winde,
For whatsoever that he be befor me I finde,
95 I wot I shal him greve!"
"Wele said!" quod Hawkyn.
"And I avow," quod Dawkyn,
"May I mete with Tomkyn,
His flail him refe!"

100 "I vow to God," quod Hud, "Tyb, sone shal thou se
Which of all this bachelery grant is the gre!
I shal scomfet thaim all, for the love of thee.
In what place so I come, thay shal have dout of me,
Min armes ar so clere:
105 I bere a reddil and a rake
Powdred with a brenand drake,
And three cantell of a cake
In icha cornare."

"I vow to God," quod Hawkyn, "if I have the gout,
110 Al that I finde in the felde presand here about,
Have I twies or thries reden thurgh the route,
In icha stede ther thay me se, of me thay shal have doute
When I begin to play!

91 *lefe behende,* stay behind

92 *Bayard the blinde:* a remarkable blind horse in the chivalric romance *The Foure Sons of Aymon,* whose extraordinary exploits must have seemed ridiculous even when these romances were still taken seriously

93 *Ich,* Each; *winde,* way (fig.) 95 *wot,* know; *greve,* injure

99 *him refe,* (I shall) take away from him 100 *sone,* directly

101 *grant is the gre,* is granted the prize 102 *scomfet,* discomfort

103 *what place so,* whatsoever place; *dout,* fear 104 *Min,* My; *clere,* bright

105 *reddil,* sieve for separating chaff from grain

106–8 Sprinkled with figures of fiery dragons, and three sections of a cake in each corner

109 *if I,* although I; MS *yf he* 110 *felde presand,* field rushing; *felde,* MS *felte*

111–12 Once I have twice or thrice ridden through the crowd, in each place where they see me, of me they shall have fear.

113 *play,* manage arms

I make a vow that I ne shall –
115 But if Tybbe wil me call,
Or I be thries down fall –
Right onis com away!"

Then said Terry, and swore by his Crede:
"Saw thou never yong boy [forther] his body bede;
120 For when thay fight fastest and most ar in drede,
I shal take Tyb by the hand and hur away lede.
I am armed at the full:
In min armes I bere wele
A dogh trogh and a pele,
125 A sadill withouten a panell,
With a fles of woll."

"I vow to God," quod Dudman, and swor be the stra,
"Whils me is left my mere, thou getes hur not [swa]!
For sho is wele shapen and light as the ro;
130 Ther is no capul in this mile befor hur shal ga.
She [wil me] noght begile;
She wil me bere, I dar wele say,
On a lang someres day
Fro Hyssultoun to Hakenay,
135 Noght other half mile."

"I vow to God," quod Perkyn, "thou spekes of cold rost!
I shal wirch [wiselier], withouten any bost:
Five of [the] best capulles that ar in this ost,
I wot I shal thaim winne and bring thaim to my cost,

114 *ne shall,* shall not 115 *But if,* Unless 116 *Or,* Before
117 *Right onis,* Even once 118 *Crede,* Creed
119 You never saw a young boy offer his body more recklessly.
120 *For,* Because; *drede,* anxiety 123 *armes,* coat of arms
124 A dough-trough and a baker's shovel 125 *panell,* saddle-cloth
126 With a fleece of wool 127 *stra,* straw
128 While my mare is left to me, you get her not so. 129 *ro,* roe deer
130 *capul,* horse; *ga,* go 133 *someres,* MS *sonerys* 135 Not a half-mile farther
136 *spekes of cold rost,* speak nonsense 137 *wirch wiselier,* act more wisely
138 *ost,* host 139 *wot,* know; *cost,* side

140 And here I graunt tham Tybbe.
Wele, boyes, here is he
That wil fight and not fle,
For I am in my jolite,
With 'yo forth, Gybbe!' "

145 When thay had ther vowes [made], furth [con they te]
With flailes and hornes and trumpes mad of tre –
Ther were all the bacheleres of that contre.
Thay were dight [in] aray as thamselfe wold be:
Thair baners were ful bright,
150 Of an old raton fell;
The cheverone of a plow-mell,
And the shadow of a bell
Powdred with monelight.

I wot it is no childer-game whan thay togedir met!
155 When icha freke in tha feld on his felay [bette].
And laid [on] stifly – for nothing wold thay let –
And faght ferly fast till ther horses swet,
And fewe wordes spoken.
Ther were flailes al [to-slaterde],
160 Ther were sheldes al [to-claterde],
Bolles and dishes al [to-baterde],
And many hedes broken.

Ther was clinking of cart sadelles and [clatering] of cannes;

140 *graunt tham,* give them (to) 142 *fle,* fly
143 *in my jolite,* in good spirits 144 *yo forth,* let's go!
145 *con they te,* they went
146 *trumpes,* trumpets; *mad of tre,* made of wood 147 *contre,* country, district
148 They were drawn up in a battle line, as (they) themselves wished to be.
150–53 (Made) of an old rat skin; the chevron (consisting) of a plowhammer and the silhouette of a bell sprinkled with moonlight; *chevron:* a heraldic figure
154 *wot,* know; *childer-game,* child's play
155 When each man in the field beat on his fellow 156 *let,* stop
157 *faght ferly fast,* fought marvelously hard
159 *to-slaterde,* smashed to pieces
162 *hedes,* heads 163 *cannes,* cans

Of fele frekes in the feld, broken were ther fannes;
165 Of sum were the hedes broken, of sum the brain-panes,
And ill ware [they besene] or thay went thens.
With swipping of swepilles,
The boyes were so wery forfught
That thay might not fight mare oloft,
170 But creped then about in the [crofte]
As they were croked crepils.

Perkyn was so wery that he began to [loute]:
"Help! Hud. I am ded in this ilk [route]!
A hors for forty pens, a gode and a stoute,
175 That I may lightly come of my noye out!
For no cost wil I spare!"
He stirt up as a snaile
And hent a capul be [the] taile,
And raght Dawkyn his flaile,
180 And wan ther a mare.

Perkyn wan five and Hud wan twa —
Glad and blithe thay ware that thay had don sa.
Thay wold have tham to Tyb and present hur with tha;
The capull were so wery that thay might not ga,
185 But stil gon thay stand.
"Allas!" quod Hudde, "my joye I lese!
Me had lever then a ston of chese

164 *fele frekes,* many men; *fannes:* wickerwork shields or winnowing shovels
165 *brain-panes,* brain pans, skulls
166–67 And ill were they treated before they went thence. With swiping of swipples (the free-swaying end of the flail)
168 *wery forfught,* exhausted with fighting
169 *mare oloft,* longer on horse back 170 *creped,* crept; *crofte,* field
171 As though they were crooked cripples 172 *loute,* sink down
173 *ded,* dead; *ilk route,* same crowd 174 *pens,* pence; *gode,* good
175 *lightly,* easily; *of my noye out,* out of my annoyance
177 *stirt,* started 178 *hent,* seized 179 *raght,* took from 180 *wan,* won
181 *twa,* two 183 *wold have,* wanted to take; *tha,* them
185 *gon . . . stand,* stood 186 *lese,* lose
187 I would rather than a stone (14 pounds) of cheese

That dere Tyb had al these
And wist it were my sand."

190 Perkyn turned him about in that ich thrange;
Among thes wery boyes he wrest and he wrang —
He threw tham down to the erth and thrast thaim amang,
When he saw Tyrry away with Tyb fang,
And after him ran.
195 Off his hors he him drogh
And gaf him of his flail inogh.
"We! te-he," quod Tyb and lugh,
"Ye er a dughty man!"

Thus thay tugged and rugged til it was nere night.
200 All the wives of Totenham come to se that sight,
With wispes and kexes and rishes ther light
To fech hom ther husbandes, that were tham trouth plight.
And sum broght gret harwes
Ther husbandes hom forto fech —
205 Sum on dores and sum on hech,
Sum on hirdilles and sum on crech,
And sum on welebaraws.

Thay gadered Perkyn about, everich side,
And graunt him ther [the gre]; the [more] was his [pride].

189 *my sand,* my sending, *i.e.,* my present
190 *ich thrange,* same throng 191 *wrest,* twisted; *wrang,* squeezed
192 *thrast thaim amang,* pushed (himself) among them 193 *fang,* start
195 *drogh,* dragged 196 *gaf,* gave; *inogh,* plenty 197 *lugh,* laughed
198 You are a brave man! 199 *rugged,* scuffled
201–2 With twists of straw and flax and rushes there alight, to fetch home their husbands, who were plighted in troth to them
203 *gret harwes,* great harrows, or sledges 205 *dores,* doors; *hech,* gratings
206 *hirdilles,* hurdles (frame sleds — in England, often used to drag criminals to executions); *crech,* latticed drag, possibly the latticed section of a horse stall or manger
207 *welebaraws,* wheelbarrows
208 They gathered around Perkyn, on every side.
209 *gre,* prize

210 Tyb and he with gret merthe homward con thay ride,
And were al night togedir, til the morn tide.
And thay in fere assent,
So wele his nedes he has sped,
That dere Tyb he [shall] wed —
215 The praise folk that hur led
Were of the turnament.

To that ilk fest com many, for the nones:
Some come hip-halt, and sum trippand on the stones;
Some a staf in [his honde], and sum two at onis;
220 Of sum were the hedes to-broken, and sum the shulder-bones —
With sorow com thay thedir!
Wo was Hawkyn, wo was Herry,
Wo was Tomkyn, wo was Terry,
And so was al the bachelary
225 When thay met togedir.

At that fest thay were served with a riche aray —
Every five and five had a cokenay —
And so thay sat in jolite al the lang day,
And at the last thay went to bed with ful gret deray.
230 Mekil mirth was them amang:
In every corner of the hous
Was melody delicious,
Forto here, precius,
Of six menes sang.

210 *con . . . ride,* rode 212 *in fere assent,* agree together
213 *nedes,* needs; *sped,* successfully pursued
215 The noble folk who led her (in the procession)
217 *ilk fest,* same festival; *for the nones:* a meaningless tag
218 *hip-halt,* limping; *trippand,* stumbling
219 *two at onis,* two (staves) together (*i.e.,* one in each hand)
226 *aray,* display
227 Every fifth person (or every tenth, or every group of five) had a bad egg. (The meaning of *cokenay* is uncertain, but this meaning, suggested in the Middle English Dictionary, conforms to the mock heroic tone of the poem.)
229 *deray,* confusion, disorder
233–34 Precious to hear, of a song for six voices.

Commentaries

LYRIC POETRY

(1) *Now goth sonne under wod.* Bodleian MS Arch. Selden, *supra* 74(3462), f. 55b. *Index* 2320; *XIII*, 1; *MEL* 6; *OML* 4.

A quatrain of 4-stress lines rhyming *abab*. This lyric is quoted in St. Edmund's *Speculum Ecclesiae* where it follows a passage in French in which the Virgin is entrusted to St. John by the dying Christ. The Virgin spoke this passage from *Cant.* 1:5. *Ne vus amerveillez mie/ que io su brunecte e haslée,/ car le soleil me ad descolurée.* (Do not consider me that I am brown, because the sun hath altered my color.)

This poem's power derives from a tension between the simple economy of its literal statement and the actual richness of meaning. It is charged with allusions, double meanings, puns — all of which were familiar to the medieval reader — whose compression allows the excitement of progressive, dramatic revelation, even within four brief lines, as the poem moves from allusion to direct statement.

L. 1 can be read literally — the sun is going down behind the wood — but another meaning is suggested, and this suggestion becomes clearer in l. 2 as the poet suddenly moves from an apparently impersonal observation of a natural event to an expression of pity for the Virgin. L. 3 then establishes explicit connection between the statements of ll. 1 and 2 by substituting the word "tre," whose double meaning is more immediately apparent than the double meaning of "wod," so that we now understand why sunset and the darkening wood should have suggested to the poet the figures of the Crucifixion. Then, as the natural image of the sunset recedes before the sharpening image of the crucified Christ, l. 4 finally fuses the two images — of Mary and the setting sun — by explicitly resolving the familiar pun on sun-son through the possessive "thy."

Multiple meanings appear in other details. The darkening of the Virgin's face, which leads the poet to pity her "faire rode," may refer to several things. First of all it describes the disfiguring agony of her grief, but it may also describe the shadows brought by the darkening of the world at the setting of the Son of God. Finally it may describe the reflection in her face of the red glow of the setting sun and thus fleetingly reveal the "courtly" element, present in many poems to the Virgin, through an allusion to the unfashionableness of a dark complexion, especially when it comes from menial activities which expose one to the sun, as Mary's vigil has exposed her. In this last sense, the reference recalls the red blood of her dying son, especially through the word "rode" which is connected orthographically with "rood" (cross), so that instead of interrupting the movement from "wod" to "tre," "rode" adds the insistence of a third reference to the Cross.

Of the four lines in the poem, then, the first three end with a reference to the Cross, while the last links the two persons whom the Cross has both joined and sundered. And it does so by connecting organically those two references – to the "sonne" and to "Marie" – which had seemed unconnected in the first two lines.

(2) *Foweles in the frith.* Bodleian MS Douce 139(21713), f. 5a. *Index* 864; *EEL* 3; *XIII,* 8; *MEL* 4; *OML* 17.

Set in *MS* as 2-part song. 3-stress lines rhyming *abbab.*

This poem is deceptive: the references to nature, the contrasting mood of the poet, the jaunty iambic rhythm all suggest that this is only a conventional love lyric, contrasting the exuberance of spring with the melancholy of the lover, until we abruptly discover in l. 5 that the poet's madness may derive not from a disdainful mistress but from a suffering Christ. The pattern of alliteration supports this discovery: in ll. 1–2 the alliteration falls twice on the soft fricative *f*; in ll. 3–4 it falls twice on the soft semi-vowel *w*; but in l. 5 it falls three times on the dramatically explosive *b,* compelling our attention and suggesting a more intense experience than casual love-longing. Of course the excitement of the poem derives from the parallel between the two experiences, secular and spiritual love, which allows the details to work at both levels. The immediacy of the secular experience emphasizes an equal immediacy in the religious: the Passion of Christ is as vividly in the present as is the passion for the mistress. Moreover, the medieval attitude toward spring is always ambivalent. It is the time of love and fruitful renewal in nature, and is therefore also the time when rejection in human love will seem most bitter, whether it lead to the languishing death of the lover or the agonizing death of Christ on the Cross. The synecdoche of the last line fully exploits this contrast between nature and man, between secular and sacred concerns. If they refer to the lover's mistress (though more commonly these two words are used in connection with Christ — see *WN*, p. 145) the two words "bon" and "blod" catch up both the earthliness and the vitality of life, with the possibility also of a pun on beste (beast). If the line refers to Christ, the "bon" and "blod" vividly symbolize the Incarnation of the incorporeal Christ, while "blod" also echoes the ambivalent feelings about spring since, in suggesting both the joy of the Incarnation and the sorrow of the Passion, it symbolizes both the life and death of Christ.

Within the poem there is, as David Daiches has pointed out,[1] a movement from impersonal description to confessional utterance — the same movement that occurs in "Now goth sonne" — so that when it first appears in l. 3, the personal statement has peculiar poignancy and force. Also, the two major variations in meter counterpoint each other: the shortened first line which gives full trochaic value to "fówelĕs" gives a mild buoyancy to the description of nature, while the heavy spondee opening l. 4 (múlch sórw) echoes a sorrow which in this poem can only be expressed, not remedied.

(3) *Wen the turuf is thy tuur*. Cambridge, Trinity College MS 323, f. 47b. *Index* 4044; *XIII*, 30; *OML* 9.

2-and 3-stress lines rhyming *aa bb cc*. An English translation of a Latin original.

Again a jaunty, almost rollicking rhythm contrasts with the familiar and serious theme of *memento mori*. The effect of the poem derives from its economy, from its vivid images, and from at least one arresting metrical variation. Each of the first two lines juxtaposes within itself single images of elegant life and of the grave: the lofty castle tower sinks to a funeral mound of turf; the ample elegance of the lady's chamber is constricted into a narrow earthen pit. Then in its middle

[1] David Daiches, *A Study of Literature* (Ithaca: Cornell University Press, 1948), p. 152.

two lines the poem expands. After the quick succession of contrasting pairs of single words in ll. 1 and 2, each image within the next contrasting pair is given a whole line to itself, so that the quick repetition of the first two lines yields to the syntactical extension of ll. 3 and 4. Moreover, the shock of contrast is further delayed by the metrical expansion of l. 3. It is the longest line (8 syllables) of the poem, and it is metrically the most uneven; and this difference in length and in regularity is additionally emphasized by its placement immediately after the two shortest, most regular lines. The effect is to draw out the warmly sensual, tactile images of soft white skin and the vulnerable throat before the quick violence of the devouring worm. This suspension is achieved not only by the additional syllable but by the addition of a third stress (wél, wí, thró) and by awkward clusters of *t*'s at the end of the line. Yet in spite of all the details which postpone the contrasting image of the worm, these two disparate images of life and the grave are linked by alliterating *w*'s. L. 4 is the only line not bound within itself by internal alliteration. The effect of the single *w* beginning the line's most powerful word is to fuse it with the *w*'s of the preceding line, so that the reluctance of line 3 to yield to line 4 is overwhelmed by the compelling sweep of the alliteration.

The effect is further heightened by the syntax, within which the main clause has been delayed by the compound subordinate clause of the first two lines whose intimations of mortality only heighten the more destructive image of ll. 3 and 4. The first four lines, then, rise dramatically to the powerful image of the worm, and we are helpless before the simple, inexorable question which closes the poem and toward which the whole rhetoric of the poem has moved.

(4) *Sumer is i-cumen in.* Harley MS 978, f. 11b. *Index* 3223; *XIII,* 6; *EEL* 2; *MEL* 3; *OML* 3.

A round (or *rota*) with musical notation. Generally alternates 3- and 4-stress lines rhyming *abcbb abcbbbb bb.*

This is one medieval lyric for which the music is as well known as the poem, both having been preserved in a commonplace book kept by the Monks of Reading Abbey. The manuscript includes also a supplementary (and musically unsatisfactory) Latin text, with elaborate instructions in Latin for the musical performance of both English and Latin versions.

The musical form is a *rota* or round, in this case a true canon for four voices accompanied by two additional, lower voices called *pes* or tenor. These two lower voices sing the two-line refrain over and over, exchanging phrases with each other, while the other four voices sing the stanzas in an indefinite round, that is, the four voices enter one after the other with the same melody and the same words (as in the familiar "Three Blind Mice"). The result is an experiment in six-part writing remarkable for the early date of 1240, now generally accepted for both the poem and the music.[1]

The racing melodic line, together with the agitated interplay of six voices, is appropriate to a poem which celebrates the resurging vitality of nature after the quiescent winter. The poem is alive with movement and sound: summer itself (often an indefinite word in Middle English, but here to be understood as spring, probably early or mid-April when the cuckoo arrives in England) has been personified; it is not merely present but has arrived, has "come in"; the imperceptible growth of plants is accelerated by the succession of simple, active verbs— "groweth," "bloweth," "springth"; and then, as the poet's eye moves from the woods and meadows to the animals themselves, not only is sound added to movement, but each becomes increasingly lively. Like the progression from the relatively quiet "groweth" to the more vigorous "springth," so now we move from bleating through lowing to the spontaneous leap of the bullock and the rich, comfortable sonorousness of the buck's sudden release.

And always this sound and movement is punctuated by the insistent call of the cuckoo, the messenger of spring, just as the two voices of the *pes* punctuate the rapid, irregular movement of the four voices singing the round. Similarly, this erratic vitality of nature is echoed in the rhythm of the poetic lines with its lively displacement of accent in the 2-line refrain and with the constant interplay between iambic and trochaic rhythms within the stanzas. In the second stanza, for instance, the individual words in ll. 6–8 set up strong trochaic rhythms; l. 9 is then perfectly poised, with the trochaic "Murie" balanced against the

[1] See *The New Oxford History of Music, II: Early Medieval Music up to 1300*, ed. Dom Anselm Hughes (Oxford: Oxford University Press, 1954), pp. 402–3.

(here) iambic "cuccu" through the pivotal "sing"; and then after the level spondees in l. 10, the last lines move in predominantly iambic rhythms. (This reading of metrical accent accords with the musical notation in the manuscript.)

(5) *Betwene Mersh and Averil.* Harley MS 2253, f. 63b. *Index* 515; *EEL* 4; *XIII*, 77; *HL* 4; *MEL* 13; *OML* 27.
3- and 4-stress lines in stanzas rhyming *ababbbbc dddc.*

The charm of this secular love lyric derives from its happy combination of the spontaneous ejaculation characteristic of the most primitive lyrics with the artificial conventions of courtly love that give shape and form to the later, literary lyric. Here the courtly tradition provides a convention within which to explore briefly the simple contrast between a lover's joy and pain, but the direct, vigorous emotions of the lover always prevent these artificial conventions from deadening the poetic statement while they are providing its formal structure.

The opening references to the conventional love-longing, to the lady's peerlessness and power could be dull enough, but they are immediately countered by the dancing rhythms of the lines themselves and by the unqualified joy of the refrain that returns after each stanza, effectively undercutting the conventional sufferings of the lover outlined in stanzas 3 and 4, and whose unqualified joy has the last word in the poem.

The traditional description of the lady in stanza 2 is similarly enlivened, first by its simple directness and the intensity of the idiom "fair inogh," then by the artless good nature of Alisoun who, unlike the "daungerous" ladies of courtly convention, smiled or laughed pleasantly at her lover. Moreover, he is courting her not as a mistress but as a wife (make). These details, together with the answering refrain, take any real sting out of his conventional fear that he may not live long.

Arthur Moore has rightly observed that the melancholy in stanzas 3 and 4 "reflects the normal apprehension of a high-spirited suitor, not that of a hopeless lover" (*SL*, p. 68). It is the intrusion of such homely allusions as "feirest may in towne" "Wery so water in wore," and perhaps even the almost too insistent alliteration of sleepless night and pale cheeks that check the seriousness of the suffering. In a curious way the heightened self-consciousness of art and the artlessness of homely allusion combine to dissipate the conventional sufferings of the lover, whose rehearsal has nevertheless been a significant means of developing the lyric statement. And these insistent good spirits receive final confirmation from the lover's philosophic recognition that short sharp sufferings are better than the endless mourning of the courtly lover. The last return of the rollicking and joyful refrain is not just automatic: it has been prepared for by the lover's perception of his state.

(6) *Now skrinketh rose and lilye flour*. Harley MS 2253, f. 80a. *Index* 2359; *XIV*, 10; *EEL* 48; *HL* 23; *MEL* 14; *OML* 31.

3- and 4-stress lines, generally in 10-line stanzas rhyming *aab aab cbcb*. Brook (*HL*, p. 85) emends "vs" in l. 58 to "me" to restore the rime of the stanza. He disagrees with Brown (*XIV*, p. 246) on the matter of the change in rhyme scheme in this stanza. Brook points out that irregularity in structure occurs in other lyrics.

Stephen Manning has observed (*WN*, pp. 100–3) that this lyric uses conventions of the French *pastourelle* to introduce and to heighten its religious theme. In the *pastourelle*, the poet goes out walking alone on a spring morning and in a specific locale. He is thinking about love and often he meets a maiden to whom he actually tries to make love. In this poem we find all of these circumstances, though they lead to reflections of a very different kind.

But it is very important to recognize that the poet does more than turn a conventional beginning in an unexpected direction. He does not simply *use* the convention; he transforms it so that the details, instead of being simply redirected, take on new meaning. In ll. 1–6 the conventional flowers are there, but instead of blooming they shrivel up; the season is established, but it is autumn, not spring. The lady is there "bright in bour," but she will be overtaken not by love but by death. In ll. 11–16 the traditional morning and specified locale (Peterborough) lead to the conventional pensiveness of the lover, but the reflections turn not to love but to folly (or, rather, love becomes folly) and the traditional lament is therefore motivated by a different kind of love, directed to a very different kind of lady, and requesting a very different kind of "mercy." Similar effects occur throughout the poem, as in l.

27 – "On o Ledy min hope is" – or in ll. 42 and 45, where the conventional service of the lover and the conventional description of the mistress reawaken our sense of the transformation which has occurred.

In their metamorphosis of a secular convention the opening six lines reveal considerable poetic art. The change of the conventional setting becomes especially poignant through reminders of what has been, and this contrast is further heightened by unusually sensitive handling of syntax, rhythm, and organization of details. The setting is presented at once, in a single line whose power derives not only from its compact economy but from the heavy opening spondee – the hammer blows of "Now" and "skrink," which between them establish the immediacy and the ugly violence of decay. The tone of the setting depends entirely on these two words: every other word in the first three lines contrasts, directly or indirectly, with this opening assertion. By themselves, the images of rose and lily would conventionally suggest not decay but bloom, and this automatic connotation is supported by explicit reminders that accumulate through two languorous lines. It is this contrast between the explosive main clause and the loosely gathered phrases and predominantly falling rhythm of the subordinate clause, between the immediately perceived details of the present and the more relaxed accumulation of details from a remembered past, which produces the startling power of this opening. And the contrast is fixed – and summarized – in the parallel positions of "Now" and "whilen." Then, in the next three lines, the poet reverses the sequence. He now moves from the present to the future, and accordingly he begins by remembering. Only after he has recalled the power and brightness of queen and lady does he acknowledge that they will be overtaken by death, as surely as the strength and loveliness of the flowers are withering at this very moment. In the first six lines the poet has thus presented certain conventions of a *pastourelle* only to deny them; and this denial, embracing past, present, and future, has been handled through a kind of structural chiasmus, so that he can open and close on a note of death – death now and death to come. Loveliness belongs only to the past or is retreating into the past. By every device he has compelled us to attend to his recommendations in the concluding four lines of the stanza.

At the same time that conventional details are being transformed, they are in another way anticipating the central theme and personage of the poem. The rose and lily are conventional images associated with the *pastourelle,* and in this role they are withering. But these flowers are also conventional symbols of the Virgin, and in this role they are reviving. So, set against the sickness and decay which affect these flowers in their secular role is the healing and restorative power attributed to the flowers when they are revived and transformed into their symbolic equivalent, the Blessed Virgin. She becomes the finest leech from Caithness to Dublin, who with her plaster of penance draws out not blood but the "folies" referred to in ll. 13, 38. Such paradoxes and contrasts can be pursued endlessly: between decay, sickness, death (the corruptions of the flesh) and health and eternal life (the purity of the spirit); between earth's flowers that fade and her flowers that are eternally reborn, between expensive earthly medicine and her medicine, which costs very little but was very dearly bought (duere boghte). And all the while there are the familiar echoes, in the relation of the poet to Mary, of the relation of the lover to his mistress.

Finally, through this devotion and this awareness the poet is enabled to act fully on his earlier advice to think on Jesus, whose side was pierced for mankind. At first he could approach Christ only through Mary — his first direct address (l. 17) is to her, "Ledy, preye thy sone for ous" — but by the end he can address Christ himself. In the last stanza he catches up all the references of the first stanza but now they are fully transformed. Women who are presently "whit and brith on ble" shall still lose all their flowers. But now, as he thinks of the past, his recollection is not of loveliness but of Christ's suffering. Now, when he appeals to a queen, he invokes one whose power will not be overtaken by death but will forever rule the heavenly mansions (boures). He has thought on Jesus, he has considered his sufferings, he has forgone lust as he complains not to his mistress but to Mary. Thus as he awaits heavenly bliss he can at last cry to Christ himself, "Jesu, have mercy of us."

(7) *Love me brouthte.* National Library of Scotland, Advocates Library MS 18.7.21, f. 121a. *Index* 2012; *XIV,* 66.

2–3 stress lines in 3-line stanzas rhyming *aab*; ll. 1–2 have 2 stresses, l. 3 has 3.

In the address of Christ to mankind, the joy of salvation overrides the suffering of the Incarnation and Passion, even though both of these are mentioned frequently. And it is partly the rollicking rhythm which, by suppressing these darker details, lightens Christ's burden.

The poem divides into two parts: stanzas 1–4, and stanzas 5–6, a division that is made clear by the careful management of details which serve both formal and thematic purpose.

Formally, the four stanzas in part I are unified by similar syntax, with its anaphoral repetition of the opening word, "Love," and by the rhyming of all the third lines. Then there is the even more exact correspondence between pairs of stanzas. Stanzas 2 and 3 correspond almost exactly in their triple repetition of "love" and in their syntax. The enclosing stanzas, 1 and 4, are alike in their double repetition of "love" and in their direct address to Man, an address which is emphasized by a return to the acatalectic meter of the first lines, and which rounds out the unity of part I.

Stanza 4 also provides transition to part II. Part I has described Love as an agency responsible for every step in Christ's activity. In this account, Christ has always been the object. Beginning in stanza 4, however, the role changes through a gradual syntactical shift. Through three stanzas "Love," as a subject, has governed a series of strong transitive verbs, with Christ as object. Now the mood shifts, through a transitional clause in which Love no longer directs Christ but is possessed by him – "Love is my pes," to a clause in which the roles of agent and object are completely reversed – "For love I ches." In the two remaining stanzas, which with their rhyming third lines constitute part II of the poem, this reversed role dominates the tone, as Christ seeks man, harbors him, and wins him in fight, much as formerly Love had brought Christ, fashioned him, and then led him through the steps of the Passion.

(8) *I have a newe garden.* Sloane MS 2593, f. 11b. *Index* 1302; *XIV–XV,* 21; *MEL* 69.

Mostly 3-stress lines in 4-line stanzas, usually rhyming *abcb.*

Though the general point of this poem is clear enough, the particulars of the joke are elusive. If the garden and the pear tree are *only* allegorical terms for the poet's sexual apparatus, then it can be assumed that "per Jonet" (an early pear) is a pun on the speaker's name, John, with reference also to his youth and his paternity. Then, the grafting episode is *only* a sexual allegory, and when he learns from the maid that the child's father *(père)* is named Robert, not John, he can sigh with relief. This is apparently the interpretation of R. T. Davies *(MEL,* pp. 375-76).

However, it seems more likely — and more amusing — that the garden and the early pear tree operate at two levels. They are first of all a real garden and a real pear tree, and the maiden really asks him to graft a slip of his pear tree onto one of her own trees. Then one graft leads to another and while her tree is bearing a new "per Jenet," she herself is bearing a pear of a different kind, named after its father, Robert, who is the poet. While it operates at this concrete level, however, the description of the garden still parallels and anticipates the physical organ that will be called into play later on.

This interpretation is supported by at least two considerations. Stanzas 4 and 5 clearly refer to two different graftings. The first has a plural object "hem," and properly refers to the trees. The second has the singular "her" as object, and refers to the maiden. Moreover, the sequence is made quite clear: after he has grafted the trees in the garden she fills him with wine and ale — a heady and aphrodisiacal mixture — and in his excitement he grafts himself to her. The first interpretation takes no account of these two parallel but different operations.

Secondly, the first stage of pregnancy is calculated so exactly (twenty weeks or five lunar months is the average time before the pregnant woman feels life) from the moment of the speaker's intercourse with her ("*I* griffed her") that it makes little sense to have the father turn out to be someone else.

(9) *As I went on Yol Day in our procession*. Sloane MS 2593, f. 34a-b. *Index* 377; *XIV-XV*, 27; *EEC* 457; *EEL* 127; *MEL* 73.

A carol with a 2-line stanza of predominantly 6- or 7-stress lines, a refrain, and a burden, rhyming *aaa BBA*.

Jankyn (Jack) is the name commonly given to the youthful clerical seducer in Middle English literature (see *EEC*, p. 452, *Index* 901). The name recalls the Wyf of Bath's fourth husband, who was also

"Jankyn clerk"; and the episode itself recalls that moment in the *Miller's Tale* when Absolon cast lecherous eyes on all the handsome young girls as he carried out his part in the church service. Even the Alysoun of that tale reappears here, for the unusual spelling "Aleyson" in line 3 suggests that it is intended to establish throughout the poem a pun linking the *"eleyson"* of the Mass to the girl's name, a pun which becomes peculiarly appropriate in light of the event.

The poem is contained within a processional Christmas Mass: it begins with the Yule-day procession into the Church, moves through various parts of the Mass, and concludes as the girl walks out of the church after the service is over. But more than this, beginning with the irreverent pun on *"eleyson,"* the poem becomes in many ways a continuous perversion or parody of the religious service which is giving the poem its structural sequence.

At first Jankyn's gaiety, established by the recurring "merye," might seem quite in keeping with the joy of the Christmas festival. But it is hardly appropriate to the particular phrase with which it is associated — *Kyrie Eleison* (God have mercy on us) — with its heavy reminder of human corruption each time it reappears in the burden. Gaiety becomes even less proper when we discover that Jankyn reserves his greatest irreverence, winking and pressing her foot, for the most solemn moment in the service — the offering of the Host (pax brede). Beyond this perversion of the serious religious service, there is the parody supplied by the girl's condition: on the birthday of Christ she too, like Mary, is bearing a child whose father is, to outward appearances, something of a mystery. But if the birth of Christ was Mary's greatest joy, the birth of her child will be Alysoun's greatest shame.

The surface tone of the poem of course always remains lighthearted: Jankyn is perpetually jolly, reads the lesson handsomely, and sings with skill and élan the difficult, involved polyphony of the 15th century ("crakit notes an hunderid on a knot"), reminding us, perhaps, that the poem itself presents a kind of counterpoint, as she speaks the stanzas, he sings the refrain, and the poet offers the burden. The girl, in spite of her condition, is delighted by his performance, takes real pleasure in remembering that she paid for his coat, and apparently enjoys the sly wink and the sudden, secret pressure of his foot against hers. But without destroying this lightheartedness, the recurring burden of *"Kyrieleyson"* constantly reminds us of these lovers' need for

Christ's mercy, at the same time that we remain amused by the impudent pun on her name which Eleyson continually suggests.

The contrast becomes particularly striking in the last stanza, in which the two Latin phrases which are used together to close a Mass whenever a procession is to follow (here, the procession out of the church) become so pointedly inadequate to the girl's real feelings. *"Benedicamos Domino"* (Let us praise God) is turned at once into a plea for mercy: "Crist fro shame me shilde"; and *"Deo gracias"* (thanks be to God) turns into her brief, moving cry of self-recognition: "alas, I go with childe" — itself an ironic transformation of the priest's closing injunction of *"Ite"* (go). The irony here becomes sharper through the internal rhyme that first joins "De*o* . . . thert*o* . . . I g*o* with childe," so that the linked words become a final irreverent — though unintentional — parody of the immaculate conception, and then joins *"gracias"* with "alas" to provide irony of the gravest sort. When the refrain returns for the last time, its impudence on one level and its seriousness on another are fully joined.

(10) *I sing of a maiden.* Sloane MS 2593, f. 10b. *Index* 1367; *XV,* 81; *EEL* 54; *MEL* 66; *OML* 54.

2- or 3-stress lines in 4-line stanzas rhyming *abcb* (stanzas 1 and 5), *abab* (stanzas 2 and 4).

This poem and the following one have received extensive critical attention. For fuller discussions of this one see especially *MEL* pp. 14–19, 23, 334–35; *WN* pp. 158–67; *MEP* pp. 67–9; B. C. Raw, "As Dew in Aprille," *MLR,* IV (1960), 411–14.

In a poem as highly wrought as this, it is safe to assume that even the number of stanzas is intended to be significant: there are five letters in Mary's name (Latin: *Maria*) and five joys are traditionally attributed to her (usually the Annunciation, Nativity, Resurrection, Ascension, and Assumption).[1] Moreover, the three interior stanzas form a unit, emphasized by a distinctive rhyme scheme and the recurring incremental element, which suggests the Holy Trinity, all of whose members participated in the central Christian mystery, both simul-

[1] In this connection, see also *Sir Gawain and the Green Knight,* lines 644–50.

taneously and individually. Taken separately, God the Father is the agent, the Holy Spirit is the means, Christ the Son is the consequence: thus the stanzas may refer successively to annunciation, conception, birth. But since the mystery of the Trinity consists in its being at the same time both divisible and indivisible, the three stanzas also suggest, through the incremental element, not only successive events but simultaneous movements within the same event. And here the event can be either annunciation, or conception, or birth – in all of which all the three members of the Trinity are involved. Nor are we prevented from this interpretation by the repeated reference to "his moder," supposing that the pronoun could refer only to Christ. Since the Trinity is indivisible, Christ simultaneously is both God and Man, and present both on earth and in heaven. Conversely, all three members are at the same time both Mary's bridegroom and her son.

So the three central stanzas of the poem play on the same mystery: they can be read as successive events each involving a different member of the Trinity; or they can represent three successive stages in any one of these events, involving simultaneously all three members of the Trinity; or they can represent all three events instantaneously involving all three members of the Trinity. To all of these readings the repeated images in the incremental element are appropriate. "Stille," "dew," "Aprille" are elements repeated in all three stanzas. Davies has shown (*MEL,* pp. 334–35) that stillness is traditionally associated both with Mary's freedom from concupiscence at the moment of conception and with the peacefulness of the Christmas night. Similarly, the silence would be appropriate both to the awful moment of the annunciation and to the serenity of the first painless birth since Creation. Dew is the conventional symbol of the Holy Ghost and grace descending; it is also the symbol of redemption, through its association with the water of baptism; it is a natural symbol of fertility; and, finally, if its mysteriously imperceptible appearance reemphasizes the silence, its evanescence suggests also the brevity of Christ's sojourn on earth – and in so doing, it not only intensifies the wonder but for a moment undercuts it. April is the month of fertility; it has also been associated with "the new age of man's redemption" (*MEL,* p. 335); and it is the month of the annunciation.

Within the incremental pattern, with its triple repetitions, the changes suggest increasing intimacy and fruitfulness. The indefinite

"Ther his moder was," appropriate to the annunciation, becomes "To his moderes bour" – in which "bour," either in its literal meaning of "chamber" or "bower," or in its symbolic meaning of "womb," is appropriate to the moment of conception. The final variation "Ther his moder lay" suggests the child bed of Christmas morning. (It is appropriate to the perfect symmetry of the poem that the variation requiring syntactical change – "To his moderes bour" – should occur in the middle of the three stanzas, which is also the exact middle of the poem.) Similarly, the movement from "grass" to "flower" to "spray" reveals a growing fruitfulness which parallels exactly the fruition taking place in Mary's womb. Moreover, grass is a traditional symbol of humility, a flower is a conventional symbol of the Virgin, and spray perhaps reminds us that the birth of Christ represents the final flowering branch of Jesse's tree. Finally, the upward movement from grass to flower to spray is set against the falling of the dew (three times repeated in "fallit") – so that we are reminded, at the moment of the incarnation, of two familiar paradoxes: Christ's descent into Mary's womb set against his ultimate ascension into heaven; his descent from the cross set against his resurrection from the tomb. And these in turn recall the fall of man which was fortunate since it led, through Christ's sacrifice, to the descent of grace that can lead to the flowering and redemption of all men.

The poem opens with a contradiction, and the three central stanzas resolve it into a paradox by exploring the larger paradox of the Trinity. Mary is presented as a woman who is matchless and mateless ("makeles" means both), that is, both virgin (maiden) and mother (who chooses a son). She is properly in the courtly tradition by her matchlessness, her power of choice, and her choice of the noblest prince ("King of alle kinges"). But the tradition is broken when we learn that the choice is of a son, not a suitor; and it is when we learn this that "makeles" first takes on its other meaning. But the problem is resolved in stanza 5, by reasserting both terms as a paradox, where contradictions have been reconciled through a meditation (in the interior of the poem) on the greater mystery of the Trinity. "Moder and maiden" reasserts her matelessness; "Was never non but she" reasserts her matchlessness; and if both are true as "makeles" had suggested, she is indeed a lady, and properly the mother of God. Appropriately, the last stanza returns to the rhyme pattern of the first stanza, whose contradiction it now resolves, but it does so by employing also the distinctive rhyme sound of the preceding stanza, whose statement has contributed to the resolution.

Within his own 3-part division, the poet has moved from the assertion of a contradiction through the meditative exploration of a greater mystery, to a resolution that grows out of the exploration but which is not fully revealed until the final identification of "God's mother" in the very last line. And like the Trinity which it celebrates, the poem exists simultaneously in its divisible units and its indivisible whole.

(11) *He bare him up, he bare him down.* Oxford, Balliol College MS 354, f. 165b. *Index* 1132; *EEC* 322A; *EEL* 81; *SCM* 86; *MEL* 164; *OML* 99.

A carol with a 2-line stanza of 4-stress lines with a burden, rhyming *aa BB.*

Critics have been consistently attracted by this hauntingly mysterious poem. They now generally agree that its allegory derives from the Grail Legend but often disagree in the interpretation of its various details.[1] Perhaps it is the elusiveness of these specific details that contributes to the mystery which has so much moved readers. Certainly the poem gains its excitement from our sense of a mystery only gradually revealed to us. John Speirs observes that "the formula of poems of rites — such as the Corpus Christi Carol must surely be — retains in its structure a sense of being initiated by stages. . . . One is led by steps as through a maze until one reaches the centre of the maze, the heart of the mystery" (*MEP,* p. 77).

It is appropriate to this movement toward delayed revelation that the lyric begins with a contradiction and then with an account of wanderings that are disconcertingly aimless and of a destination that is puzzlingly vague. The contradiction lies in the refrain, which juxtaposes a line taken from a lullaby to a line reminiscent of a ballad tragedy, in

[1] See for example accounts by Annie Gilchrist, *Journal of the Folk Song Society,* IV (1910–13), 52–66; *EEC,* pp. 411–12; *MEL,* p. 364; *WN,* p. 117. Elsewhere, Greene has read the poem as an account of Catherine of Aragon's distress over the loss of her husband, Henry VIII, to Anne Bullen: "The Meaning of the Corpus Christi Carol," *Medium Aevum* XXIX (1960), 10–21.

which a maiden weeps for her lost or slain husband (mak). Is the speaker a mother soothing her child or a wife lamenting her beloved?

The images that follow in sequence are individually precise and vivid, but they have no logical coherence until we come to the very last line in which the reference to the body of Christ suddenly makes everything fall into place and become luminously meaningful. If the dead knight is indeed Christ, then the speaker is Mary and the contradiction of the two roles can be explained. Christ as man is her son to whom as a baby she can appropriately sing a lullaby; but Christ as God also participated with the other members of the Trinity in the espousal of Mary and in the act of his own conception. So he is also her bridegroom, from whom, however, she has been separated by his death on the cross. The refrain juxtaposes the birth and death of Christ, and the dual role of Mary — as Madonna and *Mater Dolorosa* — who simultaneously mourns the death of a son and a bridegroom.

The falcon, as bird of prey, is, of course, an appropriate symbol of death, and the aimless wanderings — "he bare him up, he bare him down" — properly suggest the mysterious journey which death requires. But now we see that the falcon, a royal bird as well as a bird of prey, can also become God, while the movements up and down suggest the elevation and deposition of Christ's body, actions which, if they were performed by men, were authorized and supervised by God himself as part of his divine plan. As a location for the hall and bed, the orchard is, of course, appropriate. In recalling the fruit which was the instrument of temptation and original sin, it suggests Adam whose sin blighted the Garden of Eden, reminding us of the popular notion of Christ as the second Adam, who was, properly, buried in a second garden whose autumnal browns stand in sharp contrast to the perpetual bloom of Eden. The royal colors of purple and red-gold, which drape the hall and the bed, remind us of Christ's role as King of Kings, while the various current meanings of "pall" include a range of associations appropriate to him. As a rich cloth, traditionally purple, used ceremonially for persons of high rank, the word reinforces the other royal colors. As a cloth, usually of black, purple, or white velvet, spread over a coffin or tomb, it celebrates Jesus' Passion and death. And, in its ecclesiastical meaning of altar cloth, the linen cloth used to cover the chalice, it suggests the various Eucharistic interpretations of the images. The perpetually bleeding wounds recall both the timelessness of the sacrifice — Christ did not die just once but is eternally dying for our sins — and the perpetual availability to all men of his redeeming blood. The maid kneeling and weeping by the side of the dead knight can be, of course, the weeping Mary. But in a larger sense she can also represent Ecclesia, the whole body of Christian society (*WN*, p. 116), just as the hall and the knight represent not only the literal objects themselves but the symbols of these objects as they appear in the Eucharist (*MEL*, p. 364). Similarly the stone is not only a tablet for inscription, but at its literal level becomes the stone that sealed up the tomb in which Christ was laid.

While the images, illuminated by the last line, reveal all these coherent Christian meanings, the literal details also remind us of the simple human situations on which the mysterious poem is based — "a maiden weeping for her new-slain knight" (*MEP*, p. 78), a human situation which is still further emphasized in later versions of the poem by the addition of a faithful dog who licks his master's bleeding wounds (though this detail, too, is susceptible to religious interpretation). It is the combination of the simple, moving, human situation, the elaborate religious associations which the literal details suggest, and the mystery which suspends both levels of meaning until the very end which accounts, in large measure, for the poem's impact.

(12) *Lullay, lullay, litel child.* National Library of Scotland MS Advocates 18.7.21, f. 6a. *Index* 2024; *XIV*, 59; *EEC* 155.

A carol with a 4-line stanza of three 4-stress lines and one 3-stress line rhyming *aaab AB.*

This is possibly the only lullaby carol addressed to Christ in which the speaker is Mankind. But Mankind is represented variously, since the speaker at first seems to be Adam (in whom, of course, all mankind resides) and later Mankind in general. The shift occurs between ll. 16 and 17, and this division of the poem is supported by the shift in personal pronoun from first person singular in ll. 5–16, to the first person plural in the last stanza. More profoundly, perhaps, the apparent shift reveals the readiness of the medieval poet to recognize the participation of all mankind in Adam's particular sin, or, conversely, the continued presence of Adam in all men. This interpenetration of one man in all, of all in one, is essential to the notion of inherited, original sin, and the poem makes the inclusive responsibility strikingly vivid through the movement from "I" to "we," from one person to all men, from one act to all acts, from the first Adam to the second Adam.

Similarly the poem moves from the pain of the newborn child, a specific consequence of Adam's sin, to the greater pain of the Crucifixion (peines mo) which, voluntarily undertaken by Christ, will liberate Mankind from this sin and all of its pains. This movement is summarized in the speaker's gradual understanding of Christ's weeping. At first it is not understood at all, or understood only as the causeless weeping of any infant: "Why wepest thou so sore?" Then it is understood more fully as having been caused by Adam's sin (ll. 5–6), but still the child is crying as any infant might cry because of the pain to which childbirth had been condemned. Then (l. 12) the cause is enlarged to include the pity, which only Christ would feel, for the heritage which Adam and all men lost. But it is not until l. 16 that the poet understands fully both the double cause and the consequence of the child's tears. They derive from Christ's capacity to feel divine pity and from Jesus' capacity to feel human pain: together they become the means to Man's salvation. Through his enlarged understanding of the child's weeping the poet has illuminated the mystery of the Incarnation. In ll. 1–16 Adam describes his sin in some detail and goes as far as intimating his salvation. In ll. 17–28, Mankind accepts Adam's sin as his own (l. 19), describes Christ's Passion, and in his three ringing assertions gives the final answer to that question which has recurred in every repetition of the burden: "Why wepest thou so sore?"

The mystery of the Incarnation, of Jesus' double nature, is central to the whole poem, and through its special prominence in the opening stanza of each section, this mystery also serves as the major link between the poem's two parts. In stanza 1, the all-powerful King and the helpless child are juxtaposed through the parallel phrases "sterne and wild" and "meke and mild." And the same contrast is emphasized in stanza 5, in the progression from "litel thing" through "litel barun" to "litel king," as the persistent "litel" continues to remind us that Christ is simultaneously both child and king.

In the same way, the timelessness of Christ's redemptive act is suggested through the comparison of past, present, and future. The poem is concerned with the present moment of birth, but references to Christ's love for mankind stretch back into the past — "That thou hast loved *so yore,*" "that thou hast *ay* loved so" — and into the future — "Yet shaltou suffren peines mo."

Finally, the mystery of the Incarnation — of God made Man, of the child who is a king — is perhaps given an even larger context by the reminders of the central Christian mystery of the Trinity through the rhetorical emphasis on groups of three. The poem is composed of 4-line stanzas each made up of two parts: a 3-line unit and a single line. All three lines carry four stresses; the single line carries three. Moreover, the whole poem comprises seven stanzas (and a burden) which are, as was pointed out, divided into two units of four and three stanzas respectively. The 4-stanza unit is subdivided like the individual stanzas themselves into a single introductory stanza and then a group of three stanzas dealing with Adam's sin. These three are then matched by the three stanzas dealing with Christ's suffering on account of this sin. And within these three stanzas, groups of three constantly recur: Christ is addressed three times, three of his wounds are enumerated, and the extent of his pain is pounded into the listener by the triple repetition of the last stanza. Thus there is a primary emphasis on three, a secondary emphasis on four — which together make up the seven stanzas of the poem.

According to medieval belief, four symbolizes man and the mundane world generally, while three symbolizes the Trinity and the spiritual world generally. It is therefore symbolically appropriate that the part of the poem dealing with Adam's sin should occupy 4 stanzas; the part dealing with Christ's salvation should occupy 3. And seven therefore becomes a number of great mystical significance, uniting as it does "the triune principle of God and the quadruple principle of man" and therefore becoming "the first principle which implies totality."[1] It is a reminder of man's dual nature and, in specific terms of this poem, a reminder of his participation in both Adams.

(13) *Hale! sterne superne, Hale! in eterne.* Asloan MS ff. 303a–304b. *The Asloan MS.,* ed. W. A. Craigie, II (Edinburgh,

[1] Vincent F. Hopper, *Medieval Symbolism* (New York: Columbia University Press, 1938), p. 84.

1925), *STS,* 275–78; *SPWD,* II, 269–71; *MWD,* pp. 160–62; *WDP,* pp. 8–9; *MEL* 144.

Alternating 4- and 3-stress lines in 12-line stanzas rhyming *ababababxbab.*

The established details of Dunbar's life are scanty. He was born about 1460, and he may have been the William Dunbar who took the B.A. and M.A. degrees at the University of St. Andrews in 1477 and 1479 respectively. By 1504 he had taken religious orders. He was connected with the court of James IV of Scotland, a king who, on the account of a contemporary ambassador to the Scottish court, was remarkable for his chivalry and humanity, for his range of interests, for his skill in both learning and practical affairs, and for his patronage of art and literature. Two of Dunbar's poems refer specifically to James's marriage to Queen Margaret in 1503, and many other poems refer to life and even specific events at court. Dunbar himself received a royal pension from 1500 to 1513, after which he presumably received a benefice, since the pension had always carried the stipulation that it be withdrawn if he received a benefice above a certain amount.

In his poetry, Dunbar specifically acknowledges his indebtedness to Chaucer – particularly as a rhetorician; to moral Gower, and to Lydgate. Beyond these, he was clearly influenced by the poetry of James's court, and through it by the courtly poetry of England and France generally, as well as by the whole range of poetry in vernacular Scots. His poetry ranges widely, from courtly love to scurrilous "flyting," from court petitions to moral exhortation, from visionary ecstasy to the hallucinations of nightmare. His language reveals an appropriate variety, from the jeweled, Latinate splendor of the aureate *Hale! sterne superne,* through the quiet intensity of *Amang thir freiris,* to the broad, coarse, abusive vernacular in such a poem as *The . . . Twa Mariit Wemen and the Wedow* (Widow).

In Dunbar's aureate verse, the poetic energy is formal, verbal, rhythmical rather than intellectual. Its appeal is first of all to the ear: it must be heard (at least imaginatively) rather than read. This poem does include a remarkable wealth of imagery, but the images remain sharp, vivid, and precise, so that they can accumulate without interrupting the rapid forward thrust of the poem, at the same time that each one can also resonate with larger meanings because of the rich iconography on which it draws. The poem thus becomes something like the miracle that it celebrates. Its ornate language glows and sparkles but is also richly suggestive. Its rhetorical patterns give stately elegance, yet at the same time the rich fabric is charged with so much energy of rhythm and sound, such rapidly accumulating variations of an idea, that as Edwin Morgan observes, the reader is given "no breathing space" but is gathered up in the momentum and almost dazzled with sparks "in a pyrotechnic ascent."[1]

The poem is driven forward by the compelling repetitions of sound and an insistent meter. But there are variations in both sound and meter which avoid monotony without lowering the exultation. Each stanza is governed by two controlling sounds which alternate with each other throughout the twelve lines. But while the first sound reoccurs three times in each of its lines, the second appears only once in its lines, in the terminal rhyming word. The effect within any two lines is of alternate attention and relaxation: in stanza 1, for example, the recurring "erne" of the odd-numbered lines holds the long line in a constant single focus, while the casual vowels of the even lines diffuse this focus — or rather, these lines gather their own focus more slowly since it takes six lines of poetry before this sound has recurred as often as the first sound has recurred within a single line.

Metrically, the basic iambic meter and the regular alternation of 8- and 6-syllable lines are always being slightly varied — just enough to keep it flexible at the same time it remains insistent. L. 1 is altered dramatically by the strong initial stresses: "Hále! Stérne," which is then not repeated exactly, but modulated into the lower-keyed inversions of the second apostrophe: "Hále! ĭn." Then this irregular line is followed by the perfectly regular beat of l. 2. L. 3 is again metrically regular, but extends its rhythm by enjambing with l. 4. This same device is used still more powerfully in l. 7, when the syntax demands the enjambment even more compellingly, in order to come to the main verb, "Helpe!" which adds its own force by being an imperative monosyllable that jars the opening of its own line by introducing the first *initial* spondee to appear since l. 1. The whole supplication of the first stanza rises dramatically to this cry, which is matched by the dra-

[1] Edwin Morgan, "Dunbar and the Language of Poetry," *Essays in Criticism,* II (April, 1952), 152.

matically irregular variation of the meter. It then subsides into the liquid rhythms and soft vowels of the Latin *"Ávĕ! Măríă, gráciă plénă"*; this phrase in turn rises to the spondees of the next line before modulating into the rise and fall of "Yérne ŭs, gŭbérne, vĭrgín mătérn," and finally closing on the series of regular rising iambic rhythms: "Ŏf réuth băith rúte ănd ríne."

There does not appear to be any dramatic logic for the particular progression of sounds, or for the sequence of attributes and images which appear in the seven stanzas: in general the paean proceeds from the opening apostrophe (1) which combines adoration with solicitation, through five stanzas which successively consider the glory of the Son (2), the Virgin as combatant (3), the Virgin as flower (4), the angelic adoration of the Virgin (5), a summary of her roles (6), concluding with a vision of her enthroned in the highest heavenly spheres where God and the angels dwell (7). The number of stanzas is itself important, since 7, as the combination of the 4 and 3, carried great mystical significance (see Commentary on lyric 12). Finally, it is interesting to notice two other details. The middle stanza, 4, is the only stanza whose major sound (ene) rhymes with the Latin line, and whose minor sound (ice) also occurs as a major sound in another stanza (stanza 6). The last stanza achieves a certain internal drama found in no other stanza through the great contrast between the opening and closing images, for in it we move from the resplendent images of the "Imperiall wall, place palestrall,/Of peirles pulcritud," in the opening lines, to the dark concluding images and somber diction of Christ's earthly sacrifice: "Thy birth has, with his blude/ Fra fall mortall, originall,/ Us raunsound on the Rude."

(14) *Rorate celi desuper*. Bannatyne MS, f. 27b. *BMS,* II, 65–6; *SPWD,* II, 72–3; *MWD,* pp. 154–5; *WDP,* pp. 1–2.
4-stress lines in 8-line stanzas rhyming *ababbcbc*.

The rhetorical and visionary splendor of Dunbar's aureate verse is here replaced by a simpler, less breathless but more intense wonder and joy. C. S. Lewis has remarked that this "might almost claim to be in one sense the most lyrical of all English poems — that is, the hardest of all English poems simply to *read,* the hardest not to sing. We read it alone and at night — and are almost shocked, on laying the book down, to find that the choir and organ existed only in our imagination."[1]

But the poem is a symphony of motion and of light, as well as of sound. The whole range of creation is invited to join in the celebration: the heavens and their inhabitants, mankind, birds, beasts, fish, flowers. And if the clergy, for instance, are invited both to "read and sing" they also "incline/And bow" unto the newborn child, and they incense his altar with the gestures as well as the sounds of adoration. If the regions of air "mak armony," the heavens adore by gently distilling their "balmy shouris"; and if the birds can show their joy in song, the flowers do so by turning upward "naturaly" and unfolding their leaves "lustely." And all this music of sound and motion occurs within a large movement of space and time — a movement from heaven to earth, and a movement out of darkness into light.

The intensity of sound, of motion, and of light increases as we move through the seven stanzas of the poem; and the order of images is appropriate to the change. The light of stanza one is the first light of dawn just coming out of its heavenly towers; by l. 39 the sun is risen "with glaidsum licht"; and by l. 55 the reference to Christ "crownit abone the sky" suggests full day. At the same time the celebrants are invoked in precisely the order, first, in which Christ would meet them in his journey down from heaven, and, later, in which natural objects would respond to the growing light. First invoked are the angelic ranks which, with God, inhabit the heavenly empyrean, beyond the outermost sphere of the created universe; then the firmament of the fixed stars and the spheres of the moving planets; finally the regions of fire, air, and water which in this order encircle the earth below the sphere of the moon. Once earth is reached, the dawn begins. First to respond is the sinner, who, if he were sincere in his penance, would watch and pray all night. Next, the clergy who would rise before dawn for early Mass. Then the birds who traditionally herald the first light of dawn. Finally, the flowers whose drooping heads would respond only to the full power of the risen sun. And the response of each one shows increasing vitality — from the humble

[1] C. S. Lewis, *English Literature in the Sixteenth Century* (Oxford: Oxford University Press, 1954), p. 95.

thanks of the sinner, to the gracious but ritualized gestures and chants of the priest, to the spontaneous and full-throated song of the birds, to the lusty resurrection of the flowers — in which the image of the "rose Mary" reoccurs to round out the poem by identifying the rebirth of the flowers with the birth of Christ, celebrated in stanza 1, "fro the ros Mary, flour of flouris."

The final stanza then gathers together all the regions of created space, all varieties of created beings, all the sounds and movements which have pulsed through the poem, so that for a moment in time they are unified into one harmonious consort, *"Gloria in excelsis,"* under the blazing light of him "that is crownit abone the sky."

(15) *Done is a battell on the dragon blak!* Bannatyne MS, f. 35a. *BMS,* II, 88–9; *SPWD,* II, 156–7; *MWD,* pp. 159–60; *WDP,* pp. 7–8.

5-stress lines in 8-line stanzas rhyming *ababbcbc*. See #14.

The power of this poem is due to a number of things. First there is a procession of sharp simple images which are both vividly concrete and also, like the images in *Hale! sterne superne,* resonant with accumulated associations and symbolic meanings. The black dragon with the mortal sting; the dungeon with its gates and fetters, its jailors and prisoners; the triumphant champion raising his standard on the battle field: all these are familiar and vivid details from depictions, verbal and graphic, of the Harrowing of Hell. Other images, like the lion, the rising sun, the lamb, are not only vivid in themselves, but are also familiar iconographic representations of the triumphant and merciful Christ. Even the tiger, although a less common symbol, becomes appropriate as the figure of a dangerous antagonist who must, however, within the hierarchy of animals, succumb to the lion, who is sovereign within this area of creation, as Christ is sovereign in his.[1]

Second, there are powerful cross-rhythms set up by the individual words themselves, a great number of which carry trochaic rather than iambic rhythm. When these accumulate in considerable numbers, as

[1] Isabel Hyde, "Primary Sources and Associations of Dunbar's Aureate Imagery," *Modern Language Review,* LI (Oct. 1956), 481–92.

in the first stanza, they set up a music quite different from the iambic, even when the line as a whole scans regularly. Quite apart from obvious differences in diction and imagery, the musical feel of ll. 18 and 27, for instance, is quite different from that of l. 10, in which the self-contained trochees in "crewall," "serpent," "mortall" set up a counter-rhythm more powerful than the underlying iambic. And when words of this kind are not only numerous but central to the meaning, they control the rhythm of the whole stanza. In stanza one, for instance, "battell," "dragon," "campioun," "confoundit," "yettis," "brokin," "triumphall," "rasit," "divillis," "trimmillis" (both elided), "hiddous," "saulis," "borrowit," "ransones"—all have very strong falling rhythms. Add to these the trochees provided by inverted first feet—"Dóne ĭs," "Chríst wĭth"—and the effect of trochaic rhythm becomes overwhelming.

Finally, although the lines are basically five-stressed decasyllables, a large proportion of them carry only 4 really heavy stresses, so that they move with the stately power of the Old English alliterative line. Sometimes, as for example in the first two lines, the effect is emphasized by alliteration and the effect of a marked caesural pause.

*D*óne is a BÁTTELL on the *d*rágon BLÁK
Our *c*ámpioun *C*hríst *c*ONFOÚNDIT hes his FÓRCE

But the effect does not depend upon alliteration, for this rhythm of two against two is equally powerful in ll. 3 and 4,

The yéttis of Héll ar brókin with a crák
The sígne triúmphall rásit is of the cróce.

(16–17) *A pak, a pak, Madame, my lode alight. The mede is flowe, the grace is goon.* Harley MS 682, ff. 86b, 87a. *The English Poems of Charles of Orleans,* vol. I, ed. Robert Steele, *EETS* 215 (London, 1941), p. 131; vol. II, ed. Robert Steele and Mabel Day, *EETS* 220 (London 1946).

Roundels: no. 16 in 5-stress lines, no. 17 in 4-stress lines, with refrain, rhyming *ABbaab AB abba AB.*

These two roundels by Charles d'Orleans (for biographical note see Commentary on *The New Lady* under *Allegory and Dream Vision*) observe the normal fourteen-line pattern: rhyming *ABbaab AB abba AB,* with six lines, then the first two lines repeated, then four new lines, and, finally, the first two lines repeated again. Considerable variation was possible and was indeed practiced by Charles, who composed roundels with as many as twenty-one lines, and with great variation in the rhyme scheme. And, although the normal line was decasyllabic, he often used octosyllabics as he does in the second one here. Within these variations, however, the general pattern remains the same: a group of lines followed by the repetition of a few of the opening lines, then a shorter group of lines followed by the repetition of the same opening lines. And the rhyme is always a combination of only two sounds. Together, these two roundels reveal extremes of the lover's sensibility within the convention of courtly love: the first is a cry for help to the heartless beloved, before she has granted even her first favors; the last admits final, total rejection, but with the recognition that he may still find some proper and gracious mistress, if only he will choose more wisely before he again undertakes the chase. In between these terminal moments in love lies the familiar progress of courtly love, whose various stages are almost all represented in Charles's other roundels — like the plea for more intimate favors once his suit has been accepted, or the chilling discovery, through some chattering gossip idly overheard, that he has fallen out of favor — a misfortune that always threatened, either through slander or the mistress's own caprice.

The remarkable effect of these roundels — and it is an effect which can be lost if all 96 are read together rapidly — is their presentation of the speaking voice of the poet-lover, low-keyed but subtly modulated. The result is an emotional urgency which speaks through the artificial love convention and poetic form, and through the quiet, unpretentious diction and imagery. And Charles achieves this flexible rhythm of the speaking voice and the variations of emotional intensity without the dramatic violence to meter which will later occur in Wyatt and Donne.

A brief inspection will suggest this simple economy in his poetic art. There is, for instance, a world of difference between the exclamatory outcry which begins the first and the detached reflection which opens the second — and yet the meter of both lines is equally regular (if the French pronunciation of madame is preserved — as would seem likely). The difference in tone is achieved by less dramatic means: in the first, by the repeated ejaculation with its open "a" and sharp "k" sounds, the quick series of short interior pauses required by the exclamation, the direct address, and the sharp syntactical break at the end of the line after the imperative commands; in the second, by the modulation of soft, long vowels, the easy parallel of two simple observations, the assonance which links the first two clauses (flowe . . . goon), and the alliteration which links the two parts of the last clause (grace . . . goon). Each of these two stanzas then modulates its opening tone. In the first, the exclamation with its brief command yields first to explanation, still punctuated by exclamations, but now in a lower key (allas! lo!). Then, in the second tercet, explanation is in turn replaced by a new request, no longer a cry for help explained by practical necessity, but a moral injunction based on the strongest emotional argument — that he would do the same for her, were he in her place. In the second roundel, the opening mood is first expanded: the balanced rhythm of the two unequal clauses in l. 1 is stretched out into the single clause and unbroken rhythm of l. 2. Then follow the uneven rhythmic balance of l. 3 (with its caesura after the third instead of the second foot), the unbroken rhythm of l. 4 (which does not, however, gather rhythmic impetus from the preceding line, as l. 2 had gathered from l. 1 through parallel syntax), and the sudden sharp exclamation in l. 5 which leads, through the poem's first enjambment, to the unexpected vigor of "hay!" in l. 6. The linear organization of this sestet is 4–2, while that of the sestet in the first roundel was 3–3; and while that moved from the short ejaculatory rhythms of outcry and demand to the longer rhythms of increasing inwardness and reflection, this moves quite differently — as the rhythm first lengthens, then shortens, then breaks apart into the sudden ejaculation and the diction of the courtyard.

VERSE CHRONICLE

(18) *Layamon's Brut.* MS Cotton Caligula A ix (1200–25), upon which this text is based, ff. 130b–33a, West Midlands; MS Cotton Otho C xiii (1250–75). *Layamon's 'Brut,'* ed. Frederic Madden, 3 vols. (London, 1847); *Selections from Laȝamon's 'Brut,'* ed. G. L. Brook (Oxford, 1963); *Laȝamon: 'Brut,'* ed. G. L. Brook and R. F. Leslie (Oxford, 1963), *EETS* 250.

The verse form is modeled after the Old English alliterative line with a pattern of 4 to 7 stresses per line and a varying number of unstressed syllables. Each line has two half-lines, separated by a slight pause; a half-line contains 2 stresses, sometimes 3, infrequently 4. Often these half-lines are linked by alliteration, often by rhyme; sometimes there is neither.

The *Brut* was written about 1205 by Layamon, a priest of Kings Arley at a church on the Severn River near Redstone in North Worcestershire. In the same passage of the poem which provides autobiographical details, Layamon also refers to his three sources. The most influential was Wace's Anglo-Norman poem *Roman de Brut* (ca. 1150), itself a free rendering of Geoffrey of Monmouth's prose *Historia Regum Britanniae.* Of the other two sources, one apparently was the Old English translation of Bede's *Historia Ecclesiastica,* and the second may simply have been the original Latin version of this work, though this is not necessarily the correct interpretation of Layamon's reference to a Latin book made by Saint Alban and Saint Augustine. It is on Wace's chronicle that Layamon chiefly relied, but because of his extensive additions to the material in both Wace and Geoffrey, some scholars believe that he worked from a version of Wace different from the one that we now possess, or that he had access to some other poem – possibly the same poem that had served as Geoffrey's source.

As a result of other sources or of his own sensibilities and invention, Layamon's *Brut* differs strikingly from Wace's *Roman.* It is much longer – Wace's 15,000 octosyllabics are expanded into more than 32,000 half lines (often as long as the octosyllabics), whose diction and meter and phraseology derive not from Wace's Norman French but from Old English verse. A similar change in tone transforms Wace's chivalric knights into Layamon's heroic warriors, dominated by the fierce and bloody determination, the grim humor and weighty sententiousness, the powerful masculine loyalties of the Anglo-Saxon *comitatus* (a select band of warriors attached to a chief or hero). In his adaptation of Wace, Layamon not only incorporates new details and episodes but also adds greater vividness and dramatic power to those that he shares with his source. Just as Wace had enriched Geoffrey's spare accounts, so Layamon enlivens Wace with vigorous dialogue, powerful long speeches, and with vivid depictions of nature, of savage battle, and of elaborate festivities at court — all of which, however, evoke the heroic tone of *Beowulf* rather than the gaiety and amorousness of Wace.

In so long a work, whose form seems to be determined only by the chronological sequence of events, it is easy to overlook the poem's skillful management of formal proportions and arrangement. Much of the general proportion Layamon inherited from Wace, but it appears to even better advantage in this poem. The narrative still moves chronologically, but some episodes are expanded while others are compressed so that not only do the major units present a dramatic rise and fall, but within this pattern an irregular narrative tempo now quickens, now slackens pace.

Of Layamon's 32,000 half lines, almost exactly half are devoted to Arthurian material (reckoned to extend from the first reference to Arthur's father, Uther Pendragon, to Arthur's departure for Avalon). This material represents the focus of dramatic interest, but it achieves this prominence not only by its relative bulk but by its location within the poem: it is preceded by three-quarters and followed by one quarter of the remaining material. It thus receives the kind of emphasis given to climactic scenes in a drama when they are preceded by a leisurely introduction and followed by a rapid denouement. This Arthurian material is itself similarly proportioned, with a little less than half devoted to Arthur's immediate predecessors, a little more than half to Arthur himself.

The episodes dealing with Arthur also reveal skillful variation in narrative tempo. Arthur's first campaign, in which he struggles to establish his rule in Britain, is presented at length and in considerable detail — about 1,700 lines. But it is then followed by a series of subsidiary campaigns that are handled with increasing brevity: about 600 lines for Scotland, 200 lines for Ireland, and then Iceland, Orkney, Winetlond all tumble after each other within another 200 lines. Then follows, at somewhat greater length, the episode of the Round Table, which rounds out Arthur's consolidation of his realm by providing a domestic victory, over dissension within his own household, that parallels his earlier victory over the dissension within the country at large. A second narrative unit begins as Arthur turns from domestic to foreign campaigns, and it again reveals this irregular tempo. This time the sequence is reversed. After the briefest introductory accounts of the campaigns in Norway and Denmark, the dramatic action rises through the detailed account of the conquest of France to the still longer, climactic campaign against the Emperor in Rome, and then falls, in a rapid denouement, through the civil war with Mordred to the passing of Arthur to Avalon. Moreover, this concluding episode with its disintegration of the Court not only provides sharp contrast to that earlier scene in which the formation of the Round Table had rounded out Arthur's domestic triumphs, but it also anticipates the denouement of the entire chronicle after Arthur's death, as the realm gradually disintegrates and the Britons disperse.

The passage included here is interesting because it tells much more about the origins of the Round Table than does Wace or Geoffrey. Structurally it concludes the first group of Arthur's campaigns (see above). But at the same time that Arthur's firm handling of this household brawl parallels his triumphal consolidation of his whole realm, the sudden murderous fight within his household also looks forward to the disastrous betrayal by Mordred and the terrible battle that follows, a battle that will allow no time for the tactical withdrawal and regrouping which occurs here, and that will offer no new Round Table to reunite the scattered fellowship. Thus, as so often in the poem, Layamon obliges us to see not only the vivid events of the present but also the past which these events summarize and the future which they prefigure. At the very moment that we feel the triumph of Arthur's cumulative accomplishments, that we see the Table as a metaphor for Arthur himself from whom gleemen will draw sustenance "to there weorlde longe," we are also reminded of the other part of Merlin's prophecy, of the "unimete care" that will attend Arthur's passing. The recurrent epithets – Arthur the king, Arthur the noblest king, Arthur the young – become haunting reminders that if the young King is present in the poem, for Layamon and his audience he is the absent, aged King who, if not dead, has not yet come again as he promised.

This tension between past, present, and future is reemphasized by a number of other contrasts within this passage. There is, for instance, the contrast between the vividly realistic details of the Yule banquet and the magical details of the Round Table, fabricated by a craft that can mysteriously construct a table big enough to seat 1,600 men and yet small enough to be carried from place to place. Even Layamon suggests that the story of this marvelous table must grow out of the lies people tell about those they love. But this remark in turn leads Layamon to observe the contrary: that if too great love will lead one man to lie about another, great hate will also lead to lies — of a different sort. The effect of this reflection is to blur the distinctions not only between the true and the false but also between kinds of falsehood, since historical truth about a man can be distorted by either love or hate.

Finally, if the table itself is fabulous and the truth of its existence uncertain, the social relationship that it sets up is equally unreal. By establishing a fictional democracy among men who in fact represent very different ranks within an established social hierarchy, the Round Table reminds us of that contrast between the chivalric ideal of equality among all knights and the feudal reality of unequal social ranks. The ideal animates much chivalric literature in the Middle Ages but is consistently contradicted by social fact. Within this particular episode, this contradiction appears in the striking contrast between ll. 43–49 and ll. 130–36. And for anyone who has read the chronicle up to this point and who, with Layamon, looks ahead to Mordred's treachery, it is clear that the democracy and love which the Table imposes on Arthur's knights is as fabulous as the Table itself. Layamon knows that he is dealing with lies, even if they were originally told out of love and are retold now in the nostalgic hope that they may represent things as they could be. What is not a lie is the pride and the envy of place, the sudden anger that leads men to hurl loaves of bread and silver bowls of wine and then to plunge a knife into a man's neck, the swift and terrible anger of Arthur and his savage justice against the guilty. In the end it will be these qualities — of hate and malice and envy — which triumph, as they destroy Arthur and his knights and the whole realm of Britain.

ROMANCE

(19) *Alliterative Morte Arthure.* MS Lincoln Cathedral Libr. (Thornton), 91, ff. 53a–98b (1430–40), Northwest Midlands. *The Alliterative Romance of the Death of King Arthur,* ed. J. O. Halliwell (Brixton Hill, 1847); *Morte Arthure,* ed. George Perry (London, 1865), *EETS* 8; ed. Edmund Brock (London, 1871), *EETS* 8; ed. Mary M. Banks (London, 1900); ed. Erik Björkman (Heidelberg, 1915); ed. John Finlayson (London, 1967).

Unrhymed alliterative lines containing 4–5 stresses and 2–5 alliterations.

The Alliterative Morte Arthure is so called to distinguish it from a roughly contemporary stanzaic poem bearing a similar title — *Le Morte Arthur.* It differs from the latter, however, not only in its metrical form, but in the Arthurian episodes with which it deals and in its artistic quality.

Critics have found it difficult to assign *Morte Arthure* to one of the conventional genres. In its particular Arthurian episodes; in its careful attention to precise details of chronology, of British and Continental geography, and of military strategy; in its central focus upon Arthur himself; and in its masculine, heroic spirit that generally neglects women and the softer chivalric virtues they inspired — in all these characteristics the poem is indebted to the chronicle as it developed through Geoffrey and Layamon. At the same time, however, the poem shares with romance its lavishly extended descriptions of banquets and dress, its incredible exaggerations of the odds which Arthur and his knights overcome in battle, and its fondness for the exotic and supernatural. (These elements of course appear in chronicles; it is the degree of emphasis which recalls romance.) Finally, the unusually sustained and urgent religious invocation that opens the poem suggests a more purposeful didacticism than is usual in either chronicle or romance; taken together with the balanced two-part structure, it suggests that among other things the poem presents a medieval tragedy of fortune (see esp. *TA,* ch. iv).

This apparent confusion is in fact transformed into art, since the poem does succeed in fusing characteristics of several genres into a single, unified poetic statement. Because the two major episodes which the poem includes — Arthur's campaign against the Roman emperor Lucius and his campaign against Mordred — are not random adventures but are the last two in the traditional sequence of his campaigns as they appear in the chronicles, they can suggest the whole Arthurian legend at the same time they provide the narrower, concentrated focus essential to a tragic contrast between good and evil fortune. Similarly, the precise details of chronology, geography, and military combat give the weight of historical truth to that tragic moral which both structure and character reveal, while the emphasis on Arthur himself personalizes the tragedy within this authentic historical context. The elaborate descriptions do more than enrich the texture of the poem: they provide important changes in narrative tempo; and they also sometimes provide implicit moral comments, as when just after the dream the resplendent Arthur is juxtaposed to the austere Sir Craddock.

We have included the second section, Arthur's dream and his fight with Mordred, which occupies roughly the last quarter of the poem. The preceding 3,200 lines have presented the last and greatest of Arthur's foreign wars, his campaign against the Roman Emperor Lucius. This first section of the poem has begun with a review of Arthur's conquests to date, conquests that have made him ruler of most of western Europe. Then, on New Year's Day a Roman senator attended with sixteen knights confronts Arthur in his court, commanding him to appear before the Emperor in Rome to answer for his depradations of imperial lands, and to renew that homage to Rome which Julius Caesar had won through his conquest of Britain. Arthur's rage at these demands is so terrible that the Romans quail before him, crouching like whipped dogs. He assures them that he will come to Rome indeed, not as a suppliant but as a conqueror, and he proves to be as good as his word. As he moves victoriously through France and into Italy, his army ravages towns and destroys the people until he finally stands at the summit of his fortune: Lucius is dead, Rome is in his hands, and on Christmas Day Arthur will be crowned overlord of all the earth. (Our selection begins at this point.)

Suddenly, shortly after midnight, everything changes. Arthur has gone to bed with a light heart, but he starts up trembling with fear; he has fallen asleep with visions of the imperial crown and a holy crusade;

he awakens to the bleak reality of domestic treachery and civil war. The dream which intervenes has prepared for and explained the reversal: it appears to do so in terms of a capricious fortune; in reality it does so in terms which are wholly consistent with the events and characters as they have appeared in the first part of the poem. The dream in fact obliges us, as it obliges Arthur, to reinterpret what has seemed to be the truth of things. Accordingly, the dream itself and the events which follow are filled with contrasts which suggest the ambiguous or contradictory nature of human life and character.

At first the lady of the dream, with her elaborate garments and whirling wheel and sudden change of favor, appears to be only the familiar Lady Fortune. However, she is never specifically addressed as Fortune. Arthur refers to her simply as a duchess, while both her descent from the clouds and David's reference to her as "maiden so milde" carry suggestions of the Virgin Mary. This ambiguousness is borne out by the fortune that she dispenses. At first glance her actions seem to be capricious. But they do not seem so to the six kings whom she has already flung down from her wheel but who blame their misfortune not on her but on themselves. Nor do they seem capricious to the interpreting philosopher, who attributes Arthur's fall in the dream to the King's own selfish pride and greed.

At this crucial moment in the poem, the dream thus introduces a sudden and violent change in fortune in a way that complicates ideas and characters that might otherwise seem quite simple. Misfortune is not simply capricious chance but the clear moral consequence of human actions. Hence the purveyor of this fortune is partly pagan goddess, partly Christian. Moreover, these actions for which man is morally accountable may at the same time be both admirable and reprehensible. The philosopher accuses Arthur of pride and greed and cruelty, but at the same time Arthur remains as one of the Nine Worthiest Men in human history. Finally, the whole dream is enacted within a setting which is in its own way as ambiguous as these views of fortune and human conduct. Arthur flees in terror from the dreary wilderness, where savage beasts devour his knights, to a marvelously beautiful meadow, redolent of Paradise. Yet it is precisely here, where ripe fruit never falls, that he — like Adam before him — experiences his terrible fall.

Similar contrasts and ambiguities enrich the episodes that follow.

Arthur, splendidly dressed, is suddenly juxtaposed to Sir Craddock, in his sober pilgrim's attire. We are thus obliged to see as vividly in real life as in the fantasy of the dream the confrontation of Arthur's past with his future, Arthur still living in the world of triumphal vain-glory, while Sir Craddock reveals, in both his message and his dress, the deception and unreliability of these things and the need for the repentance already recommended by the philosopher. Within the battles that follow, Arthur's first knight, Sir Gawain, is valiant but disastrously rash. His impetuous landing is suicidal for his men and ultimately for himself, and the poet carefully reduces him to a maddened beast that fights without reason and willfully squanders his life. Yet the dead Gawain is praised on all sides as matchless among men, and Arthur, kissing the leaden lips and catching the blood in a helmet, tends Gawain in a way that is calculated to apotheosize him still further by recalling Joseph of Arimathea's tendance of the dead Christ (see *TA,* pp. 147–48). Mordred too is a far more elusive figure than usual. He remains the villain who has betrayed his trust and who shamefully disguises himself during the last battle, but he is still a complex figure. Earlier, in the first section of the poem, he has resisted his appointment as Arthur's vicegerent so reasonably that, on reflection, Arthur's highhanded insistence over Mordred's objections might seem to be as much responsible for the treachery as Mordred's own actions. Mordred's character is further complicated by his remarkable speech over Gawain, which not only eulogizes the dead hero but allows Mordred suddenly to see himself with stunning clarity. The result is the terrible access of remorse that robs him of his will to fight, so that his remaining actions lack all conviction, except for his one selfless act — his letter to Guinevere, in which he thinks only of her safety.

Elsewhere the contrast is underscored symbolically in the opposition between Arthur's two swords during his last fight, so that although Arthur is able to slay Mordred with Caliburn, the sword of battle, he is himself mortally wounded by his own ceremonial sword, Clarent, the sword of peace. Since, as Arthur says, Clarent has never been soiled by battle, it becomes a proper agent for carrying out against Arthur that spiritual retribution foretold in the dream. That the traitor Mordred should wield the weapon is not only consistent with his ambiguous character but also proper evidence of God's power to use evil agents to his own ends, as he used Satan to promote the fortunate fall. And that Arthur should be slain by his own sword underscores not only the fratricidal nature of the battle, but also Arthur's own responsibility for his fall from fortune. Imagistically, contrasts appear in the frequent and startling juxtaposition of details, as in ll. 3759–60 where the heraldic brilliance of the first line is followed by the ugly sword thrust in the throat, or in ll. 4247–48, where Mordred's severed hand, still sheathed in bright mail and clutching the jeweled hilts of Clarent, lies impotent on the heath. Thematically, contrast occurs between the fidelity of Idrous and the treachery of Mordred. Rhetorically, it appears not only in Gawain's conscious contrast between the heavenly bliss promised to the courageous and the hellish tortures reserved for the cowards, but also in the whole structure of the last episodes in which the hectic frenzy of battle is periodically interrupted by the stately, almost ritualistic laments over the dead.

In still another way, the almost clinical realism of the sea fight and the landing and some of the battle details contrasts sharply with the romantic exaggeration of the odds Arthur's knights overcome, while this exaggeration in turn stands in striking contrast to the restrained account of Arthur's death. Unexpectedly, all the familiar Celtic mystery is gone, as Avalon becomes no magical isle but a very prosaic island near Glastonbury where Arthur stops for medical attention when he can travel no farther. And Layamon's mystical sea voyage with the attending queens is reduced to a very literal death, complete with burial and Requiem Mass. Arthur may come to rule again, as the conventional epilogue promises, but in the poem he is first of all a real historical personage who has both triumphed and sinned, and whose victories led only to a terrible fall from fortune. The final emphasis is not on the brightness and magic of romance, but on the commonplace details of real life and the bleakness of a Christian morality obsessed with the consequences of original sin.

(20) *The Auntirs of Arthure at the Terne Wathelyn.* MSS: Lincoln Cathedral Libr. (Thornton) 91, ff. 154a–161a (1430–40), Northwest Midlands. Douce 324; Ireland; Lambeth Palace 491 (1400–50). This text is based on the Thornton and Lambeth Palace MSS. *Three Early English Metrical Romances,*

ed. John Robson (London, 1842), Camden Soc. 18; *Scottish Alliterative Poems,* ed. F. J. Amours (Edinburgh, 1892–1897), *STS*. Where the Thornton MS, in photostat, was difficult to decipher, Amours' readings have usually been accepted. All words and passages in square brackets are from the Lambeth Palace MS unless otherwise noted.

Fifty-three stanzas of 13 lines rhyming *ababababcdddc* with variations. Lines 1–9 of each stanza are long alliterative lines with 2–5 alliterations (a few lines have no alliteration) and 4–5 stresses. Lines 10–13 are short, have 2 alliterations, or none at all, and 2–3 stresses. The last line of each stanza is connected to the first line of the next stanza through repetition of key words. The first and last lines of the poem are similarly connected.

Critics have long noticed the apparent indebtedness of this poem to both *The Alliterative Morte Arthure* and *Sir Gawain and the Greene Knight* (for a useful summary of parallels see *TA,* pp. 156–59). Like both of these, *Auntirs* is a composite structure, but while *Gawain* fuses its various themes so that they operate simultaneously and contrapuntally, both *Morte* and *Auntirs* move sequentially so that each poem appears to divide into two parts linked by a supernatural dream or vision. In *Morte* the balance of the two parts around the pivot of the dream is managed with dramatic skill: part one — the rise of Arthur's fortune during the Roman campaign — gathers momentum slowly as the various episodes accumulate and gradually converge to focus on the crucial battle against Lucius; but after the dream, the denouement follows swiftly and economically. Also, the dream is so carefully related to earlier and later events in *Morte* that it clearly serves as a connecting link between the two parts. In *Auntirs* the vision itself is proportionally very long, becoming in fact one of the two main parts of the poem, and it is this which has perhaps obscured its linking function, and hence its relationship to the second part of the poem. Nevertheless, like the dream in *Morte,* this dream by Gawain and Guinevere serves as a link between earlier and later conduct of these two people, and of Arthur himself. Properly seen, the poem becomes a perceptive and unified moral statement about the human condition, with the vision providing an explanation for the change of character that occurs.

In the chronicle accounts of Arthur's reign there is an extended intermission between the campaigns in France and in Italy, an intermission filled with revelry and celebration of victory, chiefly at Carleon. It seems clear from the ghost's remarks (ll. 273–85) that it is during this breathing space that the adventures at Tarn Wadling occur. This terrifying reminder of another world, of another kind of fortune, thus catches Gawain, as it caught Arthur in *Morte,* at a moment when he has least reason to expect it (like the summons of Death in *Everyman*). Of course these historical campaigns do not figure in the poem, but the ghost obliges us to remain keenly aware of the larger context within which this particular adventure occurs. The result is a contrast at two levels: the larger historical contrast between Arthur's present victories and the final, terrible destruction of himself and the Round Table; and the more immediate contrast between Arthur and Guinevere and Gawain as they have been, and as they appear during the second part of the poem.

The ghost is first of all concerned about her own plight, and though she includes some general advice within her vivid *memento mori,* her chief purpose is to support her request for the thirty trentals which will release her from torment. It is not until Guinevere and Gawain ask specifically, that she is led to her remarks about human conduct and her specific condemnation of Arthur. To Guinevere's urgent question, she replies that it is pride which most grieves God, while deeds of meekness and mercy will most surely bring one to heavenly bliss. When Gawain follows with a question that in itself condemns Arthur's imperial conquests, with their destruction of people in other kings' lands "against the right," she corroborates his opinion by her blunt indictment of Arthur's greed and her prophecy of his eventual destruction.

As William Matthews has pointed out (*TA,* pp. 159–61), it is precisely these moral observations which link this part of the poem to the next: the lady who later accosts Arthur as he sits at supper twice exhorts him to do "reason and right" by Sir Galereon, whose lands in Scotland Arthur has appropriated during an earlier campaign, so that we see Arthur confronted with precisely those accusations already laid against him in part one by Gawain and the ghost. Similarly, at a critical moment in the fight which follows, Guinevere is solicited by the lady, in behalf of the stricken Galereon, for precisely that mercy which her mother had recommended. And Gawain, whom the ghost had twice urged to leave Arthur while there was still time — "Gete thee, Sir Gawayne" — is now given an opportunity to act on that advice. Both Arthur and Gawain are at first controlled by the challenge of Galereon: since he demands combat they are obliged within the knightly code to provide it. But within these terms which are imposed upon them, their actions, like Guinevere's, are directed by the moral advice of the ghost. While Guinevere responds immediately to the lady's plea for merciful intercession with the King, Arthur gives to Gawain other lands in Wales so that Gawain is able, without dishonoring himself, to return the Scottish lands to Galereon, as "right and reason" require. As a result of this charity and pity everything works out happily. Galereon marries his lady and is initiated into the fraternity of the Round Table, and these two events symbolize, as it were, an expiation for the two misdeeds, private and public, emphasized in part one by the ghost. Her own sin, deriving from love paramours, is transformed into the moral propriety of marriage, while Arthur's sins of warfare and unjust seizure are transformed into acts of restoration and reconciliation.

Both the structure and details of the poem contribute to the contrasts indicated by the theme. The two major parts of the poem are related to each other much as a moral exhortation is related to the exemplary act which it produced. Each section is given approximately equal weight (19 and 22 stanzas respectively); the first is preceded by a short introduction of 6 stanzas, the second is followed by an equally brief conclusion of 7 stanzas, and the two parts are joined by a single stanza of transition (st. 26, ll. 325–37).

The introduction is handled with skill and economy. Within the thirteen lines of one stanza the poet sets the scene, identifies the occasion and the participants, and focuses on two principal actors. The following account of Guinevere's attire and of the hunt provides vivid contrast to the apparition which will shortly appear, in both appearance and occupation. The details in st. 2, for instance, contrast strikingly with those in st. 9 (ll. 104–16), as do those of st. 4 with those in st. 15 (ll. 182–94). It is true that the ghost herself calls attention to the contrast, but the effect is all the more dramatic because we have first been obliged to see the elegant, jewelled gown and to hear the bright sounds and activity of the hunt, as we now see and hear the ghost. And although some readers have complained about the length and tediousness of the description of the hunt, the passage is not really long (only 36 lines) and it is hardly tedious when it is so much to the point, emphasizing not only the contrast between life and death, but also the contrasts within life itself — the poor crying out at the gate while the lady dines gaily within, or the injustice and suffering which are the price of Arthur's splendid triumphs. Moreover, these opening events are managed so that the details of the hunt are enclosed by the descriptions of Gawain and Guinevere, keeping the focus on them.

The apparition is introduced by changes in the weather which are so sudden as to suggest that the ordinary events of life have been not so much interrupted as suspended. The storm comes suddenly at midday; and when the sun breaks out again (l. 327) everything surges once more into life, as though a spell had been broken. And then the hunters ride directly to Guinevere, as though the isolation of the couple (suggested in ll. 31, 67–68) had never existed. The effect is to emphasize the marvelousness of the incident and, of course, to suggest a return to the real world as they all ride off together for supper at Randolphe's Hall.

But if the real world and the moral and physical world inhabited by Guinevere's mother have been set in sharp contrast in the first part of the poem, the second part fuses these two worlds — at least partly — as the moral perception of the ghost is able to penetrate and transform the world of the living through the actions of Guinevere and Arthur and Gawain, all of whom have profited from the apparition. But this resolution operates only within the limited events of the poem; simultaneously the happy resolution is ironically undercut by our awareness of the larger context. Arthur and the others may have learned for the moment, but they have not learned for long. The reader knows that Arthur will resume his wars of conquest in Italy, that Gawain will continue to follow a king who overruns rich realms against the right, and that Guinevere will follow her mother into the sin of love paramours, with Mordred. If the moral perception of the ghost transforms the events of this adventure, in the events that lie ahead it will be her world of torment that penetrates the world of Arthur and Gawain. The marriage and initiation at the end of this adventure carry with them the reminder of the betrayal and disintegration which are to come. So the poem in a sense returns on itself, just as the lines which have linked each stanza to the next now link the last stanza to the first, to reestablish that contrast with which the poem began, which has momentarily been resolved, but which will return disastrously, as the ghost has prophesied.

(21) *Sir Orfeo*. MSS: Auchinleck, 19.2.1, ff. 300a–303a (*ca.* 1330), Southwestern; Harley 3810 (early 15th c.); Ashmole 61 (late 15th c.). This text (ll. 25–32, 46–end) is based on MS Auchinleck; the sections in square brackets are from MS Harley. *Sir Orfeo,* ed. A. J. Bliss, 2nd ed. (Oxford, 1966).
Octosyllabic couplets.

Sir Orfeo probably derived from or was a translation of a lost French *Lai d'Orphée*. References to the existence of such a *lai* occur in several romances, one of which indicates that it was sung by an Irish harper. This detail, together with the Celtic elements that appear in an analogous tale in Walter Map's *De Nugis Curialium* (*ca.* 1182), suggests that the amalgamation of classical myth and Celtic legend had already occurred in the French source, either through a conscious fusion of the Orpheus story with a similar Celtic story, like *The Wooing of Etain,* or simply through an addition of Celtic elements which were already popular ingredients of the Breton *lai* and of Arthurian legend generally.

The poet of *Sir Orfeo* clearly wished to identify his poem with this popular form of romance, although in his introduction he is careful to refrain from saying that what follows is actually a *lai*: he proposes only to tell the kind of adventure from which the Bretons made their *lais*. However, neither the particular adventure that he tells nor the range of subject suggested in his outline conforms to the traditional character of the *lai* as it descended from Marie de France: Orpheus belongs to a classical, not a Breton, legend, and "bourdes" and "ribaudy" suggest characteristics quite foreign to the refinement of these romances. Both the recoloring of the classical legend and the specific references to the Breton *lai* were probably intended to take advantage of a popular literary form by associating with it a story which came from a quite different source.

Celtic influences were probably responsible for changing Orpheus and Eurydice into a king and queen, for transforming Eurydice's death into faery enchantment, for identifying the classical Pluto with the faery king, and for providing the happy ending. Moreover, the poet also chose to add onto the Orpheus story a second very popular motif — the return and recognition of an exiled ruler. These modifications have introduced problems in structure and motivation. For example, the motivation for Eurydice's disappearance becomes obscure: she does not die, as in the classical myth; and yet, since the Faery King already has his own queen, her abduction cannot be explained by the usual Celtic motivation for the abduction of a mortal woman by a faery-lover, which would in any event be inappropriate since it would compromise the story's traditional theme of marital love and fidelity.[1] It has also been argued that the structural integrity of the poem has been destroyed by the addition of the second motif, in which the elaborate test of the steward deflects attention away from what ought to be the true climax — the rescue and return of Heurodis.[2]

If we remember, however, that the poet was working with a hero who operates successfully in three roles — king, husband, harper — we discover that the poem actually reveals not disintegration but a skillful integration of all three roles, with the last episode providing an organically necessary part of the climax. Similarly, if we examine carefully the faery element in the poem, the reason for her abduction becomes clear.

The poem begins with a prologue (ll. 1–56) whose two sections are carefully linked together. The first section introduces the genre in a way that increasingly focuses on Orfeo as he will be described in the second section: from the widest range of subjects, the poet singles out faery, love, and minstrelsy — all of which are united in Orfeo, who is himself both king and harper, who will both suffer and fight for love, and who is not only descended from Pluto, the "kyng of fairye" (a similar identification between the classical Pluto and the Celtic King of Faery appears in Chaucer's *Merchant's Tale*), but will, in one sense, challenge and defeat this same faery king through the magic of his own enchanting harp. The introduction ends with a brief account of

[1] Constance Davies, "Classical Threads in 'Orfeo,'" *Modern Language Review,* XXXVI (April 1961), 162–63.

[2] H. M. Smyser's review of A. J. Bliss's edition of *Sir Orfeo, Speculum,* XXX (January 1956), 137.

Heurodis, but this is only one transitional link binding it to the first episode. The opening account of Orfeo and Heurodis has stressed a perfect harmony — in their private love and their public estate — that is summarized and epitomized in the harmony of Orfeo's music, which makes his hearers think they are in Paradise. And it is into precisely such an earthly paradise that Heurodis wanders on a May morning — into an orchard whose gentle sounds and soft odors not only express her human condition of the moment but are redolent of that other earthly paradise in Eden, and whose harmony, like Eden's, is about to be shattered by an intrusion from another world.

In the first episode, the abduction, our emotions respond immediately to the contrast between the tranquil opening scene and the horror of Heurodis' awakening, while our understanding of the cause is held in suspense. When Heurodis does at last speak, her revelation is artfully delayed still longer by her method of telling, in which she reveals the consequence before the event, and by the interruptions of Orfeo's grief, which both punctuate and intolerably protract her revelation. In the following scene contrast of a different kind operates between Orfeo's laborious defenses and the effortlessness of an abduction which does not seem even to take them into account.

The opening of the second episode, Orfeo's sojourn in the wilderness, is structurally important, since it characterizes Orfeo in a way which explains the nature and relationship of the two episodes which remain: the recovery of his wife and the recovery of his kingdom. When Orfeo announces his intention to withdraw into the wilderness, there is no suggestion that he is going to look for his wife. His ten years in the wilderness are not a search; they appear to be a self-imposed exile in honor of the lost Heurodis, in honor of love. By its nature, his vow requires political exile as well, but just as Orfeo does not expect to recover his wife, so he does not expect to return to his kingdom. He is therefore as careful to outline his political arrangements as he is to explain his private reasons. At this moment we are very much aware of Orfeo both as a faithful husband and as a responsible ruler, and it would be a structural flaw indeed if the conclusion of the poem did not take both roles into account. We are also aware, however, that his role in both areas, either by choice or necessity, has become passive. Since his active attempt to protect his wife has failed, he willfully deprives himself of the sight of women and the rule of his kingdom.

The account of his sojourn in the wilderness appropriately begins with a long series of parallels, balanced contrasts that vividly formulate, as in a lament, the fall from fortune which Orfeo has endured. Structurally they also become an extended echo of those earlier but briefer antitheses describing the stricken Heurodis (ll. 105–12).

At this lowest point in Orfeo's fortunes, the major shift in the poem occurs, and appropriately the change is associated with his harp. The account of his harping on bright days introduces the first bright touch after the long series of melancholy contrasts. Then follow glimpses of the faery world into which he will at last venture. For the moment this world still remains mysterious: the hunters take no game, the armed knights engage no foe with their drawn swords. These activities cannot yet articulate themselves into a world he understands. But these are significant moments. Orfeo, whose vow has only been to suffer, becomes aware that the other world may be available, and that he may therefore be able to change a fortune which for ten years he has simply endured. The crucial fact seems to be a renewed decisiveness in Orfeo. When he joins the ladies at their hawking, he does so partly because — unlike the hunters — these ladies actually take game, and therefore seem less mysterious, but mostly because he actively chooses to join them — his first decisive action since he left Winchester. This action may be insignificant but it is at least prompted by a wish to reexperience the life he has resigned — "ich was y-won swiche werk to se" — and in violating his vow never again to see a woman, it ironically leads to the rediscovery of his wife, in whose honor that vow had been made. The poignant meeting with Heurodis prompts his truly decisive act. Stung by the cruelty of an enchantment that would not let him speak to his wife, Orfeo resolves, in spite of death, to follow the ladies wherever they ride. It is as though this decision has unlocked the enchantment. He follows them through the rock, gains entrance to the castle, and wins back Heurodis, not only through the enchantment of his music but through a quickness of wit which seems to spring from that same determination which changed his fortune.

This whole encounter with the Faery King becomes, in its way, a version of the traditional heroic battle with some monster, although, in keeping with the gentler tone of the Breton Lai, the elements have been softened. The traditional challenge is transformed into an offer of entertainment; the weapon is not the sword but the harp; and the sign of victory is the Faery King's rash promise, won from him by the hero's enchanting music and defended, when it seems to be threatened, by an appeal to the courtly code of honor.

The recovery of Heurodis, however, is not enough; Orfeo must also recover his kingdom, and this is the business of the last episode. It requires a test of a different sort, but it is linked to the recovery of his wife not only by the symbol of the harp, which is instrumental to each of the recoveries, but also by the device of a disguise. Orfeo's unlikely appearance figured in the contest with the Faery King, and it figures again in the test of the steward. Together, the third and fourth episodes resolve the events that caused and resulted from Orfeo's withdrawal into the wilderness, and they do so in a way which verifies his nobility: his faithfulness as a husband and his responsibility as a ruler. The poem concludes by returning to those remarks about Bretons and their lays with which it had begun.

Part of the poem's art consists in the tension which operates between the mortal world and the world of faery, and part of the dramatic climax lies in the triumph of this mortal world. But the contrast between the two worlds is not always clear. The other world is not simply evil. After the abduction of Heurodis, the activities of the faeries may be mysterious but they are not especially threatening. And the faery kingdom itself, once Orfeo finds the courage to challenge it, appears altogether admirable. It is like Paradise in its gleaming splendor. Instead of the dark shadows of classical myth, everything is bright and temperate; even the dead are charmed out of their suffering and pain. Moreover, in its courtesy, its generous hospitality, its quick response to an appeal to honor, this kingdom operates within the best traditions of Orfeo's social code.

The one indication of cruelty and evil appears in the abduction itself, particularly in the Faery King's threat to Heurodis if she tries to thwart him. This threat is probably a survival from the old Celtic belief that certain groves were sacred to the gods, and that any mortal who violated these sacred precincts during a god's visits (midnight and midday were favorite times) must suffer the penalty of a hideous sacrificial death. It has been suggested that "ympe" may be a confused derivative from an old Celtic word referring to such a grove. If it is, the tree becomes more than a simple orchard tree (as its later reappearance in faeryland also suggests), and in sleeping under it through the noon hour, Heurodis has unwittingly violated a sacred place. Within these traditions, her abduction becomes justified and is in fact a more mild penalty than the sacrificial death, which reappears only in the form of a threat that can be avoided.[3] In the absence of the usual explanations for the disappearance of Heurodis (death in classical myth, love in Celtic legend) this suggestion offers a reasonable motive behind the abduction, and by so doing it also decreases the evil and cruelty which can be associated with the faery world. Moreover, this one violent detail, justified or not, is exceptional in the poem; it is not borne out by later events.

We are left with a faery world that is mysterious but hardly evil. It is in fact like the paradise that is conjured up by Orfeo's music, or that appears thematically in the perfect world of Orfeo's love and scenically in the garden where Heurodis falls asleep. But unlike these others, the paradise of the faery world is perfect and unchanging; the paradise of the mortal world can be interrupted, as it has been in the poem. It is the business of the hero to restore harmony through an act of courage, and this is precisely what Orfeo finally does, though his weapon is the harp rather than the sword. And as he moves out of suffering into action, it is perhaps significant that the faery world becomes increasingly less mysterious and less terrible as he confronts it. It is almost as if faeryland becomes what he makes of it. In the process Orfeo has become an old man, while Heurodis has remained young in the timeless world of enchantment. This is the one price of his heroic action, and it is also the detail which most strongly suggests that the romance may be remotely connected with the old fertility rites and the ideas of a perpetual return of a youthful Spring, brought in by the hand of Winter.

[3] Constance Davies, " 'Ympe Tre' and 'Nemeton,' " *Notes and Queries,* CCVII (January 1962), 6–9.

ALLEGORY AND VISION

(22) *Piers Plowman.* MS Laud Misc. 581, ff. 76b–81b (early 15th c.), South Midlands. Any corrections or emendations of this MS are from MS Trinity Coll. Cbg. B.15.17. *The Vision of William Concerning Piers the Plowman,* ed. Walter W. Skeat (London, 1869–85), *EETS* 38, 67, 81. *The Vision of William concerning Piers the Plowman in Three Parallel Texts,* ed. Walter W. Skeat, 2 vols. (Oxford, 1886).

Alliterative verse: the lines usually contain 4 stressed syllables with alliteration falling on the first 3 stresses; sometimes there are 4 to 5 stresses per line with 2 to 5 alliterations; occasionally there is no alliteration.

Little is known about William Langland (*ca.* 1330–*ca.* 1400), except that he was probably from the West of England, may have been in minor orders (lower clerical orders requiring less strict vows), was married and had a daughter. Because his name appears on none of the manuscripts of the poem, Langland has sometimes been doubted as the author of *Piers Plowman.* Recently, however, his authorship has been convincingly reestablished.[1] He wrote three versions of his book, commonly referred to by scholars as the A-, B-, and C-Texts. A is the earliest (*ca.* 1362) and shortest, C the latest (*ca.* 1387) and longest, and B — with which we are here concerned — stands in the middle, both in length and in date (*ca.* 1377).

The theme of *Piers Plowman,* with its many visions and extended allegory, is man's search for Truth or God; and Love (Charity) proves to be the way to Truth. Piers Plowman illustrates this way, and it is through his evolution that we may see the kinds of life which a man must imitate, in some measure, to ensure his own salvation. The dreamer, William, represents mankind who searches for and, through the educative process of the poem, finds the way to Truth. The way

[1] George Kane, *Piers Plowman: The Evidence for Authorship* (London: University of London, Athlone Press, 1965).

for man is to imitate the life of Piers, or rather the lives of Piers, for he has three, as he represents successively three ideal ways of life: Dowel, Dobet, and Dobest. Dowel is the way of the good Christian with simple faith who works hard and honestly for what he needs, is charitable to his neighbor whenever the occasion for charity arises, and is obedient to the Church. Dobet adds to these virtues a special concern for others: he is conscientiously charitable in his acts, is ready to teach others (and himself to follow what he teaches) and to feel compassion for their sufferings. Dobest, perfect in the qualities of Dowel and Dobet, uses these virtues to administer the Church, through which he possesses both the right to judge and the power to save other men. The movement through these ideal ways of life is thus marked by a deepening concern and enlarging responsibility for others. And if Piers, the exemplary man, reveals successively these ideals, he himself has a model to imitate in Christ who, as the poet tells us (Passus XIX: 104–89), successively lived the three lives: Dowel in the simplicity of his birth and youth; Dobet in the glory of his manhood and in his greatest act of charity, his death; and Dobest in the power of his resurrection to redeem all men, or by his final judgment to condemn them.

The poem begins with the dreamer's vision of the world (Prologue and Passus I–VII), the field of men lying between the tower of Heaven and the dungeon of Hell, a world so corrupt that the urgent need to discover the way to Truth becomes at once powerfully clear.

Passus VIII–XV contain the vision of Dowel, in which Piers, who had already appeared briefly in the first section to illustrate the life of Dowel, is now presented more fully. He is a simple, hard-working plowman, very much like Chaucer's plowman, who can lead mankind to Truth through his simple faith and his artless, instinctive charity. Already, then, the idea of Love as the way to Truth and the image of the Tree of Charity growing in the human heart have been introduced, though they are not developed until the poem moves into the life of Dobet, one of whose characteristics is to illuminate this idea and this image through teaching.

Passus XVI–XVIII present the vision of Dobet, as Piers carefully instructs the dreamer in the workings of the Tree of Charity. Later, this image becomes fully personified in the figure of the Good Samaritan, whose acts exemplify the conscious outward workings of charity. Then in Passus XVIII, when Christ appears riding into Jerusalem to joust with Death, to undergo his greatest suffering and his greatest triumph, the dreamer thinks that he looks like both Piers and the Good Samaritan, because, like the latter, he is riding on an ass, and he is wearing Piers's clothes. The Good Samaritan, as the personification of Charity, thus becomes the crucial link joining Piers and Christ, a powerful reminder to the dreamer that it is this assumption of charity within himself that is man's divine part, the Christ within him.

Passus XIX–XX contain the vision of Dobest. Christ gives Grace to Piers, and Grace in turn gives Piers the things he needs to cultivate the Christian community — the four Gospels, the Four Fathers (Augustine, Ambrose, Gregory, Jerome), the Bible, the four Cardinal Virtues, and the Church itself. Yet at the end of the poem the world is much as it was at the beginning, corrupt, besieged by the forces of Anti-Christ. Piers has disappeared, and as the dreamer awakens, Conscience (man's awareness of right and wrong in his actions) is just starting out on the search for Piers, a search which if completed in the dream vision of the poem is perpetually beginning in each human life itself.

Throughout the poem Langland reacts to the troubles, sacred and secular, that he sees about him at all levels of life. The fourteenth century in England was marked by a number of events whose consequences threatened the established order of things.

About the middle of the century, the terrible scourge of the bubonic plague, the Black Death, decimated an already dwindling population; labor became scarce, and laborers, finding themselves in demand, were tempted to sell their services to the highest bidder. In doing so they discovered a new basis of allegiance and service, in which financial gain replaced the old, personal ties to a particular lord or manor. This led in turn to a new sense of geographical mobility and social independence. The problem of securing enough labor to work the land became sufficiently acute to call forth a Statute of Laborers (1351), fixing laborers at their old work and wage. Later in the century this increasing independence revealed itself in a different and more violent way in the Peasants' Revolt (1381).

At the same time, the middle classes were continuing to gain strength and prestige, largely because of the Hundred Years War between England and France (*ca.* 1336–1453). The financing of the war required continuous support from parliament, in which the middle classes were increasingly prominent, and the great early English victories in the war, at Crécy and Poitiers, were due largely to the murderous effectiveness of the long bows of the English yeoman against the French chivalry.

Finally, one of the strongest bulwarks of tradition, the Church, was being weakened by internal abuses and dissension. Throughout the century there were increasingly vigorous complaints against the immorality and greed of churchmen, and these attacks came at a time when church authority itself was unstable. For almost seventy years (1309–1377) political unrest in Italy had led the pope to reside in Avignon instead of Rome, a decision which the English tended to interpret as evidence of the Pope's subservience to the French king. Later, there were two — sometimes even three — popes, one at Rome and one at Avignon (the Great Schism: 1377–1417). This combination of immorality and instability encouraged critics. Most notorious were John Wicliff and the "lollards," or poor priests, whose attacks on abuses within the Church came perilously close to challenging central dogma and authority themselves.

Although he was exercised by abuses and injustice, Langland was a conservative, not a radical reformer, and he was as much troubled by the reactions which they prompted as by the abuses themselves. Like his contemporary Chaucer, but to a greater degree, he was opposed to change. He had no wish to reconstruct society but only to purify its traditional forms and relationships. The exemplary Piers does not make his way by rising in the world or changing his station, but by purifying and perfecting his life within its fixed limits. Similarly, Langland's theological ideas were, more often than not, conservative. For instance, in his emphasis in Passus XVIII on Christ's legal right to the souls in Hell rather than on his absolute power to take them, he is expressing the conservative theological view of the universe governed by Divine Reason, rather than the more current notion of a universe ruled by Divine Will. "Theologians from Scotus onward, largely through their emphasis on what has been called the 'primacy of the will' in theodicy, gave more and more attention to the possible use by God of His absolute power, until the realm of the absolute becomes their only interest. All the elaborate hierarchy of means and laws [His Reason] — the clumsy but indispensable method by which the human mind can express the fragmentation of eternal Truth — disappears from sight, and the incomprehensible, illimitable power [His Will] of God alone remains."[2] Still, while insisting on legal, rational cause, Langland also emphasized the sweeter, irrational forces of Mercy and Peace. Perhaps one of the greatest miracles wrought by the Crucifixion was the reconciliation of these two opposing pairs – Truth and Justice, Mercy and Peace. Before Christ's appearance these Four Daughters of God argue and debate among themselves; after Christ's triumph in Hell they join together in a song and dance of mutual reconciliation and harmony. This insistence on God's both reasonable and willful actions reveals a mind influenced by cross-currents of fourteenth-century dispute and resolved by the transcending miracle of Christ's triumph over Death and Darkness.

Out of the poem's abundance we have selected Passus XVIII, which depicts Christ's Passion and his Harrowing of Hell, because it is the climax of the vision of Dobet, if not of the whole poem, and it is also the part of the poem where the way to salvation, which is Love, is most clearly and dramatically pictured for the dreamer. That he must allow the Tree of Charity to grow in his heart, Piers had taught him in XVI, and the Good Samaritan had shown him in XVII. Here, Christ on his tree of suffering and love and in his triumphant harrowing of Hell becomes his greatest teacher and example. His was the gift of greatest love, his life for man's, so that man could be brought from the depths of sin and death into everlasting light. As the knight-Christ rides into Jerusalem (ll. 10–11) the poet gathers the two ideal human figures, Piers and the Samaritan, into the divine ideal of Christ, yet Christ still in his human aspect. It is the spirit of love in self-sacrifice undertaken in "*humana natura*" (l. 23) which man can emulate and through which he can be saved. Later, in his totally divine aspect, which man cannot emulate, Christ appears as Light (ll. 124 ff.). When Christ is set before us, whether as man or as Light, he is a figure in an emotionally tense drama, a knight who must joust with Death and a Light who must bind the powers of Hell's darkness. As a man he dies and seems to lose, but as a Divine Light he returns to win the battle. The dreamer witnesses the major events in his trial and crucifixion, and he sees the triumph in Hell. Christ, then, is man's best example of

[2] Dom David Knowles, *The Religious Orders in England,* II (Cambridge: Cambridge University Press, 1955), 76.

love. Still, the dreamer must be instructed, and the Four Daughters of God — Mercy, Truth, Peace, Righteousness (Justice) — arrive between the two central episodes to interpret these events through their arguments among themselves, before Christ's triumphal victory over Lucifer and the dreamer's reawakening into his own local, human world.

Structurally, the Passus is held together by a sequence of Christian rituals. The dreamer, tired and wet after a long and miserable life of aimless wandering, falls asleep until Lent. Then his dream quickly draws us into the central Christian drama. The phrase "Cristes Passioun" (l. 6) probably refers to Passion Sunday which, coming one week before Palm Sunday, introduces the third and last phase of the Lenten drama, with its mood of sorrow and its focus on the historical figure of the persecuted and suffering Christ.[3] The vision itself begins with the music of Palm Sunday and ends with the ringing of the bells on Easter morning that awaken the dreamer, and throughout it is filled with echoes of the services that fill Holy Week, particularly those of Palm Sunday itself, Good Friday, the Easter Vigil, and a further ceremony, probably an early Easter morning resurrection ritual. Most of the allusions in ll. 1–17 are to the Palm Sunday services (see gloss). Many of those in ll. 36–160 are to the Good Friday services. In ll. 170–322 are frequent allusions to the Vigil service. At the end of the Passus (ll. 416–25) the allusions seem to be drawn from a resurrection ceremony which was at one time associated with the Easter Vigil, later with Easter Matins. The dreamer's visionary passage thus is clearly chronicled by these allusions to the services of Easter Week: he sees Christ's entry into Jerusalem on Palm Sunday, he witnesses the crucifixion on Good Friday; he sees the triumph of light over darkness celebrated by the Vigil, a service of light which usually occurred after midnight on Easter morning; and at the end he sees an enactment of an early resurrection ceremony, in which the Kiss of Peace is exchanged, the *Te Deum* sung, and the bells rung. (See Hardison, pp. 178–219.)

Within this familiar sequence of events and ceremonies during Holy Week, the details are handled with propriety and skill. The time

[3] See O. B. Hardison, Jr., *Christian Rite and Christian Drama in the Middle Ages* (Baltimore: Johns Hopkins University Press, 1965), pp. 109–10.

which elapses between the entry into Jerusalem and the trial before Pilate is suggested by our being withdrawn into a dialogue between Faith and the dreamer in which Faith tells him what is happening and what it will mean to mankind. Later it is appropriate that Truth should be the one to describe the Harrowing of Hell. While the earlier events — Christ's entry and death — were actually seen by men at the time and so could be accurately imagined later, the scenes in Hell, in which Christ becomes Light, are visionary and must be revealed as a deeper and more mystical kind of experience — as in the Apocryphal Book of Nicodemus they are revealed by the Sons of Simeon, who have been raised from the dead at the moment of Christ's death. Hence Divine Truth reveals this vision of Divine Light and Glory. Then we are removed from this vision by the same agents who introduced us to it, by the Four Daughters of God who, enriched by the vision which Truth has shown them, themselves exchange the Kiss of Peace and sing the *Te Deum*. The bells that celebrate this union then merge into the bells of the resurrection ceremony on Easter morning which, penetrating his dream, awaken the dreamer into his own world. He returns to ordinary life, which, however, has been transfigured by the events of his dream: within the bosom of his family, he now kneels humbly with them to reverence the Cross before going, in Passus XIX, to the Easter Mass itself.

At the same time that Langland suggests different levels of visionary experience, he also constantly reveals the two-fold purpose of his poem: instruction and example. The instruction is usually given through exposition by allegorical figures, the example through dramatic actions of real persons. Christ, the Good Samaritan, and, earlier, Abraham (Passus XVI) provide dramatic examples of how man should act, but it is such personifications as Faith and the Four Daughters of God who interpret for us the full meaning of these historical personages and events.

What holds together all the poem's variety and diversity is its form. Langland's alliterative verse is itself rhythmically satisfying. While most lines contain the usual alliterative pattern, the poet varies this pattern frequently enough to prevent monotony (see Note above). Since much of this Passus contains either urgent dramatic action or argumentative conversation or debate, the long lines with their pounding stresses provide the emphasis which strong actions and words require, recalling as they do the heroic tradition of epic and chronicle with which the alliterative line is particularly associated.

(23) *Confessio Amantis*. MS Fairfax 3, ff. 8a–9b; 16a–18b. (*ca.* 1400), London (Southeast Midlands). *The English Works of John Gower,* ed. G. C. Macaulay, 2 vols. (London, 1900–01), *EETS* 81, 82; *The Complete Works of John Gower,* ed. G. C. Macaulay, 4 vols. (Oxford, 1899–1902); *Confessio Amantis,* ed. Russell A. Peck (New York, 1968).

Octosyllabic couplets.

John Gower, like most men of his time, left few records. He was born *ca.* 1327–30 into a landed Kentish family. Though he seems to have been in touch with court circles, he was not so complete a courtier as his friend Chaucer. Marrying late, Gower lived most of his later years in the Priory of St. Mary Overies, Southwark; he died in 1408 and is now buried in Southwark Cathedral. He wrote three major works: one in French, *Mirour de l'omme* or *Speculum Meditantis* (*The Mirror of Man,* or *Mirror of a Thoughtful Man,* 1376–78); one in Latin, *Vox Clamantis* (*The Voice of One Crying Out,* 1377–86); and one in English, *Confessio Amantis* (*The Confession of a Lover,* 1392–93).

Gower's most recent critic[1] believes that the three works form a trilogy commenting upon the corrupt state of the world and tracing the origin of this corruption to man himself. When Adam and Eve disobeyed, they not only rejected their obedience to God but they turned also from the love of God to the sexual enjoyment of each other. Since that time man has been ruled by sexual love, which he shares with the beasts, not divine love (Charity), which of all earthly creatures man alone can possess. Such disobedience and misdirected love has caused division in man and in his institutions, as man the microcosm, at war within himself, creates more disorder in the macrocosm of the natural and social world around him. Correction lies within man's power, but he can reorder society only by first reordering

[1] John Fisher, *John Gower* (New York: New York University Press, 1964), pp. 135–203.

himself, by adopting a moral life ruled by reason rather than will, by eschewing temporal love and turning again to divine love. The person most responsible for reform is the King, who is divinely appointed to rule the people and who must therefore provide an example for other men to follow: before he can govern others he must first of all govern himself. All three poems were written during the troubled reign of Richard II, and Gower, apparently horrified by what he saw in the King and in the realm, becomes progressively more concerned with the need for a King to be a mirror of perfection for other men to look into and to imitate.

As the final poem of the three, the *Confessio* stresses these themes, emphasizing even more the need for royal responsibility in overseeing the realm. In his "Prologue" Gower laments the disorderly condition of England in the last decade of the fourteenth century through a discussion of the chaos within the three estates – Knights, Clergy, and Commons. Those who rule, rule with hate rather than love. The Church is avaricious. The Commons, lacking sound religious and political direction, run wild. With England in chaos, the world in its disordered old age totters on the brink of final judgment, for according to Gower, Doomsday is at hand. While there is yet time, he pleads, let man return to reason, to order, and to love.

This account in the Prologue of man's inability to rule himself and of the social conditions which result merges into the more limited events of the poem itself. The aged and decaying world is replaced by a single old man who, like the world of which he is a part, has suffered the ravages of passion because he has not properly understood the true nature of love. Unsuccessful and dispirited, the old man (identified as Gower himself in Book VIII, 2321) on a May morning seeks solitude in order to make his complaint. After swooning a number of times he awakens from his suffering to find Venus and Cupid before him. He begs them to change the course of his love affair, to make it successful. Before she will determine his case, however, Venus orders the old man to confess his sins against love to her priest, Genius, and to be shriven by him. As Gower confesses his sins, which turn out to be six of the Seven Deadly ones, Genius interrupts frequently, to explain the nature of each sin to the lover and to instruct him, through the example of others, how to avoid it.

As a collection of tales which apply these Deadly Sins to love, the *Confessio* satisfies Gower's purpose: to write a book "Somewhat of lust [pleasure], somewhat of lore [teaching]" (Prologue, 19). And it satisfies also his intention to show one old man involved in the disorder and joylessness of unsuccessful sexual passion (sexual love, Gower says, brings misrule to a man: "loves lawe is out of reule," I:18), whose bitter example reflects the disorders in the greater world, now also in its old age and disastrously unable to love. At the end of the poem, Venus gives the lover a mirror in which he sees for the first time what he is — a wrinkled old man. This is Venus' answer to his case, and it is an ugly one. She advises the lover to leave her court: it is unreasonable for an old man to yearn for sexual passion; instead, he should seek moral virtue. As soon as he consents, reason, as he says, rescues him:

> And whan Resoun it herde sein (said)
> That loves rage was aweye,
> He cam to me the righte weye,
> And hath remued the sotye (folly)
> Of thilke unwise fantasye. (VIII: 2862–66)

Venus suddenly disappears and takes her place among the stars in the sky, and the old man, amazed, knows certainly that he must abandon forever sexual love's misrule, with its interior wars and discord, and turn to the peace of charity. He thus becomes a hopeful metaphor for a kingdom and a world which should do the same, and the poem ends with a final exhortation to the Three Estates to amend themselves by seeking charity, as the old man has done.

Although it is easy to see how the poem is unified by the theme of love, divine and earthly, and by the parallel between the unhealthy passion of a senile lover and the unhealthy corruption of an aging world, it is less easy to see how the matter of kingship, so much emphasized in the Prologue, relates to this theme. Gower himself, however, provides a clue. In Book VII he interrupts the orderly examination of the Sins in order to examine the education of a prince. The last tale in Book VI had dealt with Alexander, and the old man, the Lover, is prompted to ask Genius to describe Alexander's education. Genius agrees, although protesting that such a discourse has little to do with love. Yet the account that he gives belies his protest. In emphasizing the part of Alexander's education that taught the king how to behave as a private person and as a public figure, he is in fact dealing with love on two levels. According to popular medieval belief, Divine Love had been the ordering principle which, in the beginning, called order out of chaos and created the harmonious design of the universe, ruled by reason and law. As the divinely appointed representative of God on earth, the king was expected to regulate his life so as to preserve this order in both public and private affairs. The king's personal life, his moral condition, should be spotless. He should govern his body wisely, and his household with honesty, exercising the five points of kingly policy toward those under his rule: Truth, Largesse, Justice, Pity, Chastity. If the first four speak especially to his public relationships, the last speaks especially to his private. To be chaste, Genius advises (both here and in Book VIII), is to love only one woman, to govern the body with reason, to avoid the sin of lechery, and to obey the laws of marriage. Thus Gower's idea of right sexual love is, at its level, like the king's larger love for his public realm. At both levels love should be directed by reason and law, reflecting that greater love which created and now binds together the entire universe.

Since over two-thirds of the tales in the *Confessio* deal with kings or princes, it seems clear that Gower was concerned with these two levels of love as they come together in the person of the king. The direct advice of Genius and the implicit advice of the tales both indicate how such a person should manage his life in public and private affairs. "The Tale of Florent" offers just such an example of a prince who by ruling himself wisely preserves his public honor as a knight and his private honor as a lover. This tale has become famous because it is a version of the tale told by the Wife of Bath, but it has also suffered from the comparison. If, however, Gower's tale is examined in its own right, in its relationship to the theme of the whole poem, it achieves its own kind of success.

Book I, in which "The Tale of Florent" appears, introduces the "vision" framework of the whole poem and then deals specifically with the foremost sin in love, Pride. Genius claims that there are five kinds of pride. One of these is Disobedience — the lover was expected to obey his lady and, of course, the laws of God. Since a lover was also expected to suffer the pains of love in silent submission, one kind of disobedience was complaint about one's lot in love. "The Tale of Florent" thus becomes an exemplum that illustrates this principle: by refusing to complain about his extraordinarily bad fortune in love and by submitting meekly to the old hag, Florent proves his worthiness as a lover and wins the prize. And by keeping his bargain in the first place, he has of course vindicated his public honor as a knight.

Moreover, the world in which Florent operates is the world that Gower has described in his Prologue, a world of violence and hate in which chance misfortune is sudden, and revenge is swift and relentless. Set against these actions of willful and destructive violence is Florent's patient and reasonable submission. He may not like being bound to his word or to the hag, but he makes every painful effort to reconcile himself to his fate. He brings her home, makes her his bride, and then brings her to his bed. Unwilling he may be, but he does not complain, at least not to her. To the last he struggles to accept as reasonable his horrible bargain. It is as if the poet were saying that to hate is easy — one blow, probably given in self-defense, kills a man, and revenge follows automatically. To love is difficult, or at least to govern oneself as an honorable man in all of love's vicissitudes is difficult; it requires hard work, silent suffering, and submission rather than quick and violent action.

This difficulty of love may account for the length of two passages which in Chaucer's Tale, a poem with a different purpose, are much shorter. In the first, when Florent meets the hag, is sworn to her, and receives the answer to the question, Gower's 98 lines (Chaucer, 41) dwell at length on Florent's early reluctance to accept the bargain and his difficulty in submitting his fortune to her. Later, before the wedding, Gower devotes 69 lines (Chaucer, 22) to Florent's reflections on his sorry bargain and his reminders to himself of the importance, at all costs, of upholding his honor by keeping his word. The frequency of these reminders suggest Florent's difficulty in acting as he should, and they also emphasize the importance, to Florent and to Gower, of the principles of reason and order which underlie them. Moreover, if throughout the tale Florent seems too perfect a knight, this may be another way of reminding us how difficult it was to live a life obedient to law and reason: if it is hard for such a man, how difficult it must be for the ordinary man, and yet how essential. Finally, although the ending seems anticlimactic in relation to the Tale itself, it offers a final reminder of the kind of world in which such actions as Florent's are required. The lady's transformation into the ugly hag, like Florent's torment, had been brought about by revenge and hate, so that in different ways both central figures can be seen as victims of that disordered society which so much disturbed Gower.

Metrically, the tale is regular but not rigid, as the lines flow readily over and beyond the couplet restrictions. The narrative itself is well paced, beginning rapidly with an introduction of the principal character and his problem, and then working through the solution more deliberately and painfully. Occasionally the tale lacks dramatic suspense at crucial moments, as in the scene where Florent is to give the answer: although he appears before the Court, he never speaks the answer he has won at such cost. It is true that since the answer has been revealed in the earlier scene with the hag it is not necessary to have it repeated here, but its absence results in anticlimax. Yet the Tale builds nicely to its double climax. Florent receives his reward for faithful service as a knight as, in lines 1802–03, the hag turns into a young lady. He must prove himself again, this time as a lover, by rejecting his own choice in favor of hers. She rewards him for his service as a lover, in lines 1836–39, with her promise that she will remain forever beautiful and eighteen. And Florent, the faithful, obedient knight-lover, becomes Gower's "litel world" (P:957) in harmony, and therefore a model for Prince and commoner alike to follow.

(24) *The Testament of Cresseid.* Middle Scots. There are no early manuscripts of this poem. The best early text is Henry Charteris' *The Testament of Cresseid* (Edinburgh, 1593). *PFRH; PRH; The Testament of Cresseid,* ed. Bruce Dickins (London, 1943); *WPFH; RHP; The Testament of Cresseid,* ed. Denton Fox (London, 1968).

Rhyme royal. "The Complaint of Cresseid" (ll. 407–69) is in 9-line stanzas rhyming *aabaabbab.*

Very little is known about Robert Henryson. In his *Lament for the Makaris* (Poets), Dunbar mourns the death in Dunfermline of Master Robert Henryson, and the date of this poem (*ca.* 1505) therefore establishes a date before which Henryson must have died. Other references also associate Henryson with Dunfermline, specifically as a schoolmaster, and the title "master" may refer either to this profession or simply to his learning in general, since there is no certain evidence that he took the academic M.A. degree at either of the Scottish universities, St. Andrews and Glasgow, or at any of the various continental universities attended by Scots during the fifteenth century. Whatever his formal learning, Henryson's poems reveal wide knowledge of Latin literature, both classical and medieval, and of the vernacular poetry of England and Scotland. They also reveal knowledge of rhetoric and logic and of legal language and procedures. Henryson's poetic canon comprises *The Testament of Cresseid, The Morall Fabillis of Esope the Phrygian* — thirteen beast fables, each with an appended *moralitas* (not all of which, however, can be traced to Aesop), *Orpheus and Eurydice, Robene and Makyne,* and about a dozen other short poems.

Three known sources influenced the *Testament of Cresseid*: Chaucer's *Troilus and Criseyde;* Lydgate's (?) *Assembly of the Gods,* which probably provided some details of Cresseid's trial before the assembled planets; and Boccaccio's *De Genealogio Deorum,* which probably supplied details for the description of the planets. Henryson himself refers only to the first of these identifiable sources — Chaucer's poem — but he also refers to another book, which he took down after reading Chaucer and whose account of the fatal destiny of Cresseid purports to be the primary source of his poem. Since no such work has been discovered, we can conclude either that it has disappeared, or that it is one of those imaginary sources invoked by medieval authors to give the weight of authority to their creations.[1]

Of the known sources, it is *Troilus and Criseyde* which must particularly be kept in mind, since the action of the *Testament* is embedded in — not just appended to — the events of Chaucer's poem, and therefore Henryson's art depends partly upon the power of his poem to recall parallel or contrasting moments in Chaucer. This is particularly true of the lovers' meeting at the end of his poem, with its ironic reminder of that earlier moment in Chaucer when Criseyde saw Troilus from her window as he was returning on horseback after a

[1] But see B. J. Whiting, "A probable Allusion to Henryson's 'Testament of Cresseid,'" *Modern Language Notes,* XL (1945), 46–47; and James Gray, "A Note on Henryson," *Times Literary Supplement* (March 13, 1953), 176.

skirmish with the Greeks. But it is also true of other details. The judgment of Cresseid by the assembled planets recalls the cosmological framework from whose eighth sphere Troilus, at the end of Chaucer's poem, was finally able to take a more comprehensive and objective view of his own tragic circumstances; the Temple of Venus, where Cresseid bewails her misfortunes, recalls that earlier Temple of Athena where Troilus first fell in love with her, with all the difference that the contrast between the temples of Wisdom and of Love implies. More basic even than these selected moments, however, is the general knowledge of events and characters in Chaucer's poem, for Henryson's tale of Cresseid's fortunes after she accepted Diomede is only a logical consequence of her character as it had been developed in Chaucer's poem; and similarly, her response to Troilus at the end of the poem — and our understanding of this response — depends partly upon our remembering how she had characterized him years before when she told him that she had decided to accept him as her lover not so much for his royal title or prowess in battle as for his moral virtue (*T&C* IV, 1667–73). Because she had perceived him in this way at that crucial moment in their love, Troilus can appear briefly at the end of Henryson's poem without seeming to be an undeveloped, almost allegorical figure, arbitrarily introduced to bring about Cresseid's transformation. For he appears in precisely that role which had always distinguished him, which Cresseid had most valued when she considered carefully, and which naturally predominates once again at this last, decisive moment in their history.

Critics used to contrast Chaucer's sympathetic and ambivalent attitude toward Criseyde with Henryson's stern moral treatment of Cresseid in his poem. Nothing could be more misleading. Henryson is as anxious to be sympathetic as was Chaucer: he pities her misfortune (84–91) and he later pleads with Saturn to withdraw his heavy sentence (323–29). In one sense he is no harsher to Cresseid than Chaucer had been to Troilus, who was systematically denied all the things he wanted: the return of Criseyde, the chance to kill Diomede, a speedy death in battle. If Cresseid's fate seems more severe than Troilus' this is a result of her nature as Henryson found it, not of different attitudes toward this character by Chaucer and Henryson. Both authors would have liked to be able to record a happier fortune for their characters, but their knowledge of human nature, and of the operation of fortune and of social and moral law would not allow it. There is very little reason to suppose that if Chaucer had chosen to tell of Criseyde's final fortune, he would have treated her differently than did Henryson. The Cresseid which Henryson finds in Chaucer is one who has always known herself incompletely and sporadically. She has been vague about the complex motives that dictate her actions, unable to distinguish clearly between the pressure of circumstance and of her own will, and when in doubt, she has usually taken the course of least resistance. As long as she was still with Troilus she believed, because it was easiest and most convenient to believe, that she would return on visiting day; once she is with Diomede it is easier and most convenient to yield to his persuasions. She does not calculate her infidelity in advance, but once it has occurred she is apt to rationalize so that the most convenient course of action comes to seem the most prudent — and she does this so instinctively and naturally that she deceives herself without knowing it, quite honestly believing what she concludes. Early in Chaucer's poem she determined that she could decide to love Troilus or not as she pleased; a moment later Troilus rode by and the decision was made for her, partly by chance, partly by desire, partly by the wish to take the easiest course. And the same thing happens later with Diomede, when after her moments of self-awareness and resolution about how she ought to act, Diomede intrudes, and under the pressure of his physical presence and the protection he offers in an alien world, her resolution and self-control dissolve.

Given these characters as Chaucer presents them, Henryson's projection of Cresseid's fortunes is perfectly realistic. If her fate also seems morally just, this is not due to Henryson's arbitrary handling of character and events, but to a world in which a logical or natural sequence of events is usually also a moral sequence. From what Chaucer tells us of Diomede, Henryson's conclusion, that once he had satisfied his appetite on Cresseid he would abandon her for someone else, seems almost inevitable. And it seems equally inevitable, from what we know of her character and her precarious situation within an unfriendly camp of barbarous soldiers (the Greeks were generally seen in this light by English writers through the sixteenth century), that one exchange of men should lead Cresseid to another and another as she looked desperately for support and protection, and finally to general prostitution in the "Court Commoun." Moreover, if we accept the suggestion that Cresseid's affliction was probably syphilis, whose symptoms were almost identical with those of leprosy and which was not clearly distinguished from leprosy until after 1495, it becomes quite possible that Cresseid's harsh punishment was not first of all moral retribution but a natural consequence of profligacy, a consequence that Henryson may well have seen often in the leper houses outside Dunfermline.[2]

The world of the poem, then, is first of all a world of psychological and social and medical realism. It is also a moral world, but morality does not manipulate events, it is only revealed by them. It is a world so ordered by God that the natural order of things will also be a moral order. A knowledge of Chaucer's poem — and of human nature and medieval society generally — confirms the realism of the events; the long central section of Henryson's poem, the parliament of the planets, explains this congruence between reality and the larger moral framework of God's universe.

It is probably not true, as one critic has insisted, that Henryson's audience would have seen no connection between the planetary gods in his poem and the Christian Deity.[3] In the middle ages, the influence of heavenly bodies on human events was generally accepted; the planets in particular were understood to be destinal forces whose fixed influences, working singly or in combination, were part of God's Providence. Some are malign only in certain combinations, still others are benign, but these are all judgments from a private and limited, human point of view. Seen from God's point of view, both the good and evil influences are serviceable to his providential plan, just as Adam's sin or the activities of the Devil and his agents, wicked in themselves and their particular human consequences, ultimately contribute to God's beneficent purposes. Since the planets have taken their names from pagan divinities, the characteristics of these classical gods sometimes are used to personify these planets, but almost always in a way that parallels and reinforces those qualities which they were thought to possess as planets within a Christian cosmos. That we are to under-

[2] See Beryl Rowland, "The 'Seiknes Incurabill' in Henryson's *Testament of Cresseid*," *English Language Notes*, I (1964), 175–77.

[3] Sidney Harth, "Henryson Reinterpreted," *Essays in Criticism*, XI (1961), 475–76.

stand them as agents within a Christian scheme seems clear not only from this general medieval attitude, but also from the narrator's specific reference to their power over "all thing generabill," that is, all things created, and from Cupid's reference to their participation in "devine sapience" (288–89) – a phrase with unmistakable Boethian, Christian overtones.

Thus, while Cresseid's fortunes follow the course dictated by the realities of human life, this vision of the planets indicates that this course of events is also consistent with the moral laws of God's universe. But that the actions of the planets do not so much cause these events as explain them in moral terms is suggested by the interesting fact that Cresseid may have displayed the marks of her disease even before the vision: she complains that she has been excluded from both Troilus and Diomede as an *"odious"* object, that the seed of her beauty has been slain by *frost,* and she carefully stays out of sight, always seeking darkness – all before the dream occurs. These details are of course appropriate to her state of mind, but they also suggest the particular symptoms of leprosy-syphilis.[4] Seen in this way, neither Henryson nor the planets are morally severe. Events occur in a way that is highly probable, dictated not by the planets' whims, but by their fixed natures. The vision thus operates, as Mr. MacQueen observes, at an allegorical level which is intended to suggest the full moral significance of events at the literal level – accompanying these events rather than causing them.

It is the device of the dream which integrates these two parallel levels of experience: at the literal level, the dream is a perfectly natural consequence of Cresseid's situation and state of mind and it is also natural that her dreaming self should, through the personages of the planets, recognize that self-blame which her waking self – both before and after the dream – resists. At the same time, the dream penetrates into a supra-human, allegorical world whose workings are not usually available to human consciousness, revealing God's system in its inexorably rational logic and legal justice.

Within the dream itself, it is appropriate that Cresseid should be accused by Venus and then judged by Saturn and the Moon. While

[4] See John MacQueen, *Robert Henryson* (Oxford: Oxford University Press, 1967), pp. 61, 81.

the other planets possess reasonably consistent personalities, so that contrasts between them must appear within alternating pairs — Saturn/Jupiter, Mars/Phoebus — Venus carries these terrible contrasts within herself. Her dress is half green and half black, her hair half gold and half white, her expression alternating between faithfulness and inconstancy as one eye laughs while the other weeps. She is in fact described with the variableness usually associated with Fortune, but the similarity between Love and Fortune had long been recognized. And this inconstancy of love has been precisely the experience of Troilus, of the narrator, and of Cresseid herself, and it was therefore unreasonable for her to complain that Venus had broken her promise to keep the seed of love forever green in Cresseid's face. This is not the nature of love, and she herself had hastened its changeableness and the disfigurement of her beauty through her own promiscuity.

But Venus is not the only representative of Love in the poem. The assembly is called by Cupid, who represents Love in two senses: as Venus' son, he provokes and sponsors that love which leads to human delight and generation; but he was also associated with the ordering force of the world, which at the moment of creation had bound into one harmonious whole the disparate and discordant elements that, without love, would dissolve again into chaos. This was an idea long familiar from Plato and Lucretius and easily accommodated into Christian belief about Divine Creation, and in one way or another lies behind most medieval and renaissance attempts to exalt human love by making it a shadow of the Divine. Thus he is King Cupid, who besides being appellant for his mother is in fact the author of that whole system which he asks the planets to vindicate. Cresseid has challenged the established order which controls all created things, and she has refused to take responsibility for how she has chosen to act within this order. Just as she has always done, she has taken the easiest way, blaming the nature of things — the planetary gods — instead of herself.

As judges in her case, Saturn and the Moon, the highest and lowest planet respectively, represent between them the seven planets, all of whom, as Cupid points out, share in an offense against any one of them. Moreover, because of his Greek name, Kronos, Saturn had long been identified with Chronos, Time, whose changes and ravages Cresseid had forgotten to take into account. Cynthia, the Moon, was goddess of chastity, whose purity Cresseid had flagrantly offended, both in its general sense and in its more special sense of fidelity to a single lover.

Thus Cresseid is properly judged by Time and Chastity in defense of Love, whose true nature she has misunderstood and maligned. All the planets concur in the judgment since, however different they were among themselves, they all operate within and defend the fixed system itself. And the cold, dark nature of both Saturn and the Moon, traditionally associated with disease, makes the particular sentence as appropriate on this allegorical level as it was on the social and medical levels of Henryson's world below the moon.

But the vision alone is not enough; there is no sudden epiphany, no voice out of the whirlwind or blinding light. Just as the vision grew out of natural events, so Cresseid's final understanding and acceptance of what the vision has revealed must also grow out of a human event: Troilus' dispassionate charity at the end.

As her interior disease appears on the surface in the ugly marks of leprosy, Cresseid begins to see herself as she really is. But it is not in the mirror, where she first looks at herself, that real self-recognition takes place — here she sees only the physical ugliness and concludes that the "crabbit" gods will punish anyone who offends them: she now recognizes the consequence of her action, but not yet the justice behind it. Accordingly her complaint in the leper house is still self-centered, full only of self-pity and regret for the voluptuous pleasures she has lost, and naïvely confusing her suffering, which has come about through willful and selfish actions, with that inevitable decay and change which come to all fair ladies, true or false, just in the nature of things.

Her final understanding comes only at the end, when Troilus rides by the group of lepers and throws the purse of gold into her lap (though it perhaps began a little before when she apparently accepted the leper lady's advice to make the best of a bad situation and to live according to the law of the leper folk — one version of the kind of law represented by the planets, which Cresseid has until now resisted through her whole life). As they are momentarily juxtaposed in this last scene, we see in these two human beings the same contrasting sides of love which we have seen mingled in Venus herself: truth and deception, love and lust, happiness and woe. Naturally they do not recognize each other, on the literal level because Cresseid is so disfigured and so blinded by her disease, and on the allegorical level because, except in the personification of Love itself, these two sides of love never recognize or acknowledge each other. But when Cresseid learns that the knight was Troilus, she suddenly sees in the mirror of his fairness, moral and physical, her own moral corruption, and for the first time she judges honestly, shifting the blame from the gods to herself.

Just as her fall had come about through reckless sexual love, and just as her physical punishment was intended to vindicate that harmonious order of love which she had violated, so her self-recognition has come about through love of the highest sort, through Troilus' charity, which is a higher form of love than theirs had been, even at its best. Nevertheless, this charity, however disinterested it may seem, has been stimulated by Troilus' remembrance of Cresseid and has then led to Cresseid's remembrance of that love and to the self-revelation which that remembrance brings. Thus, just as the literal events and the allegorical vision are linked by the dream which penetrates both levels, so are the various levels of love interlocked. It was sensual, earthly love, wrongly managed, which caused Cresseid's tragic fate; it was love as an ordering principle which lawfully exacted such a terrible penalty; and it was love as charity which mercifully led to awareness of sin and acceptance of the punishment. Divine love is both just and charitable, and yet charity in a human soul may be most powerfully stimulated, as it was in Troilus, by the pressures of sensual, earthly love, rightly managed.

In a number of ways the art of the poem echoes and reinforces this parallel and contrast between different levels of action and theme. For one thing, the poem alternates between sections that narrate the literal events of the story and others that, in different ways, enlarge the significance of these events. The prologue section and the dream vision – one literally, the other allegorically – connect the particular events to the larger cosmos. Cresseid's complaint and, later, her warning, apart from what they reveal about her character, relate her experience to the procession of human history. One pair of non-narrative sections thus extends the poem in space, the other extends it in time; so that the fortunes of Cresseid herself always have a deeper resonance. Then, just as the universal implications are juxtaposed against this one set of events, so within these particular events themselves, the present moment is always a reminder of what has already happened and what is still to come. Henryson calls his poem a tragedy, which for a medieval audience would mean the fall of its central character from good fortune into evil. And although we see Cresseid only in her miserable state, the remarks in the prologue and her own lament in the leper house keep us keenly aware of the contrast between her present and past fortunes. In the same way we are kept from feeling at the end that Henryson's moral conclusion is simply that virtue triumphs while vice suffers. For, although a virtuous Troilus seems for the moment to be spared the kind of suffering Cresseid must endure, we remember from Chaucer's poem what unhappy fate still lies ahead: he never recovers from his distress at Cresseid's faithlessness, yet he is obliged to linger on in his disillusioned life, not being permitted either quick death in battle or the satisfaction of killing Diomede.

Other details pick up and emphasize the kind of contrasts we have seen in love as personified by Venus. Although the narrator describes a bitter winter night as the setting for his tale, the astrological details which he lists indicate that it is in fact the very same season which Chaucer describes so joyfully in the General Prologue to the *Canterbury Tales*. Part of the difference is due, no doubt, to the colder climates of Scotland, but equally important is the familiar medieval recognition that if spring is the season of love, like love, spring has two garments, one green and filled with birdsong and new life, one black filled with storms and bitter cold and the dregs of winter: like Venus herself, spring may either laugh or weep. The narrator's belief that the setting should correspond to the story is preserved, but preserved within love's own ambivalent season, which could mark the blighting or renewal of love just as, on a higher level, it could celebrate either the crucifixion or the resurrection of Christ.

A similar contrast appears in the verse itself, with its contrasts between polysyllabic, latinate (aureate) diction and a more vigorous, monosyllabic colloquial diction, often within alternating lines[5] or in contrast between lines that are spare and economical and those that are loose and redundant.[6] On a larger scale this contrast reappears in the flexibility of the verse itself, with some lines rigidly end-stopped,

[5] MacQueen, pp. 55–57, points especially to lines 25–28.

[6] See E. M. W. Tillyard, *Five Poems* (London: Chatto and Windus, 1948), pp. 6–8.

while others overflow their linear boundaries. (Notice for example the variety with which a series of syntactically parallel phrases are distributed within the lines 316–22.) Similarly some stanzas are tightly self-contained, while others run on, enjamb, into the next (see ll. 112–13, 147–48). On a still larger scale, the contrast appears in the alternation between tightness and relaxation as the poem moves from narrative to non-narrative sections.

Finally there are parallels as well as contrasts which contribute to the poem's unity. At the beginning, the narrator makes a complaint to Venus as he stands within his oratory, just as Cresseid will later do in the oratory within the Temple of Venus; and the arctic blasts which answer his desires are premonitory of Saturn's frosty wand which will wither Cresseid's beauty. Indeed, the malevolent aspects of the planets and the darkness prefigure the tale which is to follow, though as we might expect, even these parallels conceal a deeper contrast: the contrast between the narrator's fate, which is natural considering his old age, and Cresseid's, which is unnatural considering her youth and beauty. Surely it is part of the poem's irony to suggest this parallel only to deny it, since it will be Cresseid's failure to distinguish the natural from the unnatural, the right from the wrong, which leads to her fall and requires that vindication of order provided by the natural processes of human society and confirmed, on a cosmic level, by the natural influences of the planets.

(25) *The Bludy Serk*. MS Bannatyne, ff. 325a–26b (1568), Middle Scots. *PFRH; PRH; BMS; WPFH; RHP.*

8-line stanzas, rhyming *abababab,* with alternating 4- and 3-stress lines. For biographical note, see p. 398.

The Bludy Serk may be specifically indebted to a tale about the Emperor Frederick's daughter in the *Gesta Romanorum*. More important, however, is the fact that to anyone familiar with medieval romance, Henryson's tale presents the most commonplace episodes and sequence of events: a king's daughter of matchless beauty carried off by an evil monster, the search for a worthy champion, and the maiden's final rescue by the resplendent knight after a terrible battle. The only unusual element is the death of the hero from his wounds;

in romance he more often recovers through the help of magical ointments.

The relationship between a staple plot of chivalric romance and the basic pattern of human sin and redemption reminds us that, to the medieval sensibility, connections between various kinds of human experience were not fanciful but very real and natural. Hence the reader does not feel that Henryson is consciously constructing his little skeletal romance to make it fit the details of his moral, but rather that his moral application becomes possible because *in the nature of things* there is a correspondence between basic moral truths and the recurring events of human life — at the level of romance, or of *fabliau,* or anywhere in between. The medieval poet long ago recognized that deeper psychological significance of familiar experience which modern writers have taken such pride in pointing out, as if for the first time.

The narrative is deceptively simple and straightforward, but gives no appearance of being contrived to fit some larger purpose, even though the details all turn out to be those most useful for the eventual allegory: for example, the hellish allusion in the description of the monster, or the knight who was a prince without peer and who broke the bonds of a dark prison, and so forth. Only in the last stanza is the connection between literal statement and allegorical meaning specifically made, but even here it does not occupy the full stanza, and it is offered only as a loose equivalent, like a comparison which has occurred naturally and unexpectedly. Because it is introduced so casually, we feel that we have actually participated in the poet's awakening consciousness, and we share with him the sudden shock of recognition as we perceive its larger significance.

An explicit analogy is then presented in the *Moralitas,* but its details are handled so swiftly that it does not divide the poem in two. The poem proper, both in its relatively larger bulk (12 stanzas against 3) and in its self-contained completeness, stands independently, with the *Moralitas* operating briefly and at a quite different level of statement, though clearly connected to the poem itself, as it works out the loose analogy suggested in the last stanza.

(26) *Amang thir Freiris within ane Cloister*. MS Maitland Folio, pp. 203–07 (1570–85), Middle Scots. *PWD; SPWD; The*

Poems of William Dunbar, ed. H. B. Baildon (Cambridge, 1907); *The Maitland Folio Manuscript,* ed. W. A. Craigie, 2 vols. (Edinburgh, 1919, 1927), *STS; MWD; WDP.*

8-line stanzas, rhyming *ababbcbc,* with 4 stresses per line. For biographical note see p. 359.

This poem belongs to a long tradition of devotional poetry in which the poet's — and the reader's — spiritual temperature is raised through an extended and vividly detailed consideration of a scriptural event. It moves far beyond a graphic description of the event itself to describe the result of the meditation on the poet. The poem thus produces a meditation of the highest poetic order, in which this "apprehension . . . is intensified to a point where creative transformation of the subject occurs in the poet's fancy or his imagination" (*ML,* p. 131).

For his frame, Dunbar borrows from secular love poetry the device of the dream vision. But the conventional prelude to such a vision (spring morning, bird song, the dreamer wandering in fresh meadows) is replaced by a brief rehearsal of quite different circumstances that are vividly appropriate to the vision which follows. The first part of this vision possesses all the clarity of detail we associate with dreams but without the confused organization which in actual dreams tends to dissipate this reality of detail, so that the vision becomes even more concrete and real than the experience of our waking world. The vision itself contains both a contemplation of the Passion and an account of its effect on the dreamer. In order to participate in Christ's pain without overshadowing it, Dunbar treats his own suffering (which might seem to be the climactic concern since it comes last in the poem) very briefly and abstractly. While his persecutors are only the allegorical abstractions of dream convention and include some who oppress him in order to save him, Christ's tormentors are very real persons and include only those persons, Judas and the Jews, who intend to destroy him. And while Dunbar does not endure the actual torture of the crucifixion but is only shown its instruments, "Whilk crose and nailis sharp, scurge and lance,/ And bludy crowne befoir me cest," with Christ we are made to feel that bloody crown, "persing his heid with pikis grene," and we endure the excruciation of the stretched body, the nailed hands, and the bone-breaking jolt as the foot of the cross is dropped into its deep mortise "with ane swak,/

Whill cors and corps all did crak." Finally, while Dunbar moves out of suffering and into Grace, we remember that Christ had moved out of one pain only to endure others still more terrible: the vision does allow our recollection of the Passion to move beyond the moment of his final agony.

The two parts of the vision are linked by a device which both underlines their parallel and suggests that the contemplation and reflection are occurring simultaneously, although in the poem they must be presented in sequence. The vision of Christ's Passion ends with the familiar details of the piercing lance and the earthquake. Similarly, the account of the poet's own state of mind closes with an earthquake: "The erde did trimmill whair I lay." Both levels of the vision are thus interrupted at the same moment, not only to coordinate them but also to close the poem on a note of suspense. The dead Christ hangs upon the Cross; the house of Dunbar's soul, like the tomb itself, is ready to receive Christ, but, still without its chief guest, it remains subject to the torments which precede Grace. And the earthquake not only interrupts the events of the dream vision, but it also penetrates into Dunbar's waking world, for it shook the ground where he lay. And in this world too, it is still only Good Friday. So all levels of the poem intersect: the historical moment of Christ's Passion, the interior moment in Dunbar's own soul, and the exterior moment of this particular day of commemoration. And for all of them the triumphal Resurrection of Easter Sunday still lies in the future.

(27) *The New Lady*. MS Harley 682, ff. 111a–124b (mid-15th c.). *Poems Written in English by Charles Duke of Orleans,* ed. George W. Taylor (London, 1827); *The English Poems of Charles d'Orleans,* I, ed. Robert Steele (London, 1941), II, ed. Robert Steele and Mabel Day (London, 1946), *EETS* 215, 220.

Rhyme royal; the "Complaint to Fortune," ll. 4680–4735, is in 8-line stanzas, rhyming *ababbcbc* (c-rhyme is the same throughout), with 5 stresses per line.

Charles d'Orleans was born in 1394, son of Louis d'Orleans and nephew of King Charles VI of France. He was taken prisoner by the English at the battle of Agincourt in 1415 and spent the next twenty-five years in England as a prisoner of war. During his long imprisonment he was first kept at court, at London or Windsor, but subsequently moved from place to place as he was entrusted to a series of different guardians. He was finally released in 1440, and he died twenty-five years later, in 1465.

Ever since their first printing in 1827, there has been disagreement about the authorship of the English poems attributed to Charles. Since a number of them appear also in a French version, it has been argued that the English poems were translated by someone else. However, there is evidence that Charles learned English well during his years in England; a careful comparison of parallel French and English versions indicate that the English is not simply a translation; and, finally, there are nearly 3,000 lines of poetry without any French analogues. Taken together, the evidence seems to support Charles as the author of the English poems.[1]

The unique manuscript of the poems comprises three distinct but related parts. First is an account of Charles's love affair with Lady Beauty; second, a Jubilee, or Banquet of Song and Dance for all lovers; third, the love affair with a New Lady. Only the first part is complete, containing an allegorical introduction, in which Charles is introduced to the Lady, and a complete sequence of ballades which chronicle his love affair from its beginnings through the Lady's sickness and death and his own renunciation of love. The Jubilee contains only 94 of the intended 100 roundels (and of these 94, 16 are now lost); and the third part, about the New Lady, although it contains a full introduction, has its series of ballades interrupted by Charles's release from prison in 1440.

We have included the full introduction to Part Three. Its opening line links it to the Jubilee, or Banquet of Song and Dance, which has just preceded it, and the poet's melancholy circumstances and state of mind result from the death of Lady Beauty, in Part One. The effect of this introduction depends partly upon its contrast to the parallel introduction in Part One. On that occasion, Charles had been summoned out of Childhood by Youth, who reproached him for his long idleness and then led him, on Saint Valentine's Day, to the castle of

[1] For a full discussion, see Robert Steele's Introduction, I, xi–xxix.

Humble Desire ruled by Cupid, the God of Love. Here he was invited to enter Love's service, and although reluctant and diffident at first, Charles agreed the moment he saw Lady Beauty herself. Under her protection he submitted to the service of Love, agreeing to keep Love's Ten Commandments, and received a legal patent of service, for which he left his heart as surety. In the ballades that follow we learn (Ballades 80, 81) that the castle where he had spent his Childhood – before Youth had taught him about love – was called No Care, and it is to this castle that Comfort again conducts him after the death of Lady Beauty, and from which he sends out petitions to Venus and Cupid to release him from his legal contract to Love. The petition is finally granted and he settles into the indifference of No Care, turning his attention first to the Jubilee poems of Part Two and then to the services of melancholy lovers described at the opening of Part Three.

As this summary indicates, the introduction to Part One was pure allegory in the fashionable tradition of the *Romance of the Rose,* populated by such abstract figures as Age, Youth, Nature, Bel Acueil, Plaisance. And the Lady herself, whatever real person in Charles's life she may represent, was only the most general abstraction, surrounded by the personifications of Disdain and Daunger. In the introduction to Part Three, everything is changed. Only two personifications appear, Venus and Fortune, and of these only Fortune is treated allegorically. Venus is lively and animated, arch in her withdrawal from Charles's impetuous kiss, teasing in her reluctance to identify herself, mocking in her comments upon his anchoritic dress, and delightfully feminine in her dismay at being seen by Fortune in such compromising circumstances – alone with a man, and she, as we recall, all naked except for the slender protections of her hair and a scarf about her waist. Charles, for his part, is no longer simply the conventional lover of Part One. In spite of his grief, he reacts to Venus' appearance with an interesting combination of graceful wit and innocent boldness (ll. 4772–77); he touchingly recalls vivid details in his earlier love affair; he argues cogently against taking a new mistress, and when the time comes, he solicits the New Lady with the abrupt and covert haste that a lively game of post and pillar requires. The New Lady herself is no abstraction but one of an animated crowd of knights and ladies rushing about – and stumbling – on the grass. The setting itself adds to the realism, for instead of the conventional spring meadow and purling stream, we first have a mossy ledge of rock jutting out from the cliff while the sea waves crash on the shingle below, and later the realistic scene at the edge of a wood.

Thus we have all the ingredients of the love vision but handled in such a way as to cause the waking and dreaming worlds to merge. The distinctive and realistic setting penetrates the dream itself, as Venus comes floating in on the very waves that crashed below him and Charles hurries down from his rocky ledge to meet her. Later, although it is conventional for the dreamer to be awakened by some action or sound that occurs in the dream, as Charles is awakened by his cry for help, it is not so usual for the dreamer to carry into the waking world some tangible evidence of the dream experience, as Charles carries a piece of Venus' kerchief. The effect is to confuse the two levels of experience so that we cannot altogether dismiss the dream as unreal, or even as a different kind of reality.

The great delight of the dream and the subsequent meeting is the irony of what takes place. Throughout his conversation with Venus, Charles has played the role of conventional lover, rejecting Venus' suggestion that he take a new lady, in the pious argument that his lady was unique and that he himself must be forever faithful. Yet when the New Lady actually appears, high on Fortune's wheel, Charles cannot in fact distinguish her from his former lady, in spite of Venus' assurances that the two are not the same; and later, when he meets her and confesses his love to her, he is exactly repeating his experiences with Lady Beauty, to whom he had also first revealed his love during a game of post and pillar (ll. 4834–35). The implication seems to be that in spite of all the protestations about the lady's peerlessness, the lover's fidelity, and the memorableness of certain intimate moments between them, the truth of the matter is quite different. The lover moves on to other mistresses, justifying himself by attributing to them precisely the same qualities the first one had possessed, and those memorable moments, thought to be so special, are in fact reenacted over and over again. With great humor the episode gives the lie to everything Charles has affirmed and verifies Venus' knowledge of her subject.

Throughout the poem, the rhyme royal is handled with great flexibility, as the rhythms of private reflection or of lively, urgent conversation are poised against the regular beat of the iambic line and against the formal pattern of the stanza. Lines are broken up by rapid exchanges (ll. 4781, 4865) and by colloquially broken phrases (ll. 4868, 5075–76), and at other times lines may flow into each other, two or three together (ll. 4641–43, 4677–79). Similarly the stanzas themselves may be self-contained or may flow into each other, as two flows into three, four into five and five into six.

BEAST LITERATURE

(28) *The Thrush and the Nightingale.* MS Digby 86, ff. 136b–38a (1272–83), West Midlands; MS Auchinleck (fragment). *XIII,* 52; *Early Middle English Texts,* ed. Bruce Dickins and R. M. Wilson, 2nd ed. (Cambridge, 1952).

6-line stanzas, rhyming *aabccb*; ll. 1, 2, 4, 5 contain 4 stresses; ll. 3, 6 contain 3 stresses.

The debate was a popular form in Middle English literature, for which there were copious French and Latin models. As a literary device it was as old as the debates in the eclogues of Theocritus or Virgil, but its real stimulus came no doubt from contemporary law and theology, in both of which the marshalling of evidence, the logical construction of argument, often in the form of Aristotelian syllogism, and the give and take of debate were central activities and therefore influenced all education, continuing to do so even to the time of Milton, whose companion poems *L'Allegro* and *Il Penseroso,* as well as the debates in *Comus* and *Paradise Lost,* reveal the strength and durability of this tradition. In medieval society, law was preeminently important, either in the voluntary legal contracts among the feudal nobility, or in the law of custom to which the serf could appeal against a capricious lord. In the medieval church rational argument and demonstration were natural concomitants of an orderly universe created by a rational God. Peter Abelard's *Sic et Non* (*ca.* 1135), with its tabulation of authorities who contradicted each other on almost every important theological point, no doubt popularized the tradition.

In literature, the disputants could be human or animal, and the debates could be on any issue, from the most serious to the most trivial, and in any tone, from the most dignified and abstract to the most scurrilous and personal. When a debate descended to personal invective and abuse, it might, especially in Scotland, be called a *flyting*. Regardless of the issue or tone, however, these debates, with their precise poising of one argument against its opposite, became reminders of a world in which, if everything was rational it was also, to

human minds, likely to be ambivalent. Many debates, the famous *Owl and Nightingale* among them, do not reach a conclusion; after all the arguments, the audience is left to make up its own mind. The debate is therefore an exciting form: since it may explore a question exhaustively without resolving it, the audience is both informed and perplexed, more learned but not necessarily wiser, if by wisdom we mean the ability to use learning judiciously to select a course of action. At the end of the debate the course of action is still open, and if the area of choice has been enlarged, it has also been made more complex and confusing.

The particular debate on the nature of women also has deep roots, especially within the Christian tradition with its archetypal figures of Eve and Mary, the one an agent in man's fall, the other an instrument of his redemption. In medieval literature of all sorts, women are alternately idealized and vilified — the perfect beloved and the old woman in the *Romance of the Rose* (1225–1275), the deceitful wives of the fabliaux and the virtuous ladies of romance. And in the drama, such a figure as Mary Magdalene passes in the course of her own life through both roles, as she moves from shrew and harlot to pious lady through the transforming power of Jesus.

The debate between the Thrush and the Nightingale takes up this familiar topic in a tone which lies midway between *flyting* and full dignity. And the opponents seem evenly matched as they trade arguments with a stately formality that contrasts sharply with the urgency and vitality of their language. The balanced exchanges are neatly joined, with the Thrush, especially, usually picking up some detail from the Nightingale's preceding statement.

As long as it remains on the secular level, the debate is inconclusive: argument balances argument. Only when it is suddenly raised at the end to a higher level of appeal does it resolve itself in favor of one of the disputants. The poem builds to this resolution with considerable skill. First of all the Thrush seems, on balance, to have the better case. The poet himself tips the scales, after the first pair of stanzas that set the scene and announce the topic, by dividing his introductory summary unequally, giving only three lines to the Nightingale's position and nine to the Thrush's, lines which also have the rhetorical advantage of coming last. Then, in the exchanges that follow, the Nightingale's statements have the air of naïveté and idealistic innocence, while the Thrush's cynicism seems grounded on actual experience. One reason we feel this to be so is that all the specific examples are cited by the Thrush – Alexander, Adam, Gawain, Constantine, Samson. Each of his first five statements is buttressed with an example, and taken together they are impressively comprehensive, ranging through the Old Testament (Adam, Samson) and through classical and Christian history (Alexander, Constantine, Gawain). Thus, even if abstract arguments themselves seem equal, the Thrush has the advantage of specific evidence and of the general human tendency to accept cynicism as truer to reality than optimism.

But in the end all of this works to the advantage of the Nightingale, for when she at last presents her single, consummate example of the Blessed Virgin, her triumph is all the greater because of its tactical surprise, and it suddenly diverts to her side all of the supporting evidence accumulated by the Thrush, much as a new champion transfers to his own account all of the laurels held by the defeated champion. Here, however, the effect is more subtle, for the Nightingale wins the Thrush's evidence not only by right of victory but also by a more intrinsic right, since at the moment of triumph some of his[1] evidence is transformed so that it really speaks for her side. Both Adam and Samson were familiar "types" of Christ, who is the second Adam as he becomes the spiritual progenitor of all men, and who is a second Samson in his victory over the forces of Evil. (It is also possible to reinterpret the other figures so that they too become arguments for the Nightingale's side.)

Moreover, the Nightingale's own arguments, which had seemed ineffective, are also transformed when we think of them in the special context of the Virgin Mary. Her first argument (ll. 25–36) had emphasized the power of women to heal sin and to reconcile the angry. Since, however, she also used a phrase – made to be man's companion – which is calculated to remind us of Eve, her assertion seemed absurd: rather than healing, Eve caused our sin, and instead of reconciling she brought down the wrath of God. The Nightingale returns to this idea even more insistently just before her climactic revelation, calling woman the best leech in the world to heal man's pain (ll. 151–53). Thus her own references which had seemed so effusive and

[1] For the sex of the disputants, see p. 271.

ill-considered are suddenly transformed into the most appropriate characterization of that one woman, the second Eve, before whom the Thrush crumples. It is as if the Nightingale had all along been hiding her pious secret, hinting at it obliquely but in such a way as to lead the Thrush on, until at this climactic moment she introduces it resoundingly. And the drama is still further heightened by the irony in the Thrush's last argument, in which he had repeated the phrase "maid nor wife," a phrase which the Nightingale takes up triumphantly as she summons her first and last example. Rhetorically and dramatically it has been a master stroke.

After this climax to which the poem has slowly moved the conclusion follows swiftly. Once again the Thrush has the last word, as he had in the poet's earlier summary, but now this is a position not of advantage but of defeat. Throughout the poem the Nightingale has threatened to drive the Thrush out of the grove. Now the threat is fulfilled, but by the Thrush's own choice; and as he flies off we hear echoes of an earlier expulsion from a pleasant garden and we think of the perpetual distress of the penitent setting out toward Rome, hoping for pardon.

(29) *The Fox and the Wolf*. MS Digby 86, ff. 138a–40a (1272–83), Southern. *Middle English Humorous Tales in Verse,* ed. George H. McKnight (Boston, 1913); *A Literary Middle English Reader,* ed. Albert S. Cook (Boston, 1915); *Middle English Literature,* ed. A. Brandl and O. Zippel, 2nd ed. (New York, 1949); *Early Middle English Texts,* ed. Bruce Dickins and R. M. Wilson, 2nd ed. (Cambridge, 1952); *Early Middle English Verse and Prose,* ed. J. A. W. Bennett and G. V. Smithers (Oxford, 1966).

Octosyllabic couplets, with some exceptions.

The Fox and the Wolf is a simple beast tale but managed with considerable art, especially considering its early date. It divides into two sections: the raid on the hen house (ll. 1–64) and the episode of the well (ll. 65–295). Even allowing for the probable missing lines in which the Fox kills and eats three of the hens, the second section is much longer and more complicated, to which the first stands as a briefer, simpler introduction. This relationship is made possible by links and parallels between the two parts. First, the separate adventures are linked by the natural sequence of great hunger followed by equally great thirst after a satisfying meal. Then, both adventures contain parallel accounts of a technical matter — the medical practice of bloodletting in the first, and the religious practice of confession in the second — which effectively vary the tempo of the narrative itself. The appearance of the Wolf then offers some simple structural counterpoint within this parallel: since he too is out hunting for food, he introduces into Part Two the theme of Part One, but this theme is now in a different key, since unlike the Fox he has not been successful, and when he thinks he has found some food it turns out to be a very cold collation of frogs in place of the Fox's succulent chickens. Finally Aylmer's thirst, which leads to the denouement, repeats the second theme, just as the Wolf had repeated the theme of hunger.

Like Chaucer's *Nun's Priest's Tale,* this beast fable is contained within an enclosing human framework, and part of the comic effect depends upon our alternately forgetting and remembering that the characters are aimals. At beginning and end the human framework is very prominent, first in the details of the barnyard, and later in the specific figures of Aylmer and his fellow friars, so that we begin and end with a clear perspective. But within the story we tend to forget. The author is not so skillful as Chaucer, who in his tale provides increasingly long sections in which no specifically animal reference intrudes, but something of the same effect is achieved in this poem by those long technical sections just mentioned, during which the medical and religious details tend to make us forget the animal actors so that afterward we return to our senses with something of a shock. This alternation between sympathetic identification and objective detachment is essential to the didactic purpose which most medieval poetry, even the most amusing, included, for it obliges us alternately to participate and then to judge, with the result that in judging the animals we judge ourselves.

The didacticism of this tale operates, of course, at a much lower and less urgent level than in Henryson's fables. Instead of a serious moral issue, this tale illustrates the more practical and proverbial lesson that the clever and witty get ahead of the dull and stupid. The chance for a more serious lesson actually occurs within the poem, just before the

Wolf appears, as the Fox stands helpless at the bottom of the well. In his lament he admits that he has fallen prey to his own greed and willfulness — or to the devil as he works on us through these things — which have cancelled out his cleverness. Here is where a more intensely moral fable might end. But the possible seriousness is cancelled out by what follows, with its suggestion that as long as there are stupid people in the world, the clever people do not always have to pay for their sins, even if they should. Within this practical view of life the Fox can escape, even though, like Henryson's Fox, he compounds his gluttony with a scandalously irreverent handling of the confessional. The "engine" which has trapped him becomes the "engine" of his own scheme to save himself by trapping the Wolf. This single word nicely contrasts the relative effectiveness, within this morality, of a mechanical device and calculated trickery. The Fox's ingenuity allows him to use one engine as means to the other.

Any more serious moral tone is further dissipated at the end by the fact that it is Aylmer's thirst rather than some more serious occasion which causes him to skip out of the religious service and so bring about the climax; by the vagueness about whether or not the Wolf was actually killed; and by the trivial use of such solemn words as "blisse" and "foryevenesse," which introduce serious ideas only to deny them, since they refer only to the mock-confessional which the Fox has practiced on the Wolf. Through this echo they neatly tie the end of the poem to earlier events, but also remind us clearly of the more serious poem which this might have been, but is not.

(30) *The Fox's Confession*. MS Harley 3865, ff. 18a–22b (1571), Middle Scots. Four early editions survive: Henry Charteris ed., Edinburgh, 1570; Thomas Bassandyne ed., Edinburgh, 1571; Richard Smith ed., London, 1577; Andro Hart ed., Edinburgh, 1621. *PFRH; PRH; WPFH; RHP*.

Rhyme royal. For biographical note see p. 398.

Henryson's *Morall Fabillis of Esope the Phrygian* are influenced by the medieval *Roman de Renart* as well as by their acknowledged classical source (though not all of them can be traced to Aesop), and they include satire of contemporary events and persons as well as general moral instruction. While much of the specific satire is now lost to us, it no doubt once gave topical vitality and incisiveness to the general moral exhortations, just as the medieval ambience of the *Roman* contributed the realistic details from contemporary life which invigorated the classical fables.

Henryson introduces his thirteen fables with a short prologue explaining the poetic theory behind them; and since *fabil* in Middle Scots can refer to "story" in general as well as to an animal story, his explanation is relevant to all narrative poetry. He believes that the "feinyeit fabils" of the old poets were written to reprove the sinful lives of men through some other *figure,* or symbol; therefore, although these poems were not always true, they continue to please because of their continuing moral relevance and their eloquence. To support this view he offers three different analogies, drawn from nature and the hunt, which not only explain the nature of poetry but precisely illustrate how poetry works, as he has just defined it, "be figure of ane uther thing." After explaining how he was requested by a certain Lord to translate these fables from the Latin, and apologizing for his homely language and rough style — a conventional formula of modesty which itself suggests careful training in that high rhetorical art of which he claims to be ignorant — he concludes by emphasizing the appropriateness of this kind of figural representation in which beasts speak and act like men, since men daily transform themselves into beasts through their love of carnal and filthy pleasure. The transformations of the beast fable are thus no more incredible than the unfortunate transformations that occur daily in human life.

Like Henryson's own metaphors that illustrate while they explain, the beast fable uses its transformation of beasts into men both to explain certain moral precepts and, as *figures* of human life, to remind man to shun transformations which degrade and to seek those which ennoble. The story as *figure* thus works through a convention that depends on *transformation,* and both terms have specifically religious connotations which are appropriate to their moral purpose. *Figure* recalls the tradition of Biblical exegesis which saw events and persons of the Old Testament as figures, or types, of events and persons in the New Testament.[1] *Transformations* lie at the heart of the Christian

[1] See Denton Fox, "Henryson's Fables," *English Literary History,* XXIX (1962), 341.

mystery: it was the divine Christ transformed into the human Jesus who made human redemption possible; and it is through the transforming powers of baptism and the eucharist that man fallen becomes man redeemed. It was Henryson's purpose, through the transformation of his beasts into men, to keep men from transforming themselves into beasts and to work instead toward that better transformation.

Even the structure of his fables, with the appended moral interpretation of the story, contributes to this transformation, since the effect of the *Moralitas* is always to transform the literal events of the animal story into a moral pattern of human significance. Nor is the separation of the *Moralitas* from the body of the fable necessarily inartistic or unsophisticated. Art sometimes presents different points of view simultaneously, sometimes alternately, counting on the dramatic impact of the sudden shift from one point of view to another. As an example of the second method, Henryson's appended *Moralitas* is like the final couplet of a sonnet which suddenly undercuts, ironically qualifies, or reverses the developing argument of the first twelve lines.

All three levels of transformation coalesce in this fable about the fox and the wolf. The beasts act like men, but then, as men, they allow themselves to be transformed into thieves or hypocrites, readily perverting those religious rituals which should make possible transformations of just the opposite kind. As a thief, Lowrence lives unnaturally, working by night rather than by day and living by theft rather than by charity. He thus perverts, or transforms, the natural order and proper relationships of a Christian life. At the beginning of the poem he is momentarily in touch with God's order as it is revealed by the relationships of the heavenly bodies, in which he accurately reads the unhappy consequences to which his degenerate life will lead. His concern appears to be real, but it is immediately qualified when, instead of seeking a proper confessor, he takes the first one that comes along and one who is improper on both levels of narrative. In the world of beasts, the wolf is perpetually the dupe of the fox, so that this choice suggests that, as always, Lowrence is going to use the wolf to his own ends, not to be used or directed by him, as penitent should be directed by confessor. In the world of men, the friars were notorious for giving easier penance than the secular clergy, with whom they were in competition. Hence, in spite of serious protestations from both, the very sacred acts of confession, contrition, and penance are transformed, burlesqued into farce: what might appear as a kind of blunt, naïve honesty becomes in Lowrence brazen impudence, and what might seem mercy becomes in Friar Waitskaith a combination of stupidity and irresponsibility, as Lowrence, after agreeing to penance only if it is not too hard, then talks the wolf into a series of amendments that virtually revoke even this easy punishment.

Having transformed into parody that human act which can prepare a man for grace, Lowrence then transforms the gift of grace into an act which simultaneously parodies the sacraments of both baptism and the eucharist. Rather than purification from sin and the birth into a new life that baptism is supposed to bring, his immersions of the kid confirm his sin and consecrate his old life. And in place of the miracle of transubstantiation that saves the spirit, we have the miracle that feeds the belly.

The final event is morally and artistically proper. The poem has begun in scenes of darkness that cloak Lowrence's sin, and it ends in the full plentitude of day, as the sun beats down on his belly – a proper sequence to accompany the triumph of good over wickedness and, of course, a contrast to the perverted order of things in which Lowrence has shunned the light and thrived in the dark. Moreover, certain figures in the earlier horoscope are now borne out, since the houses in which three of the most important planets were situated reappear symbolically at the end of the poem. Saturn, the most infortunate, was in his own house, Capricorn; Jupiter, the most fortunate, was in his own house, Sagittarius. And Mercury, the planet governing subtle wit, Lowrence's special talent, was in his house, Virgo. Now, Capricorn, the goat, reappears in the kid whose theft and sacrilegious treatment lead to Lowrence's death; Sagittarius, the Archer, reappears in the goatkeeper who kills Lowrence with an arrow; and Virgo, the Virgin, is the sign that governs the digestive system, the belly and entrails whose appetites motivated the theft and the sacrilege, and whose exposed vulnerability becomes a proper target for the arrow of death.[2]

In this tale the morality does not, as in some of Henryson's fables, appear only in the appended *Moralitas*. It is consciously implicit

[2] John MacQueen, *Robert Henryson* (Oxford: Oxford University Press, 1967), p. 146.

throughout the fable itself, particularly because of the flagrant travesty of religious acts. But this moral view is suppressed at the same time it is suggested by the comedy of the literal narrative, the engaging surface honesty of the fox, the lively dialogue – all of which distract us from the unpleasant truth which this diverting surface conceals. The two levels are most sharply set against each other in the fox's last remarks, which can be accepted as either admirable, since they preserve a sense of humor even in this extremity, or terrifying in their wild irrelevance to the real cause and significance of such a death. Taken either way, or both ways, it is ironically appropriate that the fox, whose great sin had been to treat the most serious matters in jest, should here be annoyed at someone who took a jest seriously.

In a simple beast tale this trivial remark would serve to dissipate the tragedy of death and so preserve the lighthearted, childlike tone in which unpleasant reality is charmed away. Here it only intensifies by contrast the serious theme which has been implicit all along and which is about to be isolated in the naked exegesis of the *Moralitas* that will transform the fable, and, Henryson no doubt hopes, the reader.

FABLIAU AND BURLESQUE

(31) *Dame Sirith.* MS Digby 86, ff. 165a–68a (1272–83), East Midlands. *Middle English Humorous Tales in Verse,* ed. George H. McKnight (Boston, 1913); *A Literary Middle English Reader,* ed. Albert S. Cook (Boston, 1915); *Middle English Literature,* ed. A. Brandl and O. Zippel, 2nd ed. (New York, 1949); *Early Middle English Verse and Prose,* ed. J. A. W. Bennett and G. V. Smithers (Oxford, 1966).

Form and meter mixed: (1) 6-line stanzas, rhyming *aabccb,* 2 to 4 stresses per line; (2) octosyllabic couplets.

The manuscript of *Dame Sirith* often gives indications in the margin of the various speakers (Narrator, Clerk, Wife, Woman). These, together with the preponderance of dialogue, suggest that the poem may have been performed dramatically, with different speakers for the several parts. It is also possible, however, that this *fabliau* may have been written to be declaimed by a single minstrel speaking all the parts (See *EME,* p. 78), since the practice of delivering comic and satiric dramatic monologues existed in France in the Middle Ages, and since *Dame Sirith* appears in a manuscript that suggests strong French influences (see p. 305). Moreover, there are five poems in Old French, either embryonic dramas or dramatic monologues written for declamation, which contain a mixture of meters, as does *Dame Sirith,* though the mixed meter of this poem no longer serves any clear dramatic function. Certainly all this evidence suggests dramatic performance of some kind; it is interesting that the only analogue to this tale in English is the fragmentary secular play *Interludium de Clerico et Puella (Interlude of the Student and the Girl).*

While *Dame Sirith* may have been intended for some kind of dramatic presentation, it remains a typical *fabliau* with the customary realistic characteristics: ordinary people who speak in colloquial idiom, coarse humor, sexual subject matter, elaborate trickery which ensnares the victim, some burlesque of courtly romance, and a tight, economical structure. It also reveals the usual attitude in *fabliau* toward character and situation. It is, for example, extremely antifeminine, scorning in somewhat parallel scenes two women of easy virtue who protest too much. Yet it lacks any explicit moral pronouncement and seems intended only to amuse its audience, though, as we shall notice in a moment, there may be some implicit condemnation of the conduct of the characters, especially the female characters.

In any comic sex chase the humor is often founded on irony deriving from the disparity between the would-be lover's intention, which is sexual gratification as soon as possible, and the terms he uses to address his "lady." These terms may be courtly and romantic or religious and sacred. In either case, such elevated diction implies a more refined and respectable pursuit than the *fabliau* is likely to deal with. Here, the lover, the clerk Wilekin, promises to keep Dame Margeri from shame, pledges secrecy, and pleads for pity and mercy. This is the rhetoric of courtly romance, not of casual sexual encounter. Later, when Wilekin swears fidelity, not to Dame Margeri as a courtly lover would do, but to the unholy bargain he has made with Dame Sirith, he reverses the satiric process by mocking the serious legal and honorable knightly custom of oath taking.

At the same time that the clerk is couching his proposition in these courtly terms and then abusing legal or knightly office, he liberally sprinkles his conversation with pious references to God, suggesting heavenly approbation of his profane proposal. In fact, all of the characters so continuously lard their conversation with references to God and Christ that the reader cannot fail to notice the gap between their righteous protestations and their disreputable actions.

This discrepancy between sacred diction and profane action is often emphasized by plays on words. As Margeri refuses Wilekin's advances, she declares that she will not love him "by our Lord who is above us" (ll. 88–90), and this protest is immediately followed by a similar reference to her other lord, her husband, who is also absent, but whose watchful presence she feels as surely as the watchful presence of God. So far so good – the analogy is traditional and appropriate. But already we feel that for her the parallel is a little too easy, too uncritical, perhaps more confusion than comparison. If she can so readily think of her husband as God, doubtless she will be equally quick to think of God as her husband, when it suits her. And this is precisely what she does at the end. Earlier she had sworn "By our Lord, Heaven's King" (l. 89) not to be unfaithful, yet at the end, convinced that she must sleep with Wilekin to save her skin, she is so pleased at the prospect that Wilekin becomes "more welcome than the king" (l. 426). With one lord out of town, she is able to dismiss with equal ease the watchful presence of the other Lord, the King of Heaven, from her conscience and welcome a wholly secular king, Wilekin, as her lover.

When both Sirith and Wilekin break fasts in the poem, both suggest a comparison of their actions to Christ's breaking of his forty-day fast. When Margeri agrees to feed the begging old woman (l. 321), Sirith replies that she hopes God, who fasted forty days until "noon," will reward Margeri ("do thee mede"). This heavenly reward recalls the profane bribe ("meding," l. 271) which Wilekin gave Sirith to pander for him. Later, when Wilekin breaks his fast — his unsatisfied longing for Margeri, the same sacrilegious comparison is implicit between Christ's fast and Wilekin's. As Christ's was supposed to have been broken at noon, so is Wilekin's: "As I ever hope to see noon" (l. 433), he says as he is about to take Margeri to bed. A similar effect is achieved through the juxtaposition of "God" and "good," during Dame Sirith's conversations with Wilekin and Margeri (ll. 322, 330), with its suggestion that the two are as nearly synonymous in meaning as they are in sound.

Perhaps the most telling irony in the poem is that Dame Sirith's threat — that Margeri will be turned into a beast if she does not submit to Wilekin — is in fact fulfilled just when it seems most successfully to have been avoided. By yielding to her lust, Margeri becomes something of the "beast" she has tried to escape; she has avoided physical at the price of moral transformation. It is here that whatever moral condemnation the poem contains is strongest: without significantly altering the comic tone, the poem has managed effectively to condemn avarice and lust in women.

(32) *The Tournament of Tottenham.* MS Harley 5396, upon which this text is based, ff. 67–76 (1456), Northern; MS Cambridge Univ. Libr. FF.V. 48, ff. 61a–65b (after 1431); emendations in square brackets which are taken from MS Cambridge are not noted in the glossary; other emendations and corrections are noted in the glossary. *The Turnament of Totenham and the Feest,* ed. Thomas Wright (London, 1836); *Remains of the Early Popular Poetry in England,* ed. William Carew Hazlitt, 4 vols. (London, 1864–66); Percy's *Reliques of Ancient English Poetry,* ed. Henry B. Wheatley, 3 vols. (London, 1876–77); *Middle English Metrical Romances,* ed. Walter H. French and Charles B. Hale (New York, 1930); *Middle English Verse Romances,* ed. Donald B. Sands (New York, 1966).

A shortened version of the stanza found in certain Northern poems: 9-line stanzas, rhyming *aaaabcccb,* roughly alliterative; in ll. 1–4, which usually contain 4 stresses, there are often 2-4 alliterations on the stresses; in ll. 5–9, which contain 2–3 stresses, there are often 2 alliterations on the stresses.

The Tournament of Tottenham is written in a Northern dialect and in a stanza form generally associated with Northern poetry; yet the action takes place, unaccountably, in what was then the rural countryside just north of London. The poem appears to burlesque courtly romance by allowing the rustic actors to travesty many of the elements associated with this literary convention; yet at the end it is a nice question to decide which has been more effectively satirized, the extravagant ideals and artificial formulas of literary romance or the boorishness of clumsy peasants who try to imitate the refinements and elegance of their betters. George F. Jones has offered interesting evidence suggesting that the peasant tournament was a familiar Shrovetide custom in Germany and Switzerland in the fifteenth century, in which the urban dwellers acted out a tournament for the amusement of the upper classes.[1] The picture of the posturing rural knights in the *Tournament of Tottenham* may reflect this tradition.

As in *Sir Gawain and the Green Knight* and other Arthurian romances, this tournament grows out of a feast. But the convivial and decorous draughts at Arthur's court degenerate here into a tavern scene reminiscent of the Gluttony episode in *Piers Plowman*: all of these celebrants are "treue drinkers" (l. 18) who have been drinking

[1] "The Tournaments of Tottenham and Lappenhausen," *PMLA,* LXVI (December 1951), 1123–40.

for most of the day. The tournament prize is, properly, a maiden, but the disparity between Tyb and the ladies of romance is immediately suggested by the various barnyard trophies which are thrown in for good measure – a hen, a cow, a mare, and a sow. The arming of the heroes (one immediately recalls the gorgeous arms of Gawain) is ridiculous: bowls for helmets, sheepskins for mail, wicker baskets for shields, flails for weapons, and mares for battle steeds. Like the lady of romance, Tyb is led forth to observe the jousts, but garlanded only with bones, seated upon a sack of seeds for her saddle, with her brood hen in her lap, and greeted with a splendid but indecorous sennet from Gyb's horse. The scene cannot help recalling by contrast the gorgeous trappings and trumpet flourishes of romance.

The following scene burlesques the heroic boast and the heraldic devices, both prominent fixtures in romance tournaments. Harry's boast is particularly amusing, because, as he vows that he will not be left behind but will strike against all before him, he is caught downwind of Gyb's horse, so that what is intended as an expression of heroic courage becomes instead a call to retreat from the flatulent barrage, and he then extends the pun by warning the others to keep out of his wind. Hud's armorial devices – a sieve, a rake emblazoned with a fiery dragon, and three pieces of cake – travesty the serious devices on such shields as Gawain's. Terry's boast invokes very unheroic guile: instead of winning Tyb fairly he will snatch her away when the fight is most furious, and his unheroic armorial devices suit his coward's plan – a dough trough and a baker's shovel. Dudman, who shouts his defiance of Terry's treachery, muddles his syntax so that Tyb seems to be compared unflatteringly to a horse, both in her shape and in her speed afoot. And the prizes that Perkyn vows to take in battle to present to Tyb are only five decrepit horses.

The fight suffers the same deflation. Banners are decorated with plow-hammers and moonlit bells, and the battle itself becomes a wearied mayhem. In the usual romantic world the men and horses fight on with renewed vigor to the end. But here Perkyn, moving like a snail, wins Dawkyn's horse simply by seizing its tail, but is then unable to take this and his other prizes to Tyb because the animals are too tired to walk. When the battle is over, no beautiful ladies or skillful surgeons appear to heal these warriors. Instead the wives come forward to drag their bruised husbands home in wheelbarrows, on doors, on

sleds and gratings. And the victory of Perkyn the potter is celebrated by a precipitous rush to bed. The customary feast is deferred until the next day, when the lame and the halt limp in unheroically on their crutches and staves.

The burlesque is often enlarged by the poem's language. "Bachelors," for example, is a term for a young knight as well as for an unmarried man, but most of the fighters are in fact neither. The heroic fictions suggested in stanza 1 — the "kene conquerours," the "dughty" and "stalworth" men — are immediately deflated by the realities of stanza 2 — "the swete swinkers" and "treue drinkers." The poetic synonym for man, "freke," rarely found outside romance, emphasizes the same disparity, as do such allusions to romance as the references to Bayard, the fabulous horse in *The Four Sons of Aymon,* and to Bernard, a famous Spanish knight. And "rereward," a correct military term for describing the placement of men and armies, is used with equal accuracy to describe the placement of a fart. If the language of narration inflates reality, the language of the characters themselves just as surely deflates this illusion: an oath is sworn on a straw, cold roast becomes a term of invective, fourteen pounds of cheese is worth almost as much as Tyb's good opinion.

The stanza of the poem is a shortened version of a type used in some Northern alliterative romances (see *The Auntirs* above), combining long, rhyming alliterative lines with short lines. This short line, properly used, can provide effective variation from the drawn-out rhythms of the long line, though in this poem the effect is often lost because the alliteration is frequently absent. It works best when the last five short lines are a series of details supporting the content of the first four long lines, as in the first two stanzas or in the sixth.

Although the separate stanzas lack real metrical coherence, a weakness due perhaps to the poorness of the two surviving copies of the poem, the structure of the poem as a whole is coherent and logical. The main action is framed at beginning and end by similar references in the first two stanzas and last two. Stanza 1 lists four of the combatants, as does the penultimate stanza. Stanza 2 describes a feast, as does the last stanza. The eventual winner, Perkyn, is rightly the initiator of the action and the first hero to speak. He is made the most important combatant in the body of the poem: not only is his boast given special prominence by being placed last, but it is he who captures

the most horses and who thwarts Terry's scheme. The narrative moves from part to part logically. The poet builds slowly to the battle (two-thirds of the poem describe the action before the battle), lingering longest, just before the battle, on the boasts of seven of the heroes. In this way he carefully makes fools of all the company so that their subsequent foolish actions delight us the more because we expect them.

COLLEGE OF MARIN
3 2555 00121696 4